On Knowing—
The Social Sciences

On Knowing—The Social Sciences

Richard McKeon

Compiled and Edited by
David B. Owen and
Joanne K. Olson

THE UNIVERSITY OF CHICAGO PRESS
CHICAGO AND LONDON

Richard McKeon (1900–1985) was the Charles F. Grey Distinguished Service Professor of Philosophy and Classics at the University of Chicago. The author of numerous books and articles, McKeon emphasized the international aspect of philosophy and its application. He served as an American representative to UNESCO and participated in the Committee on the Theoretical Bases of Human Rights, where, in collaboration with Julian Huxley, he helped draft the document which became the Universal Declaration of Human Rights by the United Nations.

The University of Chicago Press, Chicago 60637
The University of Chicago Press, Ltd., London

Printed in the United States of America

25 24 23 22 21 20 19 18 17 16   1 2 3 4 5

ISBN-13: 978-0-226-34018-0 (cloth)
ISBN-13: 978-0-226-34021-0 (paper)
ISBN-13: 978-0-226-34035-7 (e-book)
DOI: 10.7208/chicago/9780226340357.001.0001

Library of Congress Cataloging-in-Publication Data

Names: McKeon, Richard (Richard Peter), 1900–1985, author. | Owen, David B., 1942– compiler, editor. | Olson, Joane K., compiler, editor.
Title: On knowing : the social sciences / Richard McKeon ; compiled and edited by David B. Owen and Joanne K. Olson.
Description: Chicago ; London : The University of Chicago Press, 2016. | Lectures and materials from a course on "Concepts and Methods: The Social Sciences" offered at the University of Chicago in 1965. | Includes bibliographical references and index.
Identifiers: LCCN 2016002821| ISBN 9780226340180 (cloth : alk. paper) | ISBN 9780226340210 (pbk. : alk. paper) | ISBN 9780226340357 (e-book)
Subjects: LCSH: Social sciences—Philosophy. | Liberty—Philosophy. | Power (Philosophy) | History—Philosophy.
Classification: LCC H61.15 .M40 2016 | DDC 300.1—dc23 LC record available at https://lccn.loc.gov/2016002821

♾ This paper meets the requirements of ANSI/NISO Z39.48-1992 (Permanence of Paper).

To Elizabeth Allison Owen
for her patience and love

To Michael P. Clough and Renee S. Pozza
for their love and encouragement

CONTENTS

FIGURES AND TABLES

Figures

Tables

FOREWORD

Background

We live in an age of transition, from the post–World War II / Cold War era to a new, extraordinarily complex, unprecedented internationalism. This new period is reflected in the diversity of names it has been called: the age of postcolonialism, postmodernism, multiculturalism, transnational corporatization, globalization. Presented here is a scholar whose work not only reflects an early awareness of the novelty of our developing circumstances but also suggests a variety of solutions to the diverse intellectual and practical controversies and conflicts to which our circumstances are giving rise.

Richard McKeon (1900–1985) was trained as a philosopher at Columbia University and in Europe just after World War I and spent most of his professional life, from 1934 to 1974, at the University of Chicago. Philosophy is customarily considered to be a matter either of scholarship or of "pure" theory, sometimes both, and therefore of little consequence for the "real," practical world, for what are thought to be "the facts" of "what is the case." McKeon, on the contrary, argued that theory is integrally and necessarily related to practice: one cannot be understood without the other, and further, one influences, even shapes, the other. As he frequently said, "Any problem pushed far enough is philosophic." Consequently, this volume deals with the practical as well as the theoretic issues that arise in attempts to understand and to shape human behavior in individuals and in groups, that is, in what is commonly thought of as the social sciences. That this issue of the conflicts of practice and their relation to the controversies of theory was present in his early thinking can be seen in his first extended scholarship, which appeared in his *The Philosophy of Spinoza: The Unity of His Thought*;[1] however, it appears most fully after World War II. McKeon was deeply involved with the founding of the

United Nations Educational, Scientific and Cultural Organization and the creation of the Universal Declaration of Human Rights; and both the catastrophic realities of World War II and the controversies and hopes inherent in the subsequent founding of UNESCO clearly stimulated his concern with cultivating the possibilities of a more humane future worldwide. He was exceptionally well versed in retrospective knowledge, as he was one of the most learned men of his age: Bertrand Russell characterized him as "incredibly learned," and Columbia University's John Herman Randall Jr. thought he was "the most learned of American historians of philosophy."[2] Nonetheless, McKeon saw the purpose of his scholarship as ultimately being a prospective cultivation of communication among the diversity of individuals and cultures throughout the entire world. The purpose of the work presented here, then, is to provide an introductory view of his approach to preparing for the future by means of developing a set of abilities that could enable reflective individuals not only to navigate through but also to invent fruitful possibilities among the world's cultures and the philosophies of those cultures.[3]

Provenance

The course. This book derives from the second of a series of three courses on, respectively, the natural sciences, the social sciences, and the humanities. A brief sketch of the history behind these courses follows.

As dean of the Division of Humanities at the University of Chicago under president Robert Maynard Hutchins from 1937 to 1947, McKeon was "the chief founder of the undergraduate College's 'core curriculum.'"[4] That curriculum is historically important, because Chicago was the only major American university in the twentieth century which, thanks to the support of President Hutchins, had a common course of study—a true "core," or set of courses, not just a set of distribution requirements—for *all* its undergraduate students that *included* the "hard" or natural sciences. The graduate departments, especially the sciences, were unremittingly opposed to this approach. Intellectually, they argued that undergraduate education should be preparation in a specialization, that is, a "major," which would provide a method for selecting the best candidates for graduate education in that specialization. Economically, they knew that undergraduate majors provided the department with a number of students in large classes who would help pay for the much more expensive graduate program. When their opposition was joined with the retirement of President Hutchins in 1951, the original conception of the core set of yearlong courses in the natural sciences, social sciences, and humanities was soon reformulated and dismantled.

Centrally involved in the development of the undergraduate program as dean of humanities and recognizing the great pressures brought to bear on it from the forces of specialization, after World War II McKeon turned his attention to helping to form a new interdisciplinary committee at Chicago, known as the Committee on the Analysis of Ideas and the Study of Methods (referred to locally as Ideas and Methods, or I&M for short). I&M was an attempt to institutionalize his conception of education for philosophic invention, interpretation, investigation, and exploration of values. Three courses—in the natural sciences, social sciences, and humanities, respectively identified as I&M 201, 202, and 203, which in the mid-1960s were renumbered as I&M 211, 212, and 213—were created to provide not only an introduction to the approach I&M was taking but also general introductions to the broad fields of investigation undertaken by the University at large; consequently, they were open to both undergraduate and graduate students from across the whole campus, not just those focusing on I&M.

The first course, on the natural sciences, has already been published; the third, on the humanities, is in preparation.[5] This book now presents the social sciences course. It was first taught by McKeon as Ideas and Methods 202, Concepts and Methods: The Social Sciences, in the winter quarter of 1953 and repeated annually by him thereafter from 1954 through 1963, with the exception of 1961. In 1964, in connection with a reorganization of the curriculum (see the first endnote of lecture 1 in *The Natural Sciences*), the revised course was offered under the same title but listed as Ideas and Methods 212 and taught by him. McKeon taught one final revision, the one presented here, in 1965, which was the last time he taught the course. It should be noted that, reflecting his extraordinary energy and creativity, almost every time he taught this course, he rethought the content and readings and prepared a revised set of notes for the classes, as he also had for the natural sciences course.[6] Consequently, as in the case of *The Natural Sciences*, the text here reflects his most considered and final view of this material in this format.

The lectures are organized around three terms, which can be thought of as laying out the whole field: *freedom*, *power*, and *history*. By contrast, the discussions illustrate various ways in which each of the three terms can be developed, and how the interplay among the variations can work both within and among *different* positions. The readings discussed include Thomas Hobbes's *Leviathan*, Benedict de Spinoza's *Ethics* and *Tractatus Theologico-Politicus*, Immanuel Kant's *Fundamental Principles of the Metaphysics of Morals*, John Stuart Mill's *On Liberty*, and Niccolò Machiavelli's *The Prince* and the *Discourses on Livy*.

The course itself was taught within the structure of the University of Chicago's quarter system. In this context, a standard course was taught over the space of ten weeks, with three fifty-minute meetings each week.

In the case of the social sciences course presented here, it met at 2:30 p.m. on Mondays and Wednesdays in Swift Hall 200 and at 2:30 p.m. on Fridays in Swift Hall 201.

The text. Of the eleven lectures in the 1965 course, ten have been preserved on tape, and lectures 2 through 11 presented here are transcriptions of those recordings.[7] No recording exists for the first lecture; however, it has been largely reconstructed in its substance from McKeon's extensive notes, from the excellent notes that several students took and to which the editors had access, and finally from a typescript obviously compiled from several sets of notes made by an unknown group of students in the class, a typescript which is in detailed agreement with McKeon's and the known students' notes. As for the discussions, only two (the second and third Kant discussions) of the seventeen occurring in 1965 were recorded, and they have been transcribed here. The other fifteen discussions are based on a combination of McKeon's notes and notes from the known students' notebooks. An extensive overlap exists between what the students recorded as happening in class and the discussion notes McKeon prepared ahead of time, which indicates how closely his in-class analysis of the author's argument replicated what he had worked out beforehand.

Notes. Regarding McKeon's notes in general, virtually all of them for course lectures and discussions are composed of 8½″ × 11″ sheets of white paper, which, in portrait orientation, were folded widthwise to form two halves; when rotated ninety degrees clockwise, these halves were 5½ inches wide by 8½ inches tall. Consequently, the sheet, when opened, provided two 8½-inch-long columns of material for class: the right column was to be read first, rather as though one were reading a book but taking the right-hand page first, then moving to the left-hand one. Unlike a book, however, only one side of the paper was used for typing. For identification of each sheet of notes, McKeon meticulously typed at the top of each right-hand page a line stating the source or purpose of the sheet. For instance, the notes for the first lecture here are made up of three sheets, each labeled "Concepts and Methods 202 (VIII) (1963)" and numbered sequentially "1,1.," "1,2.," and "1,3." As was his custom, the full heading identifies, respectively, the name of the course with its course number; the version or revision number (if the course was taught multiple times); and finally the lecture number and, after the comma, the sheet number sequence for that lecture. These notes, therefore, were prepared for the eighth revision of this course, which was taught in 1963. The following year, the sequence of courses was changed and a new name and number assigned to it, namely, Ideas and Methods 212.[8] These notes from version VIII, however, have penciled corrections on them, indicating that they were used when he taught the first version of Ideas and

Methods 212 in 1964. (McKeon would occasionally make such changes in pencil rather than retype entire sheets.) Moreover, the notes were found in the proper sequence with other, newly typed sheets created for the course in 1965, indicating their use a third time as the basis of his introduction to his second version of I&M 212.

In addition to McKeon's own preparatory notes, the editors have had access to the notebooks of three students who took the class in 1965: Joseph Betz, Carol Gould, and Robert Hodge. Judged by McKeon's own notes prepared for class, their notes have been found to be quite accurate. Betz and Gould went on to secure doctorates in philosophy and practiced as academic philosophers; not surprisingly, then, their notes were especially informative. In addition, as noted earlier, a set of typed notes, probably combining several students' records of the first lecture, have been used in conjunction with McKeon's own notes and those of the three students just named to re-create the first lecture of the course.

Editing conventions. With respect to the transcriptions of the tapes of the ten lectures and two discussions, the editors have made minimal changes to spoken remarks, except in limited places for greater ease in reading. More important, they have tried to punctuate the material in a manner that parallels McKeon's formal writing style. In particular, since his basic argument grows out of a fourfold matrix or schematism that is often treated with pairs of binary opposites, the reader here should be aware that a series of adjectives, clauses, sentences, paragraphs, and even sections often appear with double or quadruple equivalence and that, most important, no precedence is given to any member of the set. The editors have tried to indicate some of this holding of distinctions in balance by using semicolons in a formal, periodic style. Although not common in English in the current age (though popular in earlier ages, which had greater exposure to Latin and, through it, to Roman oratory and periodic sentence structure), it represents an attempt to call attention not only to what McKeon is saying but also to what he is doing.

On a more formal level, two conventions are worth noting. First, ellipses (. . .) are used when a speaker's voice trails off into silence, as frequently happens in the discussions. In addition, since student responses are frequently hard to decipher on the recording, the editors have frequently had to use substantially greater latitude in editing their remarks than when McKeon is speaking, both by condensing and/or, in light of McKeon's response, by interpolating what students have said. Second, the editors give a brief indication [L!] when the class laughs at something McKeon has said, which occurs not infrequently. He often reveals a sense of sly humor, often delivered in a deadpan manner. For instance, a little over halfway through lecture 3, he comments that since Democritus exists only in fragments, he is therefore much easier to understand! The class doesn't always laugh at these points (as they do not at the Democritus witticism), partly, no doubt, because the remarks are subtle and go by so fast.

The editors encourage special attention to McKeon's notes as they are presented here. They are laid out and reproduced as originally typed, with any editorial changes being noted in square brackets, except for a few regularizations of spelling, which are not noted. Also, *italics* are used to indicate McKeon's penciled additions, which most usually are clearly revisions of a typewritten note and were made at a later time for subsequent versions of the course. These changes can be additional words or even new terms replacing the typed ones; numbers or letters that indicate steps in the argument or changes in his initial, typed steps; underlines or even boxes or circles around central words; or simply pencil markings that indicate breaks in the argument or points of insertion for other material. We have used a horizontal line to indicate the separation between individual sheets, which include both the typed right- and left-hand columns when opened. Finally, we would like to emphasize that the visual structure of each note is most important: the indents, underlining, numbering and lettering, particular penciled additions, all can, when focused on *by themselves*, independent of the substantive points being made, reveal in extraordinary detail and precision the architecture of the argument being made, either by McKeon in his lectures or by the author being read for class.

Figures, tables, and appendixes. Unless otherwise noted, the figures and tables used in the lectures and discussions occur in the students' notes, primarily Betz's and Gould's; where they do not, the editors have alerted the reader that they constructed them from the text in conformance with the typical way in which McKeon used such visual devices on the blackboard in his courses. They have been created to help the reader by focusing attention on relationships and distinctions among key terms and key topics, thereby summarizing the structure of McKeon's remarks. In keeping with this latter point, they have added appendixes to assist the reader in understanding the course as taught and to provide some additional material supporting the central ideas of his analysis of the social sciences.

Finally, one should note that in all the diagrams involving arrows, the arrows point *toward* the basic term.

Reading McKeon

McKeon's use of language differs from that commonly assumed in current logical discussions in philosophy. An instance is his use of *operationalism,* a term conventionally thought to equal *pragmatism*. Instead of just taking the terms at their conventional, dictionary meaning, McKeon's usage is specific to his view: meanings are to be developed out of the *relations* and distinctions between and among the terms he sets up as variables in his matrices. This leads to two important features. First, like Dewey, McKeon does not treat "isms." For instance, Platon*ism* can, in his view, reflect a wide diversity of methods of analysis, such as what he calls the logistic and operational method, and not just the dialectical, as is often assumed. Second, and as a result, McKeon also tends not to treat "schools" of thought but, rather, presents individual thinkers and their intellectual profiles. This reflects McKeon's own method, the operational, where it is important to distinguish clearly each term in its relation to others so that the relationships can open up and reveal different perspectives on the issue in question.[9]

To help the reader explore this uncommon approach to developing meaning, the editors have included a number of diagrams and tables for reference. We hope that they will be repeatedly used while reading, not just glanced at as simple summaries (though, of course, at heart they are that, too). They are designed to encourage an exploration of the structure of relationships within individual matrices, as well as between matrices, because it is not univocally defined terms but, rather, the relationships between and among terms that ought to receive attention, their distinctions and commonalities, their differences and samenesses. The definition of individual terms arises, then, only in relation to other terms. Thus, for example, the use of a matrix can be such that sets of four terms arranged in the basic knowledge matrix can change, yet the relations among each of the four terms, the structure of the set, remain similar from set to set.

Out of this operational and ambiguous, rather than deductive and univocal, use of language with its consequent importance of matrices of relations grows what may be the most important contribution McKeon's introduction to the social sciences makes—not only to a renewed, retrospective insight into the interpretation of the past but also to a uniquely powerful, prospective creativity regarding the problems and possibilities of the future. The heart of his operational approach is, as he states in lecture 1, the use of a "semantic pre-philosophic set of distinctions"—four cognate terms: *knowledge*, *known*, *knowable*, and *knower*—formed into a diamond-shaped matrix that is then used to explore three terms which organize the social sciences: *freedom*, *power*, and *history*. In his *On Knowing—The Natural Sciences*, he praises Galileo for using the operational method. He states that the latter thereby

> defined uniform motion in terms of three variables: the velocity, the distance, and the time. . . . It is an arbitrary definition in the sense of a set of variables,

> but it is not arbitrary in the sense that any old set of variables will do; therefore, we have to go on to consider other things. . . . It is a great achievement to have done this. If someone in economics at the present moment, for example, could discover three variables about which he were to say, "I want to define these, and then let's take a look at some economic processes in terms of them," he would be a genius in economics history. (p. 144)

One can argue that McKeon is doing just this. In the argument he presents here, he takes his basic knowledge matrix, examines the three pairs of relations among those four terms, which exhausts such relations, and then explores them under four equally exhaustive traditional philosophic issues: the one and the many, appearance and reality, the universal and the particular, the whole and the part. Of course, what that means exactly and how it works is the point of this course. It is hoped that the reader will soon realize that what is presented here is significantly more than just a recitation based on formidable scholarship regarding theory; it is also a call to creativity, invention, and action.

In short, McKeon is introducing students to the whole field of the social sciences by demonstrating the act of philosophizing about how to *do* philosophy.

Acknowledgments

The editors would first like to thank that group of students, undergraduate and graduate, who had the foresight, energy, and resources to make tape recordings of McKeon in a variety of circumstances. Although the student who recorded the social sciences course presented here is unknown, he or she was part of a much larger group characterized by a distinct willingness to share recordings and notes freely with others, including the editors. Without them, obviously, this transcript, like that of *On Knowing—The Natural Sciences*, would not exist. This group includes Jo-Ann Kling, Elliott Krick, Mayo Rae Roy, and Thomas Stark, plus others whose names are unfortunately unknown to us. We owe them all a great debt of gratitude.

Second, we have benefited greatly from the use of notes provided by several students who took the course presented here. We would like especially to thank, as noted above, the generous permission of Joseph Betz, Carol Gould, and Robert Hodge to do so, which was of the greatest help not only for those lectures and discussions where no recording has been found but also for providing a large number of the figures and tables that McKeon put on the blackboard to crystallize the central terms and issues that he was working with.

Third, we are grateful to Robert Hollinger, who not only carefully reviewed sections of the manuscript but also made important suggestions for making it easier for readers unfamiliar with McKeon's contribution to work with the ideas presented here.

Fourth, we would like to acknowledge the substantial help of the University of Chicago Press in the preparation of this manuscript for publication. In particular, we are grateful for the assistance Ruth Goring has given us in overseeing the entire process. Also, we want to thank Sandra Hazel for the extreme care with which she read and emended our original draft, significantly improving it. In addition, we would like to express gratitude to the individuals working "behind the scenes" who have helped bring this book to life, those whose names we know being Benjamin Balskus, production controller, Ashley Pierce, promotions manager, Kevin Quach, designer, and Kyle Adam Wagner, editorial associate. Finally, we want to extend thanks to James Farned for the reflection and care with which he created the index.

Finally, though it may appear conventional to say so, it is, nevertheless, absolutely true that without the encouragement and assistance of Douglas Mitchell, Executive Editor at the University of Chicago Press, this three-volume project, in both its conception and its execution, would never have come into existence. In fact, Doug's support has been the key factor in allowing this aspect of McKeon's work to have the opportunity to receive a public hearing.

The Editors

LECTURE ONE

Philosophic Problems in the Social Sciences

This course is the second in a sequence of three which are based on the subject matters we usually call the natural sciences, the social sciences, and the humanities.[1] The sequence is designed to be an introduction to philosophy by way of the examination of fundamental problems. It makes the assumption that philosophic problems arise in fields other than philosophy, that they arise even in everyday life. Moreover, because all three courses are concerned with similar philosophic problems and approach them by similar philosophic analyses, and because the differences in concepts and methods examined in the respective courses are, as we shall see, not fixed ones, each course is independent of the other two. In other words, these courses are an exploration of problems which are at heart philosophical and which occur in the various disciplines, but you need not to have taken the course in the natural sciences or the humanities to understand this one in the social sciences.

The method by which we shall proceed is to choose certain concepts basic to a field or discipline both as they are handled by the men in that field and as they are used by philosophers who write about work being done there. It is especially good when you can find one and the same man doing both jobs. For instance, the course on the natural sciences makes an examination of fundamental problems taken from the physical sciences. The problems of motion, to pick one example, involve philosophic aspects when different theories of motion are formed; and philosophic aspects are present either in the resolution of the problems presented by these differences of theory or in the elaboration of one position concerning motion and its related problems of space, time, and cause, even when worked out by scientists such as Einstein, Heisenberg, Bohr, and Schrödinger.[2] The results of each theoretic position taken can be ascertained and traced in experience, but the choice of position taken is not imposed on us by experience or by facts. The relation between the means by which we determine the facts and the means we employ in the science itself is, fundamentally, a philosophic problem.

This course takes its central problems from the social sciences. The social sciences treat various aspects of man's behavior in communities and in the association of individuals with one another. Philosophic problems are involved in the determination of the basic questions raised by such knowledge and its application. There are a variety of ways of identifying and considering such basic problems. As in the natural sciences, we shall use the device of examining the meanings and applications of several basic concepts, namely, freedom, power, and history. Our investigation may be viewed either as an inquiry into the meanings of the terms or as an inquiry into the nature of freedom, power, and history. Viewed the first way, our result will be a series of definitions as well as an analysis of the relations among them. Viewed the second way, the result will be a series of structures of relation among the processes involved in actions which are characterized by freedom, which employ power, and which are recorded in history, as well as an analysis of the relations among those actions. The decision concerning how to consider the actions, moreover, is itself a philosophic distinction which separates different approaches to philosophy or different philosophic schools. In short, when raised explicitly, these basic questions in the social sciences are the subject of philosophy.

We will proceed on the assumption that there is no single, true definition of any of our concepts; rather, a number of good definitions, as well as a number of bad or inadequate ones, exists. Progress occurs through the interplay of the various ideas, not the establishment of just one, and can appear either in the understanding of what freedom means or in the actual achievement of freedom. Although we will not be concerned with the history of ideas, we will see that controversies similar to current ones have occurred up and down various fields throughout history. Still, in the larger picture, progress has occurred in that the current controversies are not simply a repetition of the older ones. Over time there have been a series of significant changes; philosophers are not committing the same old mistakes. We will question the dogma, for instance, that the natural sciences have shown progress but the social sciences have not. This is not true. When we examine the question of history, we will analyze the various senses history can have. In one kind of philosophic scheme, history is progressive; in another, it is not. Consequently, we need to be clear about the definition of our terms before we see if there is progress in history or not.

What, then, is the relation of our terms to each other? Any relation is possible. Take, for instance, *freedom* and *power*. They enter into each other's definitions in the varying philosophies, and four relations are logically possible. First, *freedom* and *power* can be contraries, that is, terms on the same level and mutually exclusive. One term enters into the definition of the other, and here you have freedom when no one is exercising power over you. Second, the terms are on the same level but are not mutually exclusive: they both occur at once, overlap, and contribute to each other. In this case, the more freedom you have, the more power you have. Third, *freedom* is the basic and prior term, with *power* delimiting it and standing in its way. In this approach, freedom and right are taken together, and you get natural rights philosophers like Rousseau arguing in favor of innate rights. Fourth, you may consider *power* to be the fundamental term and prior to *freedom*. This is the position where "might makes right": might sets up the sovereign, and it is only after this that one can go on to discuss how freedom and rights fit into the state. Consequently, one has an open field for examining the meaning of freedom, and all four possibilities are present in developed philosophies and in the social sciences.

You will notice that these controversies are based on the ambiguities of the terms' definitions. This is not to say that ambiguity is a bad thing: it is not. In the history of freedom and power, ambiguous statements have been the source not only of philosophic problems but also of discussion and progress. If there were no ambiguity, if each disputant always knew exactly what position he held, there would be no need for discussion. Discussion has value in that it can lead you to clarify your ideas, change your mind, or persuade others; and it can even lead to agreement among parties about an idea that none of them had at the beginning. For instance, philosophers would generally agree on the ambiguous definition of *freedom* as "the ability to act without external restraint." The key terms here—*ability*, *act*, and particularly *external*—are all ambiguous. Acts, for instance, can be viewed as something internal rather than external. Likewise, anything that one writer holds to be an external impediment can be translated without much subtlety by another into something internal: the external irritant, for instance, may become part of an emotion, of something internal. As a result, freedom of discussion can provide both an alternative to the exercise of power as well as a basis of power.

History, our third term, enters the picture as an illustration of this process. History is the occurrences or the accounts of the occurrences in which human actions exemplify freedom or the use of power. In cases of reason and action, the appeal is to what is the case or to what the facts are; and history is the factual account, past and present, by which what is the case is determined. But examination will show that there are as many senses of history as there are senses of power and freedom; therefore, appropriate facts can be established and inappropriate facts can be rejected for proper reasons, depending on which philosophic position you take. For example, in one kind of history the sequence of what happens has the same form as the conceptual analysis encountered there. Thus, the progress of history is fundamentally the same as the evolution of thought. Hegel takes this position. In another approach to history, by contrast, your appeal is to any fact, and any explanation you can make that will account for the fact is your history. History is what you make it, because there is no simple, direct way to get at what has occurred. You will notice, therefore, that what determines the facts varies, and history will differ according to the different approaches taken. There will be a history for each idea of freedom and power, and the facts we allege will themselves have a history.

The consequence of all this is that one must examine carefully the ideas and methods of any statement, even a chance one, because in large measure they bring about the selection of the writer's facts. You will notice that in talking about ideas and methods so far, I have used a pair of expressions that refers both to the advance in freedom and to the advance in the understanding of freedom. Our analysis will try to keep both these aspects moving together; that is, we will take account of the principle of indifference. The principle of indifference says that if you have a good analysis of the terms in a statement, then you have a good analysis of the facts in the process to which the statement refers. In other words, you should be able to move back and forth between a consideration of the terms in a statement and an examination of the facts in the process. Consequently, all the way through I will draw your attention to both the formal and the material aspects of our analysis.

How should we go about examining the many ideas and methods that appear in history? Well, the first philosophic question involves asking how one goes about defining any concept or about determining the nature of the operations to which the concept refers. We will make use of a schematism which will take care of all the many possible philosophic positions by means of formal considerations. In that schematism, four elements are involved in establishing meaning. We will follow these elements throughout our lectures and discussions.

One of the four elements involves problems of *selection*. There are an infinite number of terms or data potentially related to any question we can ask, and it is out of these that we make a selection. For example, in psychology, some writers select terms that ultimately go back to physics and talk of *motions* and *forces*. Others, nonbehaviorists like Freud, borrow terms from hydrodynamics and talk of *pressures*. Still others account for social interrelations by choosing terms based on spiritual values. Thus, selection gives you the basic way in which you orient yourself to problems. Again, the question of terms or groups of terms has a double character. In its formal aspect, it involves a question of what terms are used to generate meaning, what language is employed. In its material aspect, it involves a question of what data the terms refer to—not the propositions made about the data but the isolated data the language refers to.[3] Both of these aspects, in turn, are influenced by society, ideology, the fashions of thought, or the climate of opinion in which one is working. Fundamentally, then, selection involves questions of single terms.

A second element of definition is *interpretation*. An interpretation is a statement involving two terms—when we used to speak of parts of speech, this was called a subject and a predicate; now it is done with respect to sentence functions—and it is the minimum unit of truth or falsity. The statements or propositions of interpretation make allegations that may be tested, that may be proved or disproved, about the relation of something to something else. On the one hand, a proposition can be tested formally by examining the relation between a subject and what is asserted of that subject as a predicate, which leads to establishing the proposition's truth or falsity; on the other hand, it can be tested materially by various experiential means which lead to establishing the existential relations among the data, that is, establishing the facts relevant to the case at hand. Notice, a *fact* is something that has been made,[4] something which is not fixed but, rather, is the product of an interpretation.

In order to hold that something is true or false, you must be able to prove or show it. A rich vocabulary is involved here due to the work of the German existentialists. *Explain*, *prove*, *inquire*, *discover*, all refer to processes by which you can arrive at conclusions; and the process by which you arrive at a conclusion which is either true or, at least, probable is your *method*, our third element. Method is the means by which one discovers or establishes knowledge about something, for example, freedom, or the means by which one acquires or protects freedom. It refers both to the sequence of steps leading to a conclusion, usually the exposition in words of the processes denoted, and to the sequence of steps in the actions themselves. Formally, method consists of three or more terms, the traditional example of the minimum number of terms required being the three terms of a syllogism.[5]

Finally, arguments can be organized into homogeneous sets that are compendent[6] or systematic in character; they are organized into a single whole. Any number of terms can enter at this point, so you have *n* possibilities. This is the element of *principle*. It is the basis on which knowledge is established or action is founded. Of all the terms and data which

Table 1. Four Moments of Definition.

Principle	Method	Interpretation	Selection
Set— *n* Terms	Discourse— 3+ Terms	Proposition— 2 Terms	Term— 1 Term
Basis of Entire Procedure	*How* do you achieve your result?	*What* are you saying about it?	*About* what are you talking?

might be selected, of all the truths and facts that one can interpret, of all the sequences of statements and things that one can follow, principle joins these other elements, formal and material, together into a compendent set. It grounds what you say the case is with what is the case.

This schematism is important because it corresponds to the different kinds of questions you can ask about something; and when the answers to these questions are gathered together, you have a complete definition of what it is you are talking about. Selection is an answer to the question, What are you talking *about*? What terms or data are relevant to the question? Interpretation answers the question, *What* are you saying about it? What are instances? Method answers the question, *How* did you achieve this result in fact or in argument? And principle provides the answer to the question, Where did you start? What is the *basis* ruling the entire procedure? What are the grounds for all this? (See table 1.)[7]

Let's take the concept of freedom as an example. If you begin with the ambiguous statement that freedom is the ability to act without external restraint, you can render that definition precise by answering each of these questions. The questions would look like this—and remember, they will include both formal and material aspects. Selection asks: What terms are to be used in the discussion of freedom, for example, things, institutions, natures, powers, reason, will, passions, actions, language, communication, consensus? What things or actions are free? Interpretation asks the question: What do you mean by freedom? What are the defining characteristics of freedom that allow you to recognize what things and actions are free? Method's question is: How is freedom investigated? How is it achieved and exercised? How is knowledge related to freedom? Finally, principle asks: What is the basis of freedom? How is freedom possible or conceivable? Answer each of these questions and you will have defined and located freedom unambiguously (see table 2).[8]

In this course, we will move through our three concepts by successively taking up each of their possible selections, interpretations, methods, and principles. This will be the first level of our discussion, and we will

Table 2. Four Questions in Definition of *Freedom*.

	Principle	Method	Interpretation	Selection
Formal Aspects	What is basis of concept of freedom?	How is freedom investigated?	What is meant by *freedom*?	What terms used to discuss freedom?
Material Aspects	What makes freedom possible?	How is freedom achieved and exercised?	What are characteristics of freedom?	What things or actions are free?

examine what could be meant by the various approaches. In this process, we will place various philosophers in a schema relative to each other. This part will be the semantics of the course. Philosophy here is the combination which one makes out of the various approaches and the reasons advanced in support of that combination.

We could begin from any one of our four questions, and each provides certain advantages. From each question different meanings and possibilities of analysis emerge. Each of them, moreover, is independent of the other three. In the past, at one time or another, I have started from all of them except selection.[9] I have found, however, that it would be best not to begin with principle, because principles appear too out of date. To begin with interpretation, by contrast, is to begin with statements of fact. Facts, however, are not encountered in experience as something fixed, like stones, although that is what is commonly supposed; rather, they result from interpretation, even if they have a certain amount of rigidity. So, we will not begin with facts, because we tend to be dogmatic about our facts. Consequently, we will make our beginning with method. Method involves either a process or a discourse, a sequence of antecedents and consequences in action or in statement. In a definite sense, it is easy to recognize method—or, at least, easier than the other three—and it is possible to identify it with less ambiguity and as determined by more characteristics.

But how should we discuss the differences of method in philosophy?[10] It is characteristic of philosophy that once one engages in philosophic discussion, one is committed to a method; then, any statements arrived at by other methods, after they have been translated into the terms of one's own approach, are easy to refute. To avoid such simple reductions of philosophic diversity, therefore, we shall make use of a semantic pre-philosophic set of distinctions. These will yield ambiguous propositions concerning which philosophers are in agreement before they render them precise by the use of their respective philosophic methods.

In making a semantic approach to any of the four questions, that is, to

KNOWLEDGE

KNOWER KNOWN

KNOWABLE

Fig. 1 *Knowledge Matrix*

selection, interpretation, method, and principle, the treatment of problems raised is influenced by four basic aspects in the use of language. The view one takes or the language one uses is determined by the *perspective* of an agent, observer, knower, or speaker; is influenced by the *circumstances* in which it is formed and to which it is adapted; is composed of parts or *elements* adapted to the subject matter to which it refers; or is organized on assumptions that give it an organic *unity* and govern the relations of its elements. I have arranged these different aspects in a matrix composed of cognate terms, that is, respectively, *knower*, *known*, *knowable*, and *knowledge* (see figs. 1 and 2).[11] Any one of these aspects may be taken as fundamental to any set of problems, and the remaining three can then be treated in terms indicated by that fundamental approach. Philosophies take on their characteristic properties by the combinations of such fundamental assumptions which the philosopher makes. Our concern, therefore, is to isolate these assumptions through their operation in the meanings assigned to the terms we are studying. I refer to these fundamental approaches to philosophic problems as *modes of thought*.

Let me briefly describe the central characteristics of each of these four modes of thought. If the agent or speaker—the knower—is the point of departure, a technique of discrimination or differentiation is needed to bring out the plurality of orientations in language and in practice. Reality—whether it is conceived of as references, circumstances, or assumptions, or as a combination of these—is set up relative to these differing perspectives or orientations. This is the mode of thought *discrimination*, and its typical form is *debate* and aphorism. If the elements or simples of a language or of its subject matter—the knowable—are taken as fundamental, a technique of construction is needed to build up the body of knowledge and to put in order the subject matter known. This is the mode of thought *construction*, and its typical form is *deduction*.

UNITY

(Knowledge)

PERSPECTIVE CIRCUMSTANCE

(Knower) (Known)

ELEMENT

(Knowable)

Fig. 2 *Characteristic Orientations in Knowledge Matrix*

If the circumstances determining problems encountered and positions taken—the known—are the point of departure, a technique of resolution is needed to relate hypotheses to the subject matter and to advance inquiry into the nature of the subject matter encountered and explored. This is the mode of thought *resolution*, and its typical form is *inquiry*. Finally, if inclusive assumptions, an englobing whole—knowledge—are taken as the starting point, a technique of assimilation is needed to relate the diversities encountered among the parts within the system, whether among speakers, objects, or circumstances. This is the mode of thought *assimilation*, and its typical form is *dialogue* (see figs. 3 and 4).[12]

Each of these four modes of thought can be used in questions of selection, interpretation, method, and principle. Only one can be used at a time in each question, however, if inconsistency of meaning is to be avoided; but one mode can be used in interpretation and combined with other modes in selection, method, and principle. In this fashion, a vast diversity of philosophic meanings and positions can be constructed from this simple set of distinctions.[13]

Let us return now to the decision to begin our analysis of freedom, power, and history with an investigation of method rather than of principle or interpretation. You will remember that method involves both a formal and a material aspect, that is, either a discourse or a process. Hence, we need to make a double column under method: one is for methods, strictly speaking, and the other is for modes of thought, which

ASSIMILATION

(Knowledge)

DISCRIMINATION	RESOLUTION
(Knower)	(Known)

CONSTRUCTION

(Knowable)

Fig. 3 *Four Modes of Thought*

are closely related.[14] Let me apply these modes of thought to method and set up the distinctions we will want to pursue as we examine the concepts of freedom, power, and history. There are a number of methods that you will quickly recognize, and I have chosen popular terms for them.

First, the *dialectical* method is a two-voiced affair, often employing two or more speakers. In it, you ought to come out at a place superior to the positions held initially by each speaker. A Platonic dialogue, for instance, involves a conclusion which is not the position held at the beginning either by Socrates or by any one of the disputants. Socrates does not play tricks on the other speakers; that only appears in the dialogues between master and pupil of the Middle Ages and afterwards. A peculiarity of this dialogue is that it uses the mode of thought assimilation. Whereas other approaches assume clarity exists in experience, this approach assumes that experience is filled with contradictions which must be unified by means of assimilation to a higher level. This assimilation of differences, then, is a result of the dialectical process. This is the method employed, for example, by Marx, Hegel, Plotinus, and Plato.

Another method, which looks somewhat like the dialectical, is the *operational* method. It is also two-voiced, but now the conversation is in the form of a debate, not a dialogue. Here the assumption is that the orientation of each disputant affects their point of view. Language and reality are set up relative to these perspectives or orientations. This includes the fact that since the instruments of measure also affect the position held, they must be taken into account, too. The mode of thought at work here

DIALOGUE

(Assimilation)

DEBATE

(Discrimination)

INQUIRY

(Resolution)

DEDUCTION

(Construction)

Fig. 4 *Typical Forms of Four Modes of Thought*

is discrimination. In discrimination, you need to discriminate between the positions taken by means of a debate among the disputants, which involves refutations of opposed positions; and you end the debate by refuting your opponent or by showing it is the better position. Throughout this approach of debate and aphorism, it is important to preserve the matrices of the different perspectives or the frames of reference.[15]

Both the dialectical and the operational methods have in common that they are *universal* methods (see fig. 5).[16] This means that they take the position that the same method can be applied to all subject matters. They tend to be plural-voiced in character and to set up analogical definitions to reveal relations among different positions. An instance of this is that the philosophers of science who argue for a unity of the sciences use one of these two methods. In other words, the problem of the unity of the sciences, which is usually thought to be a substantive issue, can really be a matter of commitment to a method.

Distinct from the universal methods is a group of two other methods, the particular. One of these, the *logistic* method, follows the model of Euclidean geometry. The mode of thought used is construction. Euclid's geometry is called the *Elements*, and he discusses method in the thirteenth book. He says that it is most important to begin with the least part and to build up from there. Thus, you have a constructive process by which the resultant theorems come out.[17] The uninitiated tend to assume today that this is always the best method or that "This is the method I use."

The second of these methods is the *problematic* method. This starts

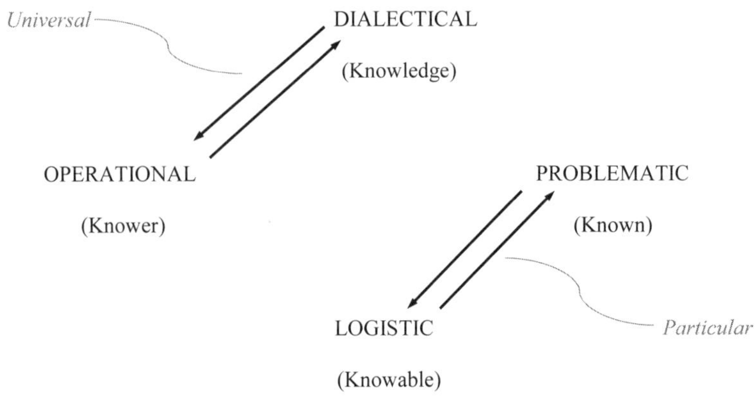

Fig. 5 *Method and Knowledge Matrix*

with the assumption that we begin to think only when we have a problem. Dewey, for example, says that we operate by habit or by instinct up to the point where we encounter a problem. It is only then that we begin to think, formulate hypotheses, test them in our mind, and then try them out in practice. The mode of thought involved is resolution. Here, instead of building up from least parts, you deal only with a difficulty, an *aporia*,[18] as it occurs and then go ahead to resolve it. Aristotle, like Dewey, uses this method.

Both of these latter methods, as distinct from the dialectical and operational ones, hold in common that they are *particular* methods. Their position is that there are a plurality of methods which are required to deal with the various subject matters of possible exploration. They are single-voiced in character, generating unambiguous definitions, and it is important to eliminate from the method any reference to the thinker or speaker involved.[19]

It is apparent at once that central philosophic issues enter into these distinctions setting up the different meanings of method. For example, dialectic is simultaneously a method of clarifying ideas, defining terms, and discovering things. The processes in thought and the processes in things are in some sense the same, and this is because the universe is fundamentally rational and intelligible. The operational method is one of action or statement, and everything else, including the external universe, is a projection or a result. Therefore, this is a method of rules and the consequent projection of the results of those rules. The logistic method functions in two fashions: construction may begin with the elements of reality, and then you have a cognitive method; or it may begin with impressions and emotions, in which case you are dealing with emotive

SYSTEMATIZATION

(Dialectical)

DISCOVERY	INQUIRY
(Operational)	(Problematic)

PROOF

(Logistic)

Fig. 6 *Ends of Four Methods*

methods. Consequently, the plurality of methods is seen in that there is one method of science, which examines the nature of things, and many other methods for morals, aesthetics, and so on. Finally, in the problematic approach, the plurality of methods comes from the plurality of ends. Thus, the ends of knowing, doing, and making lead, respectively, to the theoretic, practical, and poetic sciences, each of which has its own method, its own subject matter, and its own principles.

Each of the four methods, you should note, is especially well suited to a particular end. When assimilation is applied to the diversities of speakers, objects, and circumstances, those diversities are ordered within increasingly encompassing wholes by means of dialogue or dialectic. The result of this dialectical method is, in an ambiguous sense, *systematization* (see fig. 6).[20] When discrimination is applied, the plurality of orientations in language and reality is preserved. The result of the operational method is, again in an ambiguous sense, *discovery*. The mode of thought construction appears in method when elements or basic parts of language or of a subject matter are first isolated and then combined to build up a body of knowledge and to put in order the subject matter known. The logistic method's approach of using preliminary definitions and postulates and then deducing consequences from them leads, in some sense, to *proof*. Finally, resolution enters when the circumstances determining problems and positions are the point of departure. In the problematic method, hypotheses are related to a particular subject matter, and the investigation advances with respect to the nature of that subject matter encountered and explored, resulting in *inquiry*.[21]

We'll go on next time to explore in more detail how these four methods are related to our initial concept, freedom. At the next meeting we will discuss the selections from Hobbes's *Leviathan*.[22] Try to pay attention to the way in which Hobbes uses *liberty* and *power*. Remember, he is a systematic man.

A week later we will begin discussing Spinoza's *Ethics* and his *Tractatus Theologico-Politicus*. He is a contemporary of Hobbes, but he is not in agreement with Hobbes. Thus, we will be able to consider the way in which one can examine the relationship between two contemporary philosophers.

LECTURE TWO

Freedom: Method

At the first meeting of the class, I explained in some detail the approach that we shall follow in this course. I suspect that the meeting was only a partial one; therefore, those that were not here will need the formulation that we considered.[1] Afterwards, I will begin with the substance of what we shall do.

The part that needs repeating—and this is important by way of carrying on in the direction of the *Time Schedule*—is that we shall be concerned this quarter with the problems of philosophy that originate in the social sciences, not in the natural sciences.[2] Last time I explained further that our approach to the problems is by way of taking fundamental ideas from the social sciences and searching in them for the philosophic difficulties that anyone is engaged in whether he is engaged in technical work or is engaged in discourse about such work. We are not concerned with the definition of the terms in the sense of giving a verbal definition. We are not concerned with the solution of problems that are connected to the concepts; that would be the proper activity of the various fields of the social sciences. Rather, we look for those aspects of the problem that have a way of taking on the appearance of being substantive questions or a way of taking on the appearance of being arbitrary verbal distinctions but that are, by way of contrast, very important to the naturally philosophical problems. We proceed, therefore, on the assumption that we shall discover our philosophical problems in this region.

The three concepts that we shall be concerned with this quarter are freedom, power, and history. Last time I explained that in looking for the philosophical problems of these three concepts, we shall be looking for four elements, four ingredients, four questions that shall be asked in order to give an answer to the question of what is meant by the term. These dimensions I will repeat a great deal, so I will not go into their meaning now. Briefly, they are questions of selection of individual terms or of individual aspects; questions of interpretation, or the formulation of fact as distinct from the true; questions of method, either the manner in which one achieves, say, freedom, or the manner in which one comes to know freedom; and questions of principle, or the grounds on which you can systematize either the scheme of polity or the scheme of some science. I pointed out that we shall begin with method; in other words, one-fourth of the question of the definition of our terms will be the subject of the lecture today. I shall begin with freedom;[3] later I will go on to explain power, and then history. The portion that has to do with the method of analysis will be repeated; what I say about the three concepts will not be. But I make no apology for the repetition: I have discovered that there are philosophical truths which can be repeated before a class a half-dozen times in the course of a quarter and still be undetected on the final examination. [L!] I shall therefore come back to them again and again.

Method will be that part of the question that has to do with how one achieves freedom or how one comes to know what the nature of freedom is. It is discursive both in the sense that you need discourse or a sequence of speech in order to talk about freedom, and in the sense that you need a sequence of processes by which to establish or maintain freedom. In Latin, I would not need to apologize for using *discursus* for both of these; but in English it is perfectly correct to speak of the sequence or the consequences both in discourse and in processes, and our concern will be to move from one to the other. I also explained last time[4] that there are four fundamental ways in which we will look at things, which I called modes of thought; but I shall not repeat that now, because it is also a part of my repetition that will come out more and more.

In method, we found that there were two universal methods and two particular methods. A universal method will be a method which applies to all things. One of the characteristics of the modern period is that it looks for universal methods. The ancients and the medievals did that occasionally, but it became a kind of rallying to the banner in the Renaissance. Take Ramus, for example: his great reform in revolting against Aristotle was the defense of one method; he liked to talk about it. Descartes wanted a universal method borrowed from mathematics that would apply to all problems. And we in our own days have had our hearts raised by the cry that there is a unified science. The one method is a general schematism that is sought. On the other hand, particular methods are particular in the sense that there are more than one of them. The reason for the difference will vary as you move from one philosopher to another; but when you have more than one method, when you have the pluralism of science as opposed to the unity of science, you are

Table 3. Freedom: Method.

Mode of Thought	Method	How is freedom acquired?
	Universal	
Assimilation	Dialectical	Right Use of Choice
Discrimination	Operational	Choice
	Particular	
Construction	Logistic	Act according to Nature
Resolution	Problematic	Deliberation

down in the particular methods. One of the things I would like you to observe, therefore, is that a good part of the argument about whether science is unified or plurified is not a substantive question; it is a question of your approach, your method. It is an important issue, but it is not something you will ever discover by going out and looking at the laboratory or detecting what goes on in the mind of Helmholtz when he gets an new idea. The universal methods have familiar names: the dialectical and the operational methods. The particular methods have likewise familiar names: the logistic method and the problematic method (see table 3).[5]

As we go along, I shall want to deal in more and more detail with the peculiarities of the method, but what I should like to do as an initial introduction of them to you is to deal with them with respect to the question of freedom. That is, what is the difference that the methods have with respect to our thinking about freedom in the sense of using our reason to achieve freedom or in the sense of using our reason to talk intelligently about freedom? I am deliberately using words like *intelligently*, because sometimes the method will aim at rigorous proof, sometimes at a process of inquiry, sometimes at systematization, sometimes at a process of discovery, even of edification or aphoristic formulation and clarification (see fig. 6). There have been great philosophers who have been aphoristic philosophers; in point of fact, in our day they have somewhat more influence than most of the others. Nietzsche has an aphoristic philosophy. I hesitate to say so, but it seems to me Wittgenstein is an aphoristic philosopher. The manner of approach is one of arising, shaking off old ideas, formulating anew; then you go on and you either set up a transvaluation of values or you formulate a new language game,[6] and you're on your way. This, then, is the range of methods.

Let me make an observation at once, because methods begin to appear in radically different guises as soon as you begin to talk about them. For example, for both the dialectical and the operational methods, that is, for the universal methods in general, it is the case that all of the great practitioners of these methods hold that the sequence of thought and the sequence of things are the same. They do it for different reasons and in different ways. Hegel, for instance, holding that the dialectic is a dialectic of the spirit, likewise holds that if you have an important problem, if you wish to deal with the nature of a human institution—the philosophy of right, for example—to give its complete history and to give its rational analysis are the same thing, the same steps. The evolution of things and the evolution of thought are the same. The operational method operates differently because, being operational, it begins with a skepticism about whether there is any process that can be detected this way; and therefore, you do not measure your thinking by having it conform to the way in which the universe or spirit thinks. Vaihinger, who a number of generations ago—I nearly said "recently"—wrote a work called *The Philosophy of the "As If,"* the *Als-Ob*, is one clear formulation of the operational method. You cannot explain how, in fact, anything got to the point at which it did; but if you can give any explanation which would account for it, that accounts for it, and you do not need to ask whether or not it really happened that way. At the early point at which physicists were speculating about the nature of the atom, they had a basic theory which had great importance in the history of the development of physics. They said, let's act *as if* the atom were a universe, as if it were a sun and the various constellations, and let's have the various particles operate *as if* they were controlled by the same laws. None of the protagonists of this conception thought that the atom was a solar system, but they explained questions raised, which led to the solution of problems as if it were.

In the particular methods, neither the logistic nor the problematic method assumes that the processes of proof or inquiry duplicate the processes by which one gets to a given point. The logistic method, the prime example of it, was derived from the deductive demonstration that Euclid set up. The *Elements* of Euclid begins with elements—and he took this literally—and builds or constructs all of the aspects of geometry from these elements. Therefore, you begin with a postulate set, then you prove consequences or you construct figures, but you don't assume that every proposition in your proof has an interpretation which corresponds to a fact. If you begin from the principles that are intelligible, if you end with an answer that you can see in application, the steps of proof themselves do not correspond to anything that's been happening. The same thing would be true of the logistic method as it is practiced in physics. The other particular method, the problematic, begins with the assumption that man is in a series of circumstances, biological and natural, and he begins to think when a problem is faced. If he is merely functioning habitually or naturally, there's no thinking. When a problem is faced, he raises a question, formulates hypotheses, traces out the consequences of the alternative hypotheses, makes a choice, tries it out. Until he tries it out, there is nothing that is happening in the world that would correspond to his hypotheses. His assumption, on the contrary, is that two, one, three of the hypotheses, depending on how many he makes, won't correspond to anything. Consequently, all of the steps by which you make suppositions and try them out correspond to nothing.

As a result, in dealing with freedom we shall likewise run into a separation of the two processes, a separation which will make such a step—and this is important, because I don't think most of the discussions of freedom even notice this difference. There is a conception of freedom in which the use of reason is directly relevant to the acquisition of freedom and operation according to freedom. Those are all philosophies that use universal methods. There is a conception of freedom in which one is not dependent on reason directly; there are a whole series of indirect uses that reason would have, but you do not need to be intelligent to be free; in fact, on the contrary, freedom would even precede intelligence and set up the conditions of its possible use.

Let's now go into the differentiation of the four methods that I've set up. I will try to restrain my tendency to talk formally about them as methods and limit myself to a consideration of what the result is on freedom. In order to explain them, let me set forth the common situation or problem or knowledge that all four, that in fact, all philosophers, would face. The problems are connected to an interrelation between something called knowledge, a knower who discovers knowledge, a known which is the result of the processes that you are using when you inquire into knowledge, and a knowable that enters into the process when inquiry or discovery is involved (see fig. 1). All four of the terms that I have just put on the blackboard are deliberately and systematically ambiguous. In the first lecture, I spent a few minutes in praise of the importance of productive ambiguity. One of the compulsions of our age is to aim at an unambiguous statement, a precise statement, a univocal statement. As an objective, this is good; but as part of the situation in which knowledge is formed or transmitted, it is bad. The only possibility of discussion or of teaching would exist in a situation in which an ambiguity occurs. This is stated clearly by Plato and Aristotle; both of them, each in his own way, raise the question of what happens when a person takes a course. Why did you take this course? Well, obviously, in one sense you knew what the course was about; that's why you took it instead of chemistry. In another sense, you didn't know what it was about, because if you knew in detail what I was going to do, you could just as well go on to the more advanced course, unless you had difficulty with your adviser. [L!] Therefore, you are faced with the ambiguity of knowing and not knowing. When you enter into discussion which is genuinely a discussion, you know what you are talking about. If a meeting is called, it will frequently contain an agenda or a base paper. You don't know in detail either what you think or what you opponent thinks; if you did, there'd be no possibility of discussion. Discussion would end there, and you would move over into some other operation, an operation of warfare or of economic competition or of some other form of our second term, namely, *power*.

Knowledge, *knower*, the *known*, and the *knowable*, then, are terms of this sort. Each time I explain a method, they will take on a slightly different meaning, yet they will retain a schematic relation to each other as above, even as their meanings change. Nevertheless, the function of each term, of the *knower*, for instance, can always be easily recognized. Thus, even coming in fresh to a philosophic discussion, you can understand the other positions and perhaps even change an opinion, either yours or someone else's. Without such understanding, however, you are left with just labeling their views as wrong, lies, and so on. Now, there are two radically different ways of looking at questions of method. In one approach, you consider the way in which the knower is related to knowledge, and in the other you look at the way in which the knowable is related to the known. The former relation corresponds to what I have been calling universal methods; the latter corresponds to what I have been calling the particular methods (see fig. 5). The diagram should help make clear what the differences between these two sets of methods would be with respect, bear in mind, again, to the concept of freedom or of liberty.

Let's begin with the universal methods. I think this perspective will make you slightly more uncomfortable than the particular methods. The particular methods are kind of literal-minded, so the normal reaction of American students of philosophy is that they understand them; whereas if you start on a broad, analogical base first, you may shake them up sufficiently to get them to look at the literal meanings instead of supposing that they know what they mean. It is for this reason, then, that I will begin with the universal methods. Dialectic is a method which begins with the assumption that knowledge is fundamental. It uses the mode of thought that I called assimilation. The great example, the father of all dialecticians, is Plato. And Plato was convinced that that which *is* most truly is that which is most intelligible; and that's the reason why he called such things ideas. Ideas are not ideas that a man forms; they are instances of being which are the highest instances. So, in figure 5, anything that is—the knowable down at the bottom—merely imitates the idea that marks it off, and any knower is engaged in trying to make his opinions approximate to what the idea is. Consequently, the root form of dialectic will be that of a through-and-through intelligible universe. In fact, in the *Timaeus*, it is even more startling: it's an intelligent universe, it's a universe that is thinking.[7] And the whole problem of method is to make your thinking as good as it can be by making it as like the thinking that the universe is doing as possible. I hope that this is clear. This seems to me a perfectly reasonable approach. It's an excellent paradigm; it's one that has been repeated throughout the history of thought, and unless you take it seriously, you will miss a great deal of philosophy. Thinking is possible, because what is was thought out that way. You will never be able to think it out completely—you are finite; this is an infinite process—but you can move in particular regions and particular ways to be able to approximate to this kind of thinking. Hegel and Marx are other forms of the dialectic for which the same things could be said *qua* method. However, they have different interpretations and principles, so there are differences.

What is freedom in the dialectical approach? Let me remind you that in answering this question I shall not be telling you what freedom is in the sense of what you acquire when you acquire freedom. That's the problem of interpretation, and you'll have to come back next week to find out what the answer to that is. [L!] Today the problem is how you acquire freedom. And the answer that Plato gives is a perfectly clear one; namely, you acquire freedom by acquiring dialectic, by acquiring wisdom. And who is the free man? He is the man who can act as the wise man would. The rational procedure is the process by which one acquires freedom and is the process by which, having acquired freedom, one acts in accordance with freedom.

One of the characteristics of the universal methods is that in order to operate, they always have two conceptions which play one against the other. That's why both the dialectical and the operational methods like to work with pairs of contraries or contradictories. There are two conceptions of freedom that all of the dialecticians have engaged in. Let me give them to you in the form that Saint Augustine gave us, because he has the advantage of writing Latin; and therefore, you may think that I'm speaking in English when I talk about Saint Augustine. Plato wrote in Greek, and I'd have to do a lot of explaining. Saint Augustine's distinction is between liberty, *libertas*, and *liberum arbitrium*, between freedom and free choice; and there's a great difference between the two (see fig. 7).[8] Free choice is indifferent; I have free choice when I can take either of two courses of action. If I had some impulsion, internal or external, which limited me to only one, I would not be free; and it can be an internal as well as an external impulsion in that I might be deformed in my desire and in that situation I would not be acting freely. *Libertas*, liberty or freedom, is the right use of free choice. In a situation in which you

libertas	*liberum arbitrium*
liberty, freedom	free choice

Fig. 7 *Saint Augustine:* Libertas *vs.* Liberum Arbitrium

can do either of two things, the wise man will pick the better, the wise man is free. As I said, from Saint Augustine on, the Christian tradition is strongly impregnated with this conception, and it goes back to Plato and Plotinus. You come finally to the modern period, and it still is present. What is freedom, then? Well, the two meanings are these: the preparatory stage is the ability to act for oneself; but freedom, as opposed to free choice, is the choice governed by reason of the right course.

Let's turn to the operational. The operational conception of method is just the opposite—as figure 5 should indicate—of the dialectical. In the operational approach, you begin with the knower. He is not faced with a patterned universe or a divine spirit that has thought out the universe and laid the track which he will blaze through the wood and follow. It is he who acts; that is why it is operational. Knowledge, therefore, is the product of his activity, not the model that he follows. The mode of thought that he uses is discrimination, whereas the dialectician uses the mode of thought assimilation (see table 3). Like dialectic, the operational method is a two-voiced method. That is to say, there are two people who enter into the discussion. In the dialectic, they enter into dialogue, to use a term which is becoming very popular again in recognition of the importance of these methods of distinction;[9] that is to say, there is an assimilation of the partial positions with which the dialogue began with the higher truth which is achieved only by the dialogue. By contrast, the operational method is the method of debate, in which it is of extreme importance to continue to discriminate the different perspectives. This is true, we should recognize, not only in verbal discussion but also in physical measurement. It is important to know what the point of reference is; it is important to know where the measurer is; it is important to know what his instruments are, how they are affected by his circumstances, and the relation, therefore, that would obtain between him and another measurer measuring differently from another perspective.

This, in general, is the method that I have been calling operational.

It includes the greater number of modern philosophers who call themselves operationalists. Bridgman,[10] for example, held this very position explicitly, even to the point of arguing that one ought to differentiate three different conceptions of length: the length that you measure in visible processes by means of rulers, yardsticks, or any form of visual determination; the length that you measure between the stars, where your mode of measurement is totally different; and the length that you measure in subatomic physics. They're three totally different ways of measuring. He also was the man who, all during his life, defended the special theory of relativity. He thought the general theory of relativity was a mistake, because in the special theory of relativity the relation to the various perspectives was maintained, and all the gummy business of getting a general field theory was avoided. But in any case, this is the method of discrimination.

What is the operational conception of freedom? Well, Plato made a picture of the Sophists, who were operationalists, in order to create a prejudice against them—it is undeserved; they were among the greatest of the Greek philosophers—and therefore, we don't take their position as seriously as we might. But he also created the catchphrase for their definition of *freedom*: "might makes right." Only the man of power has freedom; therefore, *freedom* is equated to *power*. That is, in the pair of terms that we are considering in this course, *freedom* would equal *power*. As in the dialectical method, *freedom* in the operational method doubles its meaning. This is to say that in the first sense, *freedom* means "power"—I may as well use *power* instead of *might*; if I yield to poetry, I may have difficulty explaining it later—your own power. But Thrasymachus in the first book of the *Republic*, even with Plato playing around with his position, gives you the other sense, too; namely, in addition to the freedom that the powerful have, which they impose on others, there is the residue of powers that the others have. Take a man in a state ruled by the power of a tyrant: what freedom he has is in the interstices of the operation of that power. He is free to do whatever he is not controlled to do. This is at the extreme of the tyrannical state. In other states, in, let us say, a democratic state, where the freedom of the people is their ability to rule, the individual within that rule is then free when the law is silent. He has exercised his freedom in helping lay down the regulations—this is the first variety of freedom—and he exercises his residual freedom as an individual within the limitations of what he has helped set up.

Let's turn now to the particular methods. The particular methods aim to do exactly the opposite of what the universal methods do. I mention this fact with particular methods, because they come second in my exposition; if I had started with the particular methods, I would say the universal methods aim to do the opposite of the particular methods. It's a reciprocal proposition between the two; namely, the big mistake in any of the particular methods would be either to permit something that the individual knower holds to intrude into the method—that would be to ruin any scientific basis—or to permit any presupposition about the organized whole to enter in. It is important in the particular methods that you should set up whatever you are setting up in such a way that anyone else could repeat it, and that the scheme within which it works would yield to the process that goes on. Therefore, the operation is not the way in which the knower gets knowledge, whether you begin by supposing that knowledge is in the heavens—like the series of white statues which the soul drives through, following the metaphor from Plato's *Phaedrus*, in order to get a look, and then, subsequently, all thinking is the memory of that journey—or whether it is a process by which the knower creates what is known.

There are two ways in which you can do this. One, the logistic method, uses the mode of thought known as construction. Euclid's *Elements* is an example. Democritus with his examination of the atoms is another. You build what you know entirely in terms of a structure which is in the nature of things. The knowable is not yet known; but underlying things there is a pattern of bodies, and knowledge is knowledge if you can make it approximate to that preexistent pattern and the laws which it exemplifies. The human being, if he is to be examined, can, likewise, be known in the same way. For Democritus, however, there is a second kind of knowledge which arises not from the nature of things but from what happens to us, for example, sensation and emotion, both of which are passions. The difference between the various things that we know about scientifically and the various things that we engage in practically or poetically is the difference between nature and influence. All of these other modes of knowing are emotive rather than cognitive. These two, incidentally, the cognitive and the emotive, are the two methods which, for Democritus, would give you the plurality of the logistic methods.

How am I free? It's very simple. I achieve freedom when I act according to my nature; if I don't act according to my nature, obviously I act because of an external effect. And those external effects can ingrain themselves in me; that is, my past experience may put me in a situation in which I don't act according to my nature. For Lucretius, there are two causes of this: fear, and ignorance or superstition. If I act from fear or from ignorance, I am not acting according to my nature; I'm acting according to my passions. And the risk of these passions has ever increased in modern times: inhibitions, traumas, all of the forms that the logistic aspects of psychoanalysis bring in are of this sort.[11] You notice that whereas reason enters directly into either of the universal forms of freedom, into both the dialectical and the operational, it enters only indirectly into the logistic form. That is, on the one hand, it enters indirectly in the sense that if I'm in a good state, if I have no inhibitions, I'm free. On the other hand, if I need care, it's not my reason that'll help me; rather, it is the philosopher who'll write a poem for me[12] or the psychoanalyst who'll listen to me talking who will give me a therapeutic treatment, at the end of which I'll be free again. Notice, though, that then I will no longer need my poet or my psychoanalyst.

The final kind of freedom is the problematic. The problematic involves taking the known as fundamental, and the mode of thought that is used is resolution. What we are and what we know depend on our circumstances. What we know is totally different from what Descartes knew, what Descartes knew is different from what Saint Thomas Aquinas knew, what Aquinas knew is different from what Aristotle knew; and each of them would begin with the known, the known now in the sense of the accumulated knowledge. The sociologist likes to tell us that there are climates of opinion such that at a given time almost anyone who has a decent education could make the same discovery. That's why Newton and Leibniz, since they were contemporaries, discovered the calculus simultaneously—there may have been more, even. But in any case, it would have been much harder in the sixteenth century to discover the calculus than it was at the end of the seventeenth century, because a lot of work had been done in the interim. This makes perfectly good sense. That is, if you had a man trying to do this who worked before Descartes, Fermat, and Pascal had worked, it would be a very hard job; but those three were all so close to it that after them, only a few changes were necessary.[13] In fact, there are even those who argue that Fermat had it but didn't explain it fully: he didn't want other people to walk off with it too easily. So, the way in which one proceeds is to begin with a problem, a problem which would be determined by what I think the problem is, then to assemble hypotheses, and finally, to try out a possible solution on the basis of the assembled hypotheses. If I am successful, part of the knowable which was not known before now becomes known, the problematic situation changes, and we go on to other knowledge.[14]

What is freedom under the problematic method? Well, freedom is about an action relevant to the circumstances, so you would talk about the situation in which a man operates. Freedom could not be separated from the social situation, from the state; therefore, it is primarily political freedom that would come into question. You notice, as we've gone along, the concept of freedom not only shifts its base but it becomes broader or narrower. What we are talking about here is not logistic freedom, which is the laws of operation of your nature, which a scientist—a physicist, physiologist, or psychologist—could discover. What you are talking about, rather, is the situation in which, under the opinions and the laws that you are surrounded with, either you can do something in accordance with the laws to realize your own development or you can change the laws. Both of these would enter into the problematic aspect (see table 3).[15]

The time for the bell has almost come.[16] As I say, all I've done is to illustrate what freedom is in terms of the method. I want to test what I have been doing, however, by asking the class a question. All during this quarter, I will be asking you to tell me what the method is. So, I've been talking for an hour; I've used most conspicuously a method. What method have I been using?

HAND:[17] Operational.

McKEON: Operational? Why?

HAND: Well, the perspective is pretty much freedom relative to the person who knows.

McKEON: Yes, but is there any other aspect that gives it away even more?

HAND: Discrimination.

McKEON: I've used discrimination a good deal, but these are general words. I'd like it so that you could nail it down. . . . By the way, are there any other hypotheses besides the operational? [L!] Yes?

STUDENT: Not giving one of the others is the right one?

McKEON: No, the operational method is not indifferent to moral standards; you can bring morals in. The operationalist is just as puritanical as the dialectician!

STUDENT: You began with the knower.

McKEON: I began with what?

STUDENT: You began with the knower.

McKEON: Well, this is also true. But, you see, my only objection to all of these is that you are describing little traits that you can hang on to, but right in front of you all the way through, the whole schematism of the operational method has been present. Yes? . . . Well, since the bell is ringing at this moment, although you can't hear it, let me answer it. I put a schematism on the board. I've described it in purely formal terms. I could just as easily have said, "A, B, C, D: now let's try out some meanings." Knower, known, knowable, knowledge are exactly this sort of thing. In the operational method, the fundamental approach of the method is to find basic formal relations. As used in mathematics, they can always be schematized in a matrix, but they don't need to be schematized as a matrix. The word *proportion*, which we use, in Greek applies equally to language, to things, to numbers;[18] consequently, a figure of speech or a metaphor is also this kind of operational approach. The operational approach, then, when it proceeds, would give you, first, in order to clarify, a schematism in which you would test out what is involved by the meanings you give and see what the result is. Now, I've been using the operational method. If I'd used one of the other methods, we would have come out in much the same fashion; but my language would have been totally different, and my schematism would have also been quite different.

In the next lecture, we shall switch from the question of method, that is, from discourse and action, to the question of interpretation, because, you will notice, there's a kind of ambiguity in all of this. These are the various ways in which one can act so as to be free. But what is it to be free? That is not determined by the method; it is determined by the interpretation. And any full statement that I made about the acquisition of freedom would need to specify what I acquired by my method. But this would involve questions that are different; they're the questions that I will want to consider as interpretation, and therefore, interpretation will be separated from method. One further reason for this separation is that by any one of these methods it is possible to acquire freedom in any of the interpretations. Your method will not determine the concept of freedom that the method is directed to.

DISCUSSION

Hobbes, Part 1
(*Leviathan*, Part I, Chapter XIV)[1]

Discussion Summary

We have been looking at the problems of philosophy as they originate in the social sciences, and have chosen the concept of freedom for our initial focus.[2] In our analysis of the term, we have thus far been talking about the question of method, and today we turn to the first of our readings. Let me remind you that the purpose of our discussions is not to penetrate the thought, in this case, of Hobbes but, rather, to lay down the structure of different conceptions of freedom as developed by various authors.

So, how do we go about reading the first page of chapter XIV? Remember, the only way to talk about any term is to get its associations out of the way. In our approach to method, we have found that it is detected in the structure of terms and their interrelations. What, then, is the relation between liberty and power and right and law? In general, the Right of Nature is as opposed to the Law of Nature as liberty is to obligation, "which in one and the same matter are inconsistent." In the first two definitions, then, which appear in these first three paragraphs, he establishes a square of oppositions (see fig. 8).[3]

By definition, then, right is the liberty, and law is a "precept" that "bindeth."[4] To our square of interrelations, moreover, we can add another opposition, that is, an opposition in the possible sources of power. The sources will determine which column the power is in, whether it is a liberty or an obligation (see fig. 9).[5]

What is all this based upon? The first paragraph, the first sentence, is purely semantic, identifying words: "Nature" and "the preservation of his own nature." The preservation of nature has meaning only when you know what is to be preserved. We need the natural man, and all others are of the state. The distinctions are quite strong here: you cannot just jump across to the other column. Whenever one term is used, the others

Right (of Nature)	=/=	Law (of Nature)
||		||
Liberty	=/=	Obligation, Duty

Fig. 8 *Opposition of Liberty and Obligation*

Right (of Nature)	=/=	Law (of Nature)
||		||
Liberty	=/=	Obligation, Duty
Power (own)		Power (others)
Reason or judgment (own)		External compulsion*
Nature (man)		Artificial (state)

*External compulsion may be based on someone else's reason, but does not need to be.

Fig. 9 *Opposition of Power*

are implied; these are precise, definitory relations that he sets up, and they will come through as he goes along. So, in the first three paragraphs, Hobbes is defining the right of nature and the law of nature by a series of mutually exclusive terms or oppositions. Since the two sets of terms are mutually exclusive—in the sense of setting a limit or permitting a latitude—they can be used together in defining the conditions of any action.

In the next two paragraphs, the fourth and fifth, Hobbes is trying to state or deduce the two laws of nature. We've laid down definitions, established a postulate set, and are going on to two conclusions. The first law of nature is universal. We begin by defining a right of nature and want a statement of a universal obligation which is prior to the state: this is the first law. Consequently, the first law is going to link both columns together. But, notice, he doesn't dialectically unite them. The law part enjoins us to seek peace, to use all of our power to achieve peace, but we get to right when there is no possibility left of achieving peace. Then we will use all our power to preserve our own right. So, we now have the first law of nature, obtained by combining a law with a right as simply defined. Notice that in the law there is already included a right.

Next, in the fifth paragraph, he derives a second law out of the first law. Does he say that the second law of nature has two parts? In the first law, remember, law and obligation are joined but not meshed together. Your power is unlimited, but so is that of others. Now, if you are to seek peace, you must give up your power, enter into negotiations, and get back as much as others do. The only thing you don't give up a right to is life, is your own nature. (You may remember that according to Locke, you also do not give up your right to property.) For Hobbes, you can't give away your life, and you can't agree to complete imprisonment. In this second law of nature, consequently, the law part is that you lay down your right to all things, and the part regarding the right—note the prescript and satisfaction here—is to be content with as much as you give others.

Next, he goes on to analyze what is involved in laying down a right. Renouncing a right is simply giving it up; it's not a transaction across the line separating our columns. As a result of renouncing right for the first time, justice enters into the picture. It was not here before or on one side of the line or on the other. Injustice, by his careful proof, is merely doing something which is the contrary of what one did before; injustice is analogous to absurdity. Therefore, injustice exists only as a result of the abandonment of right.

Let's summarize what we have learned about Hobbes's method. It has been suggested by a student that he uses the operational method. If Hobbes were operational, a change in meaning of terms and some arbitrariness would exist. If, however, he were logistic, he would define terms univocally and stick to those terms. Remember, in universal methods, individual terms can be given different meanings. Here, however, the author sticks to his terms. Therefore, the method is logistic. A method is a way of proceeding discursively. It could do it by setting up proportions, but the logistic mode of thought does it by composition, just as we have built up laws from parts. Here we have made two compositions, two Laws of Nature, out of right and law. By contrast, the operational method uses discrimination to keep separate what could be seen to be one or the other, as if we were to say, "The law of nature from one point of view is this." The operational method never sets up laws; rather, it says, "Let's assume that *a* is to *b* as *c* is to *d*." Generally, the operational method can set up variables clean of meaning, even when starting halfway through an argument. Never are meanings sharply separated, but they help work out (always in a series of analogies, such as the atom can be to the solar system) further contrasts. They always have analogy. Here, the artificial man, the state, isn't an analogy; rather, it is itself a composition. The logistic method can use proportion; but whenever we take parts, identify them, and make a composite of things out of those parts, we are still using the logistic method.

We will next be reading Spinoza's *Ethics*. First, in your reading, contrast or compare Hobbes and Spinoza. We will culminate in book V, "Of the Power of the Understanding, or Of Human Freedom." But first, we need to go rapidly through earlier parts of the work. So, read the following sections in the *Ethics*:

Book 1: Definition VII, Prop. XVII, XXIX, XXXII with Corollaries I and II
Book 2: Proposition LX, XLIX with Corollary
Book 3: Introduction, Definitions, Proposition II with Scholium
Book 4: Preface, Definition VIII, Proposition XVIII, LVII–LXXIII (the characteristics of free men)
All of Book 5

McKeon's Notes[6]

Hobbes — Liberty 1.

Leviathan. Book I, Chap. XIV. — Actional. Logistic. Entitative

Method—detected in the structure of terms and their interrelations.

Right of Nature opposed to Law of Nature, as obligation and liberty, "which in one and the same matter are inconsistent."

Square established in the first two definitions:

Right of Nature	Law of Nature
Liberty	Obligation, Duty.
Power (own)	(External power)
Nature (man)	Artificial (state)
Own judgment, reason	External coercion

Since the two sets of terms are mutually exclusive—in the sense of setting a limit or permitting a latitude—they can be used together in defining the conditions of any action.

Method logistic—knowledge is used indirectly in securing liberty. Knowledge—nature of man—Natural liberty as opposed to own judgment, reason.

[1][7] Begin with the definition of Right of Nature—Jus Naturale—(1) liberty to use his own power, as he wills himself, for the preservation of his own nature or life, and (2) consequently of doing anything which in his own judgment and reason he conceives to be apt to that

~~Phenomenal~~ *Ontic* interpretation—~~existentialist~~*entitative*.[8]

[2] Liberty—(1) absence of external impediments which often take away man's power to do as he would, but (2) cannot hinder him from using the power left to him according to his judgment and reason.

[3] Law of Nature—Lex Naturalis—precept or general rule of reason by which mankind is forbidden (1) to do that which is destructive of life or of the means of preserving it and (2) to omit that which preserves it.

[4] Then statement of the relation of mutual exclusion of law and right. That is, one is free with respect to what one is not bound to. But that means that freedom and obligation are both involved in the definition of either.

Thus Liberty—absence of external restraint in the use of power—basic power—judgment and reason, but product of the use of reason is general precept or law.

Liberty therefore (1) power unaffected by external constraint, (2) power of reason using remaining power.

[5] Application of the condition of man.

(1) War of all against all—each governed by his own reason, therefore (2) use everything to preserve self or right to everything—no security as long as that right endures.

N.B. argument involves a right and a law: consequence of the first law of nature.

(2) seek peace and follow it (law) and (2) defend ourselves by all means (right), advantages of war.

Effect of law—men commanded to endeavor peace.

[6] From this fundamental law of nature is derived the second law of nature. (1) for peace and self-defense he shall think it necessary to lay down this right to all things (law) and (2) be content with as much liberty against others as he allows others.

Golden rule stated as law of the Gospel (positive command) and as law of all men (negative prohibition).

[7] Analysis of lay down right—divest self of liberty of hindering other. Not giving another a right he did not have before—had right, stand out of his way, to permit him to enjoy his own original right.

[8] (p. 2) Either renouncing or transferring. In either way he is obliged or bound: duty.

Consequence—injustice or injury—defined as departure from the obligation voluntarily assumed.

Similarity of injustice to absurdity—contradicting what you said originally.

Signs or bonds binding—words and actions

[9] First consequence of second natural law—duty, that is, a law of action binding men; second consequence a right.

Lay down right in consideration of right reciprocally transferred to him—object some good to self. Therefore some rights cannot be abandoned—(1) loss of life, (2) imprisonment, (3) threat to end—security of person.

[10] Mutual transfer of right called Contract.

DISCUSSION

Hobbes, Part 2 (*Leviathan*, Part I, Chapter XIV; Part II, Chapter XXI; *Philosophical Rudiments Concerning Government and Society*, Chapter XIV)[1]

Discussion Summary

As we go on interpreting philosophers, we will find that there are many interpretations and no unique one. In terms of the schematism we have been setting up, with regard to method, Hobbes is not using a dialectical method, for he doesn't begin with contradictions of experience which are assimilated and meet in a transcendental reality. Also, he is not using the problematic method, which would require that we state what the problem is and eliminate hypotheses. This does not mean that we will not solve the problem; but instead, we are not setting down hypotheses and eliminating some, as the problematic method would do. Instead, Hobbes takes the basic terms in the first three paragraphs of chapter XIV of part I. We found that they could be arranged in two columns of mutually unvarying and exclusive terms (see fig. 9). The terms going down the columns imply each other, and across the columns they are unequal and mutually exclusive. This method isn't operational, because even though we can make distinctions, what we have doesn't change with points of view. In the operational method, the writer will say that from one point of view, it is this, and from another, this. If the writer says that central concepts are mutually exclusive, the same situation cannot be interpreted in multiple ways. This is the logistic method.

We began with the right of nature, which has a two-part definition. The first part is the liberty man has to use his own power for the preservation of his own nature and life. The second part of the definition includes doing anything which in man's own judgment is of help in preserving his own nature and life. Similarly, liberty has a two-part definition. First, it is defined in terms of man's power and external power: it exists where there is an absence of external impediments, which may take away part of a man's power. Second, in the remnant of the liberty that so exists, man may use whatever power remains according to his judgment. Here again we bring in man's judgment. Our third central concept that is defined here is the law of nature. This is a contrary of right. The law of nature is a precept or a general rule of reason by which mankind is forbidden (1) to do anything destructive of his life and (2) to omit any means that he thinks may preserve it. Notice that contraries are at work here. Hobbes makes statements of the mutual exclusion of law and right, but freedom and obligation are involved in the definition of both. One is free with respect to things one is not bound by. Thus, liberty is a basic power—we come to it by judgment and reason. To summarize, liberty is that power unaffected by external restraint, and reason is using the power left over.

In the logistic method, then, Hobbes uses the method of composition in two senses: (1) where he is compounding natural units, and (2) where he is compounding passions and emotions. The chapter's fourth paragraph applies this compound distinction to the nature of man. In the first place, the condition of man is war, the war of all against all. Because man has a right to anything, even another human's body, the result is that there is no security as long as this right endures. Therefore, this argument leads to a law and a right. The consequences of argument has the law of nature in two parts here. The separation is sharp. The first law is to seek peace. The right includes the advantages of war. Note the sharpness of the separation: we do one or the other—we seek peace or the advantages of war. The second law is derived from the first. This is logistic. It is deductive. This second law also has two parts. First, man lays down the right to all things. Second, the obligation to man is to be content with as much liberty for himself as he gives others. In positive terms, this is the Golden Rule; in negative terms, this is Hobbes's Law of All Men—the second law of nature.

The sixth paragraph of chapter XIV: Since we lay down rights—we can analyze what this is—we are not giving to others a right we didn't have before. Now we turn to ways we can lay down a right. We can lay down a right by renouncing it or transferring it. Either way, we encounter an obligation. The consequence is that for the first time, an injustice or injury is defined. There is no injustice in the state of nature, but there can be inequities. To commit an injustice is the same in form as to commit an absurdity. So for Hobbes, either words or actions are signs that hold you to an obligation, a binding.

The first consequence of the second natural law is duty. The second is right. We lay down right in consequence of some good to oneself. We can't abandon some rights. We can't agree to what hurts ourselves. Thus, we cannot abandon the right to life, to resist imprisonment, or resist something which threatens the security of our person.

Thus, the step-by-step analysis proceeds. He is a careful man in this method.

In the second selection, chapter XXI of part II, which occurs some distance from the first, there are two parts. One section deals with natural liberty, and the second deals with civil liberty. In the first paragraph of the chapter, he says that freedom can apply to inanimate and irrational creatures. Why? The reason for this is that by "action" he means any local motion, and "external impediment" is anything that stops local motion. Thus, a stone is as free as a man. This is an *entitative* interpretation, because only this interpretation takes motion to be local motion and the entity involved to be a body.

In the second paragraph, Hobbes says all bodies can be free. Now let us focus on one kind of a body—a man. Man has will and wit, which a stone does not have. In those things one can do by strength and wit, he is not hindered by what he has a will to do. If he has power, he can will it. If he wills it and is able to do it, then he is free. He then goes on to point out that since freedom applies only to bodies, it's not literally correct to speak of free gifts, free speech, and so on.

In summary, the first paragraph defines freedom as the absence of hindrance in the motion of bodies. In the second paragraph, man is described as one such body. Now we can look at the third paragraph. Among things that man wants to do, some are direct, and others are distant. We may find contradictions in what he wants to do. He might want to make money by importing goods, but he wants both his life and his goods in a storm. In pursuit of one, he may be free, although he may be constrained in pursuit of the other. Among hindrances to freedom are the passions, like fear, but freedom is still consistent with fear.

In the fourth paragraph, Hobbes addresses God and man. The argument is that in my nature, I do something according to law, going back to God. Man does everything necessarily, but this is not contradictory to freedom. The freedom that a man has is consistent with the fear caused by external events and with necessity. What one wills is necessary, but on the other hand, the operations of these laws of nature allow us to act freely. In other words, the things that one wills are necessary and follow from the laws of one's nature. But if they did not follow from these laws, they would not be free but arbitrary. Wit and will explain it—this gives us freedom; nature will explain it—this gives us necessity. Again, to summarize what we have learned thus far: in paragraph one, liberty consists of bodies and their motions. In paragraph two, man is one body. In paragraph three, he is influenced by external causes which lead to fear, but he can still act freely. In paragraph four, man operates like a body and according to his nature; therefore, a free act is caused, but a free act is also necessary. Hume says the same thing one century later.

Now we can address the next three paragraphs. How do we handle the problem of civil liberty? Earlier, Hobbes described the natural man. Now

Higher Restrictions Retained

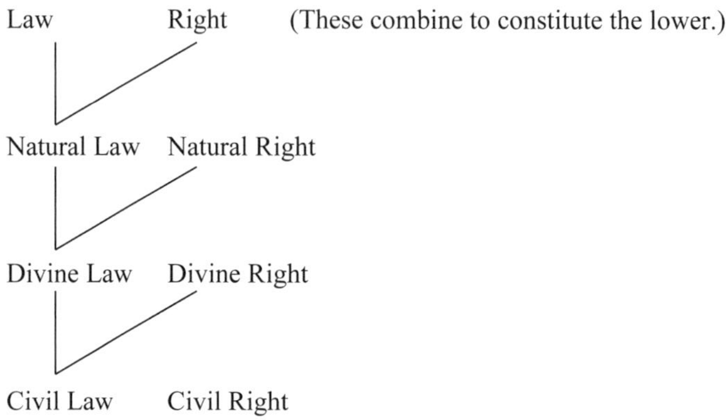

Fig. 10 *Origins and Manifestations of Laws*

we get to the artificial man—the commonwealth or state. The state has laws like natural laws that are called civil laws. (In the entitative interpretation, laws both of nature and of the state are *laws* in the same sense.) Now we are in a position to say something about the differences in the two laws. Natural law is by composition, whereas civil law is set up by covenant. So, now we can look to a twofold distinction between subject and sovereign. Liberty of subjects has two key aspects: their liberty lies in the region that the law passes over. The right of the sovereign is that he can perform no injustice to subjects, because the latter have entered into a covenant giving the former their power. The sovereign may act contrary to natural law, and therefore to God, to whom he is subject, but the sovereign would then be committing an inequity but not an injustice. The subject has his region of freedom in every state: he is free where the law is silent. Hobbes goes on to examine this freedom and argues that subjects are mistaken about it in two ways. First, freedom being physical liberty, if one is not in jail and or in chains, it is absurd to argue for freedom, because he is already free; second, if he holds that freedom is exemption from laws, as in a freedom to murder, *etc.*, that is equally absurd; for if he had that, there would be no law or social order, everyone would be at risk from everyone else, and no one would be free from injustice.

What does our remaining selection, chapter XIV from *Philosophical Rudiments Concerning Government and Society*, do? Here he adds new terms. Previously, we have defined natural law and natural right, civil law and civil right, and now we add divine law and divine right to them. The

Higher Liberties Restrained

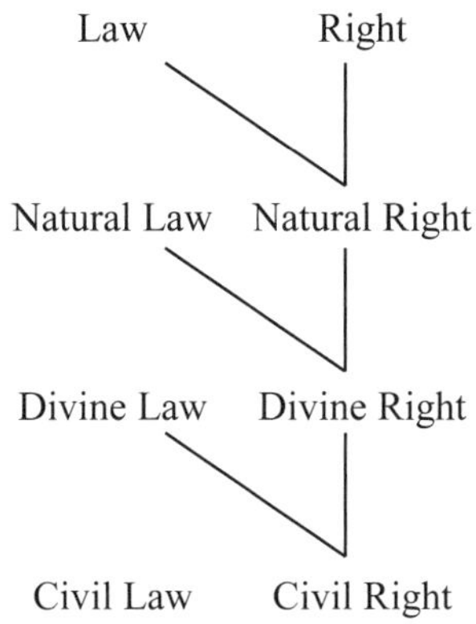

Fig. 11 *Origins and Manifestations of Rights*

basic rule is that whatever is prohibited by the higher, that is, natural and divine law, cannot be permitted by the lower, namely, civil law. This is because laws are prohibitions, while rights are permissions. We have two sequences here. The prohibitions of natural law continue all the way down, and the higher restrictions are retained as the lower add more. By contrast, in the second sequence, higher rights or liberties are restrained by the lower. Consequently, one goes from the highest to the most constricted both with regard to law (see fig. 10) and with regard to right (see fig. 11).[2]

This gets us to a double rule. First, what remains as rights may be further restrained as we go downward. Second, natural law is a restriction to which you can add, but the higher restriction is retained throughout. The point is that we get from a basis in nature to the forms that laws may take in nature and in the state. The natural law is a restriction to which we add restrictions, but that higher restriction is always retained. Hobbes writes about inferior and superior laws, and in doing so, he comes down the line in terms of allowances and prohibitions.

McKeon's Notes[3]

Hobbes — Liberty 2

N.B. Constructive sequence—literal terms. Deductive derivation, first principles. However discriminative determination of first principles—rules of mutual exclusion and discriminative determination of interpretation—liberty of self-determination of bodies.

Right =/=	law		Law (nat.)	Right (nat.)
||	||		Rule—preservation	Liberty—to all
Liberty =/=	obligation			
(principles)			Precept of reason, 1st law of nat.	
			Law—peace	Right—war
			Second law of nature	
			Law	Right
			Lay down uni. right	Retain as other
			Civil laws	Contract
			(method)	

Deduction of laws of nature from natural law and natural right

Discrimination in establishment of *principles—actional* principles: no natural difference between right and wrong. These the result of the establishment of sovereignty and the will of the sovereign.

Construction in method—first principles, literal definition of terms, univocal; one method of science—applicable to bodies but need of differentiation for artificial man or commonwealth—three sciences—bodies (de corpore), man (de homine), citizen (de cive).

Construction in interpretation—body underlying phenomena and actions. Only true liberty—natural liberty: all bodies can have liberty. Second meaning due to will in man and reason in man—power to do what one wills—not hindered from doing what he has the wit and strength to do if he wishes.

Hobbes Liberty 3

Book II Chapter XXI.
As Chapter 14 sketched the interrelations of basic terms for the construction of the state (civil) on the basis of the state (natural), so Chapter 21 deals with the applications of the terms so defined and related.

Two problems—universal applications in nature *Natural Liberty, specific applications* in civil state *Artificial Liberty.*

[1][4] *First question*—liberty and nature.

(a) Liberty applies to all creatures—inanimate and irrational as well as rational (p.2)—Liberty external impediment to motion. When the impediment to motion is in the constitution of the thing, it is lack of power not lack of liberty. All bodies—scope of freedom. Entitative interpretation.

[2] (b) Application to man—Freeman (p.3) definition—interpretation—in those things which by his strength and wit he is able to do, he is not hindered to do what he has a will to do.

"Free" applied only to bodies. Free gift, free speech, free will—all mean freedom of the man.

[3] (c) Liberty consistent with fear. Sinking ship and paying debt. Commonwealth fear of law.

N.B. Freedom here reconciled with civil obligation i.e. external power.

[4] (d) Liberty and necessity consistent. Every act proceeds from a cause—God first link. Necessity of man's voluntary actions. Necessity and liberty of many; omnipotence and liberty of God.

Natural liberty only properly called liberty.

N.B. sequence of liberty in variety of powers.

(a) Body and external bodies—liberty and power.
(b) Man—will to do and power to do.
(c) Man influenced by fear (external)—within condition may still act freely.
(d) Man and necessity (internal)—free act caused and therefore necessary.

[1] *Second question*—Relation of natural and artificial *(1)* man—commonwealth, artificial chains, civil laws.

[2] Sovereign power. Two consequences—*(a) Subject* (1) balance *(2)* of right and law—resulting in liberty being that which is left by silence of laws, actions by the law praetermitted (*(1)* if corporal liberty, not lacking; *(2)* if liberty counter to law, absurd), *[3]* (2) right of sovereign—can do no injury to subject, no injustice, want no right. But subject to God and may act counter to the law of nature.

Right and liberty of sovereign people of Athens to banish jester or just; right of Athenian to jest or be just.

N.B. Entitative interpretation fitted to literal definition of terms from logistic method and to arbitrary original distinctions from actional principles

First question—liberty applies to inanimate, irrational and rational creatures.

a. Motion—impediment. Natural liberty.
Body—external impediment

b. Man as free (only bodied free—derived sense of free gift, free will).
Power to act—will or inclination to act.

Inclination — fear of consequences

↙ ↘

Freedom to act or not to act.

c. Apparent contraction of freedom and fear removed.
d. Apparent contradiction of freedom and necessity removed.

All actions caused. God first cause. Man in his actions. Necessity as effect of God. Necessity of man's will—liberty of man.

Necessity—inevitable actions and free actions.

Second question. Civil laws and civil liberty. Artificial Liberty.

Subject	Right	Law.
	Inalienable rights of subjects and contract of subjects	Civil laws and civil rights.
	Sovereign—only natural law; rights of sovereign	No injury of subjects by sovereign

---

Hobbes Liberty 4.

Philosophical Rudiments concerning Government and Society

Confusion of law with right, and neglect of proper relation between natural, divine, and civil laws.

Questions two—what is prohibited and *what is permitted* in the sequence of laws.

Divine and civil law—what is prohibited by divine law cannot be permitted by civil law. What is commanded by divine laws cannot be permitted by civil.

What is permitted by Divine right may be prohibited by civil laws. Inferior laws may restrain what is permitted by superior.

Laws being removed, our liberty is absolute. Natural liberty is not constituted but allowed by the laws.

Restrained by natural and divine laws; residue by civil laws; remains may be constrained by constitutions or particular towns or societies.

Law—fetter; right freedom; related as contraries.

N.B. Relation of divine and civil laws.
Prohibition law; permission right. Prohibitions transitive from top to bottom; permissions may be restricted at lower level.

In the three selections.[5] Basic distinction by means of contrariety of obligation and freedom—all terms ranged under one or the other. Actional principles.

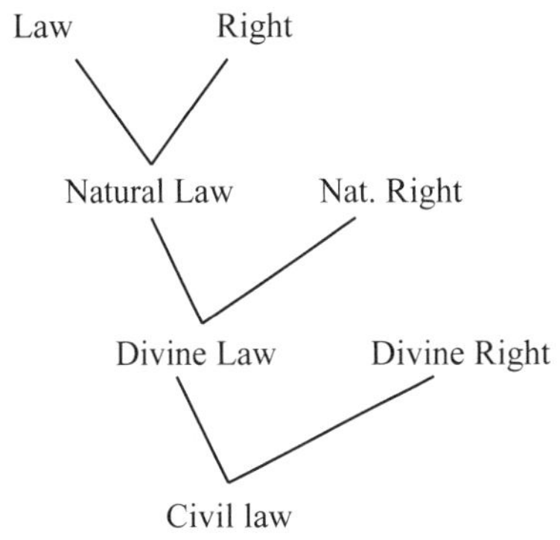

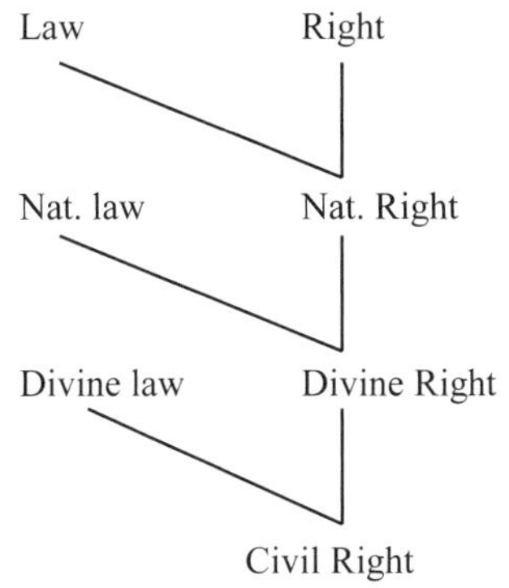

Restrictions — Liberties remaining after restrictions

Higher *restrictions* retained. — Higher liberties restrained

Deductive derivation of laws form first law of nature: determination at each stage of the obligation and the remaining right. Logistic method.

Application of laws and rights to entities—bodies and motions, preferences and contracts. Entitative interpretation.

Fundamentally the opposition between two kinds of power—external and internal. Basic opposition—principles; construction of the relations and societies to which the principles apply—method; conclusion concerning what things or actions are free or bound—interpretation.

Three arrangements of terms: (a) basic sorting—liberty and restrain, (b) construction of relations among things at liberty and constrained—nature, man, state, (c) differentiation of natural and artificial, natural and civil law.

Ch. XIV. Natural law—the natural conditions of civil society. How combine right and law: natural right universal, no security—diminution of rights for security a law of reason.

Ch. XXI. Man in state—citizen a body like other bodies. (4 respects), but sovereign is a source of civil law—command but not party to contract, restricted by no law limiting his right to anything. Establishment of asymmetry.

N.B. Principles in contrariety (defined in application); interpretation in the distinction of constructs as bodies and constructs as voluntary agreement. Bodies (motions) and values (impulses and preferences).

Rudiments

Interrelations of successive laws and rights running through natural, divine, and civil.

Begin with universal rights—restricted by series of laws—civil law can remove none of the prior restrictions, but civil law can further restrict some of the rights permitted by higher laws.[6]

LECTURE THREE

Freedom: Interpretation

Last time I discussed the concept of freedom and at the same time illustrated the variety of methods by which it is defined. Today I want to go on to a second phase of the definition of freedom which will, in turn, be an exploration of the varieties of interpretations that are possible of the term. You will recall that at the beginning of the course, I explained that the definition would consist of four parts, and that the parts can be distinguished formally by means of the number of terms that are involved (see table 1). In a method, one is engaged in a process or in discourse, and you need, therefore, three or more terms. The answer that method gives with respect to freedom has to do either with the processes by which one acquires freedom or exercises it, or with the processes by which one engages in discourse—proof, inquiry, any of the modes of discourse—in the formulation of freedom (see table 2). Interpretation, by contrast, is a matter of two terms: it corresponds to the proposition, to the sentence. It is the minimum unit to which the expressions "true" and "false" can be applied. In fact, it is the proper unit for truth and falsity, because truth and falsity in discourse are tested by the propositions in which discourse eventuates. Therefore, the question we asked last time about freedom, depending upon method, could be stated simply as the question, How is freedom acquired or understood?; and the question of interpretation is the question, What things are free? They're separate questions, separate in such fashion that the methods, any of them, would be applicable to the interpretations, any of them. You do not close the door on the interpretation of freedom in choosing the method by which it is acquired. Notice, lest it seem that "what" questions are more precise or in better odor than "how" questions, they're both "what" questions: the question of method is the question, What is freedom?; the question we shall be considering today is the question, What are free things?

In order to enter into the discussion of the modes of interpretation,

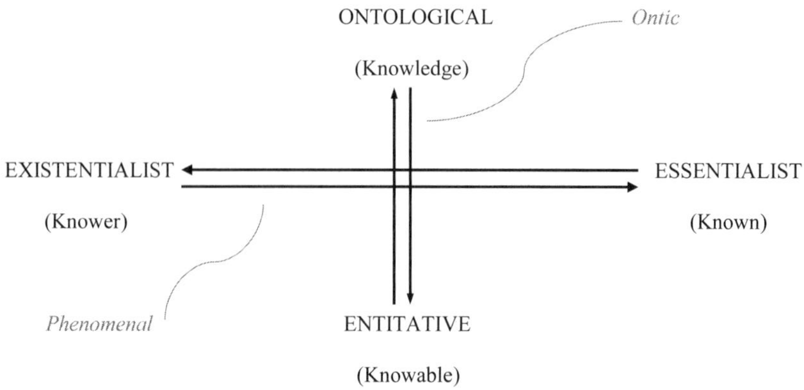

Fig. 12 *Interpretation and Knowledge Matrix*

let me use the same diagram that I used for methods. You will recall that for method, we related knowledge to knower, known to knowable (see fig. 5). These terms themselves are without definition until the method is applied. They are what the ancients would have called commonplaces, but you can call them variables—variables and commonplaces are good equivalent words. There we found that we had two varieties of method, depending upon whether method is a way in which a knower is related to knowledge—acquires knowledge or makes knowledge—or whether you conceive method in terms of the way in which the knowable is translated into the known. The connections which give us interpretation are again two: you can view interpretation either as a way in which the knowable is stated in knowledge or as a way in which the knower formulates or transmits what is known. Like the two kinds of method, the two kinds of interpretation are radically distinct. They're the subject of a good deal of discussion today; and therefore, in the differentiation of interpretations I shall be able to appropriate very fashionable words—in the case of some of my other distinctions, I had to invent them. The vertical interpretations, that is, knowledge—knowable, are *ontic* interpretations. The horizontal interpretations, that is, knower—known, are *phenomenal* (see fig. 12).[1] Let me therefore, as in the case of method, differentiate the four interpretations, going through them, to begin with, in pairs—first the ontic, then the phenomenal—and then in the subdivisions of each pair of interpretations.

In an ontic interpretation, the assumption is that the interpretation is a true or false statement about any term, like *freedom*, which depends on reference to a fundamental reality which is not directly experienced. In a phenomenal interpretation, on the other hand, it is assumed that the interpretation of true or false statements can be found wholly on the level of or on something directly in experience. Consequently, if you have a philosophic approach which deals only with experience, it is a phenomenal approach. If you have an approach in which there is a phenomenal approach and something besides, that is an ontic approach; and therefore, as in the case of the universal methods, there will be for the ontic interpretations a doubling of meanings. Some of you after the last lecture wanted to know why the universal methods doubled their meanings. Let me answer it for the interpretations, because the answer is exactly the same. That is to say, in the case of the ontic interpretations, you will grant that there is a phenomenal interpretation. There is no ontic or ontological philosopher who does not begin with experience; therefore, experience as the starting point is within his conception of interpretation, fact, or truth, but it is never enough. You need to go beyond; and that step going beyond is what gives you your second, fundamental meaning of freedom, truth, or anything else. The phenomenal interpretations are always skeptical about the appeal beyond experience. If you still read Plato's *Republic* in you previous courses, you will remember that the Divided Line divides the line into two parts, one part of which is knowledge, the other part is opinion.[2] The phenomenal interpretations are interpretations which existed when the *Republic* was written; they exist still today. The same with the ontic interpretations. The phenomenal interpretations deny that there is any upper end to the Divided Line. They say there is science or knowledge, but it is exactly the same as opinion. In the days of Plato, you need only to read Isocrates, who is mentioned by Plato himself. Isocrates says, in effect, that the entire Divided Line must be divided on the bottom half; the other half is a deception worked upon you by conniving philosophers!

Let's look at the ontic interpretation first. The ontic interpretation may be of two sorts: things may be said to be what they are either by reference to a transcending reality, a reality which is over and above, in which case it is proper to call it an *ontological* interpretation; or the things beyond may be with reference to an underlying physical body which is not directly experienced—you experience only the secondary qualities, but you can infer that there is a body with mass, with extension, with parts—this is an *entitative* interpretation. In both cases, you will observe that in order to interpret anything, including your everyday experience, either you have to go back, as Plato did, from the realm of experience to eternal ideas, which experience imitates, or you need to go down from the experiences of sense to the atoms and objects which combine and lead to the experiences of sense. The former is ontological; the second is entitative.

If you deny that there is any need to imagine, to construct, another reality which you don't directly experience, you do it in one to two ways. In the first, you begin with the knower and hold that everything that you say, do, or imagine you know must be viewed from the point of view, the perspective, of the observer. In antiquity, the best way to state this was that "man is the maker of all things";[3] but intentionalities, significances, the existentialist orientation, all would be modern versions of exactly the same thing. Beginning with that orientation, the activity of the knower will account for anything which the ontologist sets up as knowledge or the materialist sets up as matter. It is merely what is inferred or used by the knower in order to express, systematize, orient what he is doing. This is the *existentialist* interpretation. The second possibility is that you begin with the experience viewed relative to the conditioning circumstances in which the individual finds himself. If you begin with the known, that is, the body of knowledge, the biological, social, physical environment of the knower, then all interpretation will depend upon the problems that he perceives and the means he can dispose of in order to deal with the problems and to resolve them. This is the *essentialist* interpretation.

You'll observe that as I've gone along, I've used the four modes of thought again in order to get my four interpretations. In the ontic, if we are relating knowledge to the knowable with emphasis upon the intelligible whole, it is by means of the mode of thought assimilation that I come to the ontological being, or one which is the source of all interpretation. If, on the other hand, I orient to the knowable, I use the mode of thought construction in order to deal with the entities and their interrelations which are the basis of my interpretation. If I begin with the knower, it is important to differentiate all of the perspectives of the various possible knowers; and I am consequently using the mode of thought discrimination. If, finally, I begin with the known, the circumstances, the accumulated knowledge, habits, and institutions, then I begin with the problems that are resolved; this is the mode of thought resolution.[4]

We need to look now at what freedom is in these respects. Notice that the device that I used earlier for methods is much easier for interpretation. Remember, I said that when people talk about something like freedom, it is always possible to begin with an ambiguous statement on which they would all agree; interpret it more precisely, and you'd have their meaning. The ambiguous statement with which we are dealing in this process of interpretation is the statement on which I think all philosophers can be shown to agree, that freedom is action in the absence of external restraints, or more accurately, it is the ability and power to act without external restraints. You will notice that at once, the difference between ontic and phenomenal interpretations of freedom presents a radical difference. It is one that I think is not normally the subject of discussion when talking about freedom, because we're so habituated to thinking either in ontic or in phenomenal terms. For ontic interpretations, the meaning of freedom depends on something beyond experience; therefore, the phenomenal activities are measured against a real norm. Consequently, for ontic interpretations, freedom means—and there's still ambiguity here—some sense of doing what one should, whether or not one wants to, that is, one is free only if one acts according to the norm set up; whereas for the phenomenal interpretations, freedom means doing as one pleases, whether or not one should. As we go along, I want to examine these differences more fully, because the two senses of doing as one should, which correspond to ontological and entitative interpretations, are quite different; and the two senses in which doing as you please is set forth, reflecting the existentialist and essentialist interpretations, are likewise quite different.

Let's start with the ontic interpretations, the relation between knowledge and the knowable. There's a basic agreement—still ambiguous, as I have said—between the two ontic interpretations; namely, both of them say that freedom consists in acting in accordance with one's true nature, which is usually called internal—internal and external are a favorite pair in the ontic interpretation—in a context of influences, which are external. But the external influences can manifest themselves internally in a variety of ways: passions, ignorance, repressions that are contrary to one's true nature, suppressions, superstitions. They have a lot of names, and they shift according to the appropriate language in which the interpretation is made.

We will begin, then, with the ontological, the first of the ontic interpretations. This is the interpretation in which the mode of thought assimilation is used. Remember, we are answering the question, What things are free? Let me put down the mark of freedom for each of these. For the ontological, what things are free? Plato, the Stoics, Spinoza, they all give the same answer: only wise men are free, no one else. And this is quite categorical. Look at the fifth book of Spinoza's *Ethics*, where wisdom and freedom are equated. Or, Cicero wrote a treatise called *The Paradoxes of the Stoics*, and in that there's a whole chapter on freedom. It worries him, because according to the Stoics—he's quite right—only the wise man is free. And let me answer not only in terms of what things: what forms of action or motion are free? Well, the only form is—and I want to get this word in, because it is important here—autonomous wisdom; that is to say, a wisdom which rules the self is the action of freedom.

Let me explain in a little more detail the ontological interpretation.

The ontological interpretation is the assimilation of the knowable to knowledge. That is to say, it is the assimilation of the thing which is, however indeterminately, to the most perfect form of which it is capable of being. The variety of forms in which things are manifested are levels of perfection in the ontological interpretation, and there's a whole series of philosophies that have hierarchies in which the general rule is that a thing *is* more truly as it is more perfectly. The more perfectly it is what it is, the more truly it is and the freer it is, because what it is when it is truly, it's autonomous, it is its own nature. In the assimilation of the knowable to knowledge, you do it by approximation of actual or physical actions to ideal norms. There are two levels possible—this is where your two interpretations come in. On the highest level, knowledge and being coincide; on the lower levels, where you are operating by opinion and becoming, you might have right opinion, but you never know: opinion can be right or wrong. Consequently, there are two levels or senses of freedom. When a man acts according to knowledge, he acts according to his own nature, he is free. When he acts according to opinion, he acts according to his formed character, which is different from his nature. He acts according to what he has acquired of knowledge; he acts according to his passions. He may be free if he has right opinion, but he may also be a slave—Plato likes this expression—a slave to his passions. Plato likes another pair of expressions: self-mastery, and self-mastery is the only alternative to the mastery of someone else or to the mastery of the passions, which is exactly the same thing. In regions of opinion, a man may think himself free when he is really a slave, and this is the great problem that Socrates comes back to again and again.

There are two varieties of states, both with respect to law and the exercise of power. In the perfect state, there are no laws except the laws of education. I don't know how carefully you read the *Republic*, but if you'll look you'll notice that on two occasions Socrates says this very explicitly. One, he says, "Shouldn't we set down and have a few criminal laws, laws of contract, laws of torts, all the other laws?" And the interlocutor at that point says, "Well, no, not here; reason is the law. But we do need the laws regulating education."[5] Then there's a second state, which Plato called the second-best state. The title of the dialogue in which he develops it is *Laws*, and in the *Laws* there are no philosopher-kings, no dialecticians, no education leading from mathematics to dialectic. Rule is by the experienced men, the old men of the nocturnal council; and all the way through they say, *qua* law, whether you take the whole body of the laws or individual laws, there are two parts: one is persuasion—every law must have a preamble to put the citizen in the right frame of mind—and the second part is power. If the citizen is not in a state of mind to be

Table 4. Freedom: Interpretation.

Mode of Thought	Interpretation	What Things Are Free?	What Actions Are Free?	Summary Description
		Ontic		
Assimilation	Ontological	Wise Men	Wisdom, Autonomous	Self-Perfection
Construction	Entitative	Bodies, Moving	Locomotion, Unimpeded	Self-Determination
		Phenomenal		
Discrimination	Existentialist	Animals, Unrestrained	Behavior, Spontaneous	Self-Initiation
Resolution	Essentialist	Men in Society	Actions, Deliberate	Self-Development

reasonable, then you use power to prevent him from the infringement that he would otherwise engage in. What's the relation between right and law, justice and law? Remember, many of our words are more separated than the Greek: Greek words would relate *justice* and *right*—they're really the same word. When we begin talking about righteousness, we don't remember that we're translating a single Latin word and a single Greek word: *dikaiosyne* in the New Testament is translated sometimes as "righteousness," sometimes "justice." The fact that we mean the same thing—that we did when King James translated it that way with the assistance of his scholars; we probably don't any more—has been lost. In this regard, justice or right in the perfect state is action in accordance with the ideal nature of man. In an imperfect state, law is a combination of external power and external sales force, that is to say, persuasion.

What is freedom? Freedom in this sense—I'll put a third word for each of these—is self-perfection. You may think that this is a strange sense. But if you read your philosophers carefully, if you read the theologians carefully, it's not only the one which is at the very basis of much of the Western tradition; I also suspect that if you did a poll in terms of frequency of occurrence, it occurs more frequently than the conceptions of freedom that you would put down as your ordinary conception or the one expressed in ordinary language (see table 4).[6]

Let's turn to the second of the ontic interpretations, the entitative interpretation. The mode of thought is construction, that is, the building of things and of knowledge from their parts. What is it that is free? Let me put it down in the column:[7] any body can be free. When is a body free?—maybe to balance "wise men," now let me put—I said any body can be free—a body is free when it's moving; therefore, a moving body is free. We still speak of a freely falling body to distinguish it from a body where motion has been violently imposed upon it. What does freedom consist in? It consists in unimpeded motion. Bear in mind, we're here dealing in the mode of thought construction: you build your man out of bodies; therefore, it is one of the reductive modes. You can explain any kind of change by locomotion of bodies, so we're not leaving anything out. We are merely presenting a mode of interpretation which should account for the same kind of statement that your ontologist will give. For the free man, what does freedom consist in? Not self-perfection—that doesn't make any sense—but self-determination.

Remember, what we did before was to assimilate the knowable to knowledge; we are now reversing the process and constructing knowledge from the knowable. The knowable—and you can fill in your details; I'll now give you a list of them—would range anywhere from atoms to any other basic series of elements out of which you construct knowledge. When the empiricists in the seventeenth century began with simple ideas, they used an interpretation that was similar to this. If you build out of any elemental parts, your interpretation may be an entitative interpretation. When you construct knowledge from the knowable, when you begin with the constitution of things—that's what the knowable now becomes; and let me repeat to you what I said before: the word has changed its meaning, it's not what Plato would have meant—the knowable is now the underlying physical reality that is the basis. We will explain knowledge in such a construction by means of the underlying reality, both in the sense of using the nature of things as the criterion for testing the body of knowledge that we have on the top and in the sense of explaining the process by which we acquire knowledge also by means of the motions of the body of the knower. In other words, it provides both the criterion of our knowledge and the explanation of our own process of knowing.[8] I can use it to give the way in which I think and inquire as well as to give the significance of what I have discovered as a result of my inquiry. There is, as I've suggested, a variety of ways in which the nature of knowledge is determined by the constitution or structure of things. Among others, there were Democritus, Hegel, Marx, Freud, and the early Bertrand Russell—the Bertrand Russell that had atomic facts had atoms which were quite different from the atoms of Democritus.

Let me stick to just one of them. Democritus, since we have only a series of fragments of his, is much easier to understand than the others, and I'll pick Democritus. In Democritus, the atoms and the motions of the atoms in the void determine both the nature of things and knowledge. We have the process of knowledge: we have scientific knowledge only of the atoms. As a result of the interplay of our bodies with other things, for instance, the impact which the atoms of light have on the atoms of my eye, we have perceptions and emotions. Therefore, for Democritus there are two radically different ways of construction. You can construct the nature of things from the elements that are atoms—this is the cognitive construction—but you can also begin with your emotions, and from your emotions you make things of beauty or agree with other men on constitutions of states or laws of states—here the elements are emotive. He has two kinds, therefore, of construction: the cognitive constructions, which are alone scientific, and the emotive constructions, which are the basis both of aesthetics and of ethics and politics. There are, consequently, two kinds of freedom. One is the freedom which a man has when he operates according to the laws of his own nature; he is free, then, in the sense that he determines himself. The other kind of freedom is the kind that he sets up—the atomists believed in a compact theory of the state—when he enters into agreement with other men in a political community about the things that they want in common. They are free when they determine themselves.

But, notice, you'll observe that in these two senses, it is entirely possible that the second sense may be contradictory to the first. In other words, it is entirely possible that the men who build a state, although they get what they want, are not operating according to their true nature, because their passions, their repressions, the traumas of their youth, lead them to want things that they ought not to want. Therefore, they are not free in the first sense—they are being compelled by their compulsions (and we still speak this way)—although they are free in the second sense, namely, in getting what they want in this perverted way, they set up a structure of power to achieve it. I'm told that this still goes on in politics, that the politician who thinks he gets what he wants is not a free man in the sense of getting what's good—this is mere hearsay; I read this in the newspapers. [L!] The first of these two is the freedom of self-determination in the sense of a freedom from the effects of external influence. The second is a freedom relevant to ethics and politics. There are, consequently, two kinds of law and power. There's the law of one's own nature and the law imposed on the state. Think of all of the ambiguities and peculiarities that come from the question that one is asked frequently if one is a philosopher, whether the laws of nature and political laws have anything in common. The normal answer to that is "No"; but in the entitative interpretation, they're laws in exactly the same sense, for the reason that I've just explained. If the interpretations are kept straight, there is one interpretation in which the transition from one law to the other makes, interpretively, perfect sense; in fact, it is a consequence of the interpretation.

Note, then, that for both the ontic interpretations, freedom is interpreted as acting according to one's nature, but there are different conceptions of nature. In the one, one's nature is the ideas that one exemplifies; in the other, one's nature is the organization of constituent parts of which one is made up. There's a difference in the conception of knowledge that's involved. In the ontological interpretation, one talks about wisdom primarily; in the entitative interpretation, one talks about physical science primarily. The orientation is different. For both, freedom and rights are actions in accordance with law: in the ontological interpretation, it is law in the sense of the prescriptions of wisdom; in the entitative interpretation, it is law in the sense of the formula of one's own nature.

Let's turn now to the phenomenal interpretations. The phenomenal interpretations, as I said in the beginning, relate the knower and the known; and one of the regular philosophical appurtenances of the phenomenal interpretations is that you can engage in derogatory rhetoric against people who think that there's something transcendent up above, *i.e.*, knowledge, or something physical down underneath, *i.e.*, the knowable. Both are obviously nonsense: all you ever experience is what you experience. Therefore, any diremption—this is a word which is a curious English construction, but the philosophers liked it for centuries: the diremption between heaven and earth, spiritual and physical, soul and body. It's still fashionable. It's rather curious: this rhetoric never goes out of style; and you can have philosophic best sellers even in the twentieth century that still work on the discovery that someone a few centuries ago was wrong for supposing there was a soul in the body. All sorts of silly things are discovered in it. In the seventeenth century, there were people engaged in the phenomenal interpretation who made the same criticisms, but we've forgotten. We don't read them any longer; therefore, we are beguiled by the new ones.

What does freedom consist in? Well, one of the basic things you must say is that there's nothing normative in freedom. Anyone who supposes that in order to be free you must be good or act according to the true is obviously unacquainted with the proper modes of speech or what freedom means in ordinary language—I think I'm quoting someone from the seventeenth century, but it doesn't matter—because, obviously, to be free is prior to the exercise of any norm. Moreover, the phenomenal approach also can look forward to an open-ended future, and it is by the exercise of freedom that one makes advances both with respect to the true, the good, and also with respect to the beautiful. Freedom consists, therefore, in doing as one pleases without any appeal to a concern with what we ought to do, whether what we ought to do is to set up high standards of wisdom or science or piety or custom or any other way of proceeding. The primary context of freedom, then, is experience, the relation between knower and known, not of knowledge and nature.[9] One is free with respect to one's power, with no additional consideration of one's nature. One is free with respect to what falls under one's deliberation and choice and what is not prohibited explicitly by law, with no additional consideration of scientific truth.

Let's look first at the existentialist interpretation. This is by the mode of thought discrimination. This is the freedom of spontaneity or indetermination. What are the things that are free according to the existentialist interpretation? Well, neither of these ontic interpretations is correct. Any unrestrained animal is free. I'm deliberately trying to pick expressions that you'll recognize as being normal ones in the discussion of freedom. If the animal isn't tied up, if you haven't frightened the wits out of it, this is a free animal. It has to be an animal: it can't be a mere body, but it need not be a man. Freedom will be found in any animate creature under these circumstances. How does it exercise its freedom? Well, I've used the word: spontaneity. If it is not something you've drilled into it, if it is itself naturally, then it is free. And what would be the description of it, then? I suppose indetermination would be the best one; self-starting might do it—I suppose we ought to get them all "self-"s. Self-initiation is the characteristic of freedom. Jean-Paul Sartre speaks of freedom this way; the Sophists in antiquity talked about freedom this way; Descartes did; so, too, John Stuart Mill, who refers to Cicero as the model he wishes to proceed on; and the analytical philosophers and the existentialists, although they don't speak to each other, are in agreement in their interpretations here. But let's stick with the Sophists for the same reason we stuck with Democritus. Man is the measure of all things. The power that he exercises is the determination of freedom. Power determines right. Power determines law. "Might makes right," in the rhyme that gets into our discussion. Law is the imposition of power. Freedom or right is what remains when the power is imposed. And therefore, you can move up and down along this consideration.

There's a similarity between the entitative and the existentialist interpretations in this respect, namely, the balancing of freedom, of right, and law, of the exercise of power or of obligation; but there's this difference by which you can tell them apart. If the position is that the right you have, the power that is yours, can be discovered by examining your basic nature, that's entitative; but if the discussion is simply a discussion of the exercise of right without any supposition that it has any underlying reality and therefore, if you can get away with it, you've got the power, this is the existentialist interpretation.

Let me, since time marches on, get in the essentialist interpretation.

The essentialist interpretation uses the mode of thought resolution. This is the freedom of self-development. What are the things that are free? Notice, animal is narrower than body, and the wise man is less numerous than the animal.[10] Men in social situations are the only ones that are free. What action does he engage in? Well, man is free when it is deliberate action.[11]

Again, I hope that as we go along, you'll notice the words that we have used. We have dealt in the entitative interpretation with free bodies in locomotion. We move in the existentialist interpretation to animals—that is, not all bodies but merely animate bodies—and we are talking not about motion, locomotion, but we're talking about behavior, the behavior of animals. We get to a narrower group in the essentialist interpretation: these are men, not merely men who could act voluntarily but men who have acted as the result of deliberation on what they are doing. An intellectual element has come in. And now it's action that we're talking about. Motion, behavior, action has been the sequence. Then, finally, at the narrowest peak of this examination we limit it to wise men, and it is only men who engage in a self-ruled wisdom.

The sequence of the answers to the question, Who are free? varies. In the process of giving you the variation, in the interests of justice with respect to time, I've not told you enough about the essentialists; they are much more important than I've implied. But, at least, we now have our sequence of four meanings which would give the answers to the question, What things are free? As you think about them, examine the four methods that we talked about in the last lecture. It might seem that to take the narrowest of them, in which only the wise man is free, that the various methods would not succeed in making a man wise. But look at your notes, if you ever do, and consider the ways in which you might get the result of a wise man not only by the dialectical method but also by the operational method, the logistic method, the problematic method. Any one of them can be used, and in the history of thought all four of them have been used with respect to the objective, which is the ontological objective; and all four of them have been used also for the widest objective, namely, freedom as a self-determined body in locomotion.

In the next lecture, I will add a third step to the definition of freedom. We will turn around and go to principles, having dealt with methods and interpretations.

LECTURE FOUR

Freedom: Principle

Thus far in the course, we have looked at freedom from the point of view of method and interpretation. As I suggested in the opening lecture, these are two of the four parts of the definition of freedom; therefore, we have considered, first, what the process is by which freedom is possible and intelligible and, second, what the things are that are free, what the conclusions of this process are. We turn today to consider principles. Principle will be an answer to the question, How is freedom possible? A principle is something which apparently has ceased to be clearly understood today: it is the beginning point. That is what the word means in all the etymologies of all of the languages.[1] Consequently, the beginning point of an argument or an action is the discovery of some way of relating what you are saying or what you are doing to what is the fact. If you are thinking of principle in the verbal sense, it nails down among all the possible discourses which may be fantastic or removed from reality that set of discourses, proofs, inquiries, or discoveries that you have reason to say represents what is the case. The principle is what gives the discourse its actuality. And since we're talking about freedom, the principle of freedom would be that initial act or decision which would separate free actions from the other actions that we engage in which are not free or are the contrary of freedom. The explanation of the principles comes out of the same diagram that I've been using before (see fig. 1). We have explored two sets of relations thus far; without great subtlety of mathematical insight, you will recognize there's only one pair left. We will go on to that.

Bear in mind, there are two kinds of method. Let me recall to you the way we went about it. A method is either the way in which a knower acquires knowledge or something knowable becomes, in fact, known (see fig. 5); and the differences of the two kinds of method make them radically distinct. Now, a principle is either a way in which you can certify

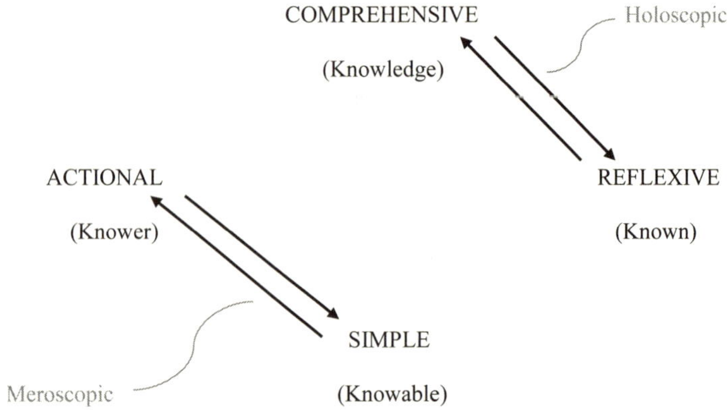

Fig. 13 *Principle and Knowledge Matrix*

that what you present as knowledge is, in fact, something that you can say is known, or it is a way in which a knower enters into relation to a knowable. They're radically distinct; in fact, the point of their difference gives you one of the main divisions among the philosophies.—This is one of the places where I had to invent a pair of terms; I invented them, and I was immediately reproached for misusing them! I want to be dogmatic about what these words mean. [L!]—There are some principles which are *holoscopic* and some which are *meroscopic*. Both words come from the Greek. You can either view—*skopein* is the Greek word *to view*—what you're dealing with as a whole—*holos* is *whole*—and then go from the whole in your exploration to the characteristics of the parts; or you can view things from the standpoint of the parts—*meros* is the Greek word for "part"—and then proceed to construct the whole out of it. The holoscopic principles are the ones that relate knowledge and known; the meroscopic are the ones that relate knower and knowable (see fig. 13).[2]

The difference between the two, I think, can be indicated by the difference of their ideal. In a meroscopic principle—for some reason, the meroscopic always seems simpler to a class, though they're really more difficult—the ideal is either to begin with something which is completely objective, into which nothing subjective enters, or else to begin with something which you can do entirely without the interference of anything external. If you can do either, then you have a principle which is repeatable: communicate to someone the character of the parts that will be put together—and they will be parts for anyone who looks at them—and you have a beginning of knowledge; or communicate to someone an act which he can repeat without any difference due to climate, height, materials, or state of mind, then you likewise have a principle. The holoscopic principles work on exactly the opposite assumption: namely, if you can find an instance in which what you allege to be knowledge cannot help being knowledge, then you have a beginning point; and in most of the beginnings that we make, what we allege to be knowledge isn't knowledge, or what we accept as known is not really known. Consequently, what we shall want to do as we go along is to look, first, at the characteristics these principles have in general and, second, at what they mean as they apply to freedom. You will see that the holoscopic principles, like the universal methods and the ontic interpretations, double their meaning; and therefore, the pattern will be similar to those other two cases.

Remember, we are dealing with an action which is free; consequently, the shape of the principle takes two forms, either the general form of the grounds of knowledge as such or the specific form of the grounds of action as distinct from knowledge. The difference between these two, which gives us our main difference of holoscopic and meroscopic, runs over into the larger philosophic problems of which half the philosophers of the world say, "You mustn't mix the theoretic and the practical, they're distinct"; the other half of the philosophers of the world say, "What you know, you can do, and what you can do, you know; the distinction of theoretic and practical is old-fashioned."

Let's begin with the holoscopic principles. They are of two sorts, comprehensive and reflexive. The comprehensive principles are the principles which make use of assimilation to assimilate anything which is presented in your experience as an experience, as something known, to the conditions of knowledge in its purity; with the result that the holoscopic principles will usually say that the ground that we're looking for, the means by which to discover a principle by finding a coincidence of knowledge with known, is to discover that the condition of being is intelligibility. There are a vast number of philosophies in the East and in the West that have argued that the world fundamentally is intelligible. It is intelligible, obviously, not in everyday experience; there are contradictions here. But whatever occurs, whatever *is*, insofar as it *is*, is intelligible; and the possibility of its intelligibility is in the intelligible universe as such. Frequently, as in the case of Plato, you carry this reflexivity even further: the reason why you can think and think truly is not only because the universe that you are part of and think about is intellig*ible*, it's also intellig*ent*, it is thinking. And your thinking is true thinking when it reproduces the processes which are the processes of reality viewed as a whole, reality in the terms in which it *is* most completely. The contradictions of experience, of phenomena, and of appearances are therefore assimilated in the unity of principle.

The unity of principle need not be put in Platonic terms, and even Platonism need not be mystical. Most of the forms of mathematical theory that make use of any general field theory engage in the same conviction, the fundamental conviction that what is known about the whole cannot be gathered by mere addition of the parts, but that on the contrary, the action and the nature of any of the parts can be understood only by placing them in the proper context of the whole which they exemplify. Even when you're dealing with knowledge in the ordinary human sense, the distinction is needed in order to differentiate the discursive proofs of reason from the simple ideas of understanding. If you think back on any of the philosophers that you've read who talk this way, you will recall that the ideas of reason, as opposed to the judgments of understanding, have a kind of simplicity, an immediateness, and the categories of understanding depend upon the ideas of reason.[3]

In the case of Plato, the assimilation ends in a unity. The One, the Good, Being, are names that he uses in different dialogues for that same unity. And if you turn from his principle to his method, the process of reminiscence[4] is a process by which from an experience, an experience which is necessary, imperfect, contradictory, you come to the idea that it exemplifies. Again, you need not be very mystical about it. Any time that you know something instead of knowing the peculiarities of its individuality, any time you can deal with it in its own terms, you have moved from opinion to this element of the principle, the principle of unity. The Delphic oracle's saying that Socrates talks about a good deal in the dialogues, "Know thyself," is interpreted this way. It is not "Know thyself" in any form; in all probability, it's not "Know thyself" in the sense in which the dedicators of the temple at Delphi had it inscribed in the marble. What "Know thyself" means is the discovery in yourself of what really is, a kind of symptomatic assimilation of the known to knowledge, which includes, also, the knower and the knowable, since for the Platonic approach you would move over into the other, lesser form of activity.

Socrates' examination of justice in the *Republic* leads to exactly this kind of a paradoxical identification. You may not remember, but the first time that he uses the expression he apologizes for it. He says he's going to explain justice by a very odd statement: it is the statement, the expression, "self-ruled." In the individual, it is the rule of the passions by reason; and in the state, the other classes are ruled by the philosopher-king. What is the function of anything we do when we do it properly or freely? It's knowledge. Knowledge is virtue, it's self-mastery, it's reason ruling the passions; it's freedom, because in no other way is a man free. That is, the principle of freedom is action in terms of one's own nature, not the nature you acquired because you were brought up in a particular state but nature, the nature you are, the nature that you are truly (see table 5).[5]

Table 5. Freedom: Principle.

Mode of Thought	Principle	What Is Freedom as a Cause or as a Value?
	Holoscopic	
Assimilation	Comprehensive	Autonomy
Resolution	Reflexive	Self-Rule
	Meroscopic	
Discrimination	Actional	Power
Construction	Simple	Nature

In the absence of knowledge, you may hit upon the right rule by opinion; the rule by right opinion is one which gives you the second-best state. In the second-best state, instead of the principle of reason ruling the entire state, you have the rule of law—the dialogue is called the *Laws*—and you establish laws by persuasion or by power.

This is the doubling of meanings. That is, on the one hand it is reason which makes freedom possible; the use of reason brings you into relation with reality, your own reality, and that of the universe. Short of reason, it is the devices of law, externally imposed by power, which will lead to security, an approximation by right reason. Assimilation makes straight use of the notion of the model, the exemplar. The comprehensive principles are the conditions of intelligibility and of action. What is most intelligible *is* most truly; what acts intelligibly acts freely, because it acts in terms of itself.

Let's turn to the reflexive principles. Reflexive principles operate on the same general conviction but also on the assumption that the universe is not intelligible, that that is not a meaningful statement—how could you even tell if it were? On the contrary, what you have is not a relation of anything that you know to perfect knowledge; it is, rather, a relation by which from what you know you can increase your knowledge. Knowledge is based upon what is previously known; it consists in increasing what is previously known. Aristotle, who uses the mode of thought resolution, spends a good part of his time refuting the eternal ideas of Plato. He denies the universal case of the intelligibility of all things. Instead, he wants a particular case; that is, whenever we know anything, what we have done has been to extract the form from something that we have experienced, and then we try to state what that form is. The principle in a science would be a reflexive instance of something that you know in such a way that you can't be wrong about it. Most empirical knowledge you can be wrong about.

Let me run through a few of the reflexive principles. God is important in metaphysics. What's the characteristic activity of God? Thinking. Thinking about what? Thinking about thinking. Reflexivity verbally is this process by which you relate the thing to itself. Science, Aristotle says repeatedly, depends upon seizing the cause. And what's the cause? Well, the cause is at once the beginning point of the process and the beginning point of the proof; therefore, the cause operates in both of these contexts. For instance, what is the state? He comes to a definition of the state in a very curious way which sometimes puzzles writers who think that he is described best as being antidemocratic. You can't define the state in itself; but you can, however, define the citizen. He runs through the definitions of a citizen. They're none of them satisfactory, for reasons that he goes into in detail, and he gives his own definition. A citizen is a man who participates in the proper activities of the state: he is the ruled who rules. The coincidence of the ruler and the ruled is the beginning of the definition of any community. He goes on to say that it might seem that this fits democracy better than any other state, but it's true even of tyranny: you need only to make your proper adjustments, and the reflexive principle will appear. Or, again, what is tragedy? Well, the differentia in the definition of tragedy is the purgation of pity and fear. And with what do you purge pity and fear? Pity and fear. I won't go into the reasons for this. I want merely to give you a list of them.

Some of the reflexive principles that later philosophers use may be easier to see at once. The *cogito, ergo sum*[6] of Descartes is a reflexive principle. Why? It comes right after the systematic doubt, and Descartes demonstrates you can doubt everything: you can doubt everything you've heard, everything you know, everything you've proved, mathematics as well as the report of the state of things in Rangoon. Where can you stop? Well, you can stop only at an instance of knowledge where what you know is knowing itself. Therefore, if you engage in a process of doubt, you cannot doubt that there is a knowing activity which involves doubting; that is, the doubting is not merely the process but the object of the knowledge. Spinoza has an even more—it isn't more obvious than the ones I've given; it's just a shorter version: God is *causa sui*.[7]

Again, you can know a thing only if you know its cause. If the cause is different than the thing, you're involved in the possibility of errors in proof; but if you have your demonstration depend upon a cause which is cause of itself, the reflexivity is present again. For the moment, what I'm doing is not praising the reflexive principles; I'm merely trying to identify them. That is, here is a beginning point in which what you know depends upon giving an instance of something indubitable, because the knowing and the thing known coincide; and until you clean up your method later on, anything else will not be a good beginning. On such a beginning, if your ingenuity and method are sufficient, you can then proceed to construct a proof.

What are the problems of freedom if you have reflexive principles? Well, one of the immediate results is that you're going to have different kinds of sciences—reflexive principles will always give you different kinds of sciences—and the problem of freedom is a problem only in the practical sciences, not in the theoretic sciences, not in the poetic or productive sciences. It is a problem of action. It might look as if it is less embracing than in the comprehensive principles, because in the comprehensive principles there isn't any difference between the theoretic and the practical sciences, and therefore there is no such restriction. I don't think there is this difference of scope, but there is this difference of way in which you talk about it. How does freedom occur? Well, the first thing that Aristotle, who is one who uses reflexive principles, does is to define the voluntary as a precondition of moral action. One may voluntarily perform actions even under the constraint of circumstances, like jettisoning a cargo to save a ship. You don't have to have reflexive principles, incidentally, to use this example; it becomes a stock example after Aristotle. In other words, you are free while being internally determined. You distinguish what you do naturally from what you do voluntarily.

In the state or in politics, the basis of freedom will go back to the coincidence of ruler and ruled. Obviously, some states will have less freedom than others by virtue of the application of the constitution after you have begun with the initial agreement that the ruler and the ruled coincide.—Incidentally, this also is an insight which the philosophers repeat a good deal. For example, even Hobbes, who is the apologist of a much more tyrannical form of state, argues that you couldn't have any state, not even a tyranny, without the initial contract, which is entered into voluntarily; and that initial contract is the place where the ruler and the ruled coincide.—What Aristotle is saying here is somewhat similar: once the state is set up, you have a variety of ends, depending upon who rules. The rich, the virtuous, the wellborn, these are among the classes that empirically have claimed the rule and have gotten away with it, and also, from time to time, the free; and when the free rule, the end of the state is freedom, just as when the rich rule, the end of the state is wealth. Let me make one further point. If you've read the *Politics*, you will remember that there are three fundamental kinds of states and there are three perversions. There is monarchy and its perversion, tyranny; there is aristocracy and its perversion, oligarchy; then there is the state whose perversion is democracy, and what is that state called?—I want to bring this in because you may have been puzzled by it.—It's usually translated as "polity." It's translated as "polity" because the Greek word is *politeia*, and that is a reasonable translation; but the other translation of polity, *politeia*, is "constitution." That is, all states have a constitution, but the undegraded democratic state is the constitution as such; that is, the ruler and the ruled are in operation together. This is the general conception, then, of freedom. Notice again the doubling up of meaning.

Let me make one other generalization. The holoscopic principles in general—and this is a very important differentiation which runs through the history of philosophy, and it still goes on today—insist that the basis of morality and of the state is natural; that is to say, there are criteria of good and evil apart from the agreements, the conventions, the preferences, the pleasures of men. This is why the law of nature takes its original meaning in this sense. The meroscopic principles, on the other hand, will say, "No, there isn't any natural state; all states are based on convention. There isn't anything in the nature of things by which you can call them good; 'good' is likewise a matter of convention, what you happen to like, what your society sets up."[8] In connection with this difference comes in the difference in freedom. In other words, freedom for the holoscopic principles will be related to something in the nature of things. For Plato, to take one example of the holoscopic principle, namely, the comprehensive, it will be knowledge. Knowledge relating you to your own nature and to the nature of things in a rational universe gives you the possibility of freedom. For Aristotle, it's quite different. He argues that the state is natural, too, but not in this sense. The state is natural because man is by nature a political animal, and all that this means is that he can't live alone. If he could live alone he would not be a man: he would either be a god because he could do it well, or he would be a brute because he'd drop all of the cultural aspects of his life. But midway between, in order to live a human life, you need to be a political animal; and man by nature—the word in Aristotle is *nature* as strongly as anywhere else in his use of *nature*—is a political animal, and consequently, a man is free only in society. What you need, therefore, is the social relations in order to get the two going.

Let me emphasize a little more the two ways in which morality and politics have a natural basis, because I think so much of what's said today about natural law is rather confused by the arguments and the rhetoric that are engaged in to support a particular principle. According to comprehensive principles, what is reasonable or rational or intelligent or intelligible is the natural basis of the state. The natural basis of the state is therefore in reason or knowledge; and this is the reason why the philosopher is a king. If you want to see the principle in Plato, the interesting thing is that he sets up the principles of the *Republic* and of the *Timaeus*, of politics and of physics, respectively, in exactly the same way: it's a proportion—usually a comprehensive principle is an equation of some sort; here the proportion is a simple one—namely, Being is to Becoming as Knowledge is to Opinion. Therefore, the whole process is to get from the region of becoming, where you have opinion, to a formulation which has the universality of a mathematical equation that will throw light upon the processes even of becoming.

In reflexive principles, what is it for morals and politics to have a natural basis? Well, you begin with a distinction between the theoretic and the practical sciences. In the theoretic sciences, what you are seeking are principles which formulate the nature of things; you're trying to know them. But in the practical sciences, the coincidence that you're looking for is found not in abstract knowledge but in what you do. The state and society are natural, because man can't live alone; and consequently, he sets up different forms of society. Aristotle examined, with a research grant that he got from the Pericles Foundation [L!], 158 constitutions before he wrote his theory. When you look through the *Politics*, you can find indicated not merely the six basic states or constitutions that I've been talking about but also a great many variants in which what you are seeking are viable ways in which the individual can live to secure both his security within the community as well as the activities which are peculiar to himself. Freedom would fall within this scope, and this is the scope which is the natural basis.[9]

Let's look now at the meroscopic principles. The meroscopic principles are, likewise, two. In both cases you deal either with the thing in itself or you deal with the agent. Actional principles come from what the knower or the agent does, and simple principles deal with what the thing is. For the first, the mode of thought is discrimination, beginning with the knower; for the second, it's construction, beginning with the knowable. Let's begin with the knower. If you are an inquirer, if you are a prover, if you are a teacher or an explainer, then any beginning you make is your principle. You decide, and once you have decided and started either on your exposition or your inquiry—and it would hold equally for both—you cannot make many steps without having the pathway well determined. Therefore, when you begin with actional principles, it is normal either to state as soon as you can what the rules of the action are—in antiquity it was the rules of business rather than the rules of the game, and you tried to do something; but it amounts to the same thing—or you lay down the rules in the beginning, that is, you begin with pure relations, symbols, forms, modes of activity, and then you attribute to them the meanings which you try out. It is obviously the case that in this fashion, knowing how a thing is made is warrant for knowledge: if you can make a beginning point, you can lay down the knowable, you can lay down knowledge, you can lay down the known.[10] In an important sense, we make nature, including our own nature, the natures of others.

According to Protagoras, "Man is the measure of all things, of the being of what is and the nonbeing of what is not."[11] I always hesitate: "measure" is the way it's usually translated. The Greek word is *metron*. "Master" would be a better translation; it's equally appropriate. And it's not "of all things"; it's *chremata*, "of all experiences." Thus, "Man is the master of all experiences. . . ." Let me try to explain that a little bit. Sartre has a similar formulation; that is, freedom for Sartre, as well as for Protagoras, is creative, and we are creative with respect to all three of the other poles of our matrix.[12] And it may look odd—I think that probably in the English translation of the French it does seem odd—to say to a person, "I create you"; but it isn't if you break your dogmatism and take a look at what we are saying. We are saying that beginning with any individual experience, all you have is the individual experience, the phenomenologically present. If you think there is some thing or some person out there, you have really only chosen pieces of this set of internal experiences and have made that thing or person. Therefore, if you take the paradoxical statement that "I make you," bear in mind that as far as this process is concerned, there isn't any *you* out there: there's only a known *you*. The only *you* that exists is my consciousness of you and everybody else's consciousness of you; and it would be entirely possible that if we entered into debate, all the members of the class would, with respect to any one of you, make as many different *you*s as there were people that entered into the debate. It would be part of method from this point on to come to some agreement, and that's what you have to do: that's why you have law courts, that's why even monuments need orations in order to make clear who it is and why the monument was set up, and so, too, all the rest.

The principle is the beginning. Any beginning you make is your principle. Some of them are no good, and they won't last very long; but if you lay down a principle which is meant to accumulate knowledge and it works out fairly well, then another person, seeing this activity of yours, may try it himself. His beginning point will, likewise, be an arbitrary beginning. Frequently, even though he meant it to be the same as yours, it won't be. One of the experiences in reading examination papers, for example, is to watch the way in which the principle which you have stated clearly is modified as it is being handed docilely back to you as precisely your product. [L!] But if it is genuinely an active activity, even though it is different, it's still an actional principle. This, then, would be the beginning point.

What's freedom, then? Freedom is power. How is freedom established once you make this beginning? It's established and defended by power. What are the limits of freedom? Well, they're discovered—the limits of authority, too—only by examining the established powers and calculating what exceeds one's own power and what could be a beginning by which you could either operate within the patterns of power or start out anew.[13] And let me say a word about this also. Like the creativity of Sartre that I defended a moment ago, this sounds cynical, because we usually move in with some attachment to comprehensive principles or to simple principles—the reflexive principles seem to be out of style these days—and with such an attachment it sounds as if the arbitrary use of power is a grave danger. But it's not, if you remain within the view of the universe that we're talking about here: for saint or sinner, this is the only mode of freedom. The differentiation between saint and sinner is just as easy once you make this beginning, but it's not laid down here at once. This is, incidentally, one of the differences that I have mentioned before. That is, in a holoscopic principle, the basis of freedom is natural and depends upon reason. In the actional principle, one of the pair of meroscopic principles, freedom is arbitrary activity out of which knowledge might develop; and if in advance you say, "Don't do it that way: a million mathematicians have tried that and it never works," you'd be interfering with knowledge. The one, the holoscopic, is not more attached to knowledge than the other; but the holoscopic assumes that reason enters directly into the free act, whereas the actional principle assumes that reason is the consequence of the free act. The diversity that would result, if only one man laid down this principle of trying it out, might enrich knowledge much better than the docile repetitions of the other actions that came before.

There remains the simple principles. If you want to begin with the knowable, if your assumption is that the way in which anything that you prove or know or talk about will have objectivity is by mapping it in against the structure of reality—and that word goes back an awfully long time—then, obviously, what you need to do is to take the structure of reality and break it into pieces that you can't be mistaken about. If you get to a simple piece—and there are many criteria of simplicity—you can't be mistaken because a mistake is always the combination of two things that don't go together; therefore, it follows immediately that if you have something simple, if you can isolate it and make it your beginning point, you're in the clear. Suppose, then, you make up a set of rules by which these simples are put into composites, always by simple steps: in a simple step, you can't make a mistake. Therefore, if you have long chains of reasoning from simple things or simple ideas or simple words[14]—it doesn't matter which one you begin with; I'm quoting three different philosophers at once here, all of them classics—in which you review your steps constantly, you have a principle from which any method would carry you unerringly to the truth.

These are simple principles; and as I've suggested, they can be any kind of simples. When they were looking for simple ideas in the seventeenth century, when they were looking for simple, indivisible bodies in antiquity, when they are looking for simple particles at present, these are all modes of simplicity, modes of seeking simple principles. If you then move on, you can go on in one of two ways: you can either make the pattern of simplicity composite, whole—notice that we're moving in the direction opposite to that in which you would move with comprehensive principles—until you get to what is all-embracing; or you can do it in terms of things that are simple within the complex structure that you have been building. In other words—let me take an ancient example—you can do you composition either by means of atoms or by means of preferences. If you are engaged in theoretic science, you begin with atoms; if you're engaged in practical science, in ethics or politics, you begin with preferences.

Therefore, to conclude the differences that we have set up, the meroscopic principles have two characteristics that are the opposite of the ones that I pointed out when I set the holoscopic principles down. Remember, the holoscopic principles involve a natural basis for good and evil. Both of the meroscopic principles, however, say, "No, the basis of the state and the basis of ethics is convention; there isn't anything natural here. It is the agreement of men about them." Second, in the holoscopic principles, the way in which you discover what is the natural basis of ethics and politics is by reason, reason with the variants that come from the kinds of principles you're dealing with, comprehensive or reflexive; whereas the basis of ethics in the meroscopic principles, namely, the actional and simple, is pleasure. From antiquity there have been two kinds of hedonism. I don't know any place where it is pointed out, except every once in a while I get mad and point it out; but then you get just a minority report. [L!] There's a hedonism that comes from an actional principle: in that hedonism, all you say is that pleasure is the mark of value, and the mere fact that it is pleasure is all there is to it. But there's a second kind of hedonism which is equally important, the one that comes from the simple principles, because there you can say, "Well, there is a pleasure which is natural to you, and then there are the pleasures that arise from the distortions that come from your experience, from your repressions, your traumas, and the rest." If you enter the state, either kind is OK; that is, the state consists in agreements to achieve your pleasure. But you can go through therapeutic advice: you're in a better state if you get rid of the false pleasures and get down to the natural pleasures.[15]

I will go on in the next lecture: we still have a fourth part of the definition, that is, selection. It is on a different pattern because, obviously, having used four terms, I can arrange them in pairs only three ways; but nonetheless, it follows from what we have been saying. I'll also want, however, in the next lecture to take you through a series of philosophers to indicate the way in which they combine their principle, their method, and their interpretation in a definition of freedom, and to indicate the ways in which these definitions of freedom will differ from each other.

DISCUSSION

Spinoza, Part 1 (*Ethics*, Books I–IV)

Discussion Summary

Today we will compare Hobbes and Spinoza to determine similarities and differences in how they approach the question of liberty.[1] What do we observe about liberty in Spinoza's *Ethics*, book I, which is the same as or different from Hobbes? It is clear that Spinoza is using the logistic method; thus, this leads to one similarity between him and Hobbes. In his interpretation, however, Hobbes says all bodies can be free; whereas according to Spinoza, only God is a free cause. Consequently, the aspects of freedom that come from method are similar, but those from interpretation are different. So, among those things following from method, Spinoza will make distinctions between law and right, and in this regard he is using the mode of thought composition. On the other hand, for Spinoza's interpretation, whatever will have to do with things other than God will have to be viewed in relation to Him.

Next, when we look at book II of the *Ethics*, we can compare his interpretation to what Hobbes said. Remember, Hobbes said that all bodies are free, and then he spoke of free men and human bodies. By contrast, in book II Spinoza is relating man's will to God. Man's body and mind are modes of different attributes of God. So, man can be free, but he has no free will. He can have an adequate idea when his idea and God's are the same. Thus, Spinoza holds that the imperfect is, to a greater or lesser extent, an exemplification of the perfect. Notice, this is the ontological interpretation. Spinoza is identifying two kinds of emotions, of affects: there are actions, which are defined as being based on adequate ideas, and there are passions, which are passive states based on inadequate ideas (see fig. 14).[2] To summarize, then, in the second book, Spinoza focuses on two things. First, he identifies the mind with man's nature. Second, he considers ways in which men interrelate with one another.

Hobbes speaks of freedom and fear and of freedom and necessity. He

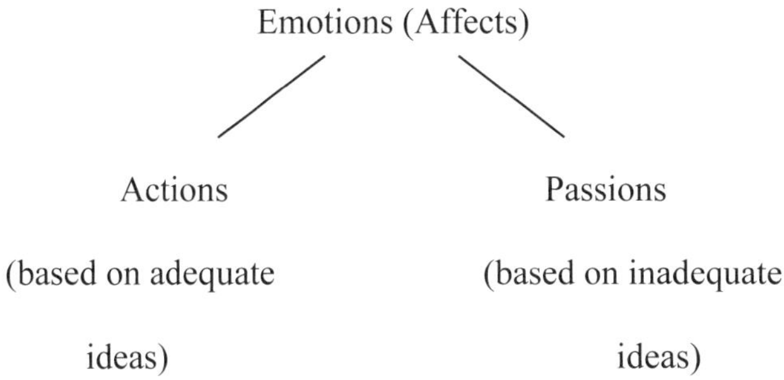

Fig. 14 *Spinoza's Kinds of Emotions*

says one can have both—they are not inconsistent. In book III of the *Ethics*, Spinoza says something like this but with some important differences. Here, as in Hobbes, on the intellectual side of an emotion are adequate ideas, whereas on the other side are passions, inadequate ideas. So, we can speak of the emotions in a cognitive way or as passions. Man's essence is his striving to continue in his true mode of being. Freedom would then be any action which flows from an adequate idea, that is, from man's nature, and a lack of such freedom is a passion. When we are active, we are free; when we are passive, we are enslaved. Thus, the nature of the passions depends on their origin, and in the mind, in the power of the intellect, is human freedom.

In book IV, Spinoza addresses human bondage and the strength of emotions. For Hobbes, after the establishment of the state, we get good and evil. For Spinoza, we call something good because we desire it—this is a relation to affect, to emotion. If we desire a thing, it's good. Notice, we don't desire it *because* it is good. The basic definition of *good* and *evil*, then, depends on the emotions. An apple is good if we want it. Now, the only way we can achieve anything is to act according to our emotions. There are two kinds of emotions, and those actions undertaken due to adequate ideas are free actions. Therefore, we are free when we act according to adequate ideas. By contrast, passions, the second kind of emotion, are based on inadequate ideas, and an inability to control the passions leads to bondage. So, a person is a slave when he acts according to passion.

For Spinoza, virtue is the power to act according to the laws of your nature. The foundation of virtue is to endeavor to preserve one's own being. And the more each person strives and is able to seek his own profit, that is, to preserve his being, the more virtue he possesses. Happiness is success in this preservation. Since men agree in nature that they desire for others what they want for themselves, we can derive concepts of what is just and what is honor. Freedom, then, is characteristic of men's actions, that is, behavior based on adequate ideas.

Now, when we look closely at objects of desire, none are good in themselves. The terms *good* and *evil* indicate nothing positive in the things considered in themselves but only in their status as being desired. So, when we look at agents of power, we see that when one increases his power, the perfecting of man is what we are talking about. Perfection of man is the means of possessing more being, more reality, more power. This is according to reason. Thus, it is man's perfection that is to be sought.

Finally, this approach leads us to consider ends. The end of politics is peace and security, the end of ethics is an increase of freedom and perfection of man, and the end of religion is piety.

For next time, in the *Tractatus*, read chapters IV and V, then skip to XVI to XX, at the end.

McKeon's Notes[3]

Spinoza Freedom 1.

Book I. Def. VII. That thing is said to be free which exists by the mere necessity of its own nature and is determined in its actions by itself alone.

That thing is said to be necessary (necessaria) or rather compelled (coacta), when it is determined in its existence and actions by something else in a certain fixed ratio.

N.B. Contraries—free and compelled. Unit involved, thing.

Prop. XVII. God acts merely according to his own laws, and is compelled by no one.

No cause of actions except the perfection of his own nature. (cor. I)

Cor. II. God alone is a free cause. Exists by the mere necessity of his own nature.

Will and intellect do not appertain to the nature of God.

Would differ toto caelo from our will and intellect. God's intellect the cause of things, differs from them in essence and existence.

God's intellect, will and power are one and the same thing.

Prop. 29. Nothing contingent in nature—everything determined by the necessity of the divine nature.

Prop. 32. Will a necessary cause, not a free one.

Cor. I. God does not act from freedom of will.

Cor. II. Will and intellect same place in the nature of God as motion and rest.

Book II. Prop. 48. In no mind absolute or free will; mind determined in willing by cause.

Prop. 49. cor. Will and intellect one and the same thing.
Sch. involves refutation of free will.
See Lemmas following prop. xiii. Nature of human body and mind.

Spinoza Freedom. 2.

Ethics III. Origin and Nature of the Emotions.
Introduction—resolve to treat the emotions in terms of nature—Nothing happens in nature that could be attributed to a defect of it.

Distinction of adequate cause and inadequate or partial cause. *Def. 1.*

Emotion (affectus) divided into action (actio) and passion (passio). Both these by definition.

Passive or suffer when something takes place in us or follows from our nature of which we are only the partial cause.

Proposition II. Scholium. Proposition on the relation of body and mind in thinking and motion.
Criticism of the doctrine that we are "free" only in respect to those things which we desire only moderately—can restrain those desires. Fact that we later regret some actions only impediment to thinking that we do all things freely—infant milk; angry child vengeance; timid child flight. Drunken man.
"Men think themselves free on this account alone that they are conscious of their actions and ignorant of the causes of them."
Moreover not within the free power of the mind to remember or forget anything.
Dreaming that we speak—think we speak freely.
Not two sorts of decisions, fantastic and free.
Decisions of the mind thought to be free cannot be distinguished from imagination or memory—nothing else than the affirmation which an idea, insofar as it is an idea, involves necessarily.
Free decrees arise in the mind from the same necessity as the ideas of things actually existing.
Actions depending on inadequate ideas and on adequate ideas.

< *Cf. Bk I Ax VII Prop XVII, incl. Cor II & Sch God's intellect, will, power same*
Prop 29
Prop 32 incl Cor. 1

BK II prop 48, 49 including Cor & Sch.

Ethics IV. On Human Servitude or the Strength of the Emotions.

Insert[4]

Preface—"Human lack of power in moderating and checking the emotions I call servitude."

Good defined as means of increasing power of acting insofar as this is understood by his nature.

Def. VIII. By Virtue and power (virtus and potentia) I understand the same thing—same as essence or nature in the case of man "insofar as he has the power of affecting something which can only be understood by the laws of that nature."

Proposition XVIII Scholium ". . . virtue is nothing else than to act according to the laws of one's own nature."

Prop. LXVI, sch. ref. back to prop XVIII—difference between a man who is led by opinion or emotion and one who is led by reason.—the former is a slave, the latter is free.

Propositions LVII—LXXIII about the characteristics of the free man.

Proof of prop LXVIII begins "I said that he was free who is led by reason alone."

Prop. LXXIII.[5] "A man who is guided by reason is more free in a state where he lives according to common law than in solitude where he is subject to no law."

Ethics V. Concerning the Power of the Intellect or Human Freedom.

Preface. "I pass on at last to that part of the Ethics which concerns the manner or way that leads to liberty. In this part then, concerning the power of reason, I shall endeavor to show what *power reason* have over the emotions, and moreover, what is mental liberty or blessedness (mentis libertas seu beatitudo): from which we shall see how far a wise man excels an ignorant."

Prop. XVI: God free from passions

Prop. XXXVI Sch. "From this we clearly understand in what consists our salvation, blessedness, or liberty (*salus* nostra seu *beatitudo* seu *libertas*), namely in the constant and eternal love for God or in the love of God for men."

Spinoza Freedom Ethics IV.

On Human Servitude of the Strength of the Emotions

Preface—"Human lack of power in moderating and checking the emotions I call servitude."

Good defined as means of increasing power of acting insofar as this is understood by his nature.

N.B. Book I. God as causa sui is cause of self and of everything else. Alone is free and acts according to the necessity of his own nature.

Book II. On the nature and origin of the mind. Man as modes of attributes of

God. Adequate ideas or natures determined by God. Inadequate ideas external causes.

Book III. On the Origin and nature of the emotions. Affects divided into actions and passions equivalent to the difference between adequate and inadequate ideas.

Book IV. therefore an internalization within man of internal and external since it is the difference between actions and passions, and the question of servitude or freedom is a question of the relative control of actions and passions in human activity.

Def. VIII. "By virtue and power (virtus and potentia) I understand the same thing"—same as essence or nature in the case of man "insofar as the power of affecting something can only be understood by the laws of that nature."

Proposition XVIII. Scholium ". . . virtue is nothing else than to act according to the laws of one's own nature." (def 8.) (p. 202) Foundation of virtue is that endeavor to preserve our own being, and happiness—that a man can preserve his own being. Men agree in nature—desire nothing for themselves which they do not desire for other men, and therefore they are just, faithful, and honorable.

N.B. two dimensions reason and desire. Internal (nature) and external (passion). Difference between acting according to one's own nature (adequate ideas) and judgments concerning what is according to one's own nature. Emotions may be in agreement with reason or contrary. Former seek the good of other men.

XXXVII "The good which every one who follows after virtue seeks for himself we will desire for other men; and his desire on their behalf will be greater in proportion as he has a greater knowledge of God."

Scholia to this proposition provide the basis for religion and the state.

Sch. 1. One who strives from emotion alone to make others love what he loves acts on impulse and is hateful. By reason—humaneness and kindness.

Insofar as we possess an idea of God—"religion."

Desire to do well in accordance with reason—"piety."

To join others in friendship according to reason—"honor." Praise and the honorable; base the opposite. Promised to prove this in prop. 18, sch.

Now explain justice, injustice, crime and merit.

Sch. 2. Promised in Appendix to Part I to explain praise and blame, merit and crime, justice and injustice. (216)

Right of nature—each person exists and does what follows from the necessity of his nature. Also judges what is good and evil, consults his advantage and avenges himself.

To live in harmony men cede their natural right. Society claims for itself the right which every individual possesses of revenging himself and judging what is good and evil. Therefore possesses power of prescribing a common rule of life, or promulgating laws and supporting them, not by *reason*, which cannot restrain the emotions, but by *penalties*.

A society firmly established by law and with power of self-preservation a "State." In natural state nothing by universal consent good or evil.

In natural state sin cannot be conceived, but only in civil state where it is decided by universal consent what is good and evil. Sin is nothing but disobedience which is punished by the law of the State alone. Obedience is merit of the citizen.

Natural state no property or rendering of due. Just and unjust in state.

Justice and injustice, sin and merit, are *external* notions, not attributes which manifest the nature of the mind. (217)

Prop. LXVI. sch. ref. back to prop. XVIII—difference between a man who is led by opinion or emotion and one who is led by reason—Former is a slave, the latter is free.

DISCUSSION

Spinoza, Part 2 (*Ethics*, Book V)

Discussion Summary

In this course, the first four books we are reading prepare us for an understanding of liberty. Their purpose is to deal with significant problems in the social sciences, of which liberty is one. When we look at the problems Hobbes and Spinoza present, they both address morals and politics. In many books of commentary, you will see Hobbes and Spinoza put together in discussions of moral and political philosophy. Both equate right and power, establish differences between law and right, and talk of a social contract; yet we need to know if they agree, because they come out at different places. Spinoza is the first philosopher who holds that democracy is the best and natural state of humans, whereas Hobbes is usually presented as pleading for absolute domination, as defending despotism. The political writings of Spinoza are pleas for freedom: his two political works are for freedom of speech and of thought and are almost the earliest to address this. Hobbes says man doesn't want to be free of what the law requires or of motion, so it's absurd to demand more freedom. How can we handle these two philosophers who look the same but come out with radically different positions? The shift between the two represents the debate between freedom and despotism.

Let us begin by examining the method, interpretation, and principle of each. Here we can see similarities and differences (see table 6).[1] In the development of what freedom is, why do their interpretations lead to radically different positions? We also need to understand what principles are and how they lead to interpretation. Remember that interpretation gives you a way of focusing on what the argument is about.

In the preface to book V, Spinoza deals with the method or way which leads to freedom, and he accomplishes two things here.[2] First, he relates power to reason. He says that a need exists for a clearer statement of the

Table 6. Differences between Hobbes and Spinoza.

	Principle	Method	Interpretation
Hobbes	*Meroscopic* Actional	*Particular* Logistic	*Ontic* Entitative
Spinoza	*Holoscopic* Reflexive	*Particular* Logistic	*Ontic* Ontological

basic idea of reason in terms of its power over the emotions. This is at the upper level of an ontological interpretation. At this point, he says, he is not going to deal with the perfection of reason, which is "the province of Logic," nor with the cure of the body, "the province of Medicine." For that, one should see his *On the Improvement of Understanding*, where he addresses these issues. There, near the beginning, he discusses the need for the improvement of medicine, a theory of education and of morals, and a science of mechanics. That work is a treatise on the improvement of understanding and deals with logic. In *Ethics*, by contrast, he addresses passions. So, the preface to book V first relates power and reason. Second, Spinoza uses this preface to look at reason and the passions: how are they related? The relationship between reason and passions is on the lower level of the ontological interpretation. What does he want to take into account regarding the relation of reason and the passions? He wants to set up the extent and nature of the control of reason over the passions, and he enumerates two groups of philosophers who made mistakes about the relation of reason to the passions. First, the Stoics said reason can control the passions through free will. For Spinoza, this is wrong. Second, Descartes said that the scope of reason and of will are different, and this is also wrong for Spinoza. So, he will need to correct both of them. He proposes to deal with the passions scientifically; thus, he will treat reason and power in the same manner.

Next in book V, what is the effect of his two axioms? These are connected with the first problem in the preface, and there should be a pattern. If we are to deal with actions, we will need to consider the contrary actions. For any affect (emotion), there will be something meeting something; that is, something moves, and so something is moved. Therefore, we need a law of motion and emotion. The power of the affect is the same as the power of the cause—internal and external cause. We need a statement of this relation and of the cause. So, there are internal causes (for actions) and external ones (for passions). These allow us to build up a table of contraries to give us a physics of the emotions. Thus, in any action, we would need to consider the relation of two actions as well as the cause or beginning of any actions. Notice that the mind-body problem now vanishes, because the axioms can handle each one: the two axioms can be stated in terms of one or the other, either of mind or of body. Whenever one changes, the other changes, too; and the order and connection of ideas, of mind, is the same as the order and connection of things, of body.

After the axioms in book V come the propositions. Proposition I says emotions are the result either of adequate ideas, that is, have an internal cause and are, consequently, an action, or of inadequate ideas, that is, have an external cause and are, consequently, a passion. In proposition III, he argues that emotion ceases to be a passion or external as soon as we form an adequate idea of it. Note the corollary to this proposition: the more a passion is known, the more of it is within our power.

In proposition IV, Spinoza establishes that everything is intelligible through a cause. Proposition VI deals with knowledge and power, and the scholium[3] addresses how to increase power of mind. Propositions VII and VIII then switch around to compare the powers of the emotions. In the scholium to proposition X, he states that the power of arranging one's affects grows "from a love of freedom." Here he addresses modification of the emotions, and argues that we cannot have knowledge of virtue without knowledge of self. Note the progression here: from knowledge of virtue as caused by knowledge of self to knowledge of God (proposition XV), then to love of God (proposition XVI), and finally to God as the only free cause (proposition XVII).

In the scholium to proposition XX, we have the mind's remedies for the emotions listed. What are they? Why doesn't he say reason can control the passions? For Spinoza, not even adequate ideas can control the passions. If we wait for the moment when we are at the interplay of reason and passion, we haven't a chance to control the latter, for the external causes will be greater; but if one prepares himself in advance, he will not become a victim of the external cause. Here Spinoza argues that one has recourse to a series of remedies to prepare himself ahead of time—a set of five. The first of the five remedies or devices would be to use knowledge itself by becoming an expert in the total psychology. But this will happen for only a few. If one knew the nature of the emotions, the whole theory, he would be a moral psychologist. The second device is this: when the external cause is coming upon you, when you are in a particular situation, see that the emotion isn't due to a internal cause, and thereby separate the emotion from the external cause "confusedly" imagined (see fig. 14).

A third device to prepare oneself against the power of passions deals with both actions and passions. Over the course of one's life, the actions are universally the result of causes that surpass in duration of time those of the passions; therefore, as we go along, actions have more strength because, in the long run, actions are what will last longer. Following passion may be stronger temporarily, but if action is what we are aiming toward, the latter will last longer. We will understand actions better than we will grasp the fleeting passions. The fourth device relates the passions to God. The modifications which are related to the common properties of things or to God are nourished by a multitude of causes rather than by fewer causes in the case of the passions. Fifth and finally, one can set up a pattern of calmness to protect his mind from the clash between reason and passion.

With regard to the force of emotion, the scholium to proposition XXXVI sets up an equivalence between salvation (safety, or *salus*), blessedness (happiness, or *beatitudo*), and freedom (*libertas*). For Spinoza, these are exactly the same thing: all are "the constant and eternal" love of God (both the love "toward God" and God's love "toward men"), and all are what the word *glory* means in scripture. Notice, this is an example of the mode of thought assimilation here: "freedom is the same as . . ." In proposition XXXVII, Spinoza establishes that there is nothing contrary to the intellectual love of God. And finally, in proposition XL, we reach another assimilation: the more perfect something is, the more active it is, the less passive, the freer, the more blessed, and so on.

So, what constitutes the difference between Spinoza and Hobbes? With regard to method, both say that substantively, the way to achieve freedom is to act according to your nature; and that formally, we should proceed deductively from an axiom set. Hobbes wrote about body, about man, about citizen. For Hobbes, the first things called free are human bodies; for Spinoza it's God. With regard to interpretation, though, Hobbes is entitative: moving bodies with wit and will are what have freedom, and the use of power as we please gives us freedom. By contrast, Spinoza uses the ontological interpretation: God has freedom, and we have it insofar as we have an adequate knowledge of it, insofar as we have the same knowledge that God does. To act according to our nature and to reason is to act according to an adequate idea. The sense of freedom, then, is the self-perfection by which you'll attain your true nature. Notice the ontological interpretation here. For Hobbes, though, using the entitative, freedom is only uninhibited motion.

Turning next to principle, Spinoza's principle is reflexive. Principle for Spinoza is related to actions and passions; both are kinds of emotion, which are modes of attributes of God (or substance, or nature). They are reflexive principles—as holoscopic, they have a kind of comprehensiveness. Everything comes to God or nature, which are the same thing. How do passions become actions? By knowing himself. One controls the emotions by knowing the nature of emotions; thus, knowledge is the prime way. This is a reflexive principle based on the nature of things caused by self-knowledge. His five remedies are less exacting as we go down the line, and this is equivalent to a plan of life. He is setting up an order, a concatenation of passions. So, based on the nature of things, he starts with self-knowledge. We are free when we are the cause of ourselves.

Next time, we will look at Hobbes's principles as they relate to law and right, and what brings these two into relation for him.

Spinoza Ethics Book V Freedom *3.*

Title Concerning the Power of the Intellect or Human Freedom. Contrast title of Book IV.

This part of Ethics concerns "the manner or way which leads to liberty." Concerning the power of reason. Show power reason has over the emotions and moreover what is mental liberty or blessedness.

Perfection of intellect—not this part—logic

Cure of body—not this part—medicine.

Power of mind over emotions.

Stoics—emotions depend absolutely on our free will.

Descartes—mind may acquire absolute power over emotions

Problem—relation of will and motion—and therefore of power or strength of mind and body.

No freedom of will.

Axioms. 1. result of contrary actions, change until they cease to be contrary.
2. The power of emotion defined by power of its cause insofar as its essence is explained or defined through the essence of cause.

N.B. result—opposition of body and mind reduced to opposition of internal and external causes. Parallelism of order of things and modifications of body (Prop. I)—emotions result either of adequate idea (internal) or inadequate (passion—external). Ceases to be passion or external as soon as we form adequate idea of it (prop III).

Cor. The more an emotion becomes known to us the more it is within our power and the less the mind is passive to it.

Everything intelligible through cause (Prop IV and Sch.)

Knowledge and power. Prop VI. Insofar as the mind understands all things as necessary it has more power over emotions or is less passive to them. Infinite connection of causes.

Sch. increase of power of the mind.

Props. VII–X comparison of powers of emotions.

Sch. Prop. X, power of rightly arranging and connecting the modifications. "He therefore who moderates his emotions and desires from a love of freedom—endeavors to obtain a knowledge of the virtues and their causes." Contrasted to false species of liberty.

Knowledge of self and emotions—knowledge of God XV.

Love of God XVI. God free from passions XVII

Remedies for the emotions enumerated in Sch. Prop XX.

1. Knowledge of emotions
2. Separate emotions from idea of external cause confusedly imagined.
3. Time
4. Multitude of causes—common properties of things or God.
5. Order in which the emotions can be arranged.

"For the force of any emotion is defined by the power of an external cause compared with our own. But the mind's power is defined by knowledge alone: its weakness or passion by privation of knowledge, that is, it is estimated by the fact through which things are said to be inadequate"

XXXVI. Sch. equivalence established between salvation, blessedness, freedom (salus, beatitudo, libertas) and the constant and eternal love of God. Also glory in Scripture

XXXVII Nothing contrary to the intellectual love of God.

XXXVIII The more the mind understands according to the second and third kinds of knowledge the less it is passive to the emotions.

XL The more perfect the more active and the less passive.

DISCUSSION

Spinoza, Part 3
(*Tractatus Theologico-Politicus*, Chapter IV)

Discussion Summary

Let's begin by reviewing where we are in the argument. For Spinoza, freedom is acquired by acting in accordance with nature, an ontological interpretation. Nature is the perfect being one has when one's ideas are adequate relative to God; thus, only the wise man or God is free. Notice, nature is defined in terms of the wise man (see table 4). Why can we undertake any action? Principle tells us that we can undertake an action because we can know ourselves. Only the wise man is free, but the citizen in the state can also be free. So, as a kind of holoscopic principle, this reflexive principle doubles its meaning here, too. A man can be wise and, according to nature, act by knowledge; but one can also undertake to improve his nature for other reasons short of having knowledge of the nature of things, that is, by having a plan of life or objectives. Hobbes also has a doubling of meaning, but it is different. For Hobbes, the method is the same as Spinoza's: he also says act according to nature. But look at his interpretation: what is free? Moving bodies. So, nature is defined in terms of a moving body, yet there is a doubling of meaning here in interpretation. One kind of moving body is that which has wit and will, that is, humans. Consequently, we can act either according to nature or according to a civil compact.

Turning to principle, then, what is Hobbes's principle? If we want to know what the principle is, we know what underlies the first law of nature. Now, a holoscopic principle involves an absolute standard of good and evil, and one would appeal to something indivisible out of which nature is built up. Spinoza, for instance, has a reflexive principle, because one could know the nature of things by knowing himself, by self-knowledge. It is not true that you can learn the nature of things from experience. The things that I know I know because of what I am, not because of what happens to me. The same is true of comprehensive principles. If one wants to know himself truly, he can know himself by knowing the nature of something, for instance, geometry, God, someone else, or by knowing the order in which one's passions are set up—then passions become actions. For Hobbes, by contrast, the first law of nature is a combination of law, namely, preserve the peace, and of right, that is, defend yourself. These are two actions; we get the first law by putting the two together. Notice, then, that for Hobbes, reason is one's own reason; whereas for Spinoza, reason is absolute: reason is only reason when it is common to all men. For Hobbes, man will know by his own reason when to preserve himself. One knows these two parts of the law by one's own reason. This is an actional principle, therefore, for both parts of the law are actions. The criteria are the results of one's actions. Reasoning is one of those actions. By these acts we set up laws. There are certain things which a man is; that is, we have only power and judgment here, but we have no nature. Reason is an act to Hobbes, a manifestation of power, and not a thing or a nature. Lay down a principle, come to a judgment, and everything follows. This actional approach is, consequently, one of the two meroscopic principles, which deal with parts as their beginning point, in this case, some action taken. Holoscopic principles, on the other hand, use a whole as a beginning: comprehensive principles deal with absolute wholes, while reflexive principles, as in Spinoza's case, deal with relative wholes.

To see further how this works, let's turn to Spinoza's *Tractatus Theologico-Politicus*, where we find that he wants to deal with religion and politics in their relation to ethics. By using reflexive principles, he shows that these three are not the same. The treatise has a purpose stated in its dedication or preface. It has been written, he says, to demonstrate "that not only can such freedom [of thought and of speech] be granted without prejudice to the public peace, but also, that without such freedom, piety cannot flourish nor the public peace be secure" [p. 6].[1] The freedom here isn't the freedom of the *Ethics*, namely, that of the wise man. Now it's the freedom of thought and speech. Notice the doubling of meaning here. This is freedom to think anything you want and to say what you think. Freedom of speech is equally as important as that of thought and essential to the security of the state. He wants to prove that it is dangerous to confuse religion and politics. He argues that there is never such a thing as a theocracy, except perhaps in the case of God and Moses. He also argues that the function of the prophet is to convey piety, to give love of God a possibility, not to give doctrine. Religion and philosophy are related in that there are many people who ought to be happy and blessed besides the wise man. The bulk of mankind will get their morals from religion.

They will not have, as the wise man does, an intelligent love of God but can still live a moral life.

Similarly, the state is based not on the natural good, though there is one, but on power. Right is the same as power. Everything you are able to do you have a right to do. This sounds like Hobbes, but Spinoza is arguing that by means of the state one achieves security, which is the end or purpose of the state. Even more, the best state, the natural state, is a democracy. Everything the sovereign can do he has a right to do, but states will be better and last longer if the sovereign uses reason. This is the line of argument, the plot, that Spinoza lays out here.

What is law for Spinoza? In chapter IV of the *Tractatus*, he addresses divine law. What does law mean for Spinoza? *Lex* is natural necessity, for instance, the motion of bodies. (Notice, he says that law is "only applied to natural phenomena by analogy" [p. 58].) By contrast, *jus* is human decree, for instance, when men are compelled to yield their right. Thus, the law of nature is not the same as the law of the state. So, law and right are both here again, as in Hobbes. For one principle, the actional, law in nature and law in the state are one; but for the other, the reflexive, the two kinds of law are different. In the reflexive principle, if one takes law absolutely, what we are talking about is the part of nature in which *X* is *X* all the way through. It's a part of nature which can be explained by these laws, ones which explain causal relations and ones where the concatenation of causes would be complete. In the second sense of the term, law is what happens when one commands or issues a decree. One can begin with an end or intention in mind and set up a formulation to achieve it. Here we cannot specify causes or talk in general terms of fate, but we can set up a plan of life, what sociologists today call a "structure of values." We can consider the same thing in terms of a way of living which will attempt to induce proper behavior in terms of morals and the state. So, we will want to distinguish between divine or natural law on the one hand and human law on the other. We have a basic distinction here. That is, we can think of what happens absolutely, even if it only gives us probabilities; or we can deal with situations in which action is desirable. For example, we can set up a law against drunken driving. All we need in this case is power and deterrents.

Reflexive principles, in other words, separate in two ways: one, by knowledge, where one begins with knowledge in general; or two, by habit, that is, where knowledge is only the concatenation of the passions. In this case, one habituates oneself, and this second way is the equivalent of a plan of life. The basic difference in reflexive principles, then, is thinking of what happens absolutely and what does not. For the latter case, he defines *law* more particularly on page 58 as "a plan of life laid down by man for himself or others with a certain object." Since few men see the true object of life, one must either promise what men chiefly desire or threaten what men fear. Here, then, is where the passions come in. So, he is dividing the law into the human and divine. For the latter, see his definition of *divine law*: it is "true knowledge of God and love" [p. 59]. Consequently, short of intellectual love, piety is needed so that others than the learned can be saved.

Spinoza is stressing separation of church and state, which in his time was a sensitive issue. In the midst of this, what was the pious plea for religion was judged to be atheism; yet Spinoza was also called a God-intoxicated man. A regular paradox!

McKeon's Notes

Hobbes and Spinoza — Freedom. *1*

Similarity of method—deductive structure of derivation of liberty.

Derived from what—Hobbes, man's nature and state going back in principles from state to man to body. Basic principles in the nature of bodies.

Spinoza—in geometric deductive order to initial definitions and axiom about Cause, substance, God—their essences and existence.

For Spinoza (but not for Hobbes) Free*dom* is one of the terms that need definition at the beginning of the system. Bk. I, Def. VII: "That thing is said to be free which exists by the mere necessity of its own nature and is determined in its actions by itself alone. That thing is said to be necessary or rather compelled when it is determined in its existence and actions by something else in a certain fixed ratio."

Spinoza—strictly only God free (man as adequate ideas identical with ideas in God).

Hobbes—word liberty and freedom abused when applied to anything other than body.

Spinoza's principles *reflexive*—God as causa sui. Consequence that God is substance and *the* only substance (demonstrated) and that God is equivalent to nature as well as substance. Operates as if comprehensive—but test of the principle or beginning is its reflexivity.

Among the definitions is the definition of "free."

Therefore demonstrated that God alone is free *cause*—prop. xvii, cor. 2., i.e. exists and acts by the necessity of his own nature alone.

Everything else modes of Attributes of God.

Principles connected with method by "cause"—two kinds, internal and external. Effect of principle twofold in application to human freedom: (1) internal and external moved into man's nature as opposition between reason and passion, adequate and inadequate ideas—definition by exclusion of contrary, and (2)

Difference of principles.

Hobbes — Natures or bodies in interrelation

(Nature ↑ Right — Nature ↑ Law) — Artificial / *State*

Reason

Freedom — *Actional Principles*

power

nature

Spinoza — God, Nature, Substance

modes ↑ reason (adequate ideas) — modes ↑ passions (inadequate)

Freedom

power

nature

freedom becomes the rule of passions by reason—reason being the equivalent to man's nature, power, perfection.

Hobbes's principles *actional*. Plurality of bodies; bodies in motion by operation of internal and external causes. Introduction of artificial man or commonwealth as something made by man.

Freedom not a basic term precisely because artificial as well as natural bonds limit it, and it is therefore discussed in terms of power (rather than in terms of reality and perfection which define power for Spinoza). (Cf. Spinoza Bk. V axiom 2. Power of an emotion is defined by the power of its cause; and Def. VIII of Book IV. By virtue and power I understand the same thing—virtues having reference to man, as his essence or nature insofar as he has the power of effecting something which can only be understood by the laws of that nature.)

Effect of this basic importance of "power" to introduce fundamental *arbitrariness*—freedom as acting according to judgment or doing as one pleases.

Principles connected with method by "power"—two natural and artificially instituted. Effect of principle twofold in application to human freedom—: (1) balance of rights and law in state of nature, natural rights and natural laws—seek peace and use all means. Rights of man unlimited but his power infinitely exceeded, (2) balance of rights and law in civil state. Rights in silence of laws promulgated by sovereign power.

Hobbes and Spinoza Freedom 2. 5[2]

Logistic method as deductive system. Three kinds of principles.
1. Simple (would depend on isolating elements philosophic in character) (Telesio?) (or hedonism of atomists)
2. Actional—(Hobbes) All basic human values dependent on establishment of sovereignty and state.
3. Reflexive—God nature of Spinoza introduction of rational principle of self rule. *(State separation)*
1. Freedom action according to laws of nature.
2. Freedom do what he pleases and is able
3. Freedom rule of reason.

4 Comprehensive (Leibniz)
Freedom—Being and perfection

Separation of questions of method from questions of principle.

Two aspects of method in practical sciences (1) examining of definition of terms and sequence of discursive connection (proof), (2) conception of relation of knowledge to control of action. (content)

(1)—~~holoscopic~~ *universal* methods—analogical terms and no first principles because assimilated or discriminated.
~~meroscopic~~ *particular* methods—literal terms and first principles because constructed or resolved. (Construction and resolution of proposition from terms; as opposed to proposition as primary—or judgment).
(2) Knowledge and power directly related—either virtue is power or power is virtue: ~~holoscopic~~ *universal* methods

Power indirectly affected by knowledge—nature is power and knowledge affects it only by habituation or external restraint: ~~meroscopic~~ *particular* methods.

Similarity of Hobbes and Spinoza—unit in both cases the thing—no free will.

In general the unit in ~~meroscopic~~ *particular* methods the agent (sometimes man, sometimes broader).

Similarity of two structures in comparison of men's interrelations as seen in the Spinoza Lemmas Bk I, II and Hobbes successive stages—body, man, state (artificial man).

In terms of method—identical equivalences of nature, power, freedom—and use of power to establish contraries.

But Hobbes's contrary to freedom is law (external power); Spinoza's is compulsion (external power) law of one's own nature.

This is the beginning of detection of principles.

Method is constructive—building of nature from interrelations of bodies—(something identical, but contrarieties of motion and rest).

Principle in Hobbes—the continuing but altering oppositions of right and law from state of nature to civil state—normative elements by force from command of sovereign. (Actional principles—i.e. discrimination or distinction). (logistic method).

Principle in Spinoza—habituation by use of reason for moral principle; power of sovereign with possible use of reason. (Reflexive principles i.e. resolution, going back to first principle causa sui, alone truly free) (logistic method.)

Leibniz and Hume[3] Principles.

Both seek principles in ideas, but difference of criteria of principles. Hume two varieties (1) simples impressions and ideas, and (2) simple relations among ideas.

Leibniz—clear, distinct, and adequate ideas.

Consequence in their treatment of knowledge

Hume—knowledge of matter of fact and of relations of ideas; Leibniz—sensible ideas clear but not distinct, ideas of common sense clear and distinct, therefore beginning of possibility of science.

Difference in treatment of cause as result—Hume one of the relations of ideas, basis of all knowledge of fact, grounded in custom. Leibniz cause a reason—of existence or of essence. In finite things cause not found in nature of thing but external to it; reason found in notion of thing.

Freedom and necessity—Hume, internal causality of will constitutes freedom; Leibniz—knowledge. (N.B. both conceived in terms of distinction between internal and external causality.

N.B. difference of conception of ideas. Hume—idea copy of impression—search for simple ideas and their relation. Leibniz—organic idea—monad as essence of existent thing, ideas influenced by other ideas in this unity.

N.B. consequence in the conception of matter—Hume body as extension—physics of external relations of bodies. Leibniz—essence of body force, laws of motion consequent on that idea.

(Knowledge of God, external world, self.)

Kant.
Characteristic approach to principles treatment of knowledge in terms of form and matter. Necessity in forms of pure reason.

Criticism of Leibniz (p. 36):[4] "This shows that the philosophy of Leibniz and Wolff has given a totally wrong direction to all investigations into the nature and origin of our knowledge, by representing the difference between the sensible and the intelligible as logical only. That difference is in truth transcendental. If a fact is not the form only, as being more or less confused, but the origin and contents of our knowledge, so that by our sensibility we know the nature of things by themselves not confusedly only, but not at all. If we drop our subjective condition, the object as represented with its qualities bestowed on it by sensuous intuition, is nowhere to be found, and cannot possibly [be] found; because its form, as phenomenal appearance, is determined by those very subjective conditions."

DISCUSSION

Spinoza, Part 4 (*Tractatus Theologico-Politicus*, Chapter XVI)

Discussion Summary

Today we continue our study of Spinoza. The *Ethics* and the *Tractatus* have as a purpose to separate ethics, politics, and religion. Let us begin the examination of the separation between ethics and religion by comparing Hobbes and Spinoza. When we started with Hobbes, we saw that he distinguished *lex* and *jus*, and he made the columns between the two concepts sharply separated. Hobbes and Spinoza use the same method and, consequently, follow this same separation. But for Spinoza, *lex* is operation according to nature, and *jus* is a divine or human decree or ordinance. Thus, Spinoza follows the same separation as Hobbes, but the terms take on different meanings. For Spinoza, strictly speaking, we can't apply *lex* (law) to nature, because a law becomes a way of life, and we don't know the universe as a whole. So, we don't know what law is in the strict sense.

When we look at *jus* in chapter IV of the *Tractatus*, there are human and divine precepts. Within this, we have divine natural law and human law. Human law is a plan of living which serves only to render life and the state secure. Divine natural law has two parts. First, the divine law is based on knowledge and leads to the intellectual love of God, which is treated in the *Ethics*. Second are the rules of life which men need to follow. Spinoza asks four questions about the divine natural law on pages 61–62.[1] The details are of two sorts: obviously, one way we can know and love God is by being a wise man, by knowing everything; or, we can wish to act with Him as an end but without this knowledge, and the guidance in this comes from scripture. Thus, scripture is for ordinary people, not sages; it does not give doctrine or knowledge, yet it uses imagination to urge us to love and piety, and so we can in this latter way also achieve happiness. Religion is hereby separated from ethics in that the latter depends on adequate ideas, while the former depends on the direction given by inadequate ideas, that is, through desires and love.

What happens to the logistic method when Spinoza turns to a discussion of religion? He needs a method of biblical criticism that begins with propositions and then deduces. What would be his mathematical proof? Notice that with the logistic method, if a philosopher is using a logistic method, we should find a postulate set. In this regard, see page 99: "I may sum up the matter by saying that the method of interpreting Scripture does not widely differ from the method of interpreting nature—in fact, it is almost the same." So, what is the difference between discussing scripture or natural history? The difference is that in both cases, we have a postulate set; but because the logistic method is a particular method, we must apply our common method differently in different regions. The postulate set applied to natural history gives one set of deductions. On the other hand, statements as to a way of life also need a postulate set, and the prophets have imagination, from which are set up precepts for behavior. Similarly, one could set up a postulate set for geometry. So, in both cases, for scripture and for natural history, we have a postulate set. We can do this because it is a particular method.

Moving on, we see in chapter XVI that "freedom of thought" is the freedom of philosophizing. To separate philosophy and theology ensures there will be freedom of thought in both. Why? Is he saying there are to be prescriptive rules for those who cannot philosophize? Does he mean to say that the religious man cannot philosophize? Philosophy and theology are distinct in their purposes, their ends. If one were to confuse them, religion, which should be a matter of belief indicating a way of life, would become a doctrine and would presume, thereby, to tell truth. Conversely, if philosophy were to prescribe for religion, it would say that all religions are false except one, the true religion. So, for Spinoza, if religion and philosophy are not separated, they interfere with each other: religion interferes by laying down a truth, while philosophy interferes by saying the state and religion are the same and there is but one true religion. So, *lex* and *jus* are to be kept apart; so, likewise, are religion and the state. For Hobbes, by contrast, the sovereign has control over everything; thus, the state determines religion. In England during the Reformation, there existed a conviction that the [Roman Catholic] Church had dominated the states of the world before the Reformation, and this view held that religion had determined the state. Note that there are four possibilities of relation between the two: that religion and the state are wholly separate; that the state is the basis of religion; that religion is the basis of the state; and the fourth possibility, that religion and the state are equal, are one and the same (see fig. 15).[2] This last is like theocracy in antiquity and Soviet Russia today, in that the state *is* religion.

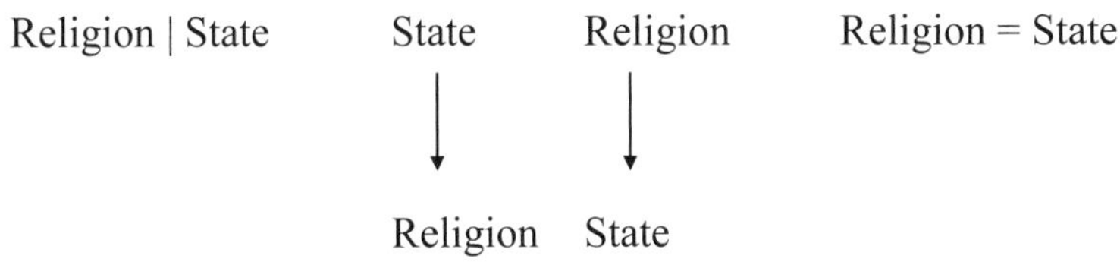

Fig. 15 *Four Possibilities of Relation between Religion and State*

So, if we separate religion and the state, we have freedom of thought in both of them. Now, Spinoza is using the logistic method and using it relative to an ontological interpretation. Therefore, if we have freedom of philosophizing, we will have two levels. On the first, freedom consists in knowing what the truth is. On the second, freedom consists in following desires. Freedom of philosophizing is important to have in this situation. Why? On the ethical side, if we have freedom of speech, we can present a pluralism of views to help us perhaps get to the philosophic truth. On the religious side, we are talking not of truth but of inspiration by God. Thus, the actions aimed at are those which are inspired by God. So, to put our answer more simply, the first sentence of chapter XVI says that we need to separate the state and religion, for then we can philosophize freely and pursue the good of man separately.

To summarize up to this point, then, we began in ethics and came down through a series of postulates. We next went to religion and distinguished it from the state. Now we go on to look for the basic components of the state; we are looking for foundations. First, we will look for the natural rights of the individual, the source of power for the individual. Then, we will move up in complexity, and we will consider the state as composed of individuals and religion as composed of individuals.

What happens in the second paragraph? He talks of the right of nature—the *lex*. He is giving "the rules of nature," the laws of motion, the laws of a thing's behavior. Anything that a thing can do, it has a right to do. By *right*, he means the laws of nature. As with Hobbes, Spinoza begins with the elemental part; and whatever that part or the composite of such parts does, it has a right to do (see pages 200–201). Notice, by beginning with the law, Spinoza defines right in terms of law. If we can tell what a law is, we can tell what a right is. We are beginning with the way a thing acts, because it has a right to do that. The determinate laws of any individual may vary among individuals and are determined by the environment. Once we have said this, right is coextensive with power, the power of nature; the power of nature is the power of God; and the universal power of all nature is the aggregate power of elemental individuals.

Spinoza, however, differs from Hobbes in interpretation. Since it is a sovereign law of nature that each individual must try to preserve its own nature, it follows that each individual has the right to act as he pleases. This is not the same right as acting according to the law of reason. The law of human reason would put us on the way to our benefit, but nature is not bound by laws of human reason. Consider where, on page 202, Spinoza states that we will be guided by reason: "it is much better for us to live according to the laws and assured dictates of reason, for, as we said, they have men's true good for their object." It is better, then, for us to operate according to reason, in which case one "will restrain any desire which is injurious to man's fellows" [p. 203], although each has a right to do so. Consequently, a compact which creates a state is set up based on a universal law that is good as long as we are convinced that we are getting a greater good. This treaty holds only either so long as its members are convinced that it is worth holding or so long as one can enforce it (by means of power).

What we are dealing with here in politics is like religion because we are working on the desires. The foundation of the state is any desire which there is. Therefore, we are trying to find out the way in which, recognizing that right and power are the same in the state, the individual will gain not only security but a type of life that is worthwhile. Notice, the handling of desire is another problem altogether from our other two inquiries, and ethics' influence on politics is meaningless. In other words, ethics is a way of achieving happiness and blessedness through knowledge; whereas politics is a way of achieving happiness and blessedness through power and the laws formulated regarding what should be done. In brief, the three ways to happiness and blessedness are either by adequate ideas, by faith and love, or by power and laws.

McKeon's Notes

Spinoza — Liberty 2

Note that in basic terms there is the same equation or equivalence as in Hobbes.

Liberty
Power
Nature.

But the oppositions which related internal to external are in Spinoza translated into an internal form (morals) which are separated form their external treatment (politics). For Hobbes ethics a part of politics—distinction between good and evil, mine and thine, just and unjust not natural—result of the decree of the sovereign after the state has been established.

Similarity to Spinoza's decision that if a man were wholly rational there would be no distinction between good and evil—since there would be no evil and therefore no good. III, Pref. Good and evil nothing positive. Similarity of conception of Right IV, prop. 37, sch. 2.

Internalization of ethics by definition of human nature—knowledge of men and—perfection from increase of his power of action, so that liberty dependent on the use of reason—liberty becomes synonymous with beatitudo, salus, wisdom and the intellectual love of God.

Spinoza Power[3] 1

Bk. 1 Def. 7. Free and compelled.

XVII. Sch. God's intellect, will and power are one and the same thing.

XXXIV. The power of God is the same as his essence.

XXXV. Whatever we conceive to be in the power of God necessarily is.

Appendix. God's "absolute nature or infinite power."

Bk. II. VII. Cor. God's power of thinking is equal to his actual power of acting.

XLV. Sch. Force by which each thing persists in existing.

Bk. III. Def. 3. Emotion—modification of body by which power of action in the body is increased or diminished.

Post. 1. Human body affected in many ways by which its power of acting increased or diminished.

VI. Everything insofar as it is in itself endeavors to persist in its own being.

VIII. dem. This endeavor not destroyed by any external cause, continues to exist by same power.

XI. What increases or decreases power of action of body, idea of it increases or diminishes power of thinking of mind.

XII. Mind endeavors to imagine things which increase its power of acting.

LIII. When mind regards self and power of acting, it is rejoiced.

LIV. Power of action. LV.

LV. cor. ii. dem. Man endeavors or desires nothing save what can follow from his given nature.

Bk. IV Strength of the emotions.

Human lack of power in moderating and checking the emotions: all servitude.
Man's nature = his power of acting. Perfection = reality or essence.

Def. 8. By virtue and power I understand the same thing, i.e. essence or nature.

LECTURE FIVE

Freedom: Selection

So far we have looked at the definition of freedom in terms of the aspect of method, interpretation, and principle.[1] There's a fourth aspect, selection, which we ought to go on to next; but I will at first only talk about selection briefly before trying to tie together the three parts of the definition of freedom in terms of selection, that is, go over again principles, methods, interpretations, emphasizing the aspect that selection brings in; and then I'll return to selection a little more fully. The reason for this is simple. You'll recall that we schematized the four parts of the definition by indicating that there is one term, which is the subject of selection; two terms, interpretation; method involves a discursive process, and therefore at least three terms; and principle, organizing either the whole of discourse or the discourse which is relevant to what we are dealing with (see table 1). It is obviously impossible to talk about selection. Selection involves only one term: you can enunciate one term; explain what it means and you are already interpreting it; justify the explanation, you're giving an argument and employing a method. And it is this—this part is review—it is this that led to the selection of the direction that we have been going in. In other words, we have begun with method, we worked from method to interpretation, and then arrived at principle. This kind of selection is involved in any intellectual discourse, not merely in philosophy but also in those more extended philosophic disquisitions that occur in other departments of the university in which you lay down what the truth is about, what the course is about.

In general, each of these headings will give us modes of something. These [method] are modes of thought—I'm going into this, because one of the questions that was asked when I permitted questions raised this issue—these [principle] are modes of being; these [interpretation] are modes of fact; and the last one [selection] is hard to name—I've been calling it sometimes modes of experience, but the modes of experience

Table 7. Aspects of Definition and the Four Modes.

Principle	Method	Interpretation	Selection
↓	↓	↓	↓
Modes of Being	Modes of Thought	Modes of Fact	Modes of Experience (Categories)

in a fixed sense—these are categories: categories organize individual terms and tell you what the schematism of the terms will be or designate the aspects of your experience on which the analysis will concentrate (see table 7).[2] We have used modes of thought, because they deal with method; therefore, any extended discourse would employ them anyway. They're a natural beginning place; in many respects, it is easier to notice the method that is being employed than to recognize what the criteria are which determine the fact—we're much more dogmatic about our facts than we are about our arguments—and as I suggested in the opening lecture when we made our choice, it is almost forgotten what principles mean, and so there was no sense in dealing with principles. But you will recall that therefore, for the explanation of each of these headings, I made use of four modes of thought: assimilation, composition or construction, discrimination, and resolution. By means of the four modes of thought I have successively distinguished four methods (which are different from the four modes of thought), four interpretations, four principles; and I want to use the modes of thought to tell you a little about categories, a very difficult subject.

Bear in mind that there is nothing sacrosanct about the modes of thought. I could have begun the exposition by giving you the modes of being; but then the orientation of the course would be metaphysical, and we would be stopped by the necessity of spending the first three weeks in explaining why metaphysics is not only meaningful but inevitable—I should, I imagine, say that the other way: it is now recognized to be inevitable but not necessarily meaningful. [L!] We might also have begun with four modes of fact; but then I would have had to get you used to the notion that even though facts are hard, irreversible, resistant, they are not necessarily always what you say they are, and therefore, the modes of fact would have to appear. Or we might have begun with the categories. Let me repeat, we made a choice. This is due, incidentally, to the fact that throughout the course we have been using the mode of discrimination: that is, the mode of discrimination is adapted to laying out the various perspectives and approaches; therefore, without more ado, as soon as you have done the job of discrimination, you have the means

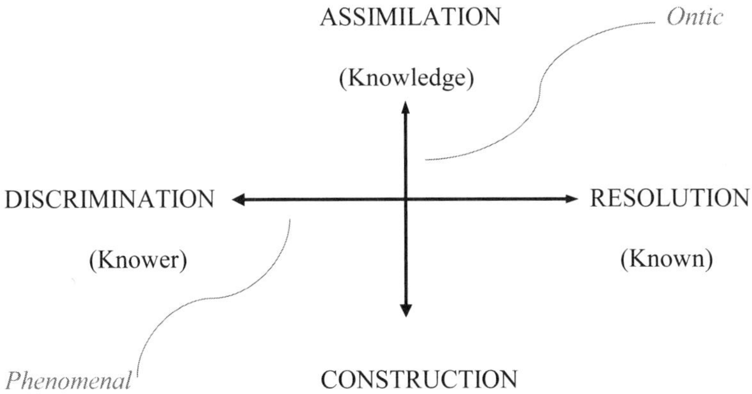

Fig. 16 *Interpretation and Modes of Thought*

of making the differentiations that are involved. Consequently, using the mode of discrimination we got our modes of thought (see fig. 3). If we had used—I'm repeating deliberately much that I have said—if we had used the mode of assimilation or the mode of resolution, we would have gotten a different set of distinctions. I've assured you that we would have come out in the same place; the only difference would have been that our selection would have been different.

What have we done? Well, in accordance with the mode of discrimination, we have used a table, a table which could be expanded to a matrix easily, and I will give you instructions to do that—knowledge, knowable, knower, and known. I've deliberately constructed it out of words that are cognates of each other, because what meaning we will assign to them will depend on their interrelations, and they'll have a different meaning for each method, for each interpretation, and for each principle. We've been underlining that. That's why we expect to come out by a combination of these four aspects with justifiable, much-used conceptions of freedom that are radically different, all of them part of the ordinary language—ordinary Greek, ordinary Latin, ordinary French, ordinary Italian, or ordinary English—-because the structure is a structure of meanings. What we have done has been, for interpretation, to set the words in pairs and to indicate in terms of the pairs the radically different basic pairs of interpretation (see fig. 16).[3] We have turned around from interpretation, and in method we have connected two other of the pairs (see fig. 17)—I shall not explain again why: this much, I hope, is in your notes; when you read your notes after the lecture, your notes will become intelligible. Finally, we connected the one remaining pair and got our principles (see fig. 18). And it requires no great mathematical intuition to see that we've

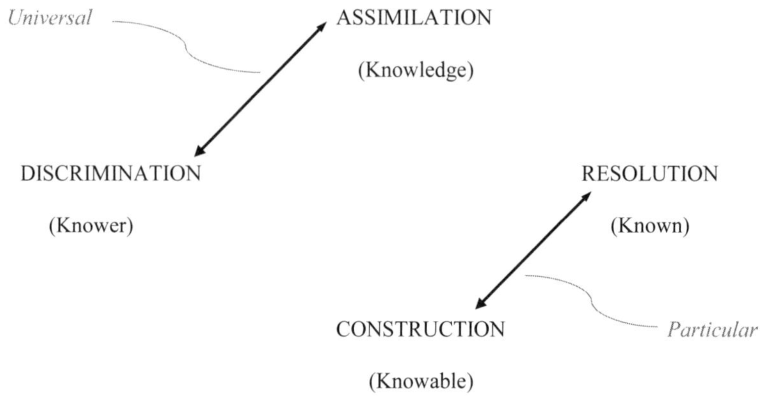

Fig. 17 *Method and Modes of Thought*

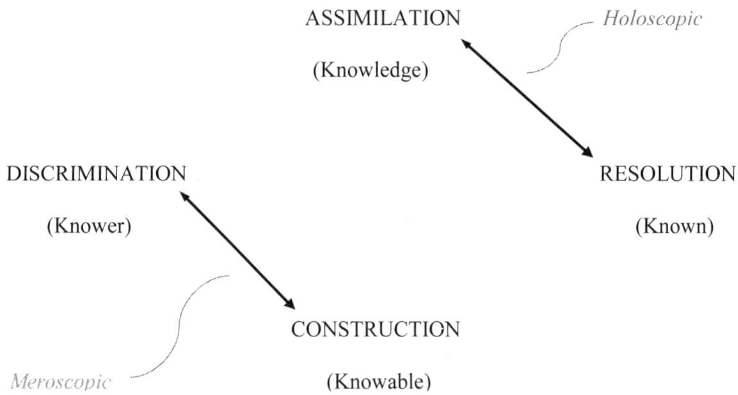

Fig. 18 *Principle and Modes of Thought*

done all the pairing that our four terms will permit. And this is quite all right, because the pairing is—I'm tempted to explain how the pairing goes on the diagram, but that would take us into mysticism and away from the literal truth that I want to introduce you to today [L!]; consequently, I will not explain—the pairing is either the pairing that you make in a statement where you have a subject and a predicate to relate; or the pairing that you make in an argument or a poetic discourse or any other mode of exposition or inquiry that you wish to engage in where you relate a beginning with an end, the known with the unknown; or it is the pairing that occurs when you begin with a basic assumption and then deal with the entire structure of what it is you are talking about, the pairing of a principle with the body of its consequences. But there is one remaining thing that we've been doing that we have not noticed: namely, for each one of these, we have used the line not simply as a line but as a vector. That is to say, if, beginning with our method, as we did, if we orient this line to knowledge, then we have assimilation. If we orient the same line in the opposite direction, to the knower, then ask what happens to all of our meanings, we have discrimination. If we orient that conception of method which involves the known and relate the knowable to known, viewed now as the body of knowledge already acquired and the problems it presents, we have resolution. If we orient the line, finally, to the knowable, giving it a character to which the known must fit, then we have construction, we will build out of the elements that must be there underlying our experience and construct the knowledge out of these parts.

Therefore, in selection it is important to recognize what goes on in these orientations, what the basis is of the vector which determines what we are doing. Selection is the group of single terms that one selects or the aspects of experience on which one concentrates. Even if you are talking about freedom in the broad, ambiguous sense in which intelligent discourse about freedom takes its start before it breaks up into parties and sects when one will select both different words and different aspects of experience, viewed as a language it can be put this way: that there is an indefinitely large number of possible terms which have been or could be constructed, going beyond even the richest of languages, out of which in any actual discourse one makes a finite selection. This is the process of selection. Putting it in terms of what you are talking about, in any experience, even a very restricted experience, such as the sight you might have of the arm of your chair, there is an indefinitely large number of aspects which could be chosen. A lifetime's research enumerating everything that could be distinguished in your experience of the chair arm would be an unending one. I don't think I need go into the details of it; I think all you need to do is to recognize that all of our experiences are of this character, and the totality of our knowledge can be focused on limited experiences no broader than the very rich experience that you have in contemplating the arm of your chair.

Consequently, there are two things that happen in selection. One is that you set up your characteristic vocabulary or your characteristic view of reality, whichever you prefer, as your basic formulation of the process; and you can broaden this to other people who agree with you. This is the way in which you move from the idiosyncratic vocabulary you have to the category of your school or your sect or the philosophic truth as you view it. Second, as soon as you do this, you have by your selection separated that selection from other selections; therefore, the second aspect is that in setting up what you think or what those think who agree with you in a right-minded way, it is the contrary, the opposite, distinct from, more complete, truer than, any of the other views. So that as the first aspect of selection is the determination of a view and a vocabulary, the second aspect gives a separation of that view from alternative separations. The relation may be amicable or it may be controversial, but even the amicable ones become controversial when you explain them fully enough to each other.

There's another aspect, however, of selection: namely, that within any given time or within any given culture, within any given system of communication, there has already been set up a selection, broader than the ones I've talked about, with more ambiguities—selections do not necessarily avoid ambiguities, they flourish on them—and it is by means of this selection that the approach of one time or one culture is separated from another. We not only adhere to a preferred approach, our philosophy, but we also frame our philosophy in a selection which is twentieth century, which makes it almost inevitable that anything that was said in the nineteenth century was wrong, meaningless or, at best, incomplete and impossible. Consequently, you have a third aspect, namely, the means by which you can characterize a system of communication—this is a selection—and the ways by which the systems of communication, of expression, of proof, differ in different ages. There is therefore the element of a philosophy of history in the selections. I say only an "element," because if you go over to the modes of thought, the philosophy of history in a strict sense is homogeneous only to assimilation. You need to be a dialectician to have a real philosophy of history, and all you need to be in order to avoid a philosophy of history and to be convinced that is meaningless is to go to the mode of construction. The other two are more or less indifferent; they'll take it or leave it. Consequently, since we're operating by discrimination, we are employing a kind of philosophy of history—one that I'll sketch in just a moment—which would constitute the entire framework of a philosophy of history that emerges from selection.

Let's begin, then, with the first, that is, the simplest, the mode of selection. What is it that each of the arrowheads that I have put on our familiar diagram would do? The answer, you see, to the problem of selection, let me repeat, is either: What words shall we use? or: What shall we be talking about? Since we're discussing the problem of freedom, we shall be using the word *freedom* all the way through, but the words we use to define freedom will shift radically with each of the arrowheads. Therefore, much of the discussion will be of such a sort that you can say, when you are in your nonbellicose mood, "Well, what he's saying may or may not be true, but he's talking about something different from what

Table 8. Orientations of Selection.

Knowledge Matrix	Mode of Thought	Fundamental Vocabulary	Characteristic of: Terms (Formal)	Characteristic of: Facts (Material)	Orientation (What are you talking about?)
Knowledge	Assimilation	Ideas and Images	Hierarchies	Transcendents	Thought
Knowable	Construction	Cognitions and Emotions	Reductions	Elements	Thing
Knower	Discrimination	Symbols and Rules	Types	Perspectives	Language
Known	Resolution	Theories and Practices	Functions	Essences	Action

I'm talking about when I talk about freedom." So, selection is the answer to the question, When you say this, what are you talking about? Let's begin with assimilation (see table 8).[4] In assimilation, where knowledge is dominant, what we are talking about when we talk about anything are ideas and images; anything else must be an idea or an image, or you can't talk about it. Consequently, there is a tendency in the selection that goes with the mode of assimilation for hierarchies to appear, hierarchies of all sorts. You can have a suspicion as soon as you see a hierarchy—there are going to be hierarchies going down as well as up, so that it's only a suspicion—when you see a hierarchy, particularly if the hierarchy emphasizes the top and if the top tends to extend transcendentally beyond what you can really talk about, that you are making a selection appropriate to assimilation.

If you go in the opposite direction and assimilate to the knowable—bear in mind, all of these lines have arrows, and consequently, there will be three aiming at the knowable in what we have said thus far—then you are engaged in construction. What are you talking about when you talk about construction? Well, you're talking about things, and therefore, the basic selection is one in which the vocabulary goes to cognitions and emotions, rarely to ideas and images, except when the philosopher is borrowing from his enemy to show how you could do it right if you really wanted to talk about ideas and images. The vocabulary runs not to hierarchies but to reductions. The reductive philosophies, reducing whatever is significant to basic subjects about which the discourse is really possible in a preferred way, would be the selection appropriate to construction. If the orientation is to the knower, the mode is discrimi-

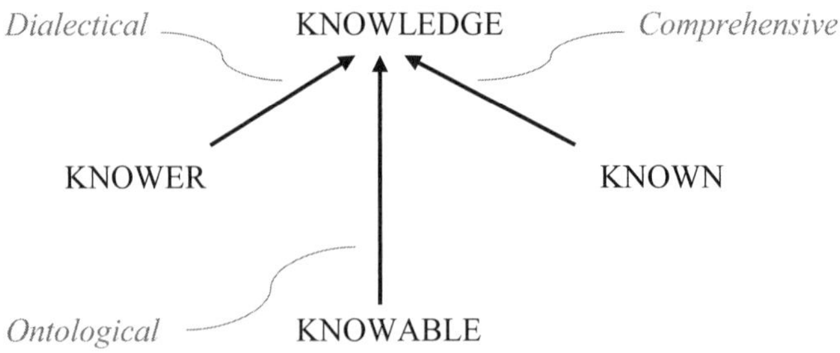

Fig. 19 *Simple Semantic Profile,* e.g., *of Plato*

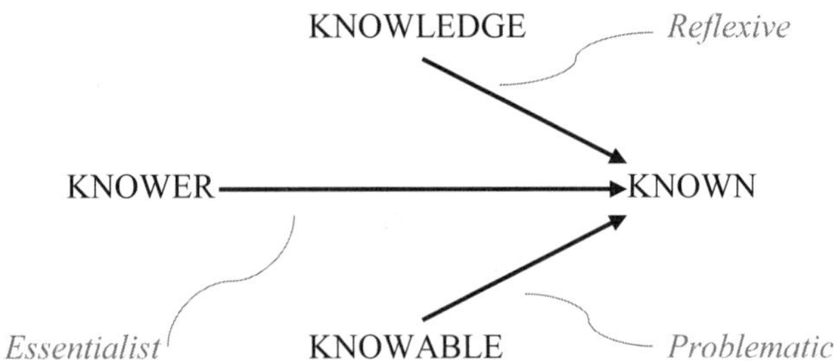

Fig. 20 *Simple Semantic Profile,* e.g., *of Aristotle*

nation; then what you are talking about is language, your fundamental terms are symbols and rules of operation with symbols, and the vocabulary runs to types. The word *type* runs all the way from the Greek, where it started, down to the present, where types take on great importance—even lead you to vice, because there is a vicious circle which can be solved only by a theory of types, it is said by this approach. [L!] Consequently, the types are arranged in perspectives. Finally, if you oriented to the known, then your selection is about theories and practices, actions are dominant, and the vocabulary runs to functions related to objectives in which you can talk about essences as you cannot if you are oriented to language—you can talk about existences if you're oriented to languages.

I've taken my examples largely from the Greek philosophers, because there are four schools that I've been using as examples in which the selection for principles, methods, and interpretations is oriented, respectively, to ideas or things or words or actions—I've said "experience" more frequently. And this was the first thing that led me to think that something like an attenuated philosophy of history was involved in the interpretation. I read a lot of philosophers from the history of philos-

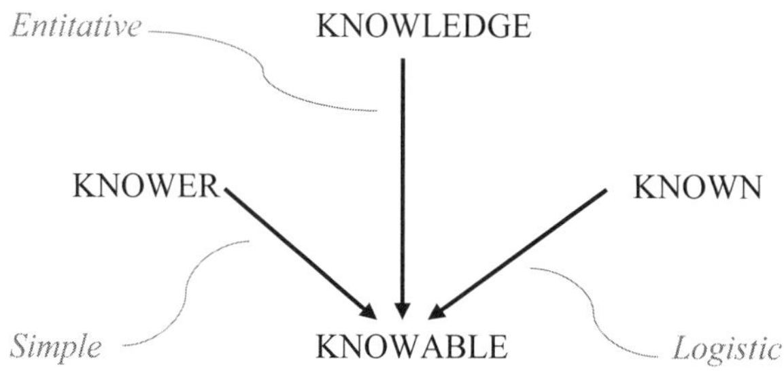

Fig. 21 *Simple Semantic Profile,* e.g., *of Democritus*

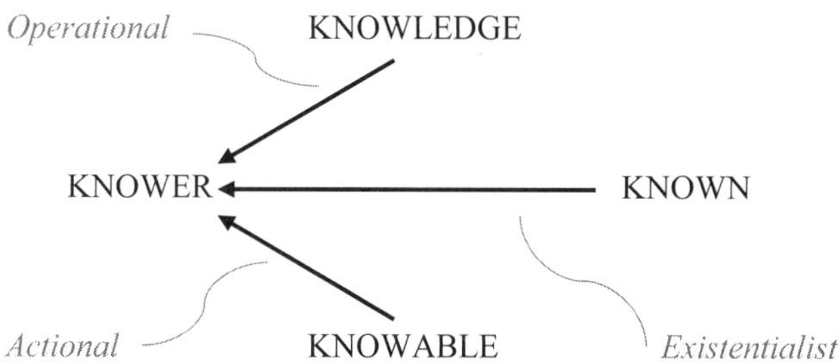

Fig. 22 *Simple Semantic Profile,* e.g., *of the Sophists*

ophy; and since I'm given to this schematic way of arranging arguments, I tend to schematize them. For the Greek writers that I've mentioned—and I think this is true for all of the philosophers who have survived; fortunately, there are only two that have survived in bulk; all the rest have survived in fragments, and you can arrange the fragments very easily, so that the experimental evidence we have, I grant, is slight—all of them use a single mode of thought for all three, for their principles, for their methods, for their interpretations. And therefore, using that scheme, the picture of Plato is that in figure 19, the picture of Aristotle is that in figure 20, the picture of Democritus is that in figure 21, and the picture of the Sophists is that in figure 22.[5]

For the pre-Socratics, if we were doing it schematically, I could give you like pictures; but thereafter I've not been able to find a single philosopher since 322 BCE[6] who uses the same mode of thought all the way through. At first I thought, since this is also a natural tendency, that this was a defect—it's always a defect if you don't do something which you observe someone else doing—a defect in later philosophy. But it seems to me now that is not the case, that you can have as good a philosophy that would diagram as that of figure 23 or that you could diagram like

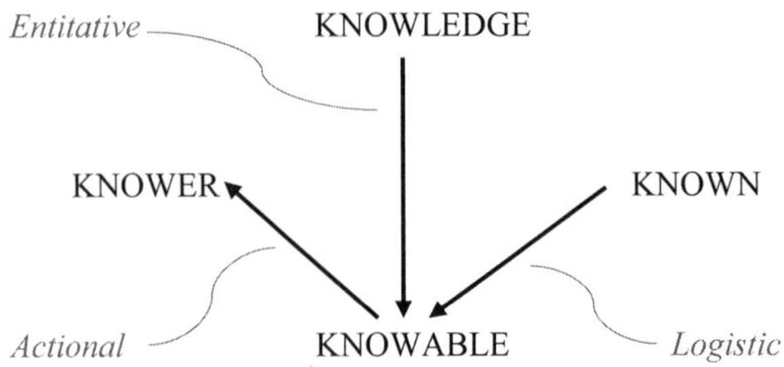

Fig. 23 *Mixed Semantic Profile,* e.g., *of Hobbes*

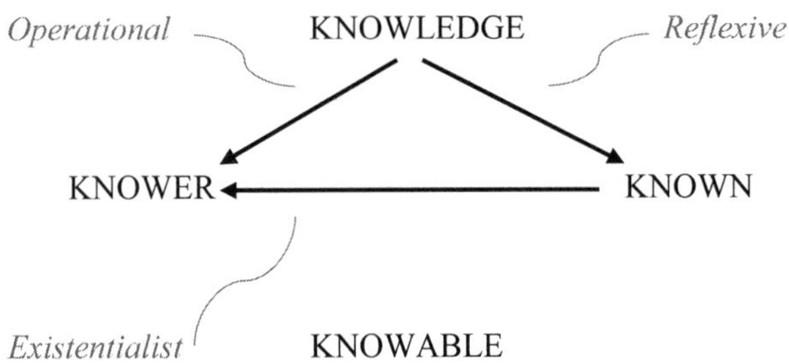

Fig. 24 *Mixed Semantic Proile,* e.g., *of Machiavelli and Mill*

that of figure 24 as the original way.[7] Consequently, there's no normative element which is involved.

The selections differ in ways, however, which can also be derived from our diagram. Let me use merely the modern period to indicate where the philosophy of history comes in. In the seventeenth century, whether you're on the continent of Europe or in England, the hunt was for principles (see table 9).[8] The important thing was to set up principles that would make philosophy and the analysis of human nature and action as solid as the analysis of nature; therefore, whether it is Bacon seeking a new method for the discovery of arts or Descartes setting up a universal mathematics or Locke imitating his friend, Mister Newton, with respect to the human understanding, the hunt is for principles. And this goes on fairly comfortably, except that so many different principles were discovered by the various philosophers that the domain of the discussion of philosophy was not very comfortable.

Then there came in the eighteenth century a change which Kant claims for himself: he says he wishes to inaugurate a Copernican revolution. The Copernican revolution had really been started before him, but he described it fairly well. It's a very curious Copernican revolution; that is—you remember, the Copernican revolution was originally one in

Table 9. Periodic Change in Selection.

Period Orientation:	Principle	Method	Interpretation
Discussion about:	Metaphysics	Epistemology	Linguistics, Pragmatics
Emphasis on:	Thing (Being or Existence)	Thought (Thoughts or Experiences)	Language, Action (Statements or Processes)
Basic Problem:	Whole/Part	Universal/Particular	Reality/Appearance

which the earth stopped being the center of things and the sun became the center of things, until it turned out that there was no center [L!]—the Copernican revolution that Kant wished to set up was one in which you stop making man merely an instance of nature like other things and you orient everything, including nature, to the forms of thought; and therefore, man becomes, in his philosophical inquiries, the center of things. The result is that we moved over to a period in which method dominated. There was enough talk about method before: the *Discourse on Method*[9] was merely one of a vast number of inquiries into method, but you'll remember that the *Discourse on Method* was one in which the important thing was to get out of the universal doubt and have a beginning point; and a beginning point is a principle. Whereas in Kant, it is the forms of thought that you investigate in detail: you can go back eventually to metaphysics, and you can have a metaphysics of nature and a metaphysics of freedom; but that's another step, you establish that possibility on a critical philosophy. One hundred fifty years, two hundred years of debate about metaphysics made people so tired of investigating the nature of being that they said, in effect, "Well, maybe if we could decide when we know something, and therefore know what knowledge is, we'll be in a position to turn around and talk about what the nature of things is." So, for one hundred and fifty years they engaged in epistemology instead of metaphysics.—Oddly enough, epistemology has not undergone the same degradation in the twentieth century that metaphysics did.—In epistemology, you likewise can debate in a variety of ways what the nature of method is. Is *Geistesgeschichte* or *Geisteswissenschaft* the same or different as *Naturwissenschaft*?[10] You can do it either way: you can either say that the knowledge of nature, the *method* of the natural sciences, should be incorporated into the social sciences and the humanities, or that there is a radical distinction between the two.

Leaving aside that large question, however, our question of liberty is,

I think, an excellent indication of the difference. When Hume and Kant, on the edge of this Copernican revolution, began talking about liberty, Hume says it rather more strikingly than Kant. Hume says, "All this time"—and usually, if it's been going on with your teachers, it always has been going on; he assumes that it's always gone on—"all this time we've set up an indefensible opposition between liberty and necessity, as if you had one rather than the other"; and he, he says, is not interested in the metaphysical question of freedom in this sense. He's interested, rather, in the moral problem of action, the consideration of choices; and in that, necessity and freedom are not the opposite. As Hume explains, if you make a moral judgment about a man, it's important that the act that you are judging followed necessarily from him or his character, because if it was merely an accident in which he had nothing to do, you can't judge *him* wrong for that; but second, it's important that it also be something that he chose freely, because if he couldn't do anything about it, there'd be no moral question—though you got into a different set of problems equally difficult. But the point that I'm trying to make is that when you come to one of these moral revolutions, it looks as if the tough problems are easily solved—that isn't quite true either, but it is possible to make statements about their being absurd in which a great many people seem to agree. [L!] In the nineteenth century, you continue, then, to talk about method, sometimes with extraordinary perception, setting up the organization of sciences. Comte, Durkheim, Dilthey, for example, wrote books that we still read about methods, adapting them to what we mean today.

Then, in the twentieth century, we had another set of revolutions—at the end of the nineteenth, the beginning of the twentieth century—this was a revolution that I've referred to several times in my lectures, a revolution against idealism and positivism. We tend, in our Anglo-American way, to forget that on the Continent and even in Latin America, positivism and Comte were ensconced in the nineteenth century, and that therefore it was a revolt against positivism that led to the modern French, German, and Italian philosophies; while the revolt against idealism in the English-speaking world introduced a neopositivism for the first time. I'm sure that our Latin American relations are seriously hampered by the fact that they were breaking the thrall of positivism about the time that we were forging the chains by which to bind ourselves in positivism. But we had a whole series of them: pragmatisms, realisms, naturalisms, phenomenologies, existentialisms, neopositivisms, neothomisms, and neoanalysis: all come in about the same way, with the same discovery that the way of posing problems previously was meaningless but, at the same time, a discovery that there is a continuing chain that binds us to the past. The twentieth century, more than most periods—this is usually

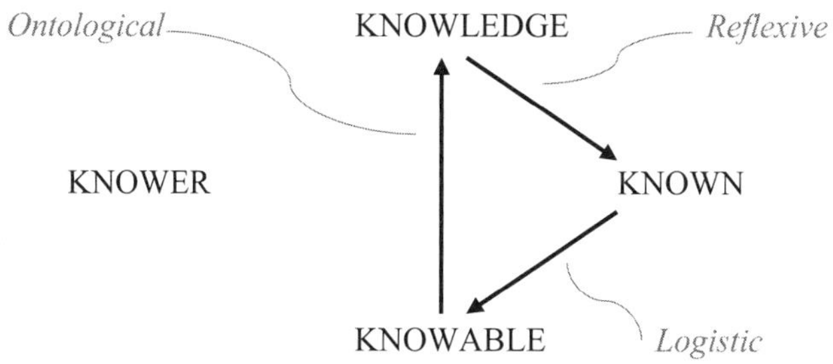

Fig. 25 *Semantic Profile of Spinoza*

the case when one moves over to interpretation as the basis of your philosophy—the twentieth century, more than most, has done two things: they have made lists of meaningless questions which all philosophies up to the beginning of the twentieth century engaged in, and they have stated more forcefully than usual the permanence of the perennial philosophy. It always turns out that in previous ages, the truth was stated in a slightly different way, opposed to the various forms of error that come in. The history of philosophy that I'm suggesting is therefore one in which the selection is one which moves from a selection of principles and things over to a vocabulary of thought, focusing on epistemology and method, to a vocabulary of facts, focusing on action and language.

Let's look for a moment—I needn't go into detail—but there are two philosophers that we have read—those of you who are in the discussion section as well as in the vaudeville section of the course [L!]—we've read two philosophers of the seventeenth century that I've just described here. We found that they had the same method but differed in principle and interpretation: Spinoza and Hobbes (see, respectively, figs. 25 and 23).[11] Both of them use freedom as a principle, a principle of human action relative to natural law and to the nature of man and to the universe. All of these words they gave slightly different interpretations to, but this was a correct statement of freedom as a principle: for both, freedom is a principle determining action "internally," with quotation marks around *internally*, as opposed to the external determination of compulsion. But for Hobbes, when you distinguish between internal and external, you do it with an actional principle, a principle which uses discrimination; namely, in any given situation, including the situation when you set up the first natural law, there is an internal and an external aspect which can be discriminated. And discrimination is written right into the law, both aspects are there: it is up to the individual in his judgment to determine whether it is the law or the right, which constitute the two parts of the first natural law, that he will follow in this case. And in each case he will follow it by performing an act in accordance with either the law or his right. For Spinoza, the distinction between internal and external is manifested reflexively, a reflexive principle, because man's nature, his essence, and his power—you'll notice the way in which a reflexive principle uses the mode of thought resolution, and the word *essence* comes in strongly when you use that mode of thought; it tends to be less respectable if you use another mode of thought—man's nature, essence, and power are manifest in his freedom. Consequently, in his freedom, which is a self-causation, the adequate ideas which he is and which are actions transform the inadequate ideas, which are passions, and actions and passions are both instances of the emotions.

We go to Kant next, and therefore, I will carefully abbreviate anything that I say about Kant. But one thing I will tell you at once. For Kant, freedom is not the principle in the sense of the beginning point. In the work of Kant that you will read, you'll get to freedom in its operation as a principle only in the third part of *The Fundamental Principles*. What you do, rather, is to examine the methods by which ordinary men operate, the methods of their transformation when you get to a philosophical way, then a metaphysical way, and finally a critical way of dealing with them; by means of the methods you'll then be able to deal with freedom.

In the twentieth century, we tend to talk about freedom not by looking at principles, in the seventeenth-century way, or at methods, in the nineteenth-century way; we rather look at the characteristics of statements which designate or which seek freedom, or at the characteristics of actions which establish or which employ freedom. We try to deal with facts, we like to be concrete, we like to go to experience; if we can't give an existential basis, we don't feel comfortable. We will then go back to the method by which we established it. One of the curious manifestations of this is that epistemology has not survived so well; but a philosophy of mind has come in, and it's the philosophy of mind which will explain both the aspects of thought and action that we deal with. Sometimes we will go from the method to the basic principles by which the validation or the processes are made possible.

Selection, then, lays the bases of agreements and differences within a period and between periods on which the meanings of freedom are examined. The three remaining basic aspects of freedom—interpretation, method, and principle, in addition to selection—each of them employs the modes of thought in a manner similar to that which I briefly indicated for selection. Let me, then, before the bell rings, move into interpretation to indicate the way in which the process now continues, because in interpretation we will not only be using the basic terms that we have selected but will also be making statements about them; therefore, we will be out of that tight situation in which you merely indicate the terms or the aspects, merely point your finger in the situation in which you can also make a statement. The basic aspect of the meaning of freedom in interpretation is found in statements which are significant or true or false in attributing freedom to some things or processes. It is by this means that we indicate our facts. The question of selection was: What are we talking about when we talk about freedom? or: What is freedom related to? The question of interpretation is, What are the instances of freedom that are distinguished from statements and processes that are not instances? That question involves the relation of knowledge to the knowable, the ontic interpretations, or the knower to the known, the phenomenal interpretations (see fig. 16). I said that for each of these, there's an ambiguous formulation on which they all agree: there's an ambiguous statement, there's an ambiguous method and an ambiguous principle. The ambiguous statement on which the interpretation is based is the statement or the fact that freedom is the power to act without external hindrance. Let's begin with the ontic interpretations, merely to start. I'll stop when the bell actually rings according to my watch.

In the ontic interpretations, we take that basic formula and we say that the power to act and the hindrances to that power are found in the nature of the universe and of man, and they can be found in the nature of the universe or of man in two different ways. Each of them involves a determination of what the nature of man and the universe would be. The ontological interpretation, oriented to knowledge, deals with the formula or gives the formula a meaning which testifies that the nature of man is his ideal nature; freedom is a freedom of self-perfection. The activity that is meant is autonomous life. Plato talking about "self-superior" is an indication of this. In the ontic interpretations, there's a doubling of meaning; therefore, among the things that are free in the highest sense are those that follow wisdom, in a lower sense those that follow a law; and the answer to the question, What is free? is that strictly only God is free, but then the divine in man. The other possibility in the ontic interpretation is that the nature of man and of the universe is physical, in any of the senses of physical—it need not be corporeal in the ordinary sense, but the corporeal usually comes into it. The nature of man for Democritus is a composition of atoms. What is freedom? It's self-determination. It is unimpeded motion, not autonomous life. This is the mode of thought composition. Again, there's a doubling: a man is free when he acts according to his nature truly, that is, what his nature really is; and a man is free if he acts according to his impulses, because he is his impulses, too, even though they depart from what they ought to be if he followed the composition of his nature. What is free? Bodies in motion, and then man with knowledge and desires. For both the ontic interpretations, then, freedom consists in doing what one should, meaning by "what one should" acting in accordance with one's nature. And therefore, on the basic question of whether freedom is doing what you should or whether that's a misuse of language—anyone who knows English and owns or has access to an *OED*[12] knows that freedom is doing as you please—this is a difference between the ontic and the phenomenal interpretations.

But unfortunately, my timing is bad: I expected to finish interpretation. We will break off here, and next Wednesday I'll complete applying selection to interpretation, method, and principle, and then go a little more fully into the nature of selection itself, to which I gave merely a brief indication in the opening words.

LECTURE SIX

Freedom: Selection (Part 2)

Last time we began with a brief discussion[1] of selection and then proceeded from selection to go back over the other three elements that enter into the definition of freedom: interpretation, method, and principle. I'd like to complete that task today. I will go on to our second concept, power, next time, and in power we shall be employing the same device; but the way in which those devices enter into the definition of power will give you a fuller idea of what is involved in basic terms, because we've already been using power as part of the definition of freedom. Consequently, when we turn around and find out what we mean by power, we shall discover that elements of freedom will enter into the definition of power. Circularity in method is not bad if the circle is big enough; it's only the small circles that become vicious. [L!]

Let me recall to you, then, where we had left off. We began with our diagram (see fig. 1). The point that we made is that in any attempt to relate the elements of the diagram, there is the vector element, which focuses on one or another of these (see figs. 16, 17, and 18); and since there is a combination of different modes of thought in most philosophies, the vector will frequently involve two or three directions (see, for instance, figs. 23, 24, and 25). Therefore, in selection what we are concerned with is, rather, the reason for the inclusion of a particular term or the reason for emphasis on a particular aspect.[2] As I went through the selections, I tried to give you a characteristic that each would have from the point of view of the mode of statement, the form, and, on the other hand, the content or the fact (see table 8). If you are making a selection which focuses on knowledge, on assimilation, your terms will tend to be arranged in a hierarchy; and there will be, in your consideration of the nature of things, an intrusion of something that will appear as transcendent, as above, as out of the region of direct experience or discourse. Insofar as your selection is in terms of the knowable, the tendency is for your terms to be reductive. The emphasis on physicalism, going back all the way to August Comte, who bequeathed it to logical positivism, is of this sort; but the physicalism need not mean actual corporeal bodies. It would mean merely that basic set of concepts out of which you construct all of your knowledge and, therefore, into which you reduce any higher form of knowledge. Consequently, on the formal side is the reductivism; on the material side is the choice of a physicalistic, elemental basis. If your emphasis is on the known, then the tendency is for your terms to differentiate according to theory and practice; action becomes dominant; and the vocabularies are adjusted to a variety of objectives. If the focus is on the knower, then your vocabulary, your selection, tends to types relative to the perspective of the knower, and your language is likewise given to two types, that is, types of things or types of words.

I went into a little detail about how the selection makes conversation among diverse points of view or diverse philosophies possible. Then I went on to say that although it is by virtue of the selection that both the differences and the communities are possible, there's a second aspect of selection, namely, the selection that moves from period to period. You will recall that I suggested the emphasis is one in which, proceeding from principles as the first concern, your selection tends to be terms that have to do primarily about being or existence, things in these two senses; and the argument about which is which, or which is more fundamental, or whether there is any such thing as being apart from things is part of the subject of discussion (see table 9). When, after discussing metaphysics for a time, one tires of that, the age turns to a discussion of epistemology: what are the grounds on which we can know anything, and then maybe we can do metaphysics. There is a tendency, consequently, for the discussion to be about thought or about experience. You'll notice, this is one of the reasons for the divisions that I suggested among your principles and methods, because when you talk about being, there is some notion that there are wholes—the holoscopic is fundamental—or there is some notion that there are parts which are fundamental; and the whole/part problem assimilates all of your other basic problems as instances of it. If thought is basic, then you either argue that there is a universal foundation or that only particulars *are*; and philosophers will argue either that all sciences are of the universal or, as Mill held, that all reasoning is from particular to particular—your fight is between these. Then, finally, your third age, the one I suggested we are now in, is when the emphasis is upon interpretation. And in interpretation one always begins with facts, data, existence, experience; but the division tends to be into processes or statements: either you have a revolt which is pragmatic or you have a revolt which is linguistic. All of these words are ambiguous. Obviously, the process that is ontic is one that would give you a title like *Process and Reality*[3]—the process is not reality, but it is oriented to reality in good ontic fashion—or if process is phenomenal, then your statements would be oriented only to the changing existences, with a denial that there is anything transcendental or anything underlying which is more fundamental.

I turned, then, to a consideration of interpretation, making it interpretation primarily as it applies to liberty, freedom; and I warned you, as I've warned you repeatedly, that as one moves from selection to interpretation, there is no carryover: you can have any interpretation with any selection and any selection with any interpretation. The richness and the diversity of the discussion depends upon this; and therefore, even though I am using the modes of thought which fall under methods to explain them all, as I explained in the lecture the reason for this is that whenever you engage in an extended discourse, you're using a method. I can use a method to explain a selection or an interpretation, but I can use any method to explain any selection or any interpretation. For consistency, I stick to one, but this does not mean that it is better. It means that I have no confidence that if I shifted my method, the class would continue to follow what I am saying. Remember that under selection we are, in effect, asking, What do you talk about when you talk about freedom? Are you going to talk about an ideal up there [*i.e.*, knowledge in the matrix of knowing—fig. 1]; are you going to talk about a body down here [*i.e.*, knowable]; are you going to talk about the region of the conditions under which men are formed out there [*i.e.*, known]; or are you going to talk about the indeterminacies [*i.e.*, knower]? You'd get, respectively, a language which would sound idealistic one way, physicalistic another way; you would get a language which would sound institutional the third way, and you'd get a language which would sound power-oriented the fourth way. And whereas there'd be overlaps with ambiguities, you would be talking about something different; and much of the difficulty in talking about anything within freedom is that you're not talking about the same thing.

Now, when we moved over to interpretation—I'll continue my oriental sequence—we are over now to the place where we make a statement which is to be true or false; and the possibilities, you will recall—I had gotten through the ontic interpretations—are either ontic or phenomenal (see tables 10 and 11).[4] We are asking what freedom is in the sense of: What is free? Is it things? Is it processes? What kinds of things? What kinds of processes? To connect the two interpretations, I said there was an ambiguous interpretation common to the two. The statement that is ambiguous, subject to the four interpretations, is that "freedom is the

Table 10. Definitions of *Freedom.*

Ambiguous Formula: "Freedom is the power to act without external hindrance."

Mode of Thought	Principle What is freedom as a cause or value?	Method How is freedom acquired or understood?	Interpretation What are free things?	Selection What am I talking about?
	Holoscopic	*Universal*	*Ontic*	
Assimilation	Autonomy	Right Use of Choice	Wisdom	Wise Man
Resolution	Self-rule	Choice	Motion, Unimpeded	Body
	Meroscopic	*Particular*	*Phenomenal*	
Construction	Nature	Act according to Nature	Behavior, Spontaneous	Animal
Discrimination	Power	Deliberation	Action, Voluntary	Humans

Table 11. Modes of Thought and the Schema of Philosophic Semantics.

Mode of Thought	Principle	Method	Interpretation	Selection
	Holoscopic	*Universal*	*Ontic*	
Assimilation	Comprehensive	Dialectical	Ontological	Thought
Resolution	Reflexive	Operational	Entitative	Thing
	Meroscopic	*Particular*	*Phenomenal*	
Construction	Simple	Logistic	Existentialist	Language
Discrimination	Actional	Problematic	Essentialist	Action

power to act without external hindrance"; and obviously, if you define *power*, *external*, *internal*, and *action* differently, you will get different regions in which the truth or falsity will occur. The ontic interpretations are interpretations where the hindrance and the power are found in the nature of the universe and of man. In the ontological, it's an ideal nature, and therefore, what you mean by freedom is an autonomous life; in the entitative, it's the nature of physical man—what you are talking about is bodies in motion—and therefore, the freedom is the freedom of self-determination, man with the addition of knowledge and desires. For both of these ontic interpretations, freedom consists in doing what one should, in two different senses: what one should either in conformity to the ideal nature of man or what one should in conformity to the laws of nature, which are human nature.

The second—it was at this point that I stopped last time—are the phenomenal interpretations. The phenomenal interpretations are the interpretations which cut across and relate knower and known (see fig. 16); and in the two of them you have a choice which involves a decision of the knower concerning what he presents or thinks of as known to him. It's freedom in two different senses. If you follow the existentialist interpretation, beginning with the knower, freedom consists in spontaneity. Whatever is known or done in general is the result of the interpretation of the knower; therefore, if you're going to engage in action, freedom consists in origination, origination either in acting or in doing. You are talking about existence from the perspective of the knower, and you are therefore concerned with spontaneous behavior. The fourth possibility is the essentialist. The known underlies all experience. All the known means is the body of those truths you already have seized or those doctrines you have taken as truths; therefore, that body of doctrine would determine your interpretation. Decision is free, not when it follows from the nature of man in the sense that the entitative interpretation would set up but when it follows the character of man as opposed to a basic nature, the character that he has acquired by virtue of the influence of his environment and of the culture—habits or virtues, they are sometimes called—as opposed to the actions which are determined externally. What is free? Man is free. He is free by virtue of his formation or character or, if you like, virtue. So we got four different answers under the four headings. Under the one, the ontological, only the wise man is free in the wise life. Under the second, the entitative, any body moving freely is free, moving bodies are free. The two phenomenal are midway between: that is to say, in the existentialist interpretation, any animal possessed of power that asserts its power is free, any animal capable of action is free when it acts spontaneously; and in the essentialist, any man who makes a decision based on the qualities that he has achieved in his environment.

What is the question of interpretation, then? The question of interpretation is, What is freedom?, in the sense of What are instances of freedom such as would make a given statement about freedom true? The selections that enter into interpretation move from existence and experience, to concreteness and individuality, to body, and to self. These are selections that you would find in dealing with the interpretations that I've just been talking about. The differences between the two interpretations are sharp. It is a difference, if you state it in ontic terms, between the real and the apparent; if you state the difference in phenomenal terms, it is a difference between the abstract, the fictive, and the concrete, the real. You notice that the choice of the way in which you state it will indicate a difference between the two in philosophy, because what is taken as real in the ontic approach becomes nonexistent in the phenomenal

Table 12. Key Topics in Definition of *Freedom*.

Aspects of Analysis	Main Division	— Key Distinctions — In General		— Key Distinctions — In Freedom	
Principle	*Holoscopic* *Meroscopic*	Nature *vs.* Convention	Basis of Values	Internal *vs.* External	Cause and Value of Freedom is . . .
Method	*Universal* *Particular*	Direct *vs.* Indirect	Relation of Reason to Action	Rational *vs.* Reasonable	Decision Leading to Freedom is . . .
Interpretation	*Ontic* *Phenomenal*	Real/ Apparent *vs.* Concrete/ Abstract (Fictive)	What Is It?	Should (Obligation) *vs* Pleases (Preference)	Freedom is Doing as One . . .

approach: it's abstract, it's fictive, or in some other way the result of an error. The difference in the answer to the question, What is freedom?, in the identification of things that are free is likewise sharp. That is, for the ontic approach, both of them, freedom consists in doing what one should. You take into account the ability to do as you please, because unless you have the two, you could not have the possibility of acting correctly. This is what I refer to occasionally as the doubling of the meaning of the terms under the ontic approach. The doubling in the ontological is perhaps the most classic: it's the difference, in Saint Augustine's terms, between freedom and freedom of choice. Freedom of choice is indifferent—unless you had freedom of choice, you couldn't have freedom—but freedom of choice can be used well or badly: the good use of freedom of choice, that is, acting as you should, is freedom. And so for the others. In the phenomenal, on the other hand, freedom consists in doing as one pleases, and any consideration of what one should do is subsequent. It's only when you act as you please that you get into the normative problems; if you couldn't act as you please, you'd not be in a position to begin to discuss, to discover, the values. You don't begin with the values by the phenomenal approach (see table 12).[5]

The third problem is the problem of method. Method is concerned with either the discourse or the action. It is the aspects of freedom which are found in the sequences or consequences of discourse and in action. I said at the beginning of the problem of interpretation that discussion is possible because there's an ambiguous statement which can be made, and all interpretations are fixed meanings of that ambiguous statement. You can't get the methods together on an ambiguous statement, but there is an ambiguous method, and all philosophers are in agreement concerning the method. The reason for this is that the question can be stated generally. The question is, What are the ways in which statements about freedom are shown to be true or false, and what are the ways in which actions are effective or ineffective in achieving freedom of the agent? How are statements or actions known to be free, and how is freedom achieved deliberately? The ambiguous method, the one on which there is agreement, is that freedom is action in accordance with knowledge and reason. One of the reasons, I think, for the proliferation of book titles about the use of arguments is precisely that this aspect, that is, the use of reason in action, the use of argument to effect action, is at the center of the problems of ethics precisely because freedom is at the center of the problems of ethics. The question is therefore a question of the relation of knowledge to action, the influence of knowledge on action. You can consider it in two different ways. You can consider it either in terms of the relation of the knower to knowledge or in terms of the relation of the knowable to the known. In terms of the relation of the knower to knowledge, the establishment of free action is possible only by the use of knowledge. When it is the relation of the known to the knowable, the establishment of free action depends on the relation of what is and what is conceived to be, and it isn't necessary that in acting this way you possess knowledge in a strict sense or use it.

Let me begin by the doubling of meanings that we have under the universal method and then go on to the particular methods. You have a doubling of meaning because both of the questions that are raised, the two that I've just given, come in; but there's a subordination of the second to the first, as in the case of the doubling of meanings in interpretation. You identify theoretic formulation and practical knowledge. They're exactly the same in either of the universal methods, whereas in the particular methods the problems of practical action are distinct from the problems of theory. In the universal methods you can ask both, What are the ways in which you are free by being wise?, and, What are the ways in which, short of wisdom, you can also be free? Let's look at them in more detail. In the universal methods, freedom is directly dependent on knowledge; so that freedom is identical with knowledge, and a man must have knowledge to be free in the true sense. There are several aspects or consequences in the universal method that need to be emphasized at this point—I stated them when we were talking about method. First is the one I've just stated, namely, there is no difference between theoretic and practical uses of knowledge; and therefore, there is one method which is applied to both. There is one method that is applied to all actions, to all inquiries, to all proofs: that is why it is a universal method. There is a second aspect which is still within method, although it sounds as if we're talking about individual terms, namely, that the terms that are used in the universal method do not have literal meanings in use. They have analogical meanings in order to fit the method. You can come to literal meaning by means of the method; but to work, the method itself requires a multiplicity of meanings for any given term, and the terms change their meaning in the course of the argument. In the third place, there aren't any fixed principles in the universal method. The universal method is universal in the sense that you can prove your principles by the same method as you prove anything else. All you do is start somewhere else, and what was your beginning point at one stage becomes the subject of proof at the second. The common characteristic of the universal methods is the position that you cannot leave the consideration of the knower out of the use of methods. It's for this reason that the analogical terms are there for the different meanings, because if the knowers are taken into account, then freedom is identical with or a consequence of their knowledge. There are two ways in which the universal methods achieve their purpose: one is by taking the scope of knowledge as being universal, thereby achieving the universality from that; the other is by taking the operation of the knower to be universal and achieving their universality that way.

What is the way that you are free by the dialectical method or by the operational method? In the dialectical method, the whole process is a process by which the knower approaches knowledge; he is adapted to knowledge. He owes his title as a knower to his success in approximating to knowledge; and freedom, his freedom, is achieved to the degree that he achieves knowledge. Only the wise man acts freely, he's the only one who has achieved truth; but—and here is your doubling—it is possible by right opinion or law or divine madness or accident to come upon truth without having established it by your own action. In Plato, for example, in the perfect state the philosophers are kings, they set up freedom, and if you look carefully in the *Republic*, you'll find freedom discussed in these terms; but in the second-best state or in all except the guardians, freedom is achieved by acting according to freedom without yourself necessarily having freedom. The devices are well known and popular in discussion today: these are the devices of myth. You will recall there are myths in the *Republic* by which those who are not able to follow the demonstration will be led to truth and freedom; and there are even myths that are lies, because this is the only way in which the motivation could operate. You'll observe that we are immediately on the edge of a controversial subject: the character of the philosopher-king bears a good deal of importance here. What is the operational method? The operational method is the reverse; that is, there is no fixed empyrean of knowledge, knowledge is the product of the knower, and knowing is any kind of action: if you can do it, you know it. Only man, or an animal powerful enough to give some objective status to what he wants and get this status beyond himself, only such an animal is free. There is a doubling; namely, weaker animals or men can achieve the freedom appropriate to their abilities by recognizing and conforming to the established rule of the stronger.

Let me pause on the universal methods before we go on to the particular methods. By the dialectical method, knowledge contributes to power by relating what different persons or knowers allege that they know, relating them by reasons based on the same truth. The good man and the wise man are the same thing, the good man and the good citizen are the same, and consequently, the methods of achieving or increasing freedom are two: education and the guidance of wise men. One is free only if one follows the path of wisdom, either because one has seized it or because one is seized by a conviction about one particular sage and one gets what he says as the path of wisdom. By the operational method, you reverse this relation of knowledge and power. Bacon's statement that "knowledge is power" is an ambiguous one. It can be reduced to the statement that I have given earlier, the operational statement that to know something is to do it, and if you can do it, you know it. If you can't do it, you don't know it, whatever else you may present as credentials for knowledge. Consequently, freedom will depend upon the power of the knower or the agent. That power may or may not be knowledge from the point of view of a dialectician; but by the criteria we have given, if he can do it, he not only knows it but this is true freedom. How do you increase freedom or exercise it or recognize its existence? Well, there are two kinds of freedom: there's the freedom of the stronger and there's the freedom of the weaker. The freedom of the weaker is likewise a power that he exercises within the circumstances, within the protection of the framework in which he lives. You will notice at once that if one is talking about campaigns to increase freedom, you have two campaigns at once—you may recognize them—one is the campaign to educate them and then they'll be free, and the other is the campaign to pressure those in power and then you'll get what you want.

The particular methods relate the knowable and the known. Freedom is now only indirectly related to knowledge, and therefore, a man may be free without himself possessing knowledge. He may need to consult an expert or even a scientist, particularly concerning means to achieve ends or means by which to relieve crises; but at most he will act according to the rules of knowledge and not *by* knowledge—that's a difference

I should like to emphasize with the two particular methods. The three consequences that I mentioned with respect to the universal methods are now reversed. The first consequence was that a single method of doing and of knowing existed; therefore, to do is to know in the two senses, the dialectical and the operational. The assumption now is that there is a different method for doing and knowing; they are not the same method, and even if you are talking about something that you know theoretically, the method of using knowledge is different from the method of acquiring knowledge—or to be more careful about it, the method of using knowledge theoretically and the method of using knowledge practically are two different methods. The result is, in the second place, that the terms you use in the particular methods are literal and univocally defined. It is in the particular methods that changing your meaning is a philosophic vice: you define your terms in the beginning and you stick to the definitions, and if you're caught changing the definition, you've made a philosophic mistake. If you're caught not changing your definition in the dialectical and the operational approach, you've made a mistake, too: you've not been doing a good philosophic job.

Finally, it is in the particular methods that there are first principles in a literal sense. You can prove your first principles dialectically and operationally. Logistically and problematically, an infinite regress would give you no knowledge at all; therefore, you must start, and you start at a point at which you can examine these principles—there are methods to examine them—but you cannot establish your principles by the same method that you employ to put the principles into theoretic or practical use. Notice, too, that these are related to the place of the knower and of knowledge. For the universal methods, you can't leave the knower out, and you can't leave the whole of knowledge out. For the particular methods, on the contrary, you *must* leave all reference to the peculiarities of particular investigators or particular agents out—your method must be repeatable with changes of persons—and you must leave out any assumption that there is anything fixed about knowledge, because the whole point of the operation in method is to change the knowledge. The purpose of the method is, obviously, to increase the body of things known or to penetrate into the things that are knowable but not yet known; and the purpose of the method, when applied to freedom, is to make action conform to the knowable. There are two possibilities: the method may be made particular, not universal, by separating theory from practice and by making both theory and practice depend either on characteristics that are found in what is the case, that is, the knowable, or on characteristics that are suggested in the body of knowledge or opinion already acquired.

Let's begin with the logistic method. In the logistic method, the assumption that we work on is that method consists in making what is known, that is, the body of the knowledge that we end with, conform to the knowable. There is a structure in things, and the whole project is to map what we say the case is onto a structure that we can justify. Practice takes its beginning from impulses, wants, and preferences of the agent. Therefore, in talking about freedom, you can, on the one hand, talk about the agent as himself a subject of inquiry, that is, a construction in which he and his motions would be the subject to be raised, and the question could be whether what he wants is actually what, according to the laws of his nature, he ought to want. The laws of his nature give you one operation of method, one particular method; this would be the scientific approach. On the other hand, when you move over into the practical, the method is precisely to set up the agreements and the arrangements by which two or more people, agreeing on the same objective, could secure for themselves what they want. In the first, if he does not want what he ought to want, then you call in the expert, and the expert through therapy fixes it up so that he returns to his proper condition.

The problematic method begins with what is known—what is known in the broad sense of what is accepted, what any individual or what the community accepts—and employs what is known in the treatment of problems. A problem is a difficulty which is detected in the body of what is taken as known. The resolution of a theoretic problem increases the body of the known. Practical problems are not theoretic problems; either they are moral and political or they're productive problems. In the moral and the political problems, you are concerned with the actions that a man takes, viewing them either in terms of his character, his virtues—in Aristotle's terms in his *Ethics*—or in terms of the institutions within which he operates. What you are concerned with is the operations that you engage in for particular ends in terms of the desire of the individual or in terms of what is taken for the common good of the community. There's a mutual influence between society and the individual. You'll notice that in the universal methods, it's perfectly correct to talk about the society in the same terms as the individual. When Plato, for example, wants to talk about the virtues of the individual, he turns to the state, because those virtues are writ large, and you would get virtues in the individual and in the state by the same means. By contrast, when Aristotle faces the same question, he assumes that the individual and society are in a relation of mutual influence. What the society is depends on the individual, and what the individual is depends on the state; but the state doesn't have any virtues, and the individual doesn't have any political constitutions. The means that would be employed, the methods, consequently, are different. By the logistic method, then, one is free only if one operates according to the laws of one's own nature. It is a kind of externalizing the internal: you need to have therapy if you're not operating well. The problematic method is the reverse: the internalizing of the external. In the problematic method, one is free when one exercises one's own choice. You have an institutional protection of rights within which you exercise your liberties.

There's a sharp line, then, between the universal and the particular methods in the answer to the question, What is freedom from the point of view of method? The universal method: freedom is achieved by rational decision, action such as the knower in any field would take. As I suggested, if you want to acquire this freedom dialectically, you put in a system of ideal education; if you want to acquire it operationally, you organize pressure groups. I said, bear in mind that for the universal methods, freedom is achieved by "rational" decision; now, for the particular methods, let me use "reasonable" decision in a sense distinct from that; namely, it is a reasonable decision based on the nature of the self or the nature of the self as conditioned by society. In both cases, it is a choice of means of achieving what one wants or deliberating concerning means of realizing what is wanted and what is possible. You may not have noted, but in the definition of the moral virtues by Aristotle, one of the four parts is that the moral virtues are in accord with the rule of right reason. The rule of right reason is known by someone who has the intellectual virtues. In order to know the rule of right reason, you need to have prudence; but you could have any of the moral virtues which operate according to the rule of right reason without yourself being a prudential man. All you need to have had was a formation in a state or in a community or in a society where the habits follow the rules of right reason—and therefore, in all probability, at some time some statesman was prudential—but you need not yourself be rational, your action has only to be reasonable. For the logistic method, too, there is the same quality.

I'll have to go rapidly—principles, as I remarked before, always get short shrift, even when one intends to spend a lot of time on them. The basic aspect of the meaning of freedom yielded by principles is in the grounds of discourse and of action. I immediately point out that I am not giving a good definition here, because *principle* and *grounds* are synonyms. But what you try to do is to explain why or for what reason or on what basis freedom is possible and desirable. What are the properties of freedom which make it an end or a means (it's both)? The question of principle is the question, What is freedom as a cause or as a value? When you read Kant's *Foundations*, watch both of those terms, they're both there: *cause* and *value*. And in many respects, it is only people who use this kind of principle [holoscopic] that give a meaning to value. There came in with Kant—it was in strong in the Hellenistic period, when the Stoics and the Epicureans were operating; however, I have difficulty with

Plato and Aristotle: I can find words that could be forced to this meaning, but Plato and Aristotle get along without a value theory—that, however, is a different question. The problem of principles is either a problem of the relation of the known to knowledge or of the knower to the knowable. The known to knowledge gives you the holoscopic principles, where you have an internal organization of freedom as a property of anything that is free. Holoscopic gives you the whole within which such a relation is possible. The meroscopic principles, the knower and the knowable, are a problem of external relations, namely, the relation of how freedom establishes value. As in the case of interpretation and of method, there's a very fundamental difference in the answers given by the holoscopic and the meroscopic principles. The holoscopic principles hold that there is a natural basis in terms of which conventional action can be recognized and evaluated. The meroscopic argues that conventional action is all that you have, and what is attributed to the natural basis is merely the result of conventions of a given kind.[6]

Let me go over the other two [columns] so that you will have them in mind. I mentioned them in passing. Between the holoscopic and meroscopic: the difference is between a natural basis of values and a conventional basis. The methods: the difference between the universal and the particular is that for the universal, the theoretic method and the practical method are exactly the same; and therefore, there's a direct entrance of knowledge into freedom; whereas for the particular methods, there is not a direct entrance, because the methods are different. In the interpretations, there is the difference between a real end and a preferential choice, a difference between an obligation and a preference. Since we are in a period of interpretation, let me merely remind you—I've referred to this once before in this class—that one of the essays that we now look back to as marking the beginning of the twentieth century is Pritchard's essay on whether moral philosophy is based on a mistake.[7] Well, it is: the mistake is that apparently all philosophers had previously depended on inclinations and preferences, whereas the truth is that there are obligations and duties. All philosophers, from Pritchard's point of view and from the orientation in which he worked, were apparently the utilitarians: from G. E. Moore on, utilitarianism is more refuted than any other view for trying to determine what is good in terms of consequences and of inclinations or preferences as part of the consequences, as opposed to—and you now jump over the Channel to Kant—looking upon a basic obligation as the foundation of ethics.

Well, I'm afraid that this is where we will have to leave our principles. We are beyond our time, and I don't want to sin any further in the name of principles, because this would endanger them. [L!] I'll go on to power next time.

DISCUSSION

Kant, Part 1
(*Fundamental Principles of the Metaphysics of Morals*, Preface)

Discussion Summary

Today we will begin our examination of Kant by looking at his method. The best way for us to proceed is to describe the method without naming it. In the preface, he begins by dividing philosophy into three parts and says that this will give the structure of all rational knowledge. If we look at the lower-left corner of our figure (see fig. 26),[1] we see that when Kant says, "Laws of Nature as object of experience,"[2] he is talking of the regularities observed in nature, which is empirical. Then, if the laws of nature are written out in formal terms—*cause*, *space*, *time*, *mass*—then one has pure rational knowledge. By virtue of these, Newton was able to write his laws of motion. So, in Kant's terms, if we connect dropping balls to formulae universally applicable, we are doing metaphysics of nature.[3]

He goes on to use two terms here, *analytic* and *synthetic*, and he uses these terms both for judgments and for methods. In Kant, judgment matters. An analytic judgment is one in which the concept of a predicate is contained in the concept of the subject; we merely need to understand the subject and analyze it, *e.g.*, "The table is solid." On the other hand, a synthetic judgment, or proposition, is one in which the predicate adds something to what we know of the subject, *e.g.*, "The table is brown." Now, if the synthetic judgment is based on experience, then it is *a posteriori*. By contrast, synthetic judgments *a priori* are the important things in science: judgments that are unchanging, although they conform to experience (see fig. 27).[4] That is, their truth does not depend on changing experience, on the fact that all laws have some variation. Physics and mathematics have synthetic judgments *a priori*, and ethics has these as well. The validity of the general law depends on the concept—this is the *a priori* part. So, we need to keep our line of distinction clear: some synthetic judgments depend on something being there; other synthetic judgments depend upon inductions from experience but go beyond them.

	Material		Formal
	Physics	Ethics	Logic
Pure	Metaphysics of Nature	Metaphysics of Morals	Logic
Empirical*	"Laws of Nature as object of experience"	Practical Anthropology	X

*Synthetic judgments where it can be asked if there are grounds in experience, i.e., "Are they there?"

Fig. 26 *Kant's Structure of All Rational Knowledge*

	Analytic	Synthetic
A Priori		
A Posteriori		

Fig. 27 *Kinds of Judgments*

Notice, anything we do can be analyzed in two different ways. First, if you perform an action and can explain it, if you are doing the explanation in terms of the individual things that motivate you, this is practical anthropology. Second, if we want to limit our consideration to morals, then, when you are faced with a problem, as soon as you begin thinking, what you are thinking about is not what leads to your action. Instead, you are trying to decide what to do by relating action to basic ideas of human duty or freedom. Consequently, any human action can be considered on both these levels.

To summarize, then, Kant begins his preface by differentiating the sciences and is careful not mix the two divisions: the pure with the empirical. Following this, he will look for moral philosophy, that is, pure morality or ethics. So, when he differentiates the sciences, he distinguishes between the empirical, where the synthetic connections that are made are connections based on experience, and the rational, where the synthetic connections that are made are based on ideas like cause. Under these circumstances, practical anthropology, being empirical, cannot be rational, because we are interested in particular instances in which we observe men. Rational anthropology, on the other hand, addresses laws of mankind independent of particular instances. So, following his differentiation of the sciences, Kant will deal with law: a metaphysics of morals. Can we base moral philosophy on the nature of man? No. One must not seek it in human nature or circumstances. If a law is to have moral force, it has to have a basis of absolute necessity and cannot be based on experience. Therefore, moral philosophy must not be done on the nature of man.

Note that Kant has been telling us that he is not using a phenomenal interpretation but, rather, an ontological one. The basis of obligation is found *a priori* in the conceptions of pure reason, which includes necessity. Therefore, this is a two-leveled interpretation. To summarize, then, if obligation were based on circumstance, it would be a phenomenal interpretation. If obligation were based on nature, it would be an entitative interpretation. But because obligation is based on *a priori* concepts, as it is here, Kant is using an ontological interpretation.

Moving on, then, Kant asks why the metaphysics of morals is "indispensable" (see page 4 [B:52]).[5] He obtains two results from this question. First, a metaphysics of morals provides a speculative result: we will come to know the source of our principles, that from which an action is done. These are the grounds of the *a priori* moral principles. Second, a metaphysics of morals provides a practical result: even though the ordinary man has a sense of duty, he will find that when he gets into trouble, the only way to correct his morals is to appeal to these principles. Kant provides a critique of this practical result which shows it is not as necessary as the first, speculative result. The reason why the practical is less important is that every ordinary man already has a sense of duty, and so he can get along.

According to Kant, then, we can deal with human action in two ways. In the first approach, one addresses consequences. In the second, by contrast, the intention, the will, is what is important and not the consequences. Since Kant is interested in the beginning point, the practical and the speculative must, for him, both have the same principles. Notice, in this procedure Kant will use both analytic and synthetic methods. The analytic will begin from common knowledge, from actual use, and will go to its ultimate principles. This occurs in the first and second sections of the text. The synthetic will go from principles to conclusions and is addressed in the third section of the *Foundations*.

For next time, consider why proceeding from principle to conclusions is synthetic.

McKeon's Notes

Kant Foundations of the Metaphysics of Morals 1.
Ref. Op. Ont.[6]

Preface.

Rational knowledge	Formal	Material	
		Objects and laws	
~~Rational~~ *Pure*	Logic	Laws of Nature Met. of Nature	Laws of Freedom Met. of Freedom
Empirical	XXXXX	Laws of Nature as experienced	Practical Anthro.

Division of labor in philosophy (4)
A priori concepts of pure reason—empirical. Ont. (5) Op. (6) Refl. (6)

Kant Fundamental Principles of the Metaphysics of Morals 1,1.
Op. Ref. Ont.

Ancient division into Physics, Ethics, Logic.
Suitable—add principle—for completeness and correct subdivisions.

All Rational knowledge—either material or formal: object, form of understanding.
Formal philosophy—Logic; material philosophy—determinate objects and laws—laws of nature and laws of freedom. Physics, Ethics.
Empirical—logic no empirical part (universal and necessary laws taken from experience—would be a canon).
Natural and moral philosophy—empirical part.
Laws of nature as objects of human experience; Laws of human will as affected by nature.
Laws of what does happen and laws according to which everything ought to happen. *(p. 4)* (p. 2)

Ont *Empirical philosophy*—based on grounds of human experience; pure

philosophy—a priori principles. Latter *when* formal—logic; *when* restricted to objects of understanding—metaphysic.
Ref Twofold metaphysic—metaphysic of nature and metaphysic of morals. Physics and ethics *empirical* and a *rational* part. Practical anthropology and morals.

Division of labor in the sciences (N.B. converse arguments for the unity of science). Separation of the rational from the empirical—name minute philosophers (3) *(4)*

Op Whether it is not necessary to construct a pure moral philosophy cleared of everything empirical or anthropological. Obviously possible from common idea of duty and of moral laws.

If law to have moral force, i.e. basis of obligation must have absolute necessity.

Ont Basis of obligation must not be sought *in the nature of a man or in the circumstances in the world*, but *a priori simply* in the *concepts of pure reason*. Empirical may be universal but not a moral law. (p. 4)

There are moral laws with distinctive principles and also all moral philosophy rests on pure part.

Oper Metaphysics of morals therefore indispensable (1) not only *(6)* for speculative reasons—to investigate sources of the practical principles, but also (2) because morals liable to corruption, without supreme canon.

Refl For action to be morally good not enough that it conform to moral law, it must be done *for the sake* of the law; otherwise conformity contingent. Principle which is not moral may produce actions conformable to law.

Pure philosophy—moral law in its purity and genuineness—must begin with pure philosophy (metaphysics). What distinguishes philosophy from other knowledge—treats in separate sciences what common rational knowledge treats confusedly. (p. 5) *6*

Distinguish this from Wolf's propaedeutic to his moral philosophy, i.e. his general practical philosophy.
Does not treat *pure will*, but *volition in general*.

Comparable to distinction of general logic (acts and canons of thought in general) from transcendental philosophy (particular acts and canons of pure thought—cognitions a priori). Acts and conditions of human volition generally—drawn for most part from psychology.

Discusses moral laws and duties, but does not distinguish *motives prescribed by reason a priori from empirical motives*. (p. 6)

These fundamental principles preliminary to metaphysics of Morals.

No other foundation for metaphysics of morals than *critical examination* of a pure practical reason. *p. 7*

(1) Critique of pure practical reason not as necessary as critique of pure speculative reason. In moral matters, human reason brought to correctness and completeness even in commonest understanding; while *its* theoretic but pure use dialectical.

(2) If critique of pure *practical reason* to be complete its identity with *speculative reason* must be shown in a common *principle*. Same reason different application. *8*

(3) Metaphysics of morals popular and adapted to common understanding. (p. 7)

Investigate and establish—the supreme principle of morality. Complete and separate from all other moral inquiry.

Conclusions would be clarified by application to whole moral system, but easy application of principle

---

Kant Fundamental Principles of Metaph of Morals 1,2.

gives no certain proof of its soundness. Rather inspires a certain partiality.

Method—proceed *analytically* from common knowledge to the determination of its ultimate principle; descend *synthetically* from examination of this principle and its sources to common knowledge in which employed.

Thence division of parts. 1. Common rational knowledge to philosophical; 2. Popular moral philosophy to metaphysics of morals; 3. Metaphysics of morals to critique of *pure practical reason.*

First section. Transition from the Common Rational Knowledge of Morality to the Philosophical. *9* (p.9)[7]

DISCUSSION

Kant, Part 2 (*Fundamental Principles of the Metaphysics of Morals*, First Section: Transition from the Common Rational Knowledge of Morality to the Philosophical)

Discussion[1]

McKeon: Last time we began our examination of Kant by looking at his preface, and in the process we were satisfied with the diagnosis that the interpretation is ontological, because Kant is making a careful distinction between the *a priori* form and the empirical procedure. We also talked a little about the method; but although a method was suggested, what it meant was not apparently clear. I propose that we go on this time to the first section, and I think it would be a good idea if we could finish the first section as a whole, because Kant is characteristically a writer in whom either you can dig endlessly or you can get the general form. If we were digging, I would spend some time asking you what the sequence of the argument in the first section is. That is a long and laborious dialectic; so I will tell you that Kant tends to divide not, like Hobbes, into two parts but into three parts, and the first section is divided into three parts. I propose, therefore, that we spend our time trying to see in large scale what he does in each of these three parts.

The first part runs from page 9—is the edition that I'm using the one that most of you have? Is page 9 the one that has "First Section" on it?

Student: Could you give the German numbers, please, too?

McKeon: No . . . Oh, well, that's the Abbott translation.[2] All right, I brought that one, too. [L!] There are three, and I just wanted to make sure. . . . Is this it?

Student: Yes.

McKeon: All right. I will have to do some mental arithmetic, because I wrote down in my notes the pages in the other edition. We will go from page 11 to—well, let's say page 15. I'll give you the exact . . . We have, then, to develop the beginning of the first part; consequently, what I would like you to tell me, first, is what in general it is that he is attempting to do in the first part, pages 11 to 15 [B:55–58], and I'll get more specific after you give me a general hypothesis. Mr. Anderson?[3] Is Mr. Anderson here? . . .

Anderson: You want a general hypothesis?

McKeon: What is it that he's trying to show in this first part? . . . The answer to it is the opening sentence. He's trying to show that there's absolutely nothing ultimate that's good "except the good will." The rest of this part will explain what this means. How does he go about justifying this statement? Notice, the flat statement right at the beginning, and then he goes on and does something to justify it . . .

Anderson: He states that the will is the cause, and . . .

McKeon: Well, go ahead.

Anderson: And he brings in duty and . . .

McKeon: No, no, Mr. Anderson, it would seem to me that the right answer is equally as apparent as the opening sentence; namely, he goes through the alternatives that would be possible. Doesn't he?

Anderson: Yes. Doesn't his thesis end with how . . .

McKeon: Well, I think as you go along, you'll discover that this is the only way in which he ever does anything. What do you think it is that a person does when he establishes a position?

Anderson: Usually, how is everything adequately shown, and then . . .

McKeon: Can you do that?

Anderson: No.

McKeon: No one can do that; consequently, no philosopher ever tries to.

Anderson: Or he can show how his position is right by going through why other positions are wrong.

McKeon: Well, well, let's go through this instead of . . . Obviously, the *a priori* construction of what the methods are has nothing to help us. Tell us what it is that we successively need to do in this argument. Mr. Berg? Is Mr. Berg here? Mr. Cummings? Is Mr. Cummings here? The bouncing ball certainly falls well. Mr. Davis, is he here?

Davis: Yeah. Would—would you repeat what you want me to . . .

McKeon: We are going to prove that only the will is good. What shall we do in order to prove that?

Davis: Well, we'll have to talk about reason and . . .

McKeon: Why do we have to talk about reason? Is there a law?

DAVIS: No, we have—man has reason.

MCKEON: Do we? I don't think man has reason. I practically never run into it in my classes. [L!] . . . No, you see, you . . .

DAVIS: Well, we'll talk about an alternative, then. One of the alternatives is the happiness he talks about at the end, which is happiness equally. He starts out by the alternative, that means discussing what people think is good, and he just shows what man has isn't suited for that.

MCKEON: Look at what he says. He makes a list of other talents of the mind in the second sentence, "intelligence with judgment and the other talents of the mind" [page 9], for which he then gives a list, the traditional list of the virtues. What's he say about them? They're all good, aren't they? . . . Why isn't intelligence as good as the good will? . . . Yes?

STUDENT: Well, it contributes to a good will, but it presupposes the good will; and therefore . . .

MCKEON: . . . and—well—let's leave "presupposes" out. What's wrong with it?

STUDENT: The goodness or badness of it will be constituted by the use the will makes of it.

MCKEON: It can be misused. Any one of these can be misused. So, the first paragraph is on the way in which the other things that could be thought to be good can be misused. As I say, we've . . . Even though they're praised, what's the difference between a thing being good and a thing being praised?

STUDENT: Something may be praised that isn't really good.

MCKEON: Well, I—no—what—[L!] that's its relevance here, but what's the difference between saying this is praised and this is good?

STUDENT: You can praise something because it can do something, but it could do something else.

MCKEON: Yes?

STUDENT: [. . . ?]

MCKEON: Well, yes. Or let's get it out of that language. That is, if a thing is good, it is because of its nature; whereas when a thing is praised, it is an indication that someone thinks it's good. Consequently, we're in the position that he is bringing us to, that whatever is good we have got to think that it's good. Therefore, you need to differentiate between the things that are merely praised and the things that can be thought to be good not because of empirical reasons but *a priori*, and then they *are* good. So that, you notice, the paragraph ends[4] that "the good will is not good because of its effects or because of its adequacy to achieve some end, but it's good in itself"—not usefulness, not fruitfulness, but worth. And this is that word *Wert* [Ger.] that I mentioned in the lecture. This is "value"; this is one of the places where value theory begins to come in.

"There are, however, suspicions about the goodness of the good will" [B:56]. This is the second way in which we go at our test of it for virtue. How do we handle the suspicions that the will isn't a good will? Mr. Engel?

ENGEL: Well, the suspicion is that the good will is not a good will, because it would be thinking of it in terms of what it does but not in terms of itself. So that whatever it does or may try to do has nothing to do with its goodness.

MCKEON: Does that really give the answer? Miss Frank? How would you say he goes about answering it?

FRANK: I'm sorry, it's not clear where we are, actually, or if he's spoken about the other alternatives and we're on the next part.

MCKEON: We're on the next paragraph, the second paragraph,[5] and we're going to speed up, hopefully.

FRANK: Oh, I thought we were . . . All right, in the second paragraph he talks about qualities which fulfill the action of the good will. And, with reference to the . . .

MCKEON: Well, let's take a larger unit. We've taken care of what leads to a good will and what is not the same as the good will. Now, let's look at the problem of what is involved if people say the good will won't do the job.

FRANK: That's where he talks about the perfection of man and the fact that the will is given to man to try and deduce it; and if it's perfect for happiness, you might have some question about whether the will's perfect [. . . ?] means to be used.

MCKEON: Well, don't tell me what he says; tell me what it is, what the mode of argument would be if a person thought that the will was not the only thing that is good. . . . Mr. Anderson?

ANDERSON: You could take any example to show how the will is the cause of it, and if the will is the cause of it, then you only have one thing which is good, which has . . .

MCKEON: I don't see that this touches the question. I say that there are lots of things that are good, but one thing that isn't good is the good will. The good will is obviously always spurious: it's what the politician says when he wants to get to Springfield.[6]

STUDENT: But you show that for all these things that you're calling good, they have a will—the will is the thing that makes them actual.

MCKEON: No, on the contrary, I say the will is what makes them bad. How do you meet this?

STUDENT: That would mean that they're only good with some qualification; that is, that the will cooperates to make them ...

STUDENT: It should, then, depend upon something else.

MCKEON: You're doing this as if it were a catechism to be recited. This is an argument that ought to be advanced. Here is a man who starts out by saying that the only thing that is good is the good will, and the thing that immediately strikes me is that there are lots of things that are good. I'm doubtful whether there is a good will, but I can conceive of nothing better than a chocolate ice cream soda with chocolate ice cream! And it's a very high good: did you ever try it? [L!] What do you do with me?

STUDENT: Show you that it can make you sick?

MCKEON: It never does. [L!] I've experimented with it. [L!]

STUDENT: Wouldn't you have to show that what you're looking for is something that has what he says is an intrinsic, unconditional value in itself, and so the method ...

MCKEON: No, no, this is what you've got to prove, not something you have to assume. If you have assumed it, then it's a pushover, naturally.

STUDENT: Well, you have to prove that there's some higher happiness which you talk about ...

MCKEON: Well, but how would I go about doing that? Happiness is self-fulfillment; it is the realization of my potentiality. What could be higher than that?

STUDENT: [... ?]

MCKEON: What?

STUDENT: I mean, by taking the thing that makes man, in respect to other objects in nature, perfectible, and that's his rationality, and then with the rationality you can act and must be higher.

MCKEON: Well, on the other—the mere assertion obviously does not achieve this. The only thing that leads to happiness is action according to the rule of right reason, rationality. If men were rational, lived rationally, then we would have to go around trying to examine their will to find out whether their will is good. This is a very sloppy approach. ... Yes?

STUDENT: Well, you don't need reasons to like an ice cream cone and ...

MCKEON: On the contrary, you do. [L!] Virtue is a meeting between extremes, and one of the virtues is temperance (see fig. 28).[7] Temperance would lead me to treat my ice cream cone in such a way that I wouldn't be greedy and I wouldn't be parsimonious. I would have the right amount of ice cream cones habitually, and that is operation according to the rule of right reason. Rule of right reason is the way it's telling me when I've got enough and when I haven't got enough.

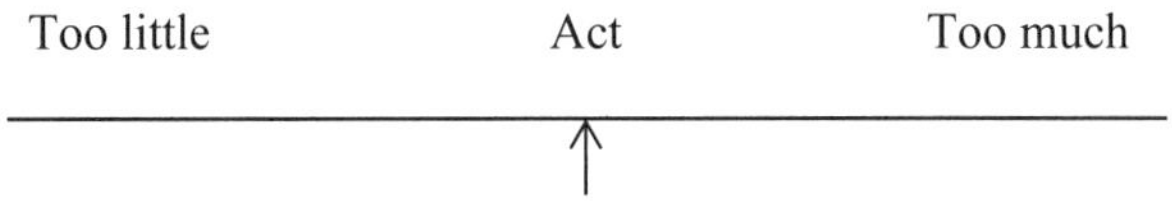

Fig. 28 *Act as Mean between Extremes*

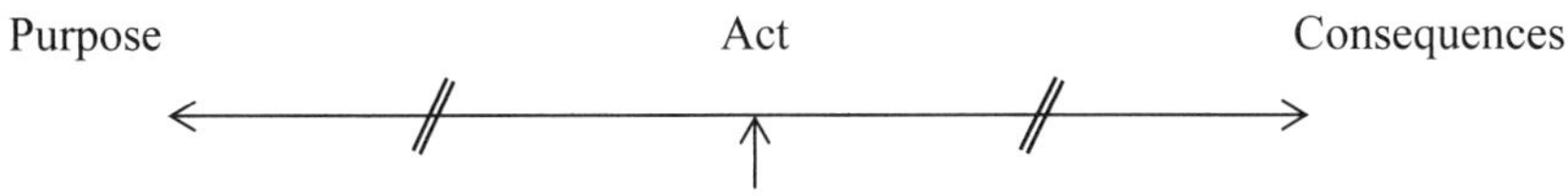

Fig. 29 *Act Good in Itself*

STUDENT: But you're basing that argument on the principle that to be temperate is something better than the excess of cones.

MCKEON: No, no, no, no. What I'm basing this on is the supposition that there are many goods. They are not goods in the separate sense of something occupying the heavens like whitened statues;[8] what they are, are realizations of potentialities that I have. I realize the potentialities by developing virtues, the virtues give me habits, habits are applying the rule of right reason. I have the proper habits with respect to the various virtues. Temperance is the one proper to ice cream cones—ice cream sodas—ice cream cones are not good. [L!] No, look, what we have done in the first paragraph is the answer you've got to deal with. That is to say, we are looking for something which is good in itself. The justification of the good in itself would be part of the question of interpretation; that is, we are differentiating between what would seem to be good for a variety of reasons and what is good in itself. This in itself does not yet give us any criterion. If we are dealing with what is good in itself, then we don't want to calculate the consequences. Let's do a picture again (see fig. 29)[9]—I've had this on the board before. This is the act; we want to call the act good, and we are saying that we won't say it's good, because it leads to the consequences we want, even happiness. We won't say it's good because we have a purpose—that's the argument that we've had thus far. If you want something which is a good, its characteristics already begin to appear, don't they? Not the consequences of the action, not the purpose of the action, but what?

STUDENT: The motive?

MCKEON: The motive?

STUDENT: Right.

MCKEON: All right. That's a little bit further on. But let's go on. Why is the maxim—well, as a matter of fact, that's in the second part; let's stick to the first part. Yes.

STUDENT: Well, he uses the word *volition*.

MCKEON: All right. Volition and will, you know, are related.

STUDENT: Yeah. [L!] But as opposed to motive are results or something.

MCKEON: Do you think volition and motive are the same?

STUDENT: They're different.

MCKEON: What's that? . . . What's is the difference between a motive and a volition?

STUDENT: A motive is related more to the results.

STUDENT: A motive depends on feelings; volition has to do with reason. A motive is the motions of the feelings.

GREEN: Volition is an activity, and motive is a cause.

MCKEON: A motive is on the empirical level. To find out what my motives are, you have to ask me questions. A volition will be on the *a priori* level. And therefore, what we're looking for would be on the *a priori* level. Now, the argument which we are engaged in here—let's get this out of the way—suppose there were some way—one of the reasons why we're dissatisfied with the argument thus far is that—notice, as a matter of fact, I was using this argument and you were assuming it, also, instead of questioning me about it—is that there are ways which are better to get something, for example, reason. Well, immediately, reason is a way of getting the consequences. And if ethics were based on reason calculating consequences, including my happiness, there'd be better ways. Reason really doesn't work, because an instinct would be better. I mean, if, in the beginning, you were making an animal that would be happy because of consequences, an immediate reaction by way of instinct would be better. There are two things against reason: first, that it makes mistakes, even in the hands of an able reasoner; and second, because of the mistakes it leads to misology. What's misology?

GREEN: Hatred of reason.

MCKEON: Why? I know, but why does it lead to misology?

GREEN: Because a man, if he has a cultivated intellect and if it dedicates itself to happiness, becomes more and more unhappy and finally ends with this kind of a longing due to the lack of pure instinct.

MCKEON: Notice the way in which our ontological interpretation is present. That is, you either deal with the ordinary man—that is the level of experience—and reason wouldn't be any good for him, because when he gets into his predicaments, his reason isn't well trained; or then you get the person with the reason well trained, and if anything, those fellows are more unhappy. Note that we're assuming the consequence that is set up, namely, the happiness: they're more unhappy than the uncultivated swain who has flocks on the hillside. That is, their sensitivities lead them astray. Consequently, we cut out all of the substitutes, including reason, as the way of getting there. If we don't deal with reason, what is our hope in order to achieve the end that we are talking about? What is reason's function? . . . And this is what I was aiming at in the beginning.

STUDENT: Well, his reason is the government of the will, the one that directs and forms the action. The will produces, the will directs.

MCKEON: What is reason's function?

STUDENT: Its practical function is to influence the will.

MCKEON: Yes?

STUDENT: It produces the will.

MCKEON: It is to produce the will, that is, to produce a will good enough in itself. Later on you can take it that you can keep it up. . . . What is the relation between practical reason—and this is a treatise on the practical reason—and will?

STUDENT: They're the same?

MCKEON: They're identical; they're exactly the same. Consequently, on the picture (see fig. 29), we're not going to deal with the problems of ethics by dealing either with the consequences or with the antecedents. We're going to deal with reason producing a good will, and Kant calls this his principle. What kind of a principle is this?

STUDENT: Reflexive.

MCKEON: Clearly a reflexive principle, isn't it? That is, the will producing a good will. This is why I tangled you up in the early discussion. It isn't that the will is a better way of getting consequences than the intellect; that's all irrelevant. The real process has been defined so that, Mr. Anderson, the answer to my first question was that what he did in the first part was to establish his principle. He has done this before, in the preface. The pagination on this book, as I said, is what I thought you had—on page 6 of this book—it's probably almost the same—it's the paragraph which begins, "A metaphysics of morals is therefore indispensable"—it's page 5 [B:52].

STUDENT: I can't find it in my book.

MCKEON: Page 5, going over page 5 to 6, the last sentence.

STUDENT: Wow . . .

MCKEON: Well, the sentence is, "For it is not sufficient to that which should be morally good that it conform to the law; it must be done for the sake of the law" [B:52]. In other words, this is a reflexive principle, that is, the law for the law, the will making the will; and as you go along, it should be possible to see this reflexive principle operating again and again. And, you notice, it makes a big difference, just as our interpretation makes a difference. Our interpretation permitted us to separate motive from will, and our principle will tell us we're going to focus at the midpoint of the line (see fig. 29).

I said that the second part of this first section began with "We have, then, to develop a notion"—well, as a matter of fact, the second part says it for you: it begins, "We have, then, to develop a notion of the will which deserves to be highly esteemed for itself and is good without a view to anything else, a notion which exists already" [B:58]. This is the reflexive principle: the will as operative on itself. My general question, then, will have to do with the second part, running from page 14 to 21 [B:58–64]. And since you've been reading it for some time, you ought to be able to give me a rough formulation. What do we do, what does Kant do, in this part? Mr. Heath? . . . Is Mr. Heath here? . . . None of the people on my list are here, but all you people are here. Mr. Isaacs? . . . Is Mr. Isaacs here?

ISAACS: Yes, here. Well, to start with, he again points out various things which . . .

MCKEON: No, no. Tell me what he does; don't tell me what he starts out to do and what he says. . . . Let me give it to you, if you had read it with attention. On page 17 [B:61], the bottom paragraph says, "The second proposition is . . ."; and then, as you turn the page, on page 18 [B:61] it says, "The third proposition . . ." And your translator in this edition very carefully says, "The first proposition was that to have moral worth an action must be done from duty" [B:61]; and he might have said, The first proposition we started to state on page 14 [B:58] at the point that we had set up. Consequently, Mr. Isaacs, I would suggest that a correct answer to my question is that in this part, he sets forth three propositions. Wouldn't that be a good slash in? If you said that, what are the three propositions? I praise you for noticing that there are three propositions. [L!] What are they?

ISAACS: Well, in order to be moral, to have moral worth, we act from duty, and duty has to be . . .

MCKEON: No, no, no. We had our duty all established for us in the preface, and this isn't that. Tell me what the first proposition is.

ISAACS: That to have moral worth, an action must be done from duty . . .

MCKEON: All right.

ISAACS: . . . from duty itself, and so . . .

MCKEON: All right. That's the first proposition. What's the second proposition?

ISAACS: Well, the action must be done from the duty, it has to be done by the maxim by which it is . . .

1. Duty

2. Maxim

3. Law (respect for)

Fig. 30 *Three Propositions in First Section*

McKeon: All right. And the third proposition?

Isaacs: Doing the action from respect for the law.

McKeon: All right (see fig. 30). What do the three propositions say, one, two, three, then, in your language? . . . Anyone who wishes to help Mr. Isaacs may step in and volunteer.

Student: Well, in terms of your chart up there, first he says it must be done from duty; then he strikes out the purpose, which would be the antecedent . . .

McKeon: No, no, we've done that. Kant is an economical writer; he doesn't do things twice if he can help it.

Student: Well, doesn't it say, first, that it must be done from duty; second, from duty and not from any purpose; and the third, from duty and not from any . . .

McKeon: No.

Student: . . . action that's moral, of morals.

McKeon: You've only described it. Tell me what the three steps are, and then we can decide whether we want to describe them in any particular way.

Student: Well, that is, having talked about the esteem we have for the will, we bring in duty as representative of moral worth, and then he . . .

McKeon: No, no. We know all that now. We bring in duty first. Let's put that down (see fig. 30).

Student: The maxim.

McKeon: We bring in the maxim.

Student: And then what the maxim is.

McKeon: No.

Student: Law.

Student: The principle?

Student: The law?

McKeon: What is that third proposition . . .

Student: [. . . ?]

McKeon: "Duty is the necessity of an action executed from respect for law" [B:61].

STUDENT: Isn't that the categorical imperative itself?

McKEON: Well, let's not trace the pedigree. Let's get the thing. [L!] . . . Let's put "law" down with respect to the form. Yes?

STUDENT: Doesn't that imply reason, the law? I just didn't understand that part.

McKEON: Practical reason and will are the same; the only thing that's good is the good will; . . .

STUDENT: I mean that . . .

McKEON: . . . consequently, he does imply reason, but so what? Yes?

STUDENT: Well, that way he establishes what he's going to talk about. He's going to talk about . . .

McKEON: No. Let me answer this, because I want to get on. What the third step is, is the way in which you state what the binding force of the law is. Obviously, you could have had a law which got its binding force from its end. But you're saying, no, this is a law which is motivated by the law itself. This is our reflexive principle. We've been climbing. Our third point would be to nail down what the reflexive principle is going to do in our treatise. And therefore, it would be natural that that will be the third proposition. The first two propositions would then be a step to that third proposition. You notice, in terms of the interpretation and the principle—we haven't got the method yet—what we are saying is that we're talking about an objective law—ontological interpretation—enforced for its own sake—reflexive principle. How do we get there? Well, we get there with a maxim, and there are two footnotes on my page to explain the difference between a maxim and a principle. What's the difference between a maxim and a principle?

STUDENT: One's a subject, and one's an object.

McKEON: One is subject and the other is object. In other words, we're now down at this level of duty (see fig. 30). And obviously, in order to know what the law is that we are going to respect, the only way that we, limited mortals, can do it is by making a maxim. But not all maxims are principles. Consequently, the line between one (duty) and two (maxim) would be the way in which you can be sure that your maxim is a principle. A maxim is subjective: any rule you can hit upon as a mode of action. It becomes objective by means that we are concerned with in our transition between duty in its ordinary sense and duty in popular philosophy, and that's what this whole treatise is about.

Consequently, we're now in a position to know what it is that the first step was. The first step is the formulation that we have been making thus far. That is to say, we have said that ethics itself will be a matter of duty; and therefore, the good will be performance in accordance with duty. In this treatise, this first section is, as he says, a transition between the ordinary conception of duty and the philosophic, and these three propositions are the transition. That is, this [duty] is our starting point: everybody has a sense of duty, and frequently the ordinary man has it better than the elevated guy, the guy who does all that thinking. He needs, however, to state it in terms of the maxim, not in terms of an objective, not in terms of a purpose, not in terms of motives, but in terms of a general rule. And the transition to philosophy is that if this general rule can then be stated in such a way that the reason for holding it is the rule itself, you've got duty. It's a beautiful argument, isn't it? I mean, you may not agree, you may not be convinced by it, but as a form of argument, there's nothing much you can object to.

Let's go back—as I say, if we were doing this in detail, there'd be some point in going over each one of these three aspects—but let's go to the beginning of the second part of the first section. I'm getting dizzy looking at two different positions [McKeon rustles papers]. [L!] It's on the bottom of your page 14 [B:58]. This is the one in which we are going to deal with the first step, namely, the proposition which is eventually stated as "To have moral worth, an action must be done from duty" [B:61]. What I would like you to tell me is what it is that he does in the first two paragraphs, because this will give you some notion, again, of what the argument is. And I warn you that the argument is not the sort of thing you've been making the argument into. Mr. Jackson? Is Mr. Jackson here?

JACKSON: Yes. . . . What he does in the first two paragraphs is examine the notion of duty. In general it'll involve various restrictions that are placed upon it.

MCKEON: That doesn't sound to me like a good description of what he does. Tell me something that would . . .

JACKSON: He also talks in the second paragraph . . .

MCKEON: "It's necessary to develop," he says, "first of all, a concept of the will which deserves to be esteemed for itself" [B:58]. You remember, we began by saying that we don't want something which is praised; but if it is esteemed for itself, then you have the reflexivity that we are talking about. "It exists already in the sound understanding"—therefore, we're beginning with the ordinary mind—"but it needs to be brought to light" [ibid.]. Paragraph two brings it to light. . . .

JACKSON: Well, doesn't he . . .

MCKEON: . . . No, all I want you to tell me is how we're going to bring it to light.

1. Duty — a) actions contrary to duty — omit

b) actions contrary to inclination — omit

c) actions we like to do and are our duty — examine

Fig. 31 *Actions from Duty*

JACKSON: Well, he gives us an example. He says that in some ways . . .
MCKEON: I don't believe it.
JACKSON: In other words, he gives that it's a duty to maintain one's life.
MCKEON: No. You're down in the third paragraph; we're talking about the second paragraph: "I omit here all actions . . ." Yes?
STUDENT: Well, he has to show that if the maxim is to be called a maxim, it must be a maxim of a man of reason.
MCKEON: Oh, no. That would be an awfully sloppy thing to do, and he doesn't do it. Yes?
STUDENT: He says [. . . ?]
MCKEON: He tells you how you're going to find it in that very paragraph, doesn't he? What are the actions which we could examine (see fig. 31)? You'll notice, all we want to do is to take the word *duty* and give it a meaning so that everyone can recognize it. Therefore, what we might do is to look at the actions that are contrary to duty. Are we going to do anything with those?
GREEN: We exclude them immediately.
MCKEON: So, we're going to omit them.
STUDENT: Yeah.
MCKEON: All right. [L!] We could also deal with those things which are according to duty but we don't want to do anyway—other inclinations don't count. I mean, the things that we ought to do and we don't like doing, too. Are we going to examine those?
GREEN: Put them aside.
MCKEON: We're going to leave those out. One and two are out (see fig. 31). You'll notice, we're proceeding by a logical device; that is, we are using pairs of contraries. There is a third possibility, namely, the things that we *like* to do—you see, the previous ones are the ones we don't want to do; and therefore, although we do our duty, we all still want to do the opposite—but these are the things that we like to do and they're also our duty. And, he says, these last are the only ones we're going to examine. Why? I mean, isn't this the key to his method? In order to make clear what a duty is, we'll examine instances in which, when a man does it, even though he says, "Now, I struggled with

1. Fair price
2. Maintaining your own life
3. Beneficence
4. Securing one's own happiness

Fig. 32 *Examples of Duty with Inclination*

myself and I done my duty," nobody knows, he doesn't himself know whether he did it because of duty or he did it because of interest. Isn't that what he's saying, Mr. Klass?

KLASS: I'm not registered for this class.

MCKEON: Well, why didn't you tell me that? . . . I mean, it's fascinating what this second paragraph . . .

JACKSON: He wants to separate out acts done from duty to others.

MCKEON: Well, all right, then, tell me, if this is what he's done, what he's doing in the next paragraph, which you had been looking at.

JACKSON: Well, this is his attempt to deal with a man who should preserve his life. It is something as duty requires, it has no advantage implied, it's not because duty requires it but action . . .

MCKEON: Well, you have to begin further up. It's in the middle of the other paragraph where he begins giving examples. "It is much harder to make this distinction when the action accords with duty and the subject besides has a direct inclination for it" [B:58]. Next he says, "For example . . . ," and then the next few paragraphs go on and do something. That's what I want you to explain to me. . . . Yes?

STUDENT: He makes the distinction between actions that are because he was for it and actions where he wasn't.

MCKEON: Well, then, how does the fair price enter as the example?

STUDENT: Well, this is—I got from a direct inclination after he acquires it, not before he acquires it . . .

MCKEON: Well, I know, but what we're going to take are instances of things that, he says, are from duty and inclination. And, he says, our first example will be to deal with someone who asks a fair price (see fig. 32).

STUDENT: Well, then he goes on to say, too, if you do something which is not from inclination but it's more from duty, whereas . . .

MCKEON: You mean, Kant just gets all balled up here and this argument goes to pot?

STUDENT: No. He's talking about—I don't think everything is done from inclination. He's saying that life isn't just inclination . . .

McKeon: What we are going to do, he says, is take an example in which you do it because of inclination and duty and you can't tell the difference. . . . Yes?

Green: The man who just charges the buyer a fair price is, in the common estimation, not called the honest man simply because of the . . .

McKeon: Yeah.

Green: . . . simply because, although what he's doing is honest, he may not be doing it for honest motives: he could be doing it from a selfish point of view. And so the ordinary opinion, the common opinion, is that you can't tell simply from this fact whether or not he is honest.

McKeon: All right. Well, then, why is this an example that we're looking for?

Green: It shows the distinction that the ordinary man makes between the honest thing and doing it because of an honest reason.

McKeon: It shows that in charging a fair price, there is no way in which not only the ordinary man but anyone can tell whether this is because of duty—and it could be; that is, honesty is one of the things you can do because of duty—or because we benefit by the result.

Let's take a look at the second example. What's the second one?

Student: Maintain one's life.

McKeon: What?

Student: Maintaining your life.

McKeon: All right, maintaining your own life. What's that going to give us?

Student: Well, it's here that he makes the distinction between "as duty requires" and "because duty requires"; and he says most men do it *as* duty requires but not because duty requires. If you do it because duty requires, then you have answered your moral worth.

McKeon: Yes, but again, we are—this is an instance in which it could be either way and . . .

Student: You can't . . .

McKeon: . . . and therefore, in the act of maintaining life, either inclination or duty could be the motive.

Student: Doesn't this imply, then, that where, in the first, inclination might be very much the controlling factor, here, in the second one, duty might very much be the controlling factor?

McKeon: No, no, we don't need to go into that. Later we're going to come back to these same examples again, and that's why I'm focusing on them now. The second section will deal with them a number of times, but all we are doing now is starting our inquiry by looking for duty in cases of an action where either inclination or duty might be the reason. Yes?

STUDENT: He uses the example where the man doesn't want life, he wants death, he has no inclination to preserve his life: is that from duty? Is it a case from duty when there's a negative inclination, you can't . . .

McKEON: That becomes even more complicated later, because it is quite clear that a person completely discouraged might avoid committing suicide because it's an old family name, he doesn't want to dishonor his parents; all of the consequences might be the reason, he says, as easily as . . . Are there any other examples? . . .

STUDENT: Helping others.

McKEON: What?

STUDENT: Help others.

McKEON: All right. What is the next position?

STUDENT: It's the same.

McKEON: What?

STUDENT: The same situation . . .

McKEON: I know, but what is another example? Don't put it in terms of similarity and that we can do it either from inclination or from duty. Are there any others?

STUDENT: Seeking happiness . . .

McKEON: What?

STUDENT: Seek happiness.

McKEON: Yes? Even when there's no happiness in living, when there's no desire for one's own happiness, duty is in again. The same generalization holds.

We have the method working again. You'll notice, the same sort of thing that we had in our list of three (see fig. 31). What are we doing? Why do you suppose he has forms? Yeah?

STUDENT: Won't he have to give an account that will verify his position?

McKEON: No. Is there anything here in the pattern of occurrence?

STUDENT: Aren't the first and the third about others, and the other two about other situations?

McKEON: All right. These, the first and third, are about others; these, the second and fourth, are about self (see fig. 33). Is there any difference between the first and third and between the second and fourth, taking the horizontal levels?

STUDENT: Is it that one's the necessary as opposed to something beyond that level?

McKEON: Well, that's roughly correct; but this top level is the very being of the thing: one is always treating oneself and the possibility of community with others. This other pair has to do with something

	Others	Self
Being (Perfect Duty)	1) Fair price	2) Maintaining one's own life
Means to it (Imperfect Duty)	3) Beneficence	4) One's own happiness

Fig. 33 *Operational Method and Examples of Duty with Inclination*

less than that, the means that are involved. So, consequently, we have a pattern. As I say, later, in the second section, he will explain this pattern himself and give names to them, relate them to duty. What method is this? . . .

Student: Discrimination.

McKeon: What?

Student: Discrimination.

McKeon: Well, this is the one that was suggested last time, and I said, "What do you mean by discrimination?" Discrimination in itself is something that all the methods would deal with. In order to make this the operational method, you would need some indication of what the operational method does.

Student: It shows relation, the different relations in terms of situations encountered.

McKeon: I don't . . . Are there any definite relations? All that I am doing here is saying self/other, transient/permanent.

Student: Those are just the formal words . . .

McKeon: That is . . .

Student: . . . definitional?

McKeon: . . . they are merely *a*, *b*, *c*, *d*, in which all I know is that they exclude each other (see fig. 34).[10] Yes?

Student: Well, you set up—you set up several analogies, analogies to pure and empirical situations.

McKeon: No, I'm afraid that's the interpretation. I thought that we'd gotten beyond interpretation and into method. That would be the difference in two propositions. We're here asking how it is that we use the method to establish the propositions.

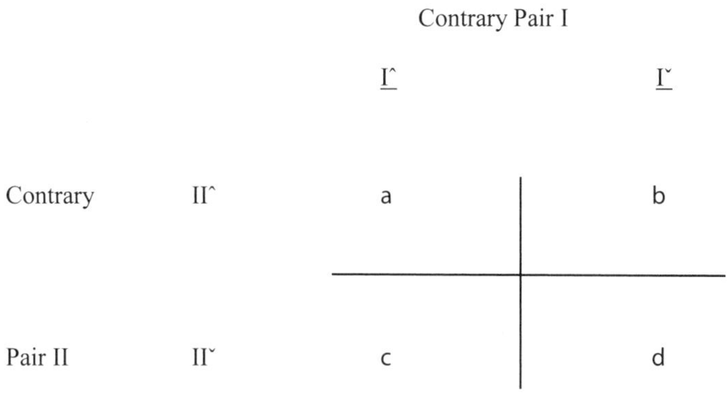

Fig. 34 *Formal Example of Operational Method*

Well, the bell has rung; and this is something that you probably ought to meditate on, because the answer to the question should eventually give you a formulation in which you can say that the operational method does *this*, the problematic, the dialectical, all the other methods do *this*, and they are different in *this* respect. And the reason why I want to impress it upon you is that I think that as you've been talking about method, you've been acting as if the operational method will prove something. On principle, it proves nothing. If you are engaged in proof, you're wrong, that is, unless you put quotation marks there. It doesn't prove the way in which the logistic method proves, and it's the logistic method that seems to be in the background of most of the answers that you've given.[11]

We'll go on from here next time. We didn't quite get the ideal of finishing part 2 of the first section. I will rapidly go through the last part, the third part of the first section, and then we'll move on to the second section, the transition from popular moral philosophy to the metaphysics of morals. We've made the transition from the ordinary view to that of popular philosophy. We will now be able to go from that to the metaphysics of morals.

McKeon's Notes

Kant. Fundamental Principles of Metaph of Morals 1, 2.[12]

gives no certain proof of its soundness. Rather inspires a certain partiality.

Method—proceed *analytically* from common knowledge to the determination of its ultimate principle; descend *synthetically* from examination of this principle and its sources to common knowledge in which employed.

Thence division of parts. 1. Common rational knowledge to philosophical; 2. Popular moral philosophy to metaphysics of morals; 3. Metaphysics of morals to critique of *pure practical reason*.

First section. Transition from the Common Rational knowledge of Morality to the Philosophical. *9* (p. 9)

(a) Nothing good except Good Will. Talents, qualities of temperament (gifts of nature) and gifts of fortune may be misused without good will. *Ont.*

Some qualities conducive to good will, but no (p. 10) intrinsic unconditional value. Moderation in the affections and passions, self-control, and calm deliberation seem part of intrinsic worth, but not good without qualification, though praised by ancients (Cf. Stoic or Spinozist principles).

Good will not *good because of its effects* or because of its adequacy to achieve some end. But good *in self*. *Usefulness* or *fruitfulness* nothing to do with worth. (11)

Value. *10*

Suspicion of absolute value of will. *Test idea* of *reason appointed as ruler* of our will. *(11)*

Assumption that in physical constitution of organized being—as fundamental principle—that no organ is found not fittest and most adapted to that purpose.

If proper object of nature its conservation, welfare i.e. its *happiness*, then reason a poor means of achieving purpose. *Instinct* better than reason. Nature would determine ends and means. (12)

The more cultivated reason, the less *true contentment*. *Misology*. Arts and sciences—difficulties, rather than happiness.

Different and *nobler end than happiness* for which reason intended. Reason not competent to guide will to its objects and satisfaction of our wants (13) but *reason a practical* faculty, one intended to *12* have an influence on the will. Reason's function to produce a will *good in itself*, not good for something else. This will is not the whole good, but the *highest good*.

Cultivation of reason for this first purpose may interfere with second purpose, *happiness*. *12*

(b) *First Proposition, p. 13*

Necessary to develop a *concept of a will* which deserves to be esteemed for itself. Exists already in *sound natural understanding*. Needs only to be brought to light. *13* (14)

Op Take notion of duty which contains that of good will.

1 Omit actions opposed to duty;

2 Omit also actions in *accordance* with duty for which no inclination.

3 Examine actions in accordance with duty for which one had direct *inclination*. (N.B. choice in order to raise question about actions done from duty).

1. Dealer and fair price. (14) Not enough to persuade us that dealer acted from duty. Also advantage. Neither duty nor inclination but advantage. *14*

2. Duty and inclination to preserve one's life (15) as duty requires vs. because of duty. Maxim moral worth.

3. Beneficence—duty and inclination. If only for pleasure, same as other inclinations, as honor.

Moral import if from duty, not inclination.

Sorrowing philanthropist. Cold temperament. (16)

4. Secure one's own happiness—duty and inclination. *15*

Gouty patient, enjoyment of moment. Duty. (17)

Examples from Scripture—love neighbor and enemy.

Beneficence rather than love (not commanded).

(From these examinations—to *have moral worth* action must be done according to duty and *because of duty*. Cause.)

Second proposition. *16* Action done from duty derives its moral worth (value) not from the purpose to be attained by it, but from the *maxim* by which it is determined. Therefore does not depend on the object of the action but on the principle of the volition.

Purposes and *effects cannot* give actions unconditioned moral worth.

Worth in the principle of the will without regard to its ends; Will stands between its a priori principle, which is formal, and its a posteriori spring which is material. Must be determined by formal principle when action done from duty. *16* (18)

Third proposition. *p. 16*

Duty is the necessity of acting from *respect for the law*. *Ref.*

DISCUSSION

Kant, Part 3 (*Fundamental Principles of the Metaphysics of Morals*, First Section: Transition from the Common Rational Knowledge of Morality to the Philosophical; Second Section: Transition from Popular Moral Philosophy to the Metaphysic of Morals)

Discussion[1]

McKeon: Last time we began looking at the first section of Kant's *Fundamental Principles of the Metaphysics of Morals*, and in the first part we undertook to demonstrate that there's nothing good except the good will. Then, in the second part of the first section, we went on through three propositions which eventually set up our principle for us. We're now ready, therefore, to go on to the third part. Remember, we saw that what our concern is, is to make the transition from ordinary modes of thinking to the philosophic in this first section. Mr. Long? Is Mr. Long here?

Long: Yes?

McKeon: Do you want to tell us what remains for us to do in the third part?

Long: To leave out the principle is going to be the consequence of the . . .

McKeon: Beg your pardon?

Long: To leave out the principle is going to be the function of this maxim.

McKeon: To leave out the principle is going to be the substance of this maxim? I'm not sure that I understand what you're saying. We've pointed out that only the will is good; we have then set up the way in which this objective can be gotten, by showing that the action is according to duty, the action is according to a maxim stating that duty is an action for the sake of itself—and this reflexivity is important. What would remain to prove if we were making a transition from ordinary knowledge to philosophical? . . . Mr. Marks? Is Mr. Marks here? . . . Mr. Norman?

NORMAN: I pass.

MCKEON: I beg your pardon?

NORMAN: Pass.

MCKEON: Well, it isn't a question of passing. Did you read this thing?

NORMAN: Yes.

MCKEON: Did it make any sense to you? . . .

NORMAN: Yes, at the time.

MCKEON: OK, then, make a statement about the third part of the first section which would justify your assertion that you made some sense of this passage. . . . What problem would remain if we have set up a moral system in which the law which we impose on ourselves is the moral precept? If you were making a transition from the common rational knowledge of morals to the philosophical, what question would remain? . . .

NORMAN: Well, you'd have to, then, say that we—what it makes of you—how much you've got—how much you could determine what you were going to do.

MCKEON: When you get through this class, you're going to have read Kant's *Fundamental Principles*. How are you going to determine how much you're going to be able to do? I don't know what sense your remark makes. I mean, suppose you think it is now your duty to understand the book that we are reading. You're saying that then you'll be informed, you'll be able to determine how much you are able to do? It sounds like nonsense to me; doesn't it to you? . . . Mr. Ott?

OTT: Well, you'd have to show the relationship between what you've done before, which was for the commonsense level, and how it relates to what you want to say about the philosophical level.

MCKEON: Yes. And having made the transition, having identified it, you would want to know what the use is, what the difference is, and what it is that the philosophic contributes that you didn't have when you started. What is it that it contributes?

OTT: Well, we would show that it contributes a position from which a principle can be brought . . .

MCKEON: I know, but why is that important? Is it important in the theoretic knowledge to have a principle?

OTT: Well, . . . yeah.

McKeon: I'm on page 23 [B:64–65],[2] in case any of you are interested in what we're going on about.

Ott: It's going to give us a principle that's going to be based on experience, as if we had . . .

McKeon: What's the difference between the theoretic and the practical?

Ott: The theoretic? Well, we're talking about the level of the practical, not the theoretic; the theoretic gives us no principle with which we would then examine the principle of morality.

McKeon: You mean, in all theory there isn't a principle?

Ott: Oh, no.

McKeon: What's the difference between the theoretic and practical since *both* of them depend on principles? . . . If you were going from common reason to the kind of reason you would use in physics, how would you do it? If you were going from common reason to the kind of reason that you would use in morals, how would you do it? What is the difference between them?

Ott: Well, one is really based on experience . . .

McKeon: Will either of them be based on experience? . . . Physics is as *a priori* as morals is. Consequently, neither of them would be based on experience. Experience is not the basis of anything in either. . . . Mr. Pearlman? Is Mr. Pearlman here? . . . Mr. Quimby? What is the difference between the theoretic and the practical—page 23.

Quimby: Well, the theoretic would try to abstract from experience—without question.

McKeon: I'm sorry; the passage is on page 23, not pages 20 to 21. I'm stuck with these two editions again. [L!] In the one that you don't have, it's 20 to 21. . . . The third part begins on page 21 [B:64] and runs over to page 23 [B:66]. What is the difference between the theoretic and the practical? . . . Anyone know the difference between the theoretic and the practical?

Green: Well, it appears that the practical is concerned with conduct, and the theoretic is concerned with knowledge.

McKeon: This is a good definition of the two. What is the difference between the theoretic and the practical with respect to principles, with respect to the laws of experience?

Green: One looks for a principle of action; the other looks for the principle of knowledge.

McKeon: Let me read you two sentences. "Here we cannot forebear admiration when we see how great an advantage the practical judgment has over the theoretical in the common understanding of men" [B:64]. You remember, this is the transition which we're going through—the common understanding of men is the theoretical. "In the latter"—that is, in the theoretical—"if common reason ventures to depart from the laws of experience and the perceptions of the senses, it falls into mere inconceivabilities and self-contradictions, at least into a chaos of uncertainty, obscurity, and instability; but in the practical sphere, it is just when common understanding excludes the principled springs[3] from practical laws that its power of judgment shows itself to advantage, it then becomes even subtle, whether it be that it chicanes with its own conscience or with other claims respecting . . ." and so on [B:64–65]. What's the difference between judgment in the practical and in the theoretical? . . .

STUDENT: The role of the principles of experience. Practical reason seeks to give principles of . . .

MCKEON: Is he saying you seek your principles in the theoretic from experience? . . . Yes?

STUDENT: No, because they don't have correspondence with the events.

MCKEON: Do you think that in the practical perhaps you can get to a rule of action which has no correspondence to anything that is done, can be done, and so forth?

STUDENT: Well, you can decide whether or not any act conforms to the right rule.

MCKEON: You mean, he can be a scoundrel and still be moral? We could take it or leave it—if he's not wise, if he's not a good physicist?

STUDENT: Practice determines the source?

MCKEON: Practice determines the source of a principle? That's *exactly* what all this book is written to demonstrate is absurd. . . . Yes?

STUDENT: Well, the practical, the common judgment of men, is likely to be more clear—more correct than—it's likely to be correct so that morality . . .

MCKEON: Once we get this difference . . .

STUDENT: [. . . ?]

MCKEON: . . . we can go into whether the common judgment of man is correct or not, but the difference is what we need first.

STUDENT: In the theoretic, you're concerned with what is; whereas in the practical, you're concerned with what ought to be.

MCKEON: Do you think Kant would hold with this notion, which has wide currency today? What's the difference between the two?

STUDENT: In the practical, [. . . ?]

MCKEON: This class is illustrating the way in which the transition of philosophy to something practical is fearsomely theoretical. [L!] I think that possibly if we were in the theoretical, you might have made an answer that I would have accepted; but in the practical, it's quite clear that the transition of philosophy is full of confusion.

STUDENT: Well, in the transition to philosophy, we will be more sure about our actions.

MCKEON: No. We will still in our moral life have as much uncertainty and impermanence as before, but we will have gotten something. Let me read it again: "But in the practical sphere it is just when the common understanding excludes all principled springs from the practical laws that its power of judgment begins to show itself to advantage." What does that mean if I am thinking of a problem and I say, "I will leave out the empirical?" What is the empirical in judgment? It is inclination, desire, want. At the moment when I leave them out, then I can begin reasoning. In the case of the theoretic, if I try to do that, leaving the empirical out, what do I have? Well, I'd have to be an awfully good mathematician, because I'd have to think completely abstractly; whereas what I need to do is to think just as purely and just as *a priori*, but I can do it better by bringing the empirical in. That's why, when I demonstrate a proposition about a right-angled triangle, I draw a picture of the right-angled triangle. I'm not talking about that picture on the board; the picture on the board doesn't conform to the laws that I have set up. But in setting up true, *a priori* judgments, as soon as I leave experiences in the theoretic, I get confused. By contrast, in the practical, as soon as I leave the empirical, namely, the pull of my passions, I'm clear. Isn't that what he's saying? And this is exactly what you've all not been telling me, the normal reaction of the class when I get through yelling at them.

If this is the case—you notice, to be subtle, the ordinary man now has as much hope as the philosopher of hitting the mark; it's almost true that he can be more sure. Why shouldn't we just stay with common reason, then, and not make this transition to the philosophical analysis?

GREEN: Because when man does begin to think or begins to reason about morals and the basis of morals, he is very easily deceived. He begins a process of dialectic, and the analysis of the principles of morality will give assurance to the basic soundness of his prior grasp of morality, a firmness and a . . .

MCKEON: What is the difference between the two dialectics?

GREEN: There are two dialectics?

MCKEON: Yeah. Natural man engages in a dialectic; we're going to engage in one, too.

GREEN: Well, this is a dialectic, he calls it a natural dialectic, to argue against the strict moral principle, and it's an attempt to kind of—to rationalize it in such a way as to be able to follow our inclinations.

MCKEON: All right. And what will the philosophical do?

GREEN: Well, the philosophical is going to give—is going to give the—the moral duties that—that are in the common feelings of man. He's going to show that this has—that this has . . .

MCKEON: And in the opposition that occurs between inclination and duty, the dialectic of the philosophic approach will give the arguments for duty; and therefore, you have a chance. Otherwise, in the natural dialectic, the principle of duty has strong forces against it.

So, we've made our transition. Bear in mind, we've done three things. First, we identified the only thing that is good; namely, it's the good will. Second, we've identified the good will by giving an action which becomes a principle without a consideration of consequences or motivation. And finally, we have shown how this philosophical consideration can reduce perplexity of opposite claims when there is a pull against the moral principle. We go on to the second section now, which is the "Transition from the Popular Moral Philosophy"—which we have just achieved—"to the Metaphysics of Morals." Remember, we will go from the metaphysics of morals to the critical philosophy in the third section. The second section is divided into three parts. The first part runs from page 23 [B:66] in your edition to the bottom of 38 [B:76]. It's the second part I'd like to get into. The first part is going to be divided into two subparts, also, but you need not make that further division. Tell me what he does in this first long part; and again, it's the argument that I'm interested in. We haven't identified Kant's method yet. Mr. Reser?

RESER: He argues that there is an insufficiency of popular moral philosophy, and that . . .

MCKEON: The insufficiency of popular moral philosophy?

RESER: Its use of the empirical . . .

MCKEON: I beg your pardon?

RESER: It uses experience.

MCKEON: Well, does popular moral philosophy use experience?

RESER: [. . . ?]

MCKEON: Listen, he starts off by saying that he has derived the concept of duty from the common use of practical reason but not an empirical concept. Does this mean that the popular conception of duty is an empirical concept?

RESER: [. . . ?]

MCKEON: Speak up, I . . .

RESER: It mixes in. . . .

MCKEON: It mixes in.

RESER: . . . from experience.

MCKEON: Is this the general impression? . . . Yes?

STUDENT: He makes a distinction between acting according to duty and . . .

McKEON: No, no, this will come later on. It is perfectly true that this first part is an argument that there's no genuine supreme principle of morality except one based on pure reason. What is he trying to say here? Does he say that therefore, the popular moral philosophy is not based on pure reason?

STUDENT: It's based on pure reason; it's not based on empirical reason.

McKEON: The difference is between *a priori* and—he doesn't speak frequently of *a posteriori*—he usually calls that empirical. What's the difference between those two?

STUDENT: *A priori* is empirical . . .

McKEON: *A priori* is not empirical.

STUDENT: *A priori* is a proposition—a proposition which connects two ideas which . . .

McKEON: On the contrary . . .

STUDENT: It might be proven, then.

McKEON: It can't be proven; that's why it's *a priori*. There are two ways—let me, instead of doing it on the up and down lines, let me do it this way. An event occurs—I'm stating the theoretic, now—an event occurs, and a whole series of consequences occur. That event is then the cause of these effects (see fig. 35).[4] If I reason back from the effects to the cause, this is *a posteriori* or empirical. My only knowledge of the cause is that there must have been a cause to account for it. If, on the other hand, I know the cause, I can reason from the cause to the effects, and this is *a priori*. I know the cause now. In the Middle Ages, the *a priori* and the *a posteriori* were contrasted by two different ways. The empirical is merely knowledge *that*. The *a priori* is knowledge *because of what*; and if, therefore, at any time you know the law of nature and go on to the effects, this is the *a priori*. If, likewise, in a difficult situation you have a sense of your duty and you're not confusing this with what your mother told you or what you read in the Good Book, this is *a priori*. It is *a priori* because the connection between the subject and the predicate is seen immediately and does not depend on induction. Anytime you have a conviction that a statement is universally true, it's got to be *a priori*, according to Kant, because you can't from the *a posteriori* get a universal, necessary proposition. So this is the difference between them.

And you notice that as a result, since—or let me take it one step further. We've agreed that this is a reflexive principle. How do I know that this is true? That is, if I say that the *a priori* is a necessary truth, what's the reflexive principle do to this?

a priori	reasoning from cause to effect	knowledge *because of what*
a posteriori	reasoning from effect to cause	knowledge *that*

Fig. 35 *Distinction between* A Priori *and* A Posteriori

STUDENT: It's from the cause to the effect which reflects it.

MCKEON: How does that reflect it? *Reflexive* means something acting on itself.

STUDENT: Well, it's the relationship between cause and effect that is reflexive.

MCKEON: If the cause is reflexive simply, it would have to be like Spinoza's cause, that is, cause of itself: *causa sui* is a reflexive cause, it causes itself. Kant isn't saying that, is he?

STUDENT: To deny it would be self-contradictory.

MCKEON: That doesn't make it reflexive. There are lots of philosophers who hold that there are necessary truths that you can't deny; when you deny such truths, you'd be involved in a contradiction or self-contradiction. A self-contradiction is not a reflexive principle; he didn't have any trouble with the alternative. . . . Yes.

STUDENT: Maybe it's circular reasoning?

MCKEON: The only reason why it's a circle is because it's a circle? [L!] And a small circle is a vicious circle? [L!] . . . All right, what's reflexive in this whole business?

GREEN: Well, the reason . . .

MCKEON: Reason—practical reason, up here on the *a priori* level, or the will. What is the will going to do?

GREEN: It'll give a law to itself.

MCKEON: It's going to impose freely a law on itself which it finds itself. And in general, the ways in which we get any of our principles for Kant are by examining the forms of thought. If we were in the theoretic part, we'd examine the categories of the mind, and from the mind's knowledge of itself you would know how it knows anything. But here, we would be dealing with the will.

I hadn't—let me rephrase that question. In the case of the ordinary man acting according to duty, without even yet having gotten to popular rational knowledge, is this reflexive principle working?

GREEN: Sure it is.

MCKEON: Sure. Consequently, it's *a priori*. The only time the ordinary man needs the philosopher is when he loses his grasp, begins going *a posteriori*, and lets his inclination start a natural dialectic with him.

Then, the popular moral philosopher, that is, the popular form of philosopher, will help him out and make the principle stick, and then it's *a priori* again. Isn't this clear?

GREEN: Make it stick, or it could also clarify it. That is, the common knowledge is not a principle you state clearly; and as a result, you sometimes might have to clarify it as well as ground it.

MCKEON: We will eventually find that there is only one principle, and then we have to go on and find out the various ways in which it's formulated. It needs various formulations as expressions of clarifying it, but that's part of the dialectic. The dialectic begins to work against the principle when inclinations have the man confused.

Well, this is what we are engaged in, then, all during this first part of the second section. There's a footnote [B:70] in which he says that pure practical philosophy or the metaphysics of morals is related to applied morals in the same way that mathematics is divided into the pure and the applied. Consequently, we will not work from examples, we will not use imitations: you need to test your examples by the principle. So, all of this is our first step. "All moral concepts have their seat and origin completely *a priori* in reason"—page 31 [B:71]—the commonest reason or speculative reason. If you wanted to nail it down, he couldn't possibly have said it more clearly. Moreover, it's going to be the pure practical reason not merely of man but of a rational being. The applications will bring in anthropology, but these are applications for man and not the principles of pure practical reason. "Our steps, therefore"—and this is the end of that subpart, on 32 [B:72], the first half of this first part of the second section—"we will advance not merely from common moral judgment to the philosophical but now from the popular philosophical to the metaphysical." Therefore, from 33 to 38 [B:72–76], he makes a series of distinctions with respect to the practical law which are essential to his argument in the second part of this second section. What distinctions do we need to make in the practical law in order to get going? Miss Stern?[5]

Discussion Summary

We can get at the distinctions in the practical law by asking, What is the difference between human beings and dogs? Humans can be rational beings, whereas animals act solely from desires. Desires are on the level of the empirical, the *a posteriori*, but to act *a priori* according to will is not aimed at getting something for oneself. Nevertheless, animals do act according to law. Therefore, we must differentiate the theoretical, which is the realm of necessity, from the practical, which is the realm of freedom. Say a human does something according to duty. We can lay down the causal chain involved so that everything one does, one does necessarily; yet freedom is not a contradiction of that necessity. The action follows from deep-seated nature, but one can also be held responsible, because there is another requirement: one must have chosen it freely. Hume, too, held that freedom and necessity don't contradict, so it's important to seek the sense of freedom involved.

So, to act according to the conception of law does not mean just knowing the law and then applying it. That would be merely treating it only on the theoretic level. If one had a moral problem, someone might know what to do; yet the act must still be worked out in terms of duty, or else it would not be acting for the sake of, that is, from, duty. Duty goes with freedom. Acting according to the conception of a law is acting for the sake of the law. If practical reason is the same as the will, we get two consequences. If one acts according to the law, we go through a sequence of things, which corresponds to empirical results, the empirical level. If, however, one acts for the sake of the law, that is, according to the concept, the end is the good will, and one acts for this end. You go through the necessary sequence, but the end is the good will.

Next, Kant introduces the terms *command* and *imperative*: "The conception of an objective principle, so far as it constrains a will, is a command (of reason), and the formula of this command is called an *imperative*" [B:72]. A command, then, is a conception of an objective principle as it operates on the will; whereas an imperative is subjective, a formula applying the command in a particular case. Thus, any maxim is subjective and can be made objective only when it can be phrased as a command. He goes on to distinguish three kinds of imperatives (see table 13).[6] There are two main kinds of imperative: the hypothetical and the categorical. The hypothetical imperative deals with actions which aim at some end outside the action itself, so that the actions are means to some other end. The categorical imperative has the doing of the action itself as its end, so that it is the basis of an act done for itself without regard to any other purpose or result. The hypothetical imperative is itself divided into two forms. One has a problematic principle and is a technical imperative; it can deal with the solutions of possible problems and thus has a specific end which may be treated with skill. The other hypothetical imperative has an assertoric principle and is a pragmatic imperative; it assumes an end which is sought by all rational creatures, namely, happiness. The categorical imperative, by contrast, is not concerned with an end and result other than itself, its form; this is the imperative that treats of morality.

Table 13. Kinds of Imperatives.

Imperatives	Principles	End	Kind	Character	Application
Hypothetical (Action Good for Some End)	Problematic	Possible (Solution of Problems)	Technical Imperative	Rules of Skill	Belonging to Art
	Assertoric	Actual (Happiness)	Pragmatic Imperative	Counsels of Prudence	Belonging to Welfare
Categorical (Action Good in Itself)	Apodictic	Form(Itself)	Moral Imperative	Commands (Laws) of Morality	Belonging to Free Conduct (Morals)

How are all these imperatives possible [B:76]? The question is not one of whether we can conceive of actions which the imperative calls for; rather, it is one of how we can conceive of the obligation of the will which the imperative expresses. That is not an issue with the first two kinds of imperative, because they both, by willing the end, also necessarily will the means; therefore, since both are thereby analytic in character, neither of these imperatives raise a problem of conceivability. However, Kant must investigate the possibility of the third kind of imperative, that of morality, though not its actuality [B:78]; and he must do that *a priori,* because it cannot be derived from experience, which is always conditional [B:79]. Consequently, the categorical imperative alone is a practical law or imperative, because the hypothetical imperatives are all conditional as principles of the will and not based on the necessity required by law. Finally, this imperative is especially difficult, because it is an *a priori* synthetic practical proposition.

He begins his analysis with an argument that only one categorical imperative is possible, namely, "Act only according to the maxim by which you can at the same time will that it should become a universal law" [B:80]. Then, to examine whether "all imperatives of duties can be derived from this one imperative as a principle," he goes on to test this imperative by listing four kinds of duties, dividing them into duties to self and to others and into perfect and imperfect duties [B:81–82], and giving examples for each (see fig. 36).[7] Exploring the first two examples, involving suicide and false promise to secure a loan, he finds that the actions called for cannot be made into an imperative, because they are self-contradictory. The latter two, neglect of one's talents and indifference to the welfare of others, are equally impossible to conceive of as being an imperative, because one simply could not will them to be such.[8]

	Self	Other
Perfect Duty	Suicide	Loan
Imperfect Duty	Talents	Welfare

Fig. 36 *Test of Duties*

Discussion

MCKEON: If Kant had shown that all forms of duty could be divided into four kinds, and therefore by trying out these four kinds and showing that anything except duty won't work to explain them, he would have accomplished something that would look like a method, wouldn't he? Too bad he didn't do that. [L!]

We'll begin next time and see whether there's any way in which we could make this into a method. In other words, we will be beginning here, and we will dash madly through the rest of the second section next time.

McKeon's Notes

Kant. Fundamental Principles of Metaph of Morals 1,3.

Only what is connected with my will as a principle, (19) *16* not as effect, but what does not subserve my inclinations, i.e. the law of itself, which can be an object of *respect* (as opposed to *approval* or even *love*).

In action done from duty, will determined *objectively* the law, and *subjectively* by *pure respect for this practical law*, maxim—follow law, thwart inclination.

A maxim is the subjective principle of volition. The *objective principle* is the practical law. *(note 1) p 17*

Moral worth not in effect or in principle depending on effect; *supreme and unconditioned* good found in will itself. Pre-eminent good—conception of law itself, possible only in a rational being. This is a good already present in the person who acts accordingly. *note 2 p. 17–18*

Respect not a feeling received, but *self-wrought* by rational concept. *Immediate determination of will by law and consciousness* of it called respect. *Respect the conception of a worth which thwarts self-love*. Object of respect law only, *law which we impose on ourselves, yet recognize as necessary*. *As law we are subjected to it without consulting self-love; as imposed by us on ourselves, it is a result of our will.* *18* (20)

Nothing remains to serve as a *principle* of the will except universal conformity of its action to law as such, which alone is to serve the will as a principle i.e. *never act otherwise* than so that I could also will that my maxim should become a universal law.

Ex. *Lying*, distinguish *prudence* and *duty*. Prudence calculation of consequences; duty very notion (21) of the action already implies a law for me. Can will the lie but not the universal law.

My maxim destroys itself. *19.*

Test—can I will maxim as universal law? cannot (22) enter as a principle into a possible universal legislation. Estimation of worth that outweighs worth of inclination. Pure respect for the practical law constitutes duty.—condition of will be good in itself.

(c) Without quitting moral knowledge of common human reason have arrived at its principle. *(21) 20*

Not conceived as *abstract universal* form, *but compass* to distinguish good and evil. Like Socrates we direct their attention to principle they employ. Do not need science or philosophy.

Advantage of the practical faculty over the theoretic (23) *20*

Theoretic—common reason cannot venture to depart from the laws of experience—inconceivabilities and contradictions.

Practical—power of judgment first shows itself to advantage when common understanding excludes all sensuous incentives from practical laws.

Subtle—ordinary ~~way~~ *man* as much hope as the philosopher of hitting the mark; almost more sure. *21*

Would it not be wiser to acquiesce in judgment of common reason, using philosophy to render systems of morals more complete and intelligible, and its rules more convenient for use (especially for disputation), but not to lead common understanding to new path of inquiry and instruction?

Innocence easily led astray. Therefore wisdom needs (24) *21* science. Not to learn from it but to secure for its precepts admission and permanence.

Against all commands *of duty*, counterpoise of *wants* and inclinations. Reason issues its commands unyieldingly. Thence natural dialectic**[9] a disposition to argue against those strict laws of duty and question their validity, at least their purity and strictness. *p. 22*

Common reason of man compelled to go out of its sphere and to take a step into the field of practical philosophy, not for speculative reasons—but on *practical grounds*, to secure *information and clear instruction* respecting the source of its principle, and the correct determination of it in opposition to maxims based on wants and inclinations.

Escape from the perplexity of opposite claims—risk of losing moral principles through equivocation.

When practical reason cultivates itself, a dialectic arises in it which forces it to seek aid in philosophy—through critical examination of our reason.

Kant Fundamental Principles of Metap. of Morals 2,1.

Second Section. Transition from Popular Moral Philosophy to the Metaphysic of Morals. *22* (p. 24)

I (a) Derivation thus far of *concept of duty* from common *(24)* use of practical reason—but not an *empirical concept*

Impossible by experience to discern with complete certainty a single case of action from duty as well as in conformity with duty. Hidden *self-love*. *23* (26)

Moreover endanger morality by conceding that notion of *(24)* duty must be drawn from *experience*. *Secure* idea of *(25)* duty by *clear conviction*, that although no action ever sprang from such pure sources, nonetheless *reason itself*, independent of all experience, ordains what ought to be done. *24* (27) *(25)*

Add that notion of morality has truth or reference of any possible object only if its law valid not only for men but for *all rational* creatures *generally*, not contingently but with *absolute necessity* (i.e. *all*, and *absolutely*). No experience could enable us to infer even the possibility of such apodictic laws.

Moreover nothing more fatal to morality than to derive it from *examples*. Examples must first be tested by principles. *moral perfection and free will* *5* (28) *(26)*

Imitation no place in morality; *examples* for encouragement.

No genuine supreme *principle of morality except when based on pure reason*. Difference between descending to popular notions after ascent to principles of pure reason (i.e. found metaphysics and then give it *26* (29) popular hearing), and attempt to be popular in establishing principles—absurd medley of *observations* and half-reasoned principles.

Principles sought in human nature, rational nature, *(27)* God, happiness, moral sense—instead of asking whether the principles of morality should be sought in human nature—or *apart from the empirical*.

Note [Pure practical philosophy or metaphysics of morals and applied *morals*—like mathematics, pure and applied. *26* (30) *(29)*

Consciousness of *worth* of pure conception of duty *27* or of moral law—contrasted to mixed ethics partly drawn from feelings and inclinations, partly from the conceptions of reason. *28* (31)

(N.B. method of discrimination—separation of *a priori* from *experience*; as discrimination in the popular dialectic of First Section.)—*inclination and duty*

All moral concepts have their seat and origin completely a priori in reason,—commonest reason or speculative (31) *28*

Cannot be abstracted from experience; purity of origin source of their worth as supreme principle.

Not make principles of *pure practical* reason depend on the particular nature of human reason (permitted in speculative philosophy) but on the *general concept* of a *rational* being. Application needs anthropology.

Steps—advance from common moral judgment to philosophical (Section I), now from popular philosophical to metaphysical (Section 2). Present the faculty of (32) practical reason from the general rules of its determination to the emergence of the concept of duty.

(b). Everything operates according to laws; man alone according to the *concept of laws*, i.e. according to principles. *Will nothing but practical reason.*
29 (30) (33)

If reason does not infallibly determine the will, actions objectively necessary, subjectively contingent. Determination of fallible will to objective laws is obligation. *(30)*

Objective principle (of reason) a *command*; formula of the command an *Imperative*.

Ought—relation of objective law of reason to will, which from subjective constitution is not determined by an obligation. Valid for every rational being—as distinguished from *pleasant*—means sensation from merely subjective causes valid only for one. *(30)* (34)

Note 1. Dependence of desires on sensations called *inclination* and indicates want. Dependence of contingently determined will on principles of reason called interest. Reason may take an interest in anything without acting from interest.

No imperatives for Divine will or for holy will—volition already necessarily in unison with law.

Imperatives—formulae to express relation of objective laws of all volition to subjective imperfection of particular wills. *(31)*

Hypothetical and Categorical imperatives. Hypothetical—practical necessity of action as means to something else willed; categorical—represent action as necessary of itself without reference to other end, i.e. objectively necessary. *(31) 32*

Kant Fundamental Principles of Met. of Morals 2,2.

Practical law—possible action as good, therefore necessary for subject practically determined by reason. *(31)* (35) *32*

Hypothetical imperative—action good for some *31* purpose, possible (problematical practical principles) or actual (assertorial)

Categorical imperative—action necessary without reference to any purpose (apodictive principle). *(32)*

1. Problematic principles—all sciences have a practical part—general *imperatives of skill*. No question of whether the end rational and good, only means.
(36) *32*

Physician and poisoner. Education of children in many things—possible ends.

2. Assertoric principle. One end assumed to actually such [*sic*] to all rational creatures. Happiness. *(33)*

Skill in choice of means to own well-being—*prudence*.

(Note 1. private prudence and knowledge of world.) (37)

3. Categorical imperative—not matter or result of action but its form—morality. *(33)*

Also difference between volitions on these three sorts of principles in dissimilarity of obligation of the will.

1. Rules of skill—*technical* imperatives (art).
2. Counsels of prudence—*pragmatic imp.* (welfare)
3. Commands (laws) of morality—moral imperatives free conduct generally.

(34) (38)

II 38 (34) Question—how are these imperatives possible? not how we can conceive accomplishment of actions which imperative ordains but how we *can conceive* the obligation of the will which the imperative expresses.

1. Imperative of skill—analytical. Imperative educes from conception of the volition of an end the conception of actions necessary. Synthetical propositions to define means.
2. Pragmatic imperative. *(35)* Notion of happiness indefinite, therefore *not analytical*. Elements of happiness almost altogether empirical, yet idea of absolute whole, maximum of welfare in present and all *35* (39) future circumstances. Imperatives of prudence not in strict sense command. Happiness ideal not of *36* (40) *reason* but *imagination*. *Analytic*—end willed means ordained.
3. How the imperative of morality is possible is *36* (40) the only question that requires answer. Cannot make out possibility 41 *37* by any example. Thus not promise deceitfully

a. We shall have to investigate a priori the possibility of a categorical imperative—reality not given in experience. *Categorical imperative alone a practical law*; other imperative principles of the will but not laws—can be free from the precept. 42 Categorical imperative unconditional law, no *liberty* to choose opposite; necessity required of law.

b. Difficulty that it is an a priori synthetical practical proposition. Difficulty of discerning possibility of speculative and practical propositions of this sort.

I First inquire whether the mere conception of a categorical imperative may not also supply us with a formula of it,

ii containing the proposition which alone can be a categorical imperative (second section)

iii How it is possible—third section. *(38)*

i ~~Categorical~~ *Hypothetical* imperative in general, do not know its content until given the condition. Conceive a categorical imperative, know what it contains—besides the law only the necessity ~~of~~ *that* the maxim. *accord with law. Note 38* (Maxim—*subjective principle of action*; *objective principle, practical law*. Maxim contains the practical rule set by reason according to the conditions of the subject (often its ignorance or its inclinations) principle on which the subject acts; *law* the *objective principle* valid for every rational being, principle on which it ought to act—imperative.)

Maxim of the action should conform to universal law. *38* (43)

[Only one categorical imperative—act only on that maxim whereby thou canst at the same time will that it should become a universal law.

If all imperatives of duty can be *deduced* from this one imperative as from their principle—know what we mean by it even though we don't know whether to call it duty.

a.~~1.~~ Since *universality of the law* according to which effects are produced constitutes nature in most general sense (as to form) imperative of duty may be expressed: Act as if the maxim of thy action were to become by thy will a Universal Law of Nature. *(38)*

DISCUSSION

Kant, Part 4
(*Fundamental Principles of the Metaphysics of Morals*, Second Section: Transition from Popular Moral Philosophy to the Metaphysic of Morals; Third Section: Transition from the Metaphysic of Morals to the Critique of Pure Practical Reason)

Discussion Summary[1]

Today we will finish our discussion of Kant and the metaphysics of morals. Let me begin by reminding you of our discussion of the first and second sections so far.

In the first section, we made the transition from the ordinary tradition of morality to popular moral philosophy. In the process, Kant sets up three propositions which give the imperatives of popular moral philosophy, and he also shows how those imperatives help the natural dialectic of reason and inclination clarify problems of action and duty when encountered. In the second part of the second section, he goes on to ask, How are the imperatives possible? [A:34; B:76][2] Having just distinguished three kinds of imperative in the first part of the second section, he shows how the hypothetical ones are easy. The difficulty arises with the categorical imperative, and he gives three formulations to the categorical imperative. We are going to want to ask, Why?

Recall that the three propositions of the first section were: (1) "to have moral worth, an action must be done from duty" [A:17; B:61]; (2) it must have a "maxim by which it is determined"; and (3) it must be "done from respect for the law" [A:18; B:61], that is, because of the maxim—note the reflexive character of this last proposition. In this first section, then, because we were trying not to act morally but, rather, to get a popular moral philosophy, we have an expression of that philosophy, we have propositions. Notice, also, that by this point we had already begun to suggest our principle, method, and interpretation. Now, turning to the second section, that is, moving to the metaphysics of morals, Kant says that his purpose is to establish his principle. He states explicitly that he needs to use an *a priori* approach, one which will be analytic in the first two sections, that is, moving away from the data of experience in order to establish the principle, and then synthetic in the third section [A: 37–38; B:79–80].[3]

So, having set up three propositions in the first section, we will now relate them to a principle. The question becomes, then, How do they relate to a principle? In the case of the third proposition, having to do with respect for the law, reflexivity appears in that the maxim is to be reflexively applied to itself. In the case of the second proposition, regarding the maxim itself, we now see that it is restated, namely, that one should always act so as to regard other men as an end, never as a means only—notice now he is working in the question of ends and means here. Finally, in the case of the first proposition, which was about duty, we will here come to see the universality of the law. Recall that in the discussion of these propositions, he began by saying, with regard to duty, that neither intention, in the sense of an empirical motive, nor consequence make an action good: an action is good only if done from duty—the center of our figure (see fig. 29). As a duty, all men have this duty. If so, to make this an imperative, what do we need to do? In the second section, to make this the first imperative, the action can't be only for the agent; it must be a universal law and not particular to the individual. We must broaden the scope of the act. In this section, the second proposition, one requiring a maxim, leads to an imperative which, because maxims can differ in many ways, must be general in character. The first imperative, remember, only stipulated that the maxim be universal. To make our maxim of such a character, we cannot talk of separating means and ends; rather, the maxim must guarantee that the person involved must be conceived as an end, not only as a means.

Finally, our third proposition insisted that action according to the maxim must be out of respect for it. Here in the second section, this gets translated into a form of the categorical imperative. Note that each of the three forms of the categorical imperative guards against a danger. In this case, where in the first section Kant treated this proposition regarding duty as based on respect for the law, an inclination, here respect is what Kant is trying to move away from. He wants it to have worth, a value in itself. Thus, the categorical imperative in this case is reflexive in the sense of the will legislating its own action. As a free agent, we are to give a necessary law to ourselves. These two aspects, then, freedom and

	Self	Other
Perfect	Suicide	False promises
Imperfect	Neglected talents	Indifference

Fig. 37 *Second Test of Duties*

necessity, are what, in fact, characterize this imperative: if it isn't free or if it isn't necessary, it is not a categorical imperative.

He will test the universality of this form of the imperative—"Act as though the maxim of your action were by your will to become a universal law of nature" [A:38; B:80]—by an examination of four sets of duties, divided into duties perfect and imperfect, to self and to others—internal and external (see fig. 37; cf. fig. 36).[4] When he examines the perfect duties, he finds that by making either set a maxim, one cannot think of them as a universal law without contradiction. Notice, this method might appear odd, because he could have taken duties which correspond to inclination, but instead took ones where inclination and duty do not correspond. For instance, it is a contradiction to take suicide as a universal maxim. In the case of false promises, the promise itself would not be impossible—it's certainly possible to fool someone—but it would be a contradiction to make that a universal law. By contrast, the imperfect duties do not involve logical contradiction. However, in the case of neglecting one's talents, all men could neglect their talents and the system of nature would continue. It could be a universal law, but a person couldn't will it as a rational being, even though it is possible without contradiction to conceive all mankind as not developing its talents. Similarly with indifference to others' welfare, one could conceive of it without contradiction but could not, as a rational being, will it. Notice how this introduces the concept of the autonomy *versus* the heteronomy of the will, which is the topic of the final part of this second section, as is shown in the headings to that part.

Recall that Kant is not deriving this universal law, his principle, empirically. At the end of the first section and into the beginning of the second section [A:22–25; B:65–67], he explicitly states he is deriving the concept of duty from practical reason and not empirically, not from experience.

He will seek its principle *a priori,* because no supreme principle of morality is possible except one based on pure reason; as he says, it "can be abstracted from no empirical and hence merely contingent cognitions" [A:29; B:71]. Therefore, when he gets to the second part of the second section, his question—"How is it possible?"—must be shown *a priori* and not empirically. Notice, that it must be *a priori* is a problem only for the categorical imperative, because nothing which we have ever experienced may be brought in. *How* it is possible will be even more of a problem, because it is, in addition, a synthetic judgment.

So, looking at all of this, what is the method that we are using? Is this nonsense or not? Let's remove the strangeness of it. At the beginning of the second part of the second section [A:34–35; B:76–77], he observes that it is a problem how we can even think of such a rule. The first step is to inquire whether the mere conception of a categorical imperative may also give us a formula for it which will provide us with its content. That is, we will give it first a form and then subsequently a content. In other words, our first step will be empty, merely an imperative, which is the opposite of the hypothetical. He says he will postpone to the end of this second part of the second section the question, "How is it possible?" He will begin by asking, "Is it possible?" His starting point is empty. That is, in the case of the hypothetical imperatives, you don't know the content until given some condition; in other words, the content is given by circumstances. By contrast, we want to conceive of a categorical imperative, and what should it contain? Besides the law, which is universal, that is, unconditional, it contains the necessity that the maxim of the act conform to universal law. Consequently, he can give us his first formulation—there is only one categorical imperative: "Act only according to that maxim by which you can at the same time will that it should become a universal law" [A:38; B:80]. If all the imperatives of duty can be deduced from this one as a principle, we will know what we mean by a categorical imperative and by duty. Then we can go on to inquire whether it is possible.

Kant immediately changes the form of the categorical imperative he has just stated. It now becomes "Act as though the maxim of your action were by your will to become a universal law of nature" [A:38; B:80]. Recall that in our distinction of the different kinds of knowledge (see fig. 38), we are on the practical side and on the pure level, which has given us our ontological interpretation. We now want a moral law that is a universal imperative, but the only kind of universal imperatives we know are theoretic. Therefore, we ask what would it look like as a universal law of nature. We find that it will give us a way of thinking about a categorical imperative, one which also leads to Kant's reflexive principle. We will take this as our first formula.

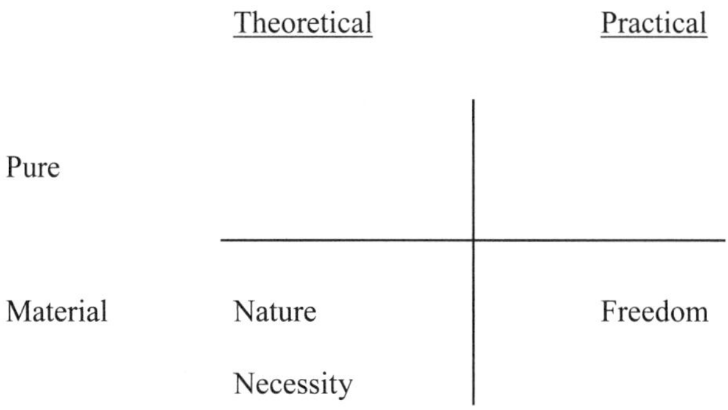

Fig. 38 *Kinds of Knowledge*

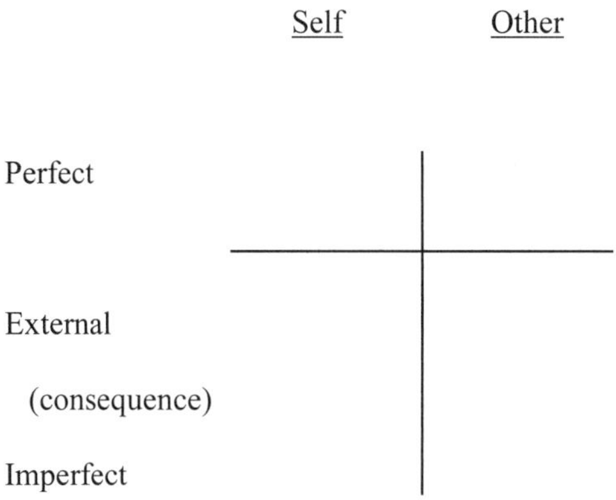

Fig. 39 *Basic Scheme of Duties*

He then enumerates his four kinds of duties on a similar scheme. How does he get this? He says in a footnote [A:39; B:80–81] that his division of duties will be defended in a future work on the metaphysics of morals. Here it is merely an arbitrary list, but it does provide formal exhaustiveness despite not saying what the duties are (see fig. 39). The list is divided into two classes. The first class, the perfect, cannot be thought of ("conceived") as a universal law without contradiction. For instance, the first duty is based on self-love; and if suicide were a universal law, the motive designed to keep man going would wipe him out. By contrast, the second class does not involve such logical contradiction; nevertheless, they cannot work because we cannot *will* them.

What have we accomplished by this first step in the method? He answers with a summary on page 42 [A:42; B:83]. We have thus far established at least this much: if duty is to have importance for our actions, it can only be expressed in a categorical imperative; in addition, we have also exhibited the content for every practical imperative. However, we have not yet proved *a priori* that there actually *is* such an imperative, that it commands absolutely, and that obedience is a duty. Still, what we have done is to give a form which is universal if morals are to be like a law of physics, are to be based on a metaphysics. He makes an additional point: the reality of this principle cannot be deduced from human nature, although its possibility can be examined [A:42–43; B:83–84]. That is, he has brought philosophy to a critical point, because it must be fixed without empirical support. Every empirical element is prejudicial to the purity of morals that he seeks.

He now poses the question, Is it? Thus far we have determined that the maxim must be a universal law. Now, if it is such a law, it must be connected *a priori* with the will of rational beings. Notice, he says that this is a step into metaphysics, not into that of speculative philosophy but into that of the practical philosophy of morals; and in the latter case, we are not going to give reasons for what happens but, rather, give laws of what ought to happen, even if it never does. So, we have a transition: we bring in that it is the will which is to do the legislating. Earlier he has shown that the will is the only thing good in itself and that it is a "faculty of acting in accordance with the conception of certain laws" [A:44; B:85]. So, what Kant wants here is laws that are going to be reflections of that good will.

He gives the second restatement of the categorical imperative: "So act as to treat humanity, whether in thine own person or in that of any other, in every case as an end withal, never as means only" [A:46; B:87]. He proceeds to take again the figure we saw earlier (see fig. 39) and, in the case of each of the duties set up by means of contraries, to ask whether we are treating the person as a means or as an end. Notice, the notion that rational creatures are ends in themselves is not derived from experience—he insists on this. He then goes on to examine three principles of the will, of the categorical imperative. First, the objective principle is the rule, and its form as universal. The second principle is that the subject of all ends is each rational being, the treatment of humanity as an end. Finally, the third principle is "the idea of the will of every rational being as a universally legislative will" [A:48; B:89]. Since "the will is subject to law and law-giving" [ibid.], this third formulation exhibits clearly Kant's reflexive principle. Once again, none of these three formulae can prove that there *is* a categorical imperative, but if it exists, it can only be expressed in the third form. This form is well adapted to the categorical imperative because it is not based on interest [ibid.]. So, to repeat, we have not proved that this *is* the categorical imperative, but we do now have a candidate.

What's going on here with regard to method? This is clearly an example of the operational method. First it sets up a series of distinctions, like self/other. From there it tries to demonstrate—to show forth, to exhibit—and give the distinctions content. If the four kinds of duties did not work, he would simply say that they didn't give the ideas needed, and he would try some other distinctions. The function of these distinctions is to give both form and content that were not there before. By contrast, if we were talking about a logistic demonstration, he would first have given universal definitions and set up some axioms and a postulate set. Kant does use the word *deduce*, but he does not mean it in this logistic sense. Rather, he gives some contraries, say, in figure 38, and merely says what the categorical imperative is not, eliminating three slots on our chart. Then he can give formulations that suit the remaining compartment and show what that result would be like. Eventually we have, by means of a will that legislates and follows the law, by means of this very reflexivity, what the categorical imperative is. We can then apply this to any imperative by a deduction which shows whether or not the latter conforms to the categorical imperative.

This is a widely used method. Demonstrations usually do not conform to those in Euclid's *Elements*. For instance, Aristotle's deductions are syllogistic, not Euclidean. Here, in Kant's first section, popular philosophy gives us the means of arguing correctly when inclination might lead us into casuistry. But then, in the second section, Kant makes the transition to the metaphysics of duty and proceeds analytically to set up the principles of morals. These, however, will only be proved synthetically. This is clearly his method. You build a structure at the beginning that gives you a set of formal relations which are exhaustive. As you explore your words or terms, the meaning of each can vary. For instance, *freedom* is defined differently in the four parts. It one instance it is contingent; in another it is self-legislating of universal law. Or take necessity: it is originally found in the theoretic, but then it has a place in the practical. Or, again, law: in one section it is necessary, in another free. This is his method.

In his next step, Kant turns to the third main part of the second section [A:49; B:90]. The key distinction becomes what the difference is between autonomy and heteronomy of the will, and it proceeds on the same scheme as his treatment of the hypothetical and categorical imperatives. Autonomy is the supreme principle of morality, because it is the property of the will by which it is a law to itself—a reflexive principle. We can't prove that this practical rule is an imperative analytically, "by a mere analysis of the concepts occurring in it, because it is a synthetical proposition. To prove it, we would have to go beyond the knowledge of objects to a critical examination of the subject, i.e., of the pure practical reason"

[A:57; B:97]. We need a universality which isn't there in the individual will. We can show, however, that autonomy is the only principle of morality by means of an analysis of the concept of morality; that is, an analysis of morality shows that its principle must be a categorical imperative, and that what this imperative commands is autonomy. By contrast, heteronomy is connected with the hypothetical imperatives and is the principle of all spurious moralities. He classifies them on the next page as either rational or empirical. Let's translate his arguments here into the terms for principles which we have been using. The empirical hypothetical imperatives involve a loss of universality, because they are based either on the particular construction of human nature—this would be our simple principle—or on human nature in accidental circumstances—this is our actional principle. Notice, both empirical hypothetical imperatives are meroscopic. On the other hand, regarding the rational hypothetical imperatives, one he calls the "ontological" principle, which is empty and useless—a comprehensive principle—though still better than the other, the "theological," which focuses on divine will—a reflexive principle [A:59–60; B:99]. So, the rational hypotheticals are our two holoscopic principles. None of these four principles works, however, because, as hypothetical, they are based on the heteronomy of the human will.

How such a synthetical practical *a priori* proposition "is possible and why it is necessary is a problem whose solution does not lie within the boundaries of the metaphysics of morals" [A:61; B:101]. What he has done is show that for the absolutely good will, its principle must be the categorical imperative, whose foundation and form are that will's autonomy. Up to this point the argument has been analytic, but to go beyond this point it must be synthetic. Note that Kant's operational method is very definite: it is distinct from the dialectical method, totally distinct from the logistic, and not at all the problematic. From here it will go on to supply a reflexive principle synthetically.

The third section is entitled "Transition from the Metaphysics of Morals to the Critical Examination of Pure Practical Reason" [A:63; B:101]. Once more we have a step upwards; this time, though, we will begin with our principle and then show its applications. We proceed to explore how "The Concept of Freedom Is the Key to the Explanation of the Autonomy of the Will" [ibid.]. Notice that in the second section, Kant made use of the selection of thought to reinforce his ontological interpretation, and so on; in fact, each of his arguments uses all four of our columns, including here. Now, how does this "key" of freedom work here? We ended the second section with the need for a synthetic proposition, one where the subject and predicate are independent. In such case, freedom would be the key if it were the reason why the subject is connected to the predicate. So, Kant needs at the beginning of the third section to look for a synthetic proposition. This leads him to observe that "an absolutely good will is one whose maxim can always include itself as a universal law" [A:64; B:102]. This proposition is synthetic, because the predicate adds to the subject. How does freedom connect these two? You couldn't have a maxim that included the will unless the will freely legislated for itself. Thus, freedom synthetically connects the subject—will—and the predicate—the maxim. Notice, we can make no propositions about freedom itself, we can say nothing about it. What we can do, though, is demonstrate, by means of the concept of freedom, that this is duty.

Next time, we will move on to Mill's *On Liberty*. Focus on the introduction and chapter 2. Try to make use of our central distinctions: interpretation, method, and principle.

McKeon's Notes

Kant. Fundamental Principles of Metap. of Morals. 2,3.

Enumerate duties, divided into *duties to self* and to others, *perfect and imperfect*. (Division of duties *38* (43) reserved to metaphysics of morals—perfect admits no exception in favor of inclination; perfect duties internal and external). Cf. examples Sect. I, pp. 14–17.

1. *Suicide*—maxim cannot exist as universal law of nature. *Principle* founded on *self-love*. *39* (44)
   Perfect duty—self.
2. *False promise* to secure loan—principle of self-love and advantage. Contradictory as universal law
   Perfect duty, others. *40* (45)
3. *Neglect of talents*. System could exist with this as universal law, but cannot will it, as rational being.
   Imperfect duty, self.
4. Indifference to *welfare* of others. Possible as universal law—but impossible to will it.
   Imperfect duty, others. *41* (46)

Two classes—some cannot even be thought as universal laws without *contradiction*; some without *internal impossibility, impossible to will.* *41–2* (47)

In fact, in any transgression we do not will maxim as universal law, but assume *liberty* of making an exception to universal law.

Consider all cases from point of view of reason—*contradiction*, principle *objectively necessary* as universal law, *subjectively not* universal. Rather. Antagonism of inclination to *precept* of reason.

Proves that we do not *recognize the validity* of the categorical imperative. *42* (48)

Have *exhibited the content* of the categorical imperative, which must contain the principle of all duty, but have not *yet proved a priori that such an imperative exists, that there is a practical law* that commands absolutely of itself, and *that following this law is duty*.

b. ~~H.~~ *(ii) (42)* Reality of this principle cannot be deduced from the particular attributes of human nature. Duty is the practical unconditional necessity of action. Law for all human wills.

Philosophy must be firmly fixed without empirical *43* (49) support. Empirical incapable of aiding principle of morality—prejudicial. Principle of action is free from all influence from contingent grounds of experience.

Question—Is it a necessary law for all rational beings that they should always judge of their actions by maxims which they can themselves will that they should serve as universal laws? *40* (50)

If it is, *it must be connected (altogether a priori) with the very conception* of will of a rational being.

Step into metaphysics of morals. Not reasons of what happens, but laws of what ought to happen, even if it never does.

Not what pleases or displeases—empirical psychology. *If reason of itself necessarily determines conduct, it must be so a priori. Will is self[-activity?]*[5] *45*

Will—faculty of determining itself to action in accordance with the conception of certain laws. End given by reason alone; must hold for all rational beings. But that which contains the grounds of the possibility of action is the means. Subjective *45* (51) grounds the *incentive*; objective grounds the *motive*. Distinction valid for every rational being.

Practical principles are *formal* when they abstract from all subjective ends; *material* when they assume them. *Relative* ends, hypothetical imperatives.

Something whose *existence* has in *itself* an *absolute worth* alone the source of a possible categorical imperative.

Man as end in self. All his actions *directed to himself* or other rational beings, *man as end*. All objects of *46* (52) inclinations only conditional worth. Distinction of *things* and *persons*.

Supreme practical principle—*objective principle of the will from the conception of that which is necessarily an end for everyone because it is an end in itself.* *(46) (52–(53))*

ii ~~Third~~ *Second restatement of the categorical imperative—So act as to treat humanity, whether in thine own person* or in that of any other, in every case as an end withal, never as a means only. *Derive all laws of the will from it*.

Return to examples.

1. Suicide. Person as means. Nec. duty to self. *47*
2. Deceitful promise. Nec. duty to others. Ex. of freedom and property of others. *47*
3. Contingent (*meritorious*) duty to self. *48* (54)
4. *Meritorious* duty to others. Harmonize with *humanity* as end.

Kant. Fundamental Principles of Meta. of Morals. 2,4.

This principle that humanity and generally every rational *49* (55) nature is *an end in itself* (which is supreme limiting condition of every man's *freedom* of action) is not borrowed from experience because (1) it is universal and (2) it does not present humanity as an end to men (subjectively) but as an *objective end.*

Ciii. Three principles of that *objective principle* (i.e. three statements of categorical imperative)—(1) objective principle in the *rule* and its form of universality as law (cf. p. 43—will maxim as universal law) while subjective principle is the end; (2) subject of all ends is each rational being (p. 53—treat humanity as end); and (3) *third* principle, which is the ultimate condition as its *harmony with reason*—the idea of the will of every *rational being as a universally legislative will. (48) 49*

On this principle all maxims rejected which are inconsistent with the *will being itself universal self-legislative legislator. 49*

Will subject to law and law-giving.

First two imperatives (conformity of actions to general laws as in physical system of nature, and that *50* based on universal prerogative of rational beings as ends in themselves)—*only assumed* to be categorical, to explain conception of duty.

None of the three formulae can *prove that there is a categorical imperative*—but can be indicated in *third form* that in *volition from duty* all *interest is renounced*—i.e. by idea of will of rational being as a *universally legislating* will.

Will subject to law—interest; *will* as supreme lawgiver not dependent on interest.

This principle, if otherwise justified, well-adapted to be categorical imperative—because not based on interest and unconditional

In volition from duty the renunciation of all interest the *specific mark* of the *categorical imperative.*

III. ~~III.~~ ***57*** *51 (49)* Looking back at previous attempts—failed because they observed that man bound to laws by duty, *but not that the laws those of his own making, but universal.*

He is only bound to act in conformity with his own will.

Labor of finding supreme principle of duty lost, only necessity of acting from a certain interest.

Principle of *autonomy of will* vs principle of heteronomy. Leads to conception of *kingdom realm of ends*. Kingdom *realm* union of rational beings by laws.

(58) *51 (50)*

A rational being belongs as a member to the kingdom *realm* of *ends, when subject*, and as *sovereign, when giving* laws.

Kingdom of ends possible by *freedom* of the will.

Morality consists in reference of all action to *legislation* (51) that renders kingdom of ends possible. *Duty necessity of acting according to maxims as universal laws, since maxims not coincident with objective principle. End in itself, not interest.*

Duty applies to members not sovereign. *52* (59) *(51)*

In kingdom *realm* of ends everything has a *value* (something equivalent) or a *dignity* (above value).

General inclinations—*market value*; without want—affective *value*; end in itself—*dignity*. *53* (60) *(51)*

Morality is condition under which rational being can be end in himself. (52)

Skill and diligence—*market value.*

Wit, imagination—*affective value*. (fancy value).

Fidelity to promises, benevolence—*intrinsic worth*.

Morally good disposition and virtue *justified* because it permits rational beings to participate in giving universal laws and *legislating in kingdom of ends—free from laws of physical nature*. *54* (61) *(52)*

Nothing has any worth except what the law assigns it (cf. Hobbes). *(52)*

Legislation which assigns the worth must have dignity

Three ways of presenting principle of morality; different formulae of same law; all maxims have: *(53)*

1. *form*, universality—maxims chosen as if universal laws of nature. *54*
2. *matter*—rational being an end in self.
3. a *complete characterization* of all maxims by means of the formula—all maxims ought by *own legislation* to harmonize with a possible kingdom of ends as with a kingdom of nature. *55 (53)*

Progress in the order of the categories of *unity* of form of the will (universality), *plurality* of matter (ends) and *totality* of the system of these.

End where we started—conception of will unconditionally good. *(54)*

(1) *universal law*. The validity of the will as universal law for possible actions analogous to the universal connection of existence of things by general laws.

First *formula* that of absolutely good will.

(2) Rational nature distinguished from all others *56 (54)*

Kant. Fundamental Principles of Metap. of Morals 2,5.

by fact that it sets before self an end. End of *56* (63) *(54)* absolutely good will—an independently existing end. conceived only negative—not means.

Formula—act so that every rational being is end, equivalent to, Act upon a maxim which involves its own universal validity for every rational being. *56* (64) *(54)*

(3) In such laws he must also be able to regard himself as legislating universally. *Worthy as end, dignity*.

Persons and mundus intelligibilis. *57 (55)*

Every rational being must so act as if he were by his own maxims a legislating member in the universal kingdom of ends.

Formal principle of these maxims—to serve as universal law

Kingdom of ends possible on analogy of a kingdom of nature—self-imposed *rules, laws* of efficient *causes*.

Categorical imperative not universally followed—Act according to the maxims of a member of a merely possible kingdom of ends legislating in it universally. *57* (65) *(55)*

Paradox—*mere dignity of man*, without any other end serves as inflexible precept of will

Paradox—*sublimity of maxim* in its independence of other springs of action. *(56)*

Essence of things not altered by their external relations

Morality the relation of actions to the autonomy of *58* (66) the will, that is, to the potential universal legislation by its maxims.

Action consistent with autonomy permitted; inconsistent prohibited.

From this clear—*duty subjection to law, yet dignity—legislator*. Have also shown actions have moral worth, not from fear or inclination, but only respect for the law.

III. ~~3.~~ Principles of actions (66) *59 (57)*

1. The Autonomy of the will as the supreme principle of morality.

Autonomy of the will is that property of it by which it is a law to itself independently of any property of the objects of volition. Cannot prove principle, since it is a *synthetical proposition*—go beyond knowledge of objects to critical examination of the subject. *59* (67)

Principle of autonomy can be shown by analysis of conception of morality to be sole principle of morality.

Analysis of morality shows its principle to be a categorical imperative, and what this commands is autonomy.

2. The heteronomy of the will as the source of all spurious principles of morality. *59 (57)*

Any other source of laws for will, whether inclination or concepts of reason, only *hypothetical* imperatives: I ought to do something because I wish for something else. *Moral imperative*: I ought to do so and so, even though I should not wish for anything else. Latter abstract from all objects.

Classification of all the Principles of Morality which can be founded on the Conception of Heteronomy. *60 (58)*

|| *Reason* in pure use, without criticism, always tries *all the possible* wrong ways first.

Principles taken from this point of view either *empirical* or *rational*.

Empirical—principle of *happiness*—either physical or moral feeling. *Rational*—principle of *perfection*—either rational conception of perfection as a possible effect or on concept of independent perfection (will of God) as cause of our will. *60* (69)

Empirical incapable of serving as foundation of moral law. Universality lost, if foundation taken from particular constitution of human nature or accidental circumstances. (N.B. ~~Entitative and essentialist or circumstantial interpretations~~ *Simple and actional principles—meroscopic*). Principle of *private happiness* (prosperity) most objectionable—not merely because false, contradicted by experience, and contributes nothing, but because it undermines and destroys sublimity of morality—calculation.

Empirical—*moral feeling*, alleged special sense, nearer to morality, but no general laws.

Rational principles—ontological conception of perfection empty and indefinite, but better than the (70) *61 (59)* theological (divine will), because no intuition of divine perfection or attribute to him glory and dominion. Both vicious circles. *(60)* (N.B. ~~Ontological and existen. Int~~ *reflexive and comprehensive principles*)

Moral sense and perfection do not weaken morality; latter preferable.

62 (71) *(60)*

All these principles—heteronomy of will; absolutely good will autonomy.

63 (72) *(61)*

How is such a *synthetical practical a priori possible and necessary*? *Problem beyond the bounds of metaphysics*

Kant. Fundamental Principles of Met. of Morals 2,6.

of morals. Have not affirmed its truth or proved it.

Have shown only by the development of the universally received notion of morality that an autonomy of the will is connected with it, or rather is its foundation.

This section, like the first merely analytical.

To prove that morality is no creation of the brain, supposes the possibility of a synthetic use of pure practical reason.

Kant. Fundamental Principles of Met. of Moral 3,1.

Third Section. Transition from the Metaphysics of Morals to the Critical Examination of Pure Practical Reason *64* (73) *(63)*

The Concept of Freedom is the Key which explains the Autonomy of the Will.

Will is a kind of causality of living things so far as they are rational; *freedom* the property of this causality by which it can be effective independently of foreign causes; just as *natural necessity* is the property of the causality of all irrational beings under influence of foreign causes.

Negative def. → positive

Freedom not lawless even though not a property of the will according to the laws of nature. *Physical necessity* a heteronomy of efficient causes. Freedom of the will—autonomy, i.e. property of will to be a law to itself. *Free will and will subject to moral laws identical.* Negative definition of freedom. (74) *65 (63)*

On hypothesis of freedom of the will, morality together with its principle follows by analysis of concept. Yet this is a *synthetic preposition*, viz. *an absolutely good will is one whose maxim can always include itself regarded as universal law*. Cannot be discovered by analyzing concept of good will.

Good will connected with *property of its maxim* by third concept—*freedom*. Further preparation to show what this third is to which freedom points.

Freedom must be presupposed as a Property of the Will for *all* rational beings. *66 (64)*

Morality must hold valid for all rational beings (75)

Not enough to prove freedom from alleged experiences; must prove it generally.

Every being *that cannot act except under the idea of freedom* is just for that reason in a practical point of view *really free*. Must attribute to every rational being which has a will that it also has the idea of freedom and acts entirely under this idea.

Reflex Prin It must regard itself as the *author of its principles* independent of foreign influences. As practical reason or will it must regard itself as free. (76)

Of the Interest *End* attaching to the Ideas of Morality. *67 (65)*

Have reduced the definite concept of morality to the idea of freedom, but could not prove freedom to be real in ourselves and the human race.

Oper Method Why submit myself and other rational beings to this law? No interest urges me; but I must take interest in it. *Subjective necessity* distinguished from *objective*. *68* (77) *(66)*

Not enough to prove it subjectively and objectively. Why must universal validity of law be condition restricting our actions, on what ground worth of this manner of acting, why by this a man believes he feels his personal worth?

Sometimes take interest in personal quality without interest in external conditions. Mere worthiness to be happy even without motive of participating in it, can have interest of itself. *68* (78) *(66)*

Have not discerned whence the moral law derives its obligation. *Circle*—assume we are free in the order of efficient causes so that we can conceive ourselves as subject to moral laws *69 (67)* in the order of ends. Then think we are subject to these laws because we have ascribed freedom of the will to ourselves.

One resource left—*distinguish points of view Int. Ontol* when we think of ourselves as *causes efficient a priori* and when we form our conceptions of ourselves from our actions as effects which we see before our eyes. *69* (79) *(67)*

Apparent to *commonest understanding*—difference between ideas given us from without in which we are *passive*, and ideas which we produce simply from ourselves in which we are *active*. *Appearances* and *things in themselves*; world of *sense* and world of *understanding*. Differences due to observers in former; identity of latter. Self as belonging to world of sense and also to intellectual world. Reflecting man and commonest (80) *70 (68)* understanding. Latter sensualizes invisible.

Faculty by which man distinguishes himself from *(69)* everything else. Reason—*pure spontaneous* activity, raised above understanding. Reason transcends everything that sensibility can give to it; *distinguishes world of sense* from that of understanding, and prescribes limits of the understanding itself.

Rational being must regard *self as intelligence*; qua intelligence *71* not belonging to world of sense but of understanding. Two points of view of self, faculties and actions—(1) world of sense, laws of nature, heteronomy, and (2)

Kant Fundamental Principles of Met. of Morals 3,2.

intelligible world, independent of nature—reason.

As rational being man can never conceive the causality of his own will otherwise than on condition of the idea of freedom. Independence of the determining conditions of sensible world is freedom. Idea of *freedom* inseparably connected *with autonomy*, and this with the *universal principle* of morality, which is ideally the foundation of all actions of rational beings, as law of nature is of all phenomena.

Suspicion of latent circle removed. *(70)*

Free—world of understanding, *morality*; *obligation* belonging to *world of sense* and *also understanding*. <

How is the Categorical Imperative Possible? *72 (70)* (82)

Rational being, qua intelligence belongs to *world of understanding*; as efficient cause belonging to that world calls his causality a *will*.

Consciousness of self as part of *world of sense*, actions appearances of that causality. Cannot discern how they are possible from that causality—viewed as determined by phenomena—desires and inclinations.

If only world of understanding, actions conform perfectly to principle of autonomy—morality; if only sensible world, conform to natural laws of desires and inclinations—happiness.

Since *world of understanding* contains the *foundation* of the *world of sense* and consequently of its *laws*—must regard the laws of world of understanding as imperatives and actions that conform to them as duties. *(71)* (83)

Categorical imperatives possible because idea of freedom makes me a member of an *intelligible world*; also intuit myself as a member of *world of sense*, my actions ought to conform. Categorical ought implies synthetic a priori proposition—besides *will* affected by sensible desires, added idea of *same will* belonging to world of understanding, which contains the supreme condition according to reason of former will—similar to concepts of pure understanding in knowledge of physical nature.

Practical use of *common human reason* confirms this reasoning. *Desire* to follow maxims of *honesty*, *steadfastness*, *sympathy*, and *benevolence*. Prevented by inclinations and impulses. *Will free from impulses*—greater intrinsic worth of own person. Acknowledges authority of this law even when transgressing it.

On the Extreme Limits of all Practical Philosophy. (84) *(72)*

This freedom not a conception of experience. Experience shows contrary of what on supposition of freedom are conceived as its necessary consequences. On other side, everything fixedly determined by natural law—this necessity of nature likewise not empirical conception.

But conception of system of nature confirmed by (85) experience, and freedom is only an Idea of Reason whose objective reality in itself is doubtful while nature is a concept of understanding whose reality proved in examples of experience.

Dialectic of Reason, since *freedom attributed to will (73)* appears to contradict the necessity of nature. *Speculative purposes—necessity*; *practical purposes* freedom. Philosophy must assume that no real contradiction will be found between freedom and physical necessity. Remove apparent contradiction.

Impossible to escape contradiction if freedom and necessity conceived in the same sense. Can coexist 86 and must be thought as necessarily united in the same subject.

Settlement of the controversy belongs to speculative not practical philosophy.

Now touching on the bounds of practical philosophy—only *(74)* demand from *speculative* reason that it put an end to discord.

Claims to freedom of will made by common reason based on consciousness of independence of reason from merely subjectively determined causes of sensibility

No contradiction between a thing in appearance being subject to certain laws from which it is independent as a thing or being in itself. Must think of self in twofold way. (87)

Hence man claims will—conceives actions as possible and even necessary only by disregarding all desires and sensible inclinations. Causality of such actions lies in himself as an intelligence and in the laws of effects and actions depending on principles of an intelligible world—knows of it only that pure reason *gives laws independent of sensibility*. Laws apply to him *directly* and *categorically*. *(75)*

When the practical reason thinks itself into a world (88) *(75)* of understanding, it no way transcends its limits; as it would have to if it tried to enter it by intuition or sensation. *Intelligible world* only a negative thought with respect to the world of sense. *Positive* only in

---

Kant. Fundamental Principles of Met. of Morals. 3,3.

this single point that it is also conjoined with positive faculty and even with a causality of reason, called will. Overstep bounds if it borrowed an object of will. World of understanding a point of view by which Reason conceives self as practical,—rational cause. Involves idea (89) of an order and *system of laws different* from that of the mechanism of nature belonging to sensible world.

Can think only of its formal condition, i.e., the universality *(76)* of the maxims of the will as laws and therefore autonomy of will which alone consistent with freedom.

But reason would *overstep its bounds* if it undertook to explain how pure reason can be practical, which is the same as explaining how freedom is possible.

But *freedom a mere Idea*, the objective reality of which can in no wise be shown according to laws of nature or in any possible experience. Cannot be comprehended or understood. Holds good only as a necessary hypothesis of reason in a being which believes itself conscious of a will, that is, of a faculty determining itself distinct from desire.

Explanations cease—*defense*, i.e. *refutation* of objections. 90 *(76)*

Supposed contradictions from considering man as an appearance, to apply laws of nature to human actions. Removed when recognize behind appearances *things-in-themselves—laws of action different* from those of appearances.

Subjective impossibility of *explaining freedom* of the *(77)* will same as impossibility of *explaining interest* in moral laws.

Note. Interest is that by which the reason becomes practical, i.e. a cause determining the will. *Rational being—interest; animals—appetites*. Reason—direct interest in action only when universal validity of its maxims alone sufficient to determine the will. When determined by another object of desire, indirect.

Foundation of this interest—moral feeling, which 91 *(77)* is not, as some suppose, standard for moral judgment but subjective effect of law upon will, the objective principle of which is furnished by reason alone.

Impossible to explain how and why the universality of maxim as law interests—how thought containing nothing sensuous produces sensation of pleasure or pain. *(78)*

Certain only that it is not because it interests us that it has validity; it *interests* us *because it is valid* for us as men, because its source in our will as intelligences.

Only *hypothesis* on which the categorical imperative is possible is *idea of freedom*. Can discern its 92 *(78)* necessity, but not how hypothesis is possible

Hypothesis that *the will* of an *intelligence* is free—its *autonomy as essential formal* condition of its determination is a necessary consequence.

Shown not merely quite *possible speculatively*; unconditionally *necessary practically*. But cannot show how pure reason can be practical.

Same as trying to find out how freedom itself is possible as the causality of the will. *(79)* 93

Intelligible world remains when determinations of world of sense excluded. Have Idea but no knowledge of it.

Of *pure reason* only *form remains*, i.e. the *practical law of the universality* of maxims and *conception of reason as possible efficient* cause determining the will.

This is the extreme limit of all moral inquiry.

LECTURE SEVEN

Power: Selection and Interpretation

When I started lecturing about freedom, I pointed out that the three concepts that concern us this quarter are intimately interrelated, that they enter into the definition of one another; and therefore, when we turn to power, we shall be turning to a concept which is not only subject to a similar four-part analysis, but at each part of the analysis a relation to the concept of freedom—differentiated by similar selection, interpretation, method, and principle—will be apparent.

In the analysis of freedom—let me pause for a moment—we tried to show that there is no unique or proper meaning of freedom, that each of the meanings of freedom that we built up from our four terms is justifiable and subject to a consistent analysis in a complete philosophy. We tried to show, also, that each one is subject to degradation and misuse. Therefore, it is *not* the case that anything you say is equally good or that no philosopher ever makes a mistake, but it is the case that he doesn't make the mistakes that you can attribute to him if you use his words in a different sense. Consequently, the entire function of the analysis is to bring out the different senses and their interrelations. There's a second aspect, one equally important to this first, which is a purely theoretic aspect; namely, we're working with concepts in moral and political philosophy, in practical philosophy, in philosophy directed to action. It would seem *a priori* improbable that by any device which employed freedom there would ever be a uniform philosophy accepted by all mankind. Therefore, one of the first transitions from freedom to power would be to recognize that there are two ways in which you can get agreement, even on ideas: either you can get it by use of reason, coming to an agreement freely, or you can get it by a use of force—overt force, the threat of force, the suspicion of force, the concern about force—in which the position is accepted. So, one of the problems that we shall want to consider is precisely the problem of what the prospects, possibilities, and devices are of achieving freedom on the basis of a diversity of basic opinions: basic opinions in all the departments that we've been talking about as practical, basic opinions about metaphysics, basic opinions about theology, basic opinions about politics, basic opinions about economics, basic opinions about social relations. And so the analysis, by indicating the interrelations of meanings, may reveal the possibility of sound meanings different from the ones that you are accustomed to use; may clarify the differences of method properly employed to achieve freedom in these various senses; and may raise the question of whether the various methods are necessarily antagonistic or whether they are the related aspects of the action that is necessary to achieve freedom by the use of power.

With this in mind, let me merely recall to you that the four parts of our definition were, respectively, what we thought we were talking about when we talked about freedom (this is selection), what we mean when we apply freedom to things or to processes (this is interpretation), how we can achieve freedom either in fact or induce an acceptance of our meaning (the material or the formal aspect of method), and finally, on what grounds it is possible to think about freedom and to operate to achieve freedom. Let me turn now to power.

What is the relation of power to freedom? Well, in connection with the interpretation of freedom, I said that it is possible to enter into discussion and cooperation because there is an ambiguous formula which, so far as I can discover, all philosophers and all practical men would accept, namely, that freedom is the ability to act without external hindrance and impediment—it's ambiguous because what you mean by "ability," what you mean by an "internal/external hindrance," will shift not only on the high levels of philosophy but on the low levels of controversy and debate—but you'll notice that power is in that ambiguous formula. The ability to act is a power, a hindrance is a power; therefore, we have defined freedom in terms of two opposed powers, and we have already introduced one of the most powerful of all of the paired terms in philosophy and practice—*internal* and *external*—because anything that is internal in one analysis is equally plausibly—or more plausibly, if you feel that way—made external in another. So, the transition between internal and external in the placing of powers will be one of the things that we need to analyze. In the same fashion, when I give you an ambiguous formula about power, freedom will be in the formula about power. Let me try an ambiguous formula—again, I think one that no reasonable man, not even a reasonable philosopher [L!], differs from: "Power is the condition or possibility of originating rather than undergoing change." The exercise of power is therefore dependent on the freedom of the agent and the freedom of the circumstances or persons that surround the agent, an internal freedom and an external freedom—but again, with internal and external in the same condition of ambiguity that it had when we talked about freedom. "Condition or possibility" in this definition of power, in this statement about what power is, involves freedom; that is, the condition is a freedom to act, the possibility is a situation in which the act is possible and therefore a freedom. Thus, the exercise of power is freedom to act rather than to be acted on.

Let's consider the relation between freedom and power in the process of giving this ambiguous formula some definition. The interrelation of the two terms in the formula, the ambiguous definition, does not mean that they are equivalent, although this is one of the possibilities, and we will encounter philosophers who equate freedom and power. It means, rather, that you have the probability, which we will be examining by looking at arguments that philosophers make or that we make in the guise of philosophers if we don't find any, the probability that all the possible relations will be realized in some philosophy. Let's enumerate the terms that we have for freedom and power as they occurred in Hobbes and Spinoza: since they were using a logistic method, it's easy to draw up the list. And bear in mind, since we're dealing with human action, we're taking our beginning with human power; as in the case of freedom, it will sometimes move out and have the same meaning beyond the human being and be a power in inanimate or animate as well as in rational beings—and in other situations human power will be different from any of these, and therefore will be a narrowing.

One opposition, starting from this human level, is obligation and freedom (see fig. 40).[1] Going down this list, remembering that they are mutually implicative, this is law on one side and this is right on the other. In English, these are uncomfortable words, because we don't remember that they're both words for "law"; although we still do remember this in the similar words in French, German, and Italian. Therefore, this is *lex* and this is *ius*. When we talk about natural law, for example, in English, sometimes it is *lex naturalis*, sometimes it is *ius naturale*: sometimes they mean the same things, sometimes they mean the opposite things, and so the operation of our column begins to work. This is a duty; this is an independence. And finally, the statement in the term that we are interested in, this is power of others; this is power of our own. The equivalent that we ran into, sometimes in a disturbing way, is that this is the freedom—we're going to the social level now, leaving out the metaphysical—of the individual; this is the freedom of the community, the group, or the state.

I put the list on the board in the logistic form, because it looks like a separation; but from the list what I would like to ask is, What is the real relation? Let's take these two—since I did it before in these terms;

OBLIGATION	⟵ (mutual implication) ⟶	FREEDOM
law	⟷	right
lex	⟷	*ius*
duty	⟷	independence
power of others	⟷	power of our own
freedom of state, community, or group	⟷	freedom of individual

Fig. 40 *Logistic Form of the Relation of Power and Freedom*

strictly, you can do it with any of the two—and ask, What is the relation between *lex* and *ius*? What is the relation between law and right? What is the relation between obligation and freedom? As I said, when I say *lex* and *ius*, substitute the one that you feel more comfortable with. *Lex* and *ius* I like because, since they are in Latin, you can take the distinction that is sharply made rather than subject to the peculiarities that you learn to associate with English as it is spoken. One of the possibilities is that one of the two terms is more inclusive and prior to the other, prior in the sense of being a basic principle from which you can define what goes on. *Ius,* or right, is sometimes taken as prior (see *a* in fig. 41).[2] Then the natural rights with which a man is born, the inborn rights, the innate rights that God gave man—the "God" dropped out of the formula when it got into the "Universal Declaration of Human Rights,"[3] because the Soviets didn't like it [L!], but it is the same formula that they gave, though with this omission—would mean that they are coextensive with power: every man has a right to everything that he has a power to—bear in mind that both words are still ambiguous, *right* and *power*—and the limits to his power and therefore to his universal rights are introduced by

RELATION OF *LEX* and *IUS*	INTERPRETATION	MODE OF THOUGHT
a) *lex* ⟶ *ius*	Existentialist	Discrimination
b) *lex* ⟵ *ius*	Ontological	Assimilation
c) *lex* = *ius*	Essentialist	Resolution
d) *lex* ≠ *ius*	Entitative	Construction

Fig. 41 *Interpretation and Relation of* Lex *(as Power) and* Ius *(as Freedom)*

law. Law is posterior to right, in this sense. Suppose we try the opposite direction (see *b* in fig. 41): *lex* is fundamental, and *ius* is derived from *lex*. It makes perfectly good sense, namely, that there is in the nature of things—this is the law of nature when it is *lex naturalis*—there is in the nature of things a basic pattern discovered by science or identical with reason, a rational pattern, which is then particularized to objectives in applications that men make. Consequently, it's extremely plausible: the universe as a whole has a natural law, the human being has a natural law, but the human being operating according to natural laws can employ his intelligence to achieve ends. When he does, he has set up a right subject to the result of his employment of his powers according to the laws of nature.

There is a third possibility (see *c* in fig. 41). The two may be on the same level of generality and coincident; that is to say, any right that you have is coincident with your power, any freedom that you have is likewise coincident with your power. Your rights, your freedoms, the law, are the same. You cannot, obviously, operate contrary to the laws of nature and of the civil state; the conditions of nature, the conditions of the civil state, with their laws determine your rights. As you go along, rights are increased by the addition of laws. In fact, within the last year we've passed a civil rights law,[4] and we obviously did it in spite of the fact that in one sense those rights were already in the Bill of Rights, because you needed a law; that is to say, you needed to empower administrators of the state to go in and enforce these rights. Therefore, the right and the law go together. As you pass your laws, you increase your rights. There's only one possibility left—that is, you have to recognize I'm merely opening up the diamond, the knowing matrix, I've put on the board a number of times before[5]—namely, that *ius* and *lex*, right and law, are mutually exclusive (see *d* in fig. 41). This makes perfectly good sense. I think that probably, in some respects, this is more nearly what we would commonly think of as the relation when we talk; namely, I'm free to do things that the law is silent about: if there is a law, I'm obliged to do it; if there is no law, then there is the possibility of a difference. Consequently—you'll remember, we began running down this in the last selection from Hobbes (see fig. 11)—you have a process by which the restrictions remain, but you add to the restrictions: the rights are always the negations that the restrictions have not taken in; and whenever the restriction is there, you do not have any more freedom with respect to that, because the provision is made to invoke a sanction if you attempt to act freely with respect to that which is prohibited by law, custom, or by any other effective force.

Well, now, it is possible—in fact, as we go along we will more and more do this—to find a philosophy that exemplifies each one of these. It would be possible, if we did it in terms of action groups, in any problem that concerns either the use of power or the achievement of rights to find an action group that postulated its entire action on one or another of these and, indeed, criticized other groups for doing something which, according to their conception of the proper use of power relative to freedom, is impossible. Let's go, then, into the steps of our analyses.

What are the selections? Since we have been through all four, I will abandon the cautionary device I used in the beginning. You will remember, I began with method because this was the easiest way to initiate you into the distinctions that I was going to make, since a method permits a long discourse. Having already defined liberty, then, let's go from one to two to three to *n* terms. What are the terms that will be used in the discussion of power and freedom? What are the aspects of experience that are relevant to the determination of power, the use of power in the context of freedom? You will have, let me remind you, a selection in each one of the interpretations that are made; that is, within a given time, there will be a difference concerning whether you are talking primarily about things in motion, about animals with impulses, about men with institutions, or about rational beings with intelligence. These are the four selections that we will eventually make; and as I tried to show as we went along, there's nothing wrong with any of these. Whatever you can say by reducing intelligence, the most restrictive of the interpretations, to motion, the most extended of the interpretations, you can say by the other; in other words, there is no limitation in the possibility of talk. There is a totally different orientation to what you want to say, but you are not precluded from taking into account any aspect of the situation which your opponent will take in: you can argue with him and even focus your argument on the same issue that you have with him.

Then there was a second aspect of selection, you will recall, which moved from age to age; and roughly, as we put it in terms of freedom—we can take it over now into power—there are three dominant aspects. The first, which was in terms that were used in the seventeenth century and in the first part of the eighteenth century, was an attempt to deal with power as—I hesitate to say "metaphysical"—but as an entity in the nature of things, a process in the nature of things. In this period, Hobbes, for example, got into a long controversy with a bishop[6]—both of them wrote tremendous volumes on it—on the relation between freedom and necessity. And in at least one metaphysical approach, the two are contradictory—that metaphysical approach is on the board, but I won't pause to identify it.[7] In this period, Spinoza, whom you read, is another example: the power that a man has and the being that he has are the same; the more powerful you are, the more you *are*. Consequently, in this selection it is a reference back to the basic principles that would differentiate the exercise of power, political power included, as distinct from the exercise of other kinds of power in any of the approaches. The second selection, which occurred after the Copernican revolution celebrated by Kant, deals with power and freedom relative to forms of thought. Put it in Kant's language—you'd have to do it a little bit differently if you moved over to Bentham and Mill, but the British tradition is likewise dealing with the interrelations of ideas; therefore, the formulations that you would make would be the same: it's not political power as opposed to natural power now; it's practical philosophy in the sense of constitutional power. It was about the time of the Copernican revolution that the two written constitutions of the modern world, the French and the American, were made. As was often the case, this led to the discovery that the British had an unwritten constitution, which had been there before, and they'd had a revolution a century earlier; but even if this is true, it wasn't until the British contemplated the American and the French constitutions that they began to see their own constitution and its advantages. This is a structure like the framework of political power, like the framework that we are now seeking in the forms of thought; it is a shift.

Finally, the second Copernican revolution, which came at the beginning of the twentieth century, is one which moved from political, false constitutional power to something I would like to speak of as social power. Political power and freedom: seventeenth century; constitutional power and the political, you see, is then assimilated to that framework in the nineteenth century; then, social power. *Society* had been used before, but now *society* became a basic term. In the twentieth century, we begin to get uncomfortable about the notion of political democracy and to fall into the argument more and more that you can't have a political democ-

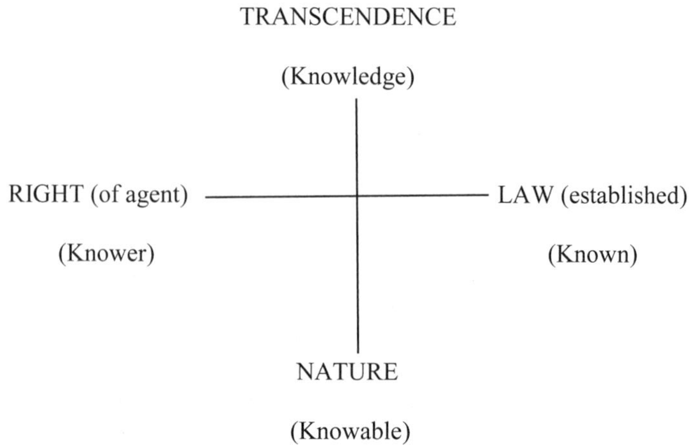

Fig. 42 *Interpretation of Power and Knowledge Matrix*

racy unless you have a democratic man living in a democratic society, and then you can put the constitution on him. So, this is roughly the context of our current selection. We will therefore be talking about concrete action, not about the nature of man and his agreements, not about the constitutions that he has set up and their effect on him, but the actions that we take forming groups and uniting groups for further action.

Let us proceed to interpretation. Interpretation deals with the cross relations between knowledge, known, knower, and knowable. I've told you repeatedly that these are variables or commonplaces. Let's particularize them. Knowledge in the sense that lands on the top of our scheme—knowledge can circle all the way round in the different meanings—is knowledge which has become transcendent, in the sense that it's not something that the human mind has thought up, but it's in the nature of things; and therefore, in dealing with power it is this transcendent structure that we will be dealing with (see fig. 42).[8] Let's put nature in again, remembering that in one lecture I went around the diagram and gave a definition of nature for each of these. Now, this [*i.e.*, knowable] is nature in the sense of elementary things underlying the processes of motion or of social change or of political action which can enter into various composites as you go along; therefore, it is an underlying nature as opposed to a transcendent idea that you would appeal to. When you talk about the knower—and this is probably even a more dangerous particularization—the emphasis is on the rights of the agent. When you talk about the known, the emphasis is on the laws established in what it is that you are talking about and doing. The perpendicular line are the ontic interpretations; the horizontal line are the phenomenal interpretations. We'll take them in that order and ask, What do we mean by power in the sense of what things have power and what processes or actions exhibit power?

The basic agreement among the ontic interpretations, ambiguous like the agreement about the nature of power among all four interpretations, is that freedom—we'll begin with freedom and move to power—freedom consists in the ability to act according to one's own nature. Obviously, this means that one will have power in the exercise of this freedom. Let's take the two possibilities that the ontic interpretation opens on this ambiguous agreement. Remember, we're talking about power now; I'm leaving freedom. Either there are transcendent determinants or there are natures which will determine the exercise of power; that is, the meaning of power will depend on determinants of relations between internal and external power which underlie what we are doing or transcend our experience. There will be an appeal, in other words, beyond experience in the determination of power. You will begin with experience—the ontic interpreters are never *a priori* in the sense that you can think without thinking—but in order to come to anything that would look like resolution, you make an appeal either to the laws of nature, which you can write out and which are approximated in the things that occur, or to the harmony to which the entire process aspires or tends and which gives meaning to what it is doing. On the phenomenal interpretations, the horizontal line, existent or experienced law or right, one or the other, are the basic terms. That is, the meaning of power involves reference only to experience and facts and their relation; there are no atoms underneath, unless by your interpretation you bring them in as a result, and there are no ideas above. Let me repeat what I have said before (see table 10). Since in practical or political philosophy, our concern is with freedom and power in human relations, the coincidences of meanings among the different approaches when they cooperate or understand each other will be with respect to human action. Nonetheless, the reference or the applications of power and of freedom may extend in some approaches beyond to take in the motions of inanimate bodies, the impulses of animals; or it may be restricted to human action alone or only to human action when it is proceeding reasonably or rationally—that is, social action or wise action are the two possibilities.

What's the question of interpretation: What is power and what has power? As we go along, I'll try to answer that by using four different power words. I do it with some hesitation because, as I said before, although in a strict sense the power word will indicate the peculiarity of power in this interpretation, any one of the power words can, with a use of the appropriate method, be approximated to the other interpretations;

therefore, it is the interpretation that I state for each of these words which is the one that I am attributing. The fact that you can remember somebody who uses the word differently is no refutation; it merely indicates that you are now adapting for this word one of the other interpretations which I've attached to another word. The first of the ontic interpretations is the ontological interpretation; the mode of thought, assimilation. What is power? Well, power in the good, old-fashioned sense is being. There's a famous passage in the *Sophist* in which Plato says, "By being I mean *dunamis*, I mean power." Cornford almost has a baby about this. [L!] In his introduction to the translation of the *Sophist*, he quotes Whitehead, who is a very good philosopher; and Whitehead says, "Like Plato, by power I mean being." Cornford says, with the superiority proper only to us classical scholars [L!], "Whitehead was misled by a bad translation; this is what old man Jowett said Plato said, but Plato didn't say that." His resultant statement is not meaningless, because he's operating on another interpretation. But Plato said, I reassure you, by *being* he means "power," that's what he meant. There is, consequently, in the ontological interpretation, a tendency to distinguish being from becoming—you will recognize this in most of the ontological interpretations that we have engaged in. I don't think you have any difficulty in distinguishing the two, even in your own thought: what anything *is* is its power; what it does at any given moment is its power. It's never using its whole power: any instance of operation will be power as appearance; but if you believe that there is a thing itself in addition to what it's doing at a particular moment—and that's the whole point of the ontological interpretation—then, obviously, what the thing is does not limit it to what it is doing right now, because a moment from now it's going to be doing something else, and it is that, too. Consequently, the relation of power to freedom is perfectly clear; that is to say, we said that on the ontological interpretation, liberty or freedom is self-perfection and power is being. The two will obviously be working together. That is to say, at any given moment what you are is the power you have; if in the process of operating you increase your power, that is, you become wiser, you increase your perfection, and therefore, you also increase your freedom.

You'll notice, this is the interpretation in which power and freedom become the same. The more being you have, the more power you have; and operating on a higher level is precisely what constitutes freedom and therefore the more freedom that you have. If you prefer it in a proportion—you can use matrices and be set for a long time; also, you can write the proportion four different ways and you will get our four interpretations—the proportion is simply: transcendence is to nature (that is the first of our interpretations) as law is to right.

TRANSCENDENCE : NATURE :: LAW : RIGHT

The doubling of the meaning of *power* that you have is, consequently, the two proportions that enter into the equation with the confidence that the first one is what gives you the nature of the thing in terms of which the operations within the changing conditions of the state or man's life would appear. Let me read that proportion in English, then, beginning with the second ratio. Law is more than a human enactment: it's based on or approximates to a rational reality which the society or the lawgiver is trying to achieve. Or stated in a basic schema, knowledge as constituting reality and the foundation of nature—that is, the true reality is the nature of ideas—will give us an insight into a rational understanding of the concrete structure of the universe at any given time as stated in physics or in any science; consequently—we're coming across [the equation] now—the institutions that we set up either will be an attempt to achieve this rationality or will operate by power within the structure of that rationality.

Well, let's move into the two varieties of power and forget about the proportions and equations. They fascinate me, but I don't have the feeling that the orator has that my audience is entirely with me. [L!] Let's move around, then, away from the regularities into the two varieties of power. There's a kind of power that's based on adequate knowledge or on the true nature of things. There's a kind of power that's based upon the organizations or institutions or laws that men set up short of knowledge. They may be set up on right opinion—in which case they'll be right, even though you don't know the reason why—or on agreement—in which case you'll get what you want, even though you oughtn't to want it—or on mistakes or on force. All of this would be part of your picture. For Plato, to limit ourselves to him for a moment, power is inseparable from wisdom or self-perfection; this is the true sense of power. For this reason he says, or he has Socrates say, that there are no laws in the *Republic*. There is a passage—if we were doing it, I'd give you the reference; but take my word for it[9]—in which one of the interlocutors says, "What about contracts? What about crime? What about torts?" And Socrates says that in the *Republic,* these won't exist. There will be the law of reason, he says; if the law of reason is departed from, the state has changed, and you're on the degradations of the state that occur in the eighth and ninth books. The one law which we must hold to—and he says this twice[10]—is the law of education: keep education going, the state is there, this is the only law that there is. But then he wrote another book, the book called the *Laws*; and in the *Laws*—Socrates isn't there, but there is an Athenian Stranger there who talks very much like Socrates—the Athenian Stranger and all of the interlocutors say that this is a second-best state—the *Republic* is a perfect state—and then they vary it: it's an actual state. Actual states would always be second-best states. Socrates says in the *Republic* that the state they have described never did exist, never will exist; it occurs, rather, as a model for existent states, but will not in its fullness be.[11] And how does the second-best state work? Well, it works by law, and law has two parts: in general—in fact, the whole book is based on this—and for each of the particular laws, you have a preamble to the law and you have the law. The purpose of the preamble is to persuade the citizens to follow the law, while the law states the sanctions that are applied if you don't: persuasion and force. When we get to method, the way in which this is set up, again, is not by having philosopher-kings—this is not part of interpretation; this is method—you get men of experience, old men, old men who meet in a nocturnal council and then, to free themselves from the habit of long years, get drunk: drunken old men late at night [L!] are the makers of laws in actual states, "philosopher-kings" in the perfect state. But you'll notice, this is our second level.

Since the bell will ring in a few seconds, let me put in the rest of this schematism (see table 14).[12] The ontological will deal with—let me quote a good modern word—energy, energy in the sense of that structure of interrelations which hold any system together, a physical system, one you can write a field equation for, or an organic system, an organism, which likewise possesses the energy of organization. The power term is one inseparable from order and organization. The entitative deals with nature, as you will recall. Consequently, if you want power, you don't go to being; you take a look, rather, at motion, motion and rest, and the exercise of power are the laws of motion, the laws of the continuation of a body in the state in which it was unless it meets an external hindrance, or the transfer of motion when one thing moves another. What's our power term here? It's *force*. You'll notice, what power does is to move or to repel in this latter case, what energy does in the former is to order something; consequently, the power operation is quite different in the two interpretations.

When you get to the phenomenal interpretations, you are not dealing with power in either of these senses. You'll notice, these are ontic in the sense that motion *is* and being *is*; but in the phenomenal you will be dealing, rather, with potentialities and possibilities. What is power in the existentialist approach? Well, power is really—taking the whole situation in, in good Sartrean fashion—possibility. And what does power do? It initiates. Sartre likes the word *creates* better, but *creates* has too much of a theological ring in my ear in spite of Sartre's supposed atheism. It initiates or dominates. What is the essentialist's conception? Well, for

Table 14. Power: Interpretation and Selection.

Mode of Thought	Interpretation: Name	Interpretation: What is Power?	Selection: What am I Talking About?	Description of Freedom
	Ontic			
Assimilation	Ontological	Energy/Being	Wise Man	Self-Perfection
Construction	Entitative	Force/Motion	Body	Self-Determination
	Phenomenal			
Discrimination	Existentialist	Possibility	Animal	Self-Initiation
Resolution	Essentialist	Potentiality	Reflective Human	Self-Development

the essentialist, power, again, is not actuality, as it would be in either of the ontic interpretations; power is potentiality, and there is a vast difference between potentiality and possibility for any of these philosophers—many of them discuss this in considerable detail. What is it that the operation of power does? Well, it actualizes.

You notice, you have four different ways in which the power will manifest itself. You had to move our columns, because power manifests itself ontically either in being or in motion, which continues to be until something external changes it but which is as eternal as being is, even in a good Newtonian system; that is to say, the very character of motion or rest is to continue unchanged unless hindered from the outside. What is it that power does in the phenomenal interpretations? Well, beginning with the knower or beginning with the person who has the right to start something, it initiates; or beginning with the law or the person who is concerned with what the situation is, with the circumstances of what is known, it actualizes what is there. Notice, also, that the senses of power correspond in different ways with the senses of freedom. We had freedom in the sense of self-perfection; the freedom which we found for the entitative was self-determination; the freedom that we found for the existentialist was spontaneity; the freedom that we found for the essentialist was self-development (see table 14).

Well, I'll go on from here next time. I have really only done the first of the interpretations. I will finish the interpretations and at least start on the methods.

LECTURE EIGHT

Power: Interpretation (Part 2) and Method

Last time I began our analysis of power and spoke briefly about the problem of selection in relation to freedom and to power. I then went on and started our second problem, namely, the problem of interpretation. The problem of selection would be merely what we talk about when we talk about freedom. The problem of interpretation is the problem of what we say in the sense of answering the question, What things are free or what actions are free? In dealing with interpretation, I'd gotten through only the general considerations of the difference of the ontic and the phenomenal, then the first of the ontic interpretations, the ontological.

You will recall that we are back again to our basic diagram, except that for the purposes of more precise formulation, I gave you the significance these terms would have with respect to our freedom-power problem (see fig. 42). I started to write a series of proportions, of which the ontological is the transcendent, the proportion indicating the source of the two meanings, the doubling of meanings that I've referred to all along; namely, in order to talk about power, one needs to consider the nature of things as it depends on the understanding of something that transcends.

TRANSCENDENCE : NATURE :: LAW : RIGHT

The ideas of Plato, the god of Spinoza, would be instances of this, or the noumena of Kant. In terms of this basic meaning, there is then an exercise of power that arises from actual institutions. I won't go into the detail of the analysis, since I gave it to you once; but I did want, before we go on to the other four so that we can see the different meanings of power, to recall the main point of the ontological.

Power, in the ontological approach, means "being"; and consequently, the answer to the question, What has power or who has power? is the wise man in wise action (see table 14). The wise man is usually the surrogate for something above the wise man, the demiurge or god; but the basis of freedom, the basis of power, is precisely acting according to one's nature as realized in the highest. Therefore, freedom as self-perfection and power as access of being become equivalent. One of the things I want you to watch as we go along is that the ontological meanings of power are equivalent to the ontological meanings of freedom. Strictly speaking, what is anything? What is a man? Well, a man is what he has the power to do, and he has the power to do it when he has realized himself as fully as possible and is therefore free to do it. Being, freedom, power are the same. And this needn't surprise you, since in your rapid excursion through the fifth book of Spinoza's *Ethics*, he says exactly this: substance is power is perfection is freedom is beatitude—they're all equivalent terms.[1] As we go along, let me continue to assert, this is not an esoteric meaning of freedom; this is an essential meaning that's present in even the everyday discussions that we engage in in our attempts to achieve our freedom.

Well, let's go on, then, to the second of our ontic terms. We've done the ontological. What is the entitative meaning? This is the meaning that we get by composition; and power in this meaning is not "being," it is "motion." There's a doubling of meaning again, because in the entitative interpretation, since motion is basic, you need to be able to determine what the absolute motion is; all the motions that you experience are relative motions which are interpreted in terms of the absolute motion. Apparent motions are so interpreted. Therefore, you will always have a real power as well as an apparent power, and the apparent power is one that you exercise in the region of appearances. Your basic proportion is therefore a simple transmutation.

NATURE : TRANSCENDENCE :: RIGHT : LAW

Nature becomes important: it is the explanation of the transcendence; that is to say, if nature underlies everything that is, then it is the underlying thing we go to for reality, and the transcendent is the region of appearance. You just inverse the previous scheme, and your right is based on your nature, and the laws you establish are an exercise of your rights. The first part of the equation, then, is a pattern in the nature of things—that's including men—and the second part is the pattern of convention and agreement which men set up in their societies and in their associations. The two kinds of power are—and again, it's easy to distinguish—the power which you have by nature and, second, the power that you're able to exercise in any particular circumstances. Those of you who had the class on the natural sciences may recall that when you got to Newton, you dealt with the kinds of motive centripetal force; the first one was the absolute motive centripetal force, and the second one was the accelerative. What's the difference between the two? Newton uses the example of the lodestone.[2] When you go and buy a magnet, it's stamped, you know what its power is: that's its absolute power. Whether or not it will move a piece of iron will depend upon how close it is: that is the accelerative power. And the two need to be distinguished. Here in the political sciences we are making exactly the same distinction, that is, an absolute power in the nature of the individual and the apparent power, or the social power let's call it. In other words, if we grant that a man has abilities that might be more effective socially in another society than his, what he can actually do depends upon the society, upon the relative determinations that are involved.

Let me pause for a minute for these two different meanings in the entitative interpretation as related to the two different meanings in the ontological interpretation. True power, in the ontological interpretation, is the power of man when he becomes as able as possible; that is, it is a more complete wisdom and rationality. The second power is action according to the laws that are imposed in the state by virtue of power. In Plato, the difference between the *Republic* and the *Laws* would involve this difference. In the entitative, the true power is the power of motion—bearing in mind that motion runs all the way up and down from walking to thinking (these are all behaviorists)—the true power would be the power that a body has to move, and the second power is the right or the potential power that one has because of one's position and circumstances. In the old-fashioned physics which was taught on the basis of Newton, it was always customary to talk about the difference between kinetic energy and potential energy—our language today, meaning selection, makes it harder to make this distinction. Kinetic energy was the energy of the body in motion; therefore, you had power in this sense—*force* would be a better word—only when you were actually in motion. My briefcase has potential energy, because it is up from the floor on the desk; all I do is push it over, and then it has kinetic energy, it plops! It is this difference that would make the two forces different. What has power? A big body in motion, in actual motion. Remember, in the ontological the answer to the question, What has power? was that it was the wise man engaging in wise action. We're now down at the other extreme; that is, we're at nature. We can explain everything the same way if we do it well, and some of the philosophers who use this have done it extremely well. What is the relation between this conception of power and the conception of freedom which goes with it, the entitative interpretation? We said that freedom in the entitative interpretation was self-determination. All that's involved in motion is local motion, and you move either because you're pushed or because you move. If you move by virtue of the laws of your own nature, you determine yourself, you're free; and as in the case of the ontological interpretation, freedom and power are strictly the same. When a body is actually moving, it has power, not otherwise except in the potential sense. When it is actually moving, it is free. That's why we say a "free-falling" body, only because it is free and it is determining itself in that this is not a violent motion imposed by an outside force. The difference between a projectile and gravitation from Galileo on is precisely that the one is free and the other is violent, you have it imposed.[3]

Well, these are our ontic interpretations. What are the phenomenal interpretations? Well, the phenomenal interpretations we said differed from the ontic interpretations in that in the phenomenal interpretations, there is no assumption that there is anything transcendent or that there is anything underlying. You can talk that language; you can even borrow terms from these interpretations. You would show, however, that all that the transcendent means is not that there is something apart up there but that the mind, beginning with experience, abstracts; and similarly, you would show that there aren't any least parts but that the mind, in the process of explaining anything, can show what underlies any particular process. It is a process of the mind rather than a body of things that we appeal to. There are two interpretations. One is the interpretation in which you begin with the agent or the knower or with right, and from it explain all the rest. Again, it's a simple transformation in the case of the two ratios and inversion of them.

RIGHT : LAW :: NATURE : TRANSCENDENCE

In the existential interpretation, in discrimination, what is force, what is power? Well, power now is the possibility of initiating a motion relative to the frame of reference or the circumstances or the perspective of the agent. What exercises power? Well, neither wise men nor moving bodies—the two answers we had previously—but animate bodies, any animal. It is the initiation of a motion because the animal is able to, it can achieve this; that is, the power includes not only physical power but any guile, skill, or persuasion that will also get the motion initiated. How is it related to freedom? Well, there's an existentialist interpretation of freedom, too: the existentialist interpretation of freedom was that it was lack of constraint in the sense of spontaneity, indetermination to any course of action. Power is the initiation of an action.

Let's try to get a little bit further in this. You notice, you have the basic character of the entire process in the right—the first word in each case of the proportion is the basic word which throws all of the interpretation in line with it. We're talking about animate creatures and therefore somewhat broader than the political power of free men—free men are animate creatures—but there will be power in this sense and, consequently, freedom in the discussion of any animal. You can take into account law if you begin with a right, because if rights are basic, among the rights are the civil and political rights by which you make laws; and if you are initiating, if you recognize this initiative that is present, the only reason that we have nature is that men of power and freedom initiated the idea. Newton's three laws of motion didn't operate before the seventeenth century: nature as we've known it since Newton was not known. When you begin, you remember, you don't suppose that nature was there industriously working out the three laws of motion for centuries until Newton came along and then announced them; you suppose, rather, that in the immense complexity of experience there was the initiative that threw a sense, an organization, and a harmony on experience. What Newton set up was then pushed further and spoiled by Clerk Maxwell, and then it was patched up by Einstein; and these are all the ways in which nature is made.[4] And in the same fashion, any transcendent influence—remember, our other word is *knowledge* (see fig. 42)—any body of knowledge is likewise made by the thinkers. This, then, is our basic proportion.

Power is initiative; there's no power except exercised power, not merely in the entitative sense—there, you remember, there is no power except things actually in motion—but it is now in the sense not of motion but of action, and an action is a motion plus a motive or a motivation. One's own action is initiated, and one can also initiate the actions of others. If you want to do it on the level of the animal that I started with, there are two aspects of an animal's power that would relate to freedom. If the animal is uncaged, he is free. If, uncaged, he starts on a movement because he wants something, like drink, he is likewise free in this first sense. But now put the animal in a herd led by a leader—at the beginning of this century, in fact, the whole of anthropology was influenced by the herd theory moving from herds into human beings; it was perfectly serious, and we still have remnants of it, though probably not as popular as it was in 1920–25—but here again you have the exercise of power and of freedom in the initiative that any creature unrestrained by external restraint and unrestrained in the exercise of the impulsions would have. Freedom is self-initiation; power is the ability to initiate. And you'll notice, what I said before, in the ontic interpretations power and freedom become the same. They're not the same here in the phenomenal interpretations; that is, there is a difference in the two. Power is related to freedom, but they're not the same. Let me repeat again the way in which the ontological and the entitative are the same. In the ontological, power and freedom are both being. In the entitative, power and freedom are both motion. In the existentialist, freedom is a perspective or a frame of reference in which it is possible to initiate; power is the ability to initiate. You can have the uncaged animal I spoke about a moment ago unable to move, too weak; therefore, it has freedom—nothing's stopping it—but it doesn't have power. So, there is a difference in this approach between the things that you don't do because you're not free to and the things that you don't do because you're not able to. The question of freedom and power is a question of how to start or stop, accelerate or diminish, an action, one or the other; that is, the initiative is what is important.

Let me move from the social sciences to a related field. This is the line of interpretation in which the use of statistical laws is important, and there's always a temptation to make the social sciences up to date by means of quantum mechanics. Let's go to Darwin instead. Darwin's doctrine was that there was an aggregate of independent determining agents which was the reason for the occurrence of variation; therefore, you could set up statistical laws which would account for the occurrence of the variation. From that point on, it was a problem only of the transmission of the variations that had occurred. The statistical laws, you notice, tell you what nature is over here.[5] In a strict sense, statistical laws don't tell you what nature is in the sense of representing the way something could be; it is nature viewed through a screen. And consequently, it would be knowledge of nature that we would have.[6] What's power, then? Power is animate bodies capable of self-initiated action in circumstances in which they actually initiate action.

There remains one interpretation: that's the essentialist interpretation. By now you can write your proportion: law becomes fundamental.

LAW : RIGHT :: TRANSCENDENCE : NATURE

If I may interpolate again, the only point of these equations is that you could be able to read them in such a way that each of the four words take on totally different meanings in each of the proportions; otherwise, they're gimmicks. In the essentialist interpretation, the basic character is institutionalized, whether in the individual or in the state: in the state it is the institution of law in a constitution, in the individual it is the institution of a law of operation. You may not have noticed that when Aristotle, who is given to this interpretation, talks about even the moral virtues, one of their characteristics is that they are operation according to the rule of right reason. The person who exercises the virtue need not know what the rule of right reason is, but he operates according to it. If it were an ontological interpretation, this wouldn't be a moral situation. Those of you who've been struggling through Kant will recognize this: this is operation *according to* law, but for the ontological you have to operate *for* law. Law becomes the end; respect for the law is the cause of the operation. Let me go back to What is it that is power? Power is now potentiality—remember, it was possibility for the existentialist. It is potentiality in the sense that a man becomes actually what he is potentially as a result of actions; these actions form institutions in the community and habits in his own person which, in turn, are the causes of actions like the ones that formed them. Aristotle has a very moving passage which I think ought to be recalled here. Potentiality is quite different from power in the sense of force or possibility. In youth, a child has a potentiality which is broad but not very deep. He could become an engineer, a general, a divine, a saint; all of these are potentialities which he possesses. As he develops and is trained, the range of his potentialities narrows, but they move up in actualization. Even those of you who came to the University of Chicago for the undergraduate course of study, when you came in you could have been a chemist or a historian. By the time you get out, you're on the way to becoming either a chemist or a historian; and if you want to start over again, you've got to go back and start over again. This is the nature of potentiality. And you'll notice, it is a power word, but a power word totally different from the ones that we have been talking about thus far.

What's the relation of this conception of power to the equivalent conception of freedom? Well, we said that the essentialist conception of freedom was a freedom of self-development. We are now saying that power is a potentiality. And you notice, once more, as in the case of the other phenomenal concepts, power and freedom are not the same. If you don't have the potentiality, you won't make it; but with the potentiality, you may not have the freedom. The two therefore need to go together in order to have action operate.

Let me take the four senses of power and arrange them in a line, and let me underline four different power words that I've been using (again, see table 14). Don't get the idea from this that the word *power* disappears: these are merely synonyms of *power* which emphasize the meanings that we have given them. The ontological is power as energy or a unitary ordering force which constitutes the being of anything. What does power do? Well, you've already answered this: power orders; if it doesn't order, it isn't power. Let me pause again to illustrate this. You may remember that at the end of book I of the *Republic*, Thrasymachus does a very good job on the relation of power to justice—in the ontological interpretation, the fact it's done by justice rather than freedom makes no difference—and making use of an existentialist interpretation, he defends in very good fashion the position that power is right or *ius*—*right* and *just* are synonyms (see fig. 40). And Socrates asks him the question, "Now, do you mean that it is just for a man who has the power to do anything he wants even though he makes a mistake, even though he does something which isn't going to be good in the sense that he wants?" Thrasymachus slips here: he says, "Well, no. A powerful man is not a dumb man; he wouldn't make mistakes." He has lost his existentialist position; that is, the right existentialist answer is that the powerful man does as he wants, and there isn't any sense in asking whether it would have been right for him to do otherwise. But for the ontological interpretation, there is: there is an order; therefore, it is not a mistake, not just in language, to say that a man who has power to do something does something wrong. Only the wise man has power: the use of power is inseparable from wisdom. This is our first meaning, and as I say, I am giving an extra sentence to it because you might think that this is somehow idealistic. This is as down-to-earth, as realistic, as free from category mistakes [L!] as any of the other interpretations. Now the second meaning: power is force in the sense of a material system of interrelated motions. Whenever you do your parallelograms of forces, you're engaging in something of this sort. And what does power do? Well, power does only one thing: it moves. If it isn't moving, it isn't power; if it is moving, it is power, and that's the way you know it. In this scheme, freedom is self-determination as motion, just as in the first scheme freedom is action according to order or self-perfection.

What's the third meaning of *power*? Well, power is now possibility. Bear in mind, possibility does not mean the same as potentiality; even when you are speaking within the same scheme, they are different. Power, therefore, is the actual occurrence of spontaneous variation. What does power do? Well, it does only one thing: it originates—I said "initiates" before, but *initiates* or *originates* is the same thing. Between this existentialist interpretation and the entitative interpretation there's a total difference. In the entitative, if the body is moving—and as I say, the body is either a ball rolling or a larynx vibrating, that is, a theoretic process—if the body is moving, you have power; that's it. But here it isn't a question of the motion of the agent; the question is whether he starts anything. He might be in motion simply because he is pushed. That would be no paradox in the entitative, because, however the motion came, the body in motion continues in motion or at rest until it meets another and contrary force. Whereas here, you don't have anything called ineffective power: you could have the body and the mind of the agitator going off at great rate; but if you don't initiate anything, it is not a power. It's a noise or something else.

Finally, the fourth meaning of *power*? Potentiality. And what does power as potentiality do? Well, it does only one thing: it actualizes, it moves from potentiality to actualization, and the related concept of freedom is self-development. Now, it's possible if you like one of these interpretations to reduce them all to that one. After all, if you can think, as most of you do, that power appears only in motion, it's quite clear that motion orders things and motion starts things and motion actualizes things. But I've blunted the original meaning of these three terms. I could have as easily started from one of the other of the three and reduced the other conceptions to that one.

I want in the remaining ten minutes to do what I did last time, that is to say, to start on the new dimension of the definition. I want to move on to method. I won't try to complete method; but the reason why I want to tack it on to interpretation is to show in a little more detail what I've tried to illustrate repeatedly, namely, that fixing the interpretation does not fix the method. Therefore, for any of the four interpretations I have on the board, any one of the methods could set it up. Let's move over, however, into method. Method, we said, is a discursive device by which consequences are set up and ordered, either in language—in discourse—or in fact. You get the meaning of power from the relation of terms arranged *seriatim*. The method is related to the interpretation: the method is the way in which you justify an interpretation. If you're trying to prove it, the interpretation is the conclusion of the proof. But it does not predetermine the kind of interpretation that you would set up. We have two problems, you will recall, the formal and the material one. One is the problem of how power is acquired, maintained, and exercised—that's the material consideration; the other is the question of how discourse about power is given meaning. The basic differentiation in the methods will, therefore, bear both on reason and on the exercise of power; and in point of fact, the whole question of method is the question of to what extent and how can reason be used in the exercise of power.

There are the two methods, the universal and the particular methods. In the universal methods, reason is used directly to influence power. In the universal methods, there's the doubling of meaning that is like the ontic doubling: you can use reason in two ways, or you can get a meaning for method, either when the use of reason is direct or when it is not direct and the possibility of direct use of reason is irrelevant. They're universal methods because there's one method for all processes, there are analogical meanings, not single meanings, and there is a variety of principles. But for the universal methods in general, it is significant to say that power is acquired. For the particular methods, it is not. In the particular methods, reason is used indirectly in the utilization of power. You have one method, that is, they are particular, in the sense that you have methods suited to different problems and subject matters. For the

Table 15. Power: Method.

Mode of Thought	Method	What does power do?
	Universal	
Assimilation	Dialectical	Orders
Discrimination	Operational	Initiates
	Particular	
Construction	Logistic	Moves
Resolution	Problematic	Actualizes

particular methods, power is realized or utilized or developed; but it's there, it isn't acquired.

Let me begin with the universal methods and move at once to the dialectical method, because I want to use that to illustrate at once the fact that, with respect to the mode of thought, it is very much like the ontological interpretation; but second, this does not mean that the only interpretation you can use with the dialectical method is the ontological (see table 15).[7] I want to include the other interpretations in connection with the dialectical method. The dialectical method uses the mode of thought assimilation: the emphasis is on knowledge or transcendence—I've put it there (see fig. 42). The use of power is the use of reason in operation—first meaning—or it is operation in a rational manner. That's the double meaning, the two meanings, that I spoke of a moment ago. Power orders; therefore, it is reason that enters into action for the ordering of power. How do you acquire power? Well, power is acquired when you understand the ordering principles, as opposed to using power without knowing the ordering principles, that is, when you might by chance or experience or opinion operate according to the ordering principles. But those are your only two possibilities: you either know it and you are the wise man acting; or, using Plato's language, you may be the experienced statesman—and, according to Plato, all of the good statesmen in Athens apparently operated according to right opinion, they didn't know the reason. The conditions which determine power in the individual and the state are exactly the same. This is the reason why in the *Republic* Socrates is looking for justice in the individual, but he's going to find it writ large in the state. It's very simple: there are three classes in the state, there are three powers in the mind, and the interrelations are the same. Consequently, there are four virtues in the state, there are four virtues in the individual, and one of them is the virtue of justice.

Moreover, once you begin this, you will always run into a hierarchy, a hierarchy which runs from the ideal state to the degradations that are short of the ideal state, and they are always the actual states. The transcendent, you see, is transcendent because it's the model for everything we do. But Socrates says in the *Republic* that the state they've just described never did exist and never will exist; its importance is, rather, to guide us for the states that do exist.[8] And in this hierarchy, the difference between the transcendent and the actual turns up again and again. In antiquity, there was the ideal state and the actual states. In the Hellenistic and Christian periods, it was the city of God and the terrestrial city.[9] It was transformed in the nineteenth century to the classless society and the various degradations that preceded the classless society, ending with the cataleptic society, which is the last of four.[10] You get, consequently, the two meanings, that is, the doubling and the degradations. In the perfect state, there is no need for power in the sense of restrictive force, compulsory force, restrictive law. What you have is the operation of reason and love, and they are sufficient; you don't have anxiety and opposition. One of the things that you might look into sometime when you're investigating is the use of the term *love*—and there are a half dozen of them—the way in which *love* is used as a term which is the transcendent explanation of how a state occurs. If all men were friends, you wouldn't need a state; on the other hand, the best way to explain the bond of justice, the association of men in *philia* [Greek for *love*], is by considering friendship. At the second level, in actual states, you need law; and law involves both persuasion and force. In the *Laws*, the book itself, the entire work and each law that the Athenian Stranger writes is broken into two parts: the prologue, which is persuasive—it brings people into the right frame of mind—and the law itself, which states the sanction, what the punishment is if you don't obey the law. Both of these are forms of force. That is, it is not the case that persuasion is the way in which you come freely to agreement. The existence of the medium of mass communication is an excellent illustration that persuasion is a mode of force; sometimes it's more extreme than the actual physical force. But this would be the second level on which you would have force operating.

The operation of power dialectically, therefore, is an ordering and—this is where I will be ending—it is an ordering which may be related to the ontological interpretation. If you order the state or society or the individual in such a way that there is a preexistent distinction between right and wrong, if there is, in other words, a law of nature which lays the pattern according to which you do your organizing, then you are using the dialectical method with the ontological interpretation. Or you could use dialectic to order a state in such a way that the state would map out a pattern of nature (see table 16).[11] You would investigate in detail what the motivations of man are. You would argue, as an endless series of

Table 16. Power: Dialectical Method with Four Interpretations.

Mode of Thought	Method	What Does Power Do?	Interpretation	
	Universal			*Ontic*
Assimilation	Dialectical (Direct Use of Knowledge to Achieve Power)	Orders	Energy (in Perfection)	← Ontological
			Forces (from Motivations)	← Entitative
				Phenomenal
			Possibilities (of Initiation)	← Existentialist
			Potentialities (in Circumstances)	← Essentialist

moral and political tracts are doing today, that you can't in the modern world know what political justice or a moral act is without knowing the nature of the political man and the moral agent. Therefore, you investigate human nature: you go to sociology, anthropology, psychoanalysis, psychiatry, and all the other basic sciences, and you discover the laws of human nature and get your dialectical order, your state, on this basis. Or, again, you can proceed dialectically—that is, to order action using reason directly—bearing in mind that there isn't any pattern that you have to order for, neither a transcendent pattern nor an underlying pattern; but you can find out that the whole hope of mankind—and this is in, at least, the language of men like Justice Holmes—the whole hope of mankind is to have an open-ended, progressive possibility. Have ideas compete in the marketplace, the best will come out better; and in any case, the only way in which you discover the truth is to admit everything that is said to be examined. Don't imagine in the beginning that you know what the truth is, but examine the arguments on either side; then you'll be ordering the state on the basis of the existential interpretation. Finally, there's a fourth possibility, the essentialist. Again, you can use dialectic to order; but you will recognize that the important thing is not the individual initiative, which you are preserving in your existentialist interpretation, but the question of circumstances. You can't have one constitution for all mankind, you can't have one state: this is monolithic. You need to have as many constitutions as the circumstances require. The circumstances will depend on the characters of citizens, their past, their industries, the geographic character, the climate, all of the aspects which will form the group, from their past history to their physical, biological, or spiritual environment.

Well, then, this is the way in which with one method you can get all four interpretations in. I won't do this frequently, but I have illustrated it in pieces before. I'll go on next time and give you the four methods.

DISCUSSION

Mill, Part 1
(*On Liberty*, Chapter I: Introductory)

Discussion Summary

Today we begin our discussion of Mill by looking at chapter I in *On Liberty*. We will see that he is not interested in freedom and necessity in the form, as he states it at the very beginning of the chapter, of "the so-called 'liberty of the will'" as opposed to the "philosophy of necessity" [E:65; L:3];[1] rather, he wants to talk about liberty in social situations. Liberty, he says, has always been defined by the social situation for any philosopher, but now new conditions require a more fundamental treatment. In so doing, we will need to look closely at Mill's arguments (his method), assumptions (his principle), and applications (his interpretation).

First, notice that for Mill liberty changes as the social situation does. That shows clearly that this is a phenomenal interpretation; he wants nothing to do with absolute natures. Moreover, this is an existentialist interpretation and not an essentialist one, for it is not related to anything connected with a constitution. What things are free? What actions are free? Liberty is individual spontaneity. This is his basic definition of *liberty*, the individual as spontaneous. Who is free? Only that kind of object which is capable of initiating actions is free, especially men. He is thus concerned with animate individuals.

Now, how would liberty as a principle operate? Why is it that a man is capable of being spontaneous? Notice that this is a different question from that regarding liberty as an interpretation. If you take a look at page 13 [in L; E:72–73],[2] you will see that he says, "The object of this essay is to assert one very simple principle . . . that principle is that the sole end for which mankind are warranted, individually or collectively, in interfering with the liberty of action of any of their number is self-protection." Here he is stating a reflective principle, namely, that man will protect himself. The only way in which we can set up conditions in which spontaneity is possible is by making the principle depend on self-protection. Thus, the principle is reflexive, and without this, spontaneity is impossible. Notice, the nature of a principle indicates where the operation and action are possible: if self-protection isn't possible, then it isn't a free society. The point of the essay, therefore, is to promote the extension of freedom to where it does not exist. In other words, a principle indicates what the range is that you talk about. For Mill, one could not talk about freedom in relation to an individual who lacked the power to protect himself, such as an institutionalized person. We could not discuss such people or societies; they are not in discussions of liberty because they are excluded by principle. Immature people are viewed similarly, because others protect them; that is, the principle excludes them.

Turning now to the method here, we can see that it is operational. Why? What is the argument? Mill starts with "the struggle between liberty and authority" [E:65; L:3] and proceeds to distinguish between two ages. Until recently, the state was divided into the *ruler* and the *ruled*, and it was assumed that their interests were different by nature, the rulers having "derived their authority from inheritance or conquest" [E:65: L:3]. This led to attempts to limit the power of rulers in order to create liberty by (1) recognizing immunities called political rights that the ruled could be presumed to hold or (2) establishing constitutional checks on the rulers. Next, in the second period of time, we get self-rule in the form of popularly elected government. Now we face the question of how the *individual* is related to the *society*. We have self-rule in that society rules, and the individual is ruled by the society of which he is a part. So, each individual is ruled by all the rest, not each by himself. It might be supposed that when we have self-rule, it is true that we don't need to protect the ruled from the ruler. However, in the situation of self-rule, we get both (1) the tyranny of the majority and (2) the tyranny of opinion. Mill will try, therefore, to discover how to preserve for society its proper function while at the same time preserving for the individual his own true function.

Notice, we thus have created a schematism that is formally exhaustive (see fig. 43).[3] By contrast, if this were the logistic method, he would have demonstrated something through a method of proof using axioms and definitions, and we can see that he is not doing that. To state it once more, in the logistic method we would lay down propositions that form a postulate set and then prove that postulate set. Alternately, if he were using the problematic method, we would not have discussed general terms. Say we had collected 150 constitutions, as Aristotle did for his *Politics*. We would proceed to separate them, in today's terms, into (1) underdeveloped countries, whose problems would be unique; (2) revolutionary societies; (3) mature states, where democratic institutions are operating; and (4) utopias. The problems that arise in each category are different.

	Liberty (Freedom)	Authority (Power)
1st Age — (Different)	Ruled (Immunities — Rights)	Ruler (Limitations — Constitution)
2nd Age— (Same)	Individual (Self-rule)	Society (Problems: Tyranny of Majority & of Opinion)

Fig. 43 *Forms of Rule in Mill*

We couldn't talk about the problems of France and Nigeria at the same time. We would differentiate the problems and then, rather than engage in deduction as in the logistic approach, use inquiry to achieve resolution to our problems. Or, to pick another approach, what would we have done if we had proceeded dialectically? We would systematize as Hegel does.[4] We would develop that kind of schematism in which all problems are reformulated to fit into one ruling organization; and in that systematization, we would have the readjustment of contraries such that one contrary would ultimately explain another. In other words, the dialectical method would always have an overarching pattern where we aspire to achieve that level where we have identity, the integration of all the parts in an englobing whole.

Now, with Mill we haven't done any of this; instead, what we have here is a series of successive discriminations. We are interested in the discovery of the legitimate exercise of the power of the individual and the legitimate exercise of the power of society. We discover what actions a man is accountable for only to himself and what ones he is accountable for to society. This is characteristic of the operational method.

To conclude, notice that Kant and Mill have the same method and the same principle but that they differ greatly in interpretation. What happens when the difference centers squarely here? We see that the philosophies of the two are radically different. They should have much in common, but interpretation makes a great deal of difference. As you continue to read Mill, note the operational method in successive chapters and the relation of the last chapter to this introductory chapter. So, watch the sequence of chapters: does he do what he says he is going to do? Does he forget, or does the operational method cause this? Next time, we will address chapter 2, "Of the Liberty of Thought and Discussion."

McKeon's Notes

Mill *Ref. Op. Ex.* On Liberty 1
(Everyman edition)
(*Liberal Arts edition*)[5]

1. Introductory

Subject of essay not so-called Liberty of the Will as opposed to Philosophical Necessity, but "civil or social liberty: the nature and limits of the power that can legitimately be exercised over the individual." (p. 65). *(3)*

Question seldom stated and hardly ever discussed in general terms—but not new; has divided mankind almost from the remotest ages. But requires new and more fundamental treatment.

Method

Struggle between *Liberty* and *Authority*. Previously between subjects and government. "By liberty was meant protection against the tyranny of the political rulers." Conceived as necessarily antagonistic relation.

Liberty—limit on power of ruler—two ways (66) *(4)*

(1) recognition of *immunities* called political rights or liberties, (2) *constitutional* checks.

Historical change—men have ceased to think it a necessity of nature that their governors be an independent power opposed in interest to themselves.

With elective governors, limitation of power not the objective. Experience in popular government showed continued need of limitation: the tyranny of the majority.

Not only political tyranny but tyranny of prevailing opinion and feeling (68) *(7)*. (Notion that the people have no need to *limit their power over themselves*

Reflexive (6) (67*)[6] *Tyranny of Majority*

(Self government, power of people over themselves).

Not each by self, but government of each by all the rest.

General proposition not contested but practical question of how to make fitting adjustment between individual independence and social control almost untouched (68–9) *7–8*

Need of restraints on actions of other people. Rules of conduct imposed by *law* and by *opinion*.

Reason and feelings. Practical principle feeling that everyone should be required to act as one, and those with whom one sympathizes, would like them to act. (69). *(8)* Multifarious causes of opinion. *(9)*

Concern with what society ought to like and dislike rather than with question whether its likings and dislikings should be a law to individuals (70–1) *(10)*

Alter feelings of mankind rather than make common cause with heretics in defense of freedom. Exception in case of religious beliefs. *(10)* reason (71)

England—yoke of opinion heavier, of law lighter. (72) *(11)*

Principle

No recognized principle by which the propriety or impropriety of government interference is customarily tested. *(12)*

Interference of government improperly invoked and improperly condemned.

Purpose of essay—assert one very *simple principle*—the sole end for which mankind are warranted, individually or collectively, in interfering with the liberty of action of any of their number is *self-protection*. Prevent harm to others.

Limited to persons and societies. (73) *(13–14)* Despotism for barbarians.

Interpretation

Argument uses principle of utility (74) *(14)* in largest sense—grounded on permanent interests of a man as a progressive being. Individual *spontaneity* subjected to external control only when *interests* of others involved. Injury. External relations of individuals. Law and conscience.

Sphere of human liberty (interest of society only indirect) (75) *(15)*—(1) consciousness and expression, (2) liberty of tastes and pursuits, (3) liberty of combination among individuals. *(16)*

The *only freedom which deserves the name*, is that of *pursuing our own good in our own way*, so long as we do not attempt to deprive others of theirs, or impede their efforts to obtain it. Each is the proper guardian of his own health, whether bodily, or mental and spiritual. *(17)*

Ancient commonwealths and philosophers—regulation of private conduct.

Modern world—greater size of political communities, separation of spiritual and temporal authorities.

Formation of new sects (Comte) *(18)*

Disposition of mankind to impose own opinions and inclinations as rule of conduct on others.

Examine first liberty of thought.

N.B. Sequence of argument. *Ruler—ruled*

Liberty—Authority *Society—individual*

Limit power—tyranny of political rulers

rights, checks

———

Self-government (no need of limit?)

Tyranny of majority—law, opinion

Individual independence—social control.

Mill On Liberty 2.[7]

[Chapter 1. Initial statement of interpretation—liberty to be examined in existentialist sense, in order to establish reflexive principle of self-protection, argument to use the "principle of utility" grounded on permanent interests of a man as a progressive being. The argument itself to proceed by examining human spontaneity and its proper subjection to external control when the interests of others are involved. Spontaneity and external relations to others (injury). Sphere of liberty (1) consciousness and expression, (2) liberty of tastes and pursuits, (3) liberty of combination among individuals.

Historical sketch of this operational argument.]

Chapter II. Of the Liberty of Thought and Discussion.
[Elaboration of the first stage of Operational Method.]

Mill On Liberty 1.
Method and Principles

operational—opposed opinions (see pp. 96–97)
Method—~~problematic~~; principles—reflexive.
Interpretation. Freedom spontaneity (efficient) (existential)

Ch. 1. Introductory. Problem—civil and social liberty, not liberty of the will—doctrine of philosophical necessity.

Struggle between liberty and authority.

Early states—liberty protection against the tyranny of political rulers. Limits to powers of rulers (1) immunities, (2) constitutional checks (66)

Later stage—governors not independent power by necessity of nature opposed to ruled. Self-rule—thought no need to limit power over themselves. (67) "Self-government" and "power of people over themselves" not expressive of true state of affairs. Not government of each by himself but of each by all the rest (67)

Tyranny of the majority—by law and by opinion.

Limit to the legitimate interference of collective opinion—to find and maintain it as indispensable to good condition of human affairs as protection against political despotism.

Adjustment between individual independence and social control. Some rules of conduct must be imposed by law and by opinion. (69) Differences in different ages and countries—appear to be self-evident and self-justifying. (69) People believe their feelings better than reason.

Each feels everyone should be required to act as he would like them to. Their legitimate or illegitimate self-interest.

Position of an ascendant class. (70)

Also servility of mankind toward temporal masters. Baser influences and the general and obvious interests of society.

Those in advance of society have occupied themselves with inquiring what things society ought to like or dislike rather than inquiring whether its *likings and dislikings should be a law to individuals*. Alter *feelings of mankind* rather than make *common cause with heretics generally*.

Progress of religious liberty. (71) Duty of toleration admitted with tacit reserves.

England—yoke of opinion heaver than that of law.

Persistence of habit of regarding government as representing an opposite interest to the public.

Majority has not learned to feel the *power of the government* as their power or its opinions their opinions. Opposition to extension of control of government in things not previously controlled.

No recognized principle to test propriety and impropriety of governmental interference. (72) Consequence—interference of government is, with about equal frequency, improperly invoked and improperly condemned.

Object of essay—one simple principle. The sole end for which mankind justified, individually or collectively, in interfering with the liberty of action of any of their number is self-protection. (73) Prevent harm to others—his own good not sufficient warrant for interference.

Not rightfully compelled because it will be better for him, or because it will make him happier, or because in the opinion of others it is wise or right.

Independence is of right absolute—over himself, over his own body and mind, the individual is sovereign.

Exception of children and minors, backward societies. Despotism the legitimate government of barbarians. Free and equal discussion.

No idea of abstract right independent of utility. (74)

Individual *spontaneity* and external control. Control of positive acts for benefit of others as well as negative acts harming others. Latter rule, former exception.

Society—indirect interest in sphere of action which affects only individual.

Appropriate region of human freedom (1) freedom of thought and feeling absolute; freedom of expressing and publishing opinions, (2) freedom of tastes and pursuits, (3) freedom of combination.

No society in which these freedoms are not respected is free.

Although doctrine is not new, contrary to practice. Compel people to conform to notions of personal and *social excellence*. Ancient commonwealths; modern—larger, separation of spiritual and temporal authority. Religion—Comte and opposition to religion, but establishes despotism over individual.

Tendency to stretch unduly the powers of society over individual—*opinion* and *legislation*; limited only *by want of power—need of moral conviction.*

Mill On Liberty—Method and Principles 2[8]

Operational method apparent in the balance and opposition—and preservation of opposed opinions. *Also in the equality* of power and opinion. The insistence on consequences and on the causal efficacy of actions.

Existential interpretation—freedom spontaneity

Reflexive principles operate in the determination of the scope of the discussion and the course of action.

Movement from opposition of governors and government to discovery of self-government (removal of natural basis of the difference because of development of power)—apparently reflexive principle, but seen not to be one actually by the recognition of a new pair of opposites—majority vs. minority—in opposition of power.

Power of officials in law and of majority in opinion.

Imposition of opinions by those in power.

The single "simple" principle advocated by Mill—sovereignty (power) of individual over himself (i.e. reflexive, operational method), over body and mind. Sovereignty of state over consequences of his actions—prevent harm to others and even require beneficent actions in particular circumstances.

Region therefore of freedom determined by the principle, not of self-rule but of self-protection.

Not what is better for him, or what makes him happier, or what is wise or right (N.B. these the criteria of comprehensive, *reflexive*, and simple principles). Furthermore, not what others have the power to impose (actional principles). Need to impose a moral principle—reflexive.

N.B. however that the method is not problematic—would require the determination of natural basis of society and enumeration of problems of kinds of states and individuals. Rather the preservation of a framework of discussion—test by hearing the reasons for opposed positions. *Opinion*

Contrast to logistic method of Hobbes + Spinoza—Freedom – power – nature. Omission of nature. Freedom = power Opinion. Operational.

Ideas and Methods 202[9]

Kant and Mill

Kant — Reflexive, Operational, Ontological.

Mill — Reflexive, Operational, Existential.

Hobbes — Actional, Logistic, Existential

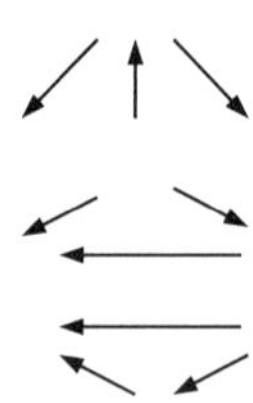

Begin with differences of interpretation—

Liberty as *spontaneity* for Mill, differences of opinion and their discrimination as method, limited only by self-protection in interference with the liberties of others—individual and society in balance in method.

Liberty as the means by which the good will (which is alone good) related to the maxim in which absolute duty set forth. Liberty *doing as one should*—all men, men as end, rule self-imposed. Difference of kinds of law natural and moral—therefore kinds of reason—pure and practical—and realms of necessity and freedom. *Two duties* within realm of freedom—to self and others nearest to selfish and other regarding duties of Mill—former not duty. Reflexivity not in self-protection but in examination of the forms of reason in critical philosophy and self-legislation in morals.

Difference of interpretation—between the existential and the ontological—affects the methods and principles in their operation. One interpretation Ontic, involving appeal to reality beyond phenomenal experience; the other phenomenal, involving continued appeal to discriminated perspectives from which judgments of reality are evolved.

Kant schematism of duties therefore involves distinction between perfect and imperfect (or medium) duty, as well as distinction between self and others.

Mill in virtue of his interpretation drops perpendicular distinction (all phenomenal) but retains distinction between self and other regarding duties.

Center of the difference between the two therefore becomes methodological—human actions with a beginning and end. Utilitarianism the method of consequences, the critical philosophy the method of the a priori. Judgment of the one by the other in this inverse: Kant no morality without duty with an a priori rule; Mill no morality without consideration of utilities.

(Cf. Cicero and the stoic consideration of duties—honesta and utilia).

Further consequence—what is discriminated by Mill is opinions—what men think are true and false, and the method leads to the recognition of the need of freedom of thought and expression (to maintain the vitality even of opinions which happen to be true—true doctrines without knowledge of reasons lose force). What is discriminated by Kant is kinds of imperatives, categorical and hypothetical, which are basically practical and theoretic, and the possibility of morality depends on maintaining that distinction.

Similar changes in the principles. Both reflexive principles. But for Kant the reflexivity of freedom consists in self-legislation, since the operational method discriminates imperatives. For Mill the reflexivity of freedom consists in self-protection, the operational method discriminates opinions, and in that discrimination recognizes the danger that the concern might be focused on what society ought to like and dislike rather than on whether its likings and dislikings should be a law to individuals. Therefore the need to preserve individuality and spontaneity while recognizing the importance of the social virtues. N.B. the priority of the practical in both—Practical reason and its ideas prior to pure reason; utilitarianism and the test of truth.

Note finally that these differences due to difference in interpretation leave open the question whether in spite of philosophic differences, the applications of the morality to the same situations would yield different decisions.

DISCUSSION

Mill, Part 2
(*On Liberty*, Chapter II: Of the Liberty of Thought and Discussion)

Discussion Summary

Today we will continue our discussion of Mill. Students have asked me, What is the value of learning your schematism, Professor McKeon? Well, my answer is that knowing a philosopher's principle, method, and interpretation leads to concrete questions. This does not mean that we will have the right understanding of Mill, or of any philosopher, for that matter. There are as many interpretations of any philosopher as there are of nature itself. Examining the systematic interrelation allows us to be clear about what we are assuming.[1]

So, let us look at chapter II. Does the earlier treatment by Mill afford guidance to the treatment in this chapter? Why do we start where we do? In the introductory chapter, he said we will take up three questions. Does he follow his outline? How will we discuss the problems of liberty? Remember that in his schema in chapter I, the schism began with the ruler and the ruled, then turned to society and the individual. Thereafter we found that there are three ways in which liberty manifests itself and why they are different: (1) consciousness and expression; (2) tastes and pursuits; and (3) combination among individuals. We see this on page 75 [in E; L:16].[2] These three set up the state, which results, for all we know, from accidental circumstances. Notice, there is nothing prior in the operational method. He rarely talks of freedom of thought but, rather, mostly of freedom of expression. Freedom of thought cannot be suppressed, whereas expression can. Expression comes in, then, in that it is hard to think without thinking in words; thus, thinking and thinking explicitly are on the same general level.

In the operational method, man is often at the center with what he says and does. So, let us look more closely at what man says and does. First, we deal with man, and we are talking of things that go on in a man's mind, what he really thinks and wants to say. This is man thinking and expressing his thought. Note that this is a product, not a potentiality. Second, having expressed his thought, man does something. One of the assumptions of the operational method is that although thinking and doing are both instances of doing, we can differentiate them. Whatever man does comes about because it is what he wants to do, whether based on a flaw in thinking or on human desire. This, then, is taste, which includes what he thinks and feels and is not something innate to his nature. From this, consequently, we get pursuits. For example, if we have a taste to paint or to make money, we will get a difference in pursuit; that is, we will have a difference between the freedom of expression and the freedom to act, which, finally, leads us to character. Thus, we now have the basis and performance of two freedoms: the first is man, and the second is character. Significantly, we have shifted away from nature and to exercise. So, to repeat, Mill's principle is reflexive, his method is operational, and his interpretation is existential. Consequently, to make a distinction, we can only bring in an individual agent and the agent to which it addresses itself; in other words, we can only bring in the speaker and the one spoken to. This is the commitment of the operational method.

Spontaneity is one of the key ingredients here. How is spontaneity possible? Remember that in chapter I, man first expresses himself spontaneously. Second, he has character and acts spontaneously. Third, this occurs in a variety of circumstances, but we can have spontaneity only if we can have a variety of circumstances. It is this third freedom that makes the first two meaningful; in other words, if man had no freedom of the circumstantial sort, the other two are meaningless. In chapter II, Mill begins with the first two, because they are generally accepted, but he also begins here for another reason. Because he is using the operational method, he can begin with a negation of liberty, namely, the suppression of an expressed opinion, since it hasn't a nature. Remember that Kant, also using the operational method, similarly began with a negative form of his contrary duties by treating the issue of the violation of duty.[3] Here, Mill starts by saying that "the peculiar evil of silencing the expression of an opinion" [E:79; L:21] can be explored by asking what happens if we do two opposite things. The result is that we get two contraries; namely, the opinion expressed is either true or it is false, and that suppression of either would be bad; that is, we would be "robbing the human race" in two ways:

> If the opinion is right, they are deprived of the opportunity of exchanging error for truth; if wrong, they lose, what is almost as great a benefit, the clearer perception and livelier impression of truth produced by its collision with error. [ibid.][4]

Thus, chapter II divides according to these two hypotheses, and to them Mill adds a third possibility, one that is not a new hypothesis but merely follows from the first two. This third hypothesis arises

> when the conflicting doctrines, instead of being one true and the other false, share the truth between them, and the nonconforming opinion is needed to supply the remainder of the truth of which the received doctrine embodies only a part. [E:105; L:56]

So, we have two branches, plus a third. Our three hypotheses are that the opinion is true, the opinion is false, and the opinion is neither—a mixture of true and false.

How does our three-step argument develop? If the opinion is true—and notice, we are beginning with the assumption that no one can tell whether it is true or false—we are assuming our infallibility if we deny or suppress it. In the operational method, we can only act short of certainty: probability is the best we can hope for. Setting ourselves up as infallible leads to a tendency to condemn the best, those, Mill states, like Socrates, Christ, Dr. Johnson, and the Christians. Mill is pointing out that the assumption of infallibility would tend to lead to a condemnation of the best along with the worst. The penalties here involve both the legal ones as well as the social stigma the former strengthen. What is the price paid for this? The result is that by being careful in expressing our opinions, we give up our originality and lose the "moral courage of the human mind" [E:93; L:40]. Moreover, we can also do a disservice to mankind by quashing truth.

Moving on in Mill's outline, in the second section of chapter II [E:95; L:43][5] we address what happens if we suppress something we assume to be false. Notice what he does here: he first said we would assume that the opinion expressed is true, but now he seems to be going on to say that it is not relevant whether it is true or is false, that is, is false in that it is contrary to accepted opinion. Since we are talking of freedom of expression, what is false is only false for its being contrary to the accepted opinion, to the situation where no one else holds the view being expressed. So, expressions are being divided into true and false only because it is wrong to express one or the other. Therefore, if we have two social situations with loose definitions of true and false, we can end up suppressing true or false opinions. In short, the mere statement that an opinion is true or false is not adequate. Unless we can give the reasoning for any particular position, it cannot be judged as true or false; both sides are possible. The only way in which we can talk about true or false is to examine, as Cicero said,[6] the opposing side of the argument even more carefully than your own; moreover, we should want the contrary opinion expounded by those who believe it. Thus, we must not suppress the other views.

We will go on next time and look at chapter III. As you read, ask yourself, What happens to our outline?

McKeon's Notes

Mill On Liberty 2.[7]

Method

Chapter 2. Of the Liberty of Thought and Discussion. 78 *(19)*

Liberty of the press now universally recognized—but footnote on the press persecution of 1858. *(20)*

Government and people: *power of coercion illegitimate.*

If all mankind minus one of one opinion, neither justified in silencing the other.

Peculiar evil of silencing expression of an opinion that it robs the human race:

(1) if right, of opportunity to change error for truth;

(2) if wrong, of clearer perception of truth provided by collision with error

Consider these two *hypotheses*, each of which has a distinct branch of argument corresponding to it. We can never be sure the opinion we are endeavoring to stifle is a false opinion; and if we were sure, stifling it would still be an evil. (79) *(21)*

First: opinion may be true. (79) *(21) 17 (a)* Lack of infallibility—individual and group. Responsibility to act, short of certainty. Test: argue those who hesitate to push defense of freedom too far. *83 26 (b)* Truth and utility of an opinion. 84

Not being sure of a doctrine, but undertaking to decide for others—assumption of infallibility

Immorality and impiety. Condemnation of best—Socrates 86 *29*, Christ 86 *30*. Marcus Aurelius 87 *31*. Dr. Johnson persecutors of Christianity right 88 *33*.

Error of assumption that persecution does *truth* no harm (88–89). *33–34* Real advantage of truth—periodic rediscovery 90. Persecution of atheism 90.

Penalties of social stigma as well as legal penalties 92.

Price paid for intellectual pacification—sacrifice of *the entire moral courage of a human mind. Makes conformers to common-place or time-servers for truth*. 93

Harm of *failure to discuss* heretical opinions to those who are not heretics. 94.

Three periods of casting off yoke of authority—Reformation, latter half of eighteenth century, Germany of Goethean and Fichtean period. 95.

Second: Opinion may be false 95. *Assume they are true. 43, 34* Assent to what is true without arguments not enough. Learning grounds of arguments against. Mathematics—nothing on other side; natural philosophy other explanation possible; morals, religion, politics, social relations and business of life. *Cicero*—and the principle of examining opposed arguments. Not only hear them explained by one's teachers, but by those who believe them.

Imagine opponents if they do not exist. If not all mankind, at least the experts—ex. of Catholic Church 98.

Not only the grounds of an opinion forgotten in absence of discussion but also its meaning.

Degradation of ethical doctrines of religions. 99ff.

Average Christian and Christian morality 101

Early Christians. 102

Prudence and knowledge of life as well as religion and morality. 102. But is absence of unanimity an indispensable condition of true knowledge? 103

Progress—lessen number and gravity of truths uncontested. Seek substitute for opposition—but instead abandoning of Socratic dialectics, medieval disputation. Need of opponents to contest opinion.

Finally—no choice between the conflicting doctrines 105 *45*. Share truth between them. Each a portion of the truth.

Paradoxes of Rousseau 106. Simplicity of life vs. artificial society.

Politics—party of stability and party of progress

Democracy-aristocracy; property-equality; cooperation-competition; luxury-abstinence; sociality-individuality; liberty-discipline—each expressed with equal freedom. 107.

Intolerance in England of differences on these.

Some privileged principles more than half-truths? 107 Christian morality. N.T. and Paul—preexisting morality; theological morality later. Christian morality a reaction—negative and passive. Omits duty to state—Koran. 109. Sayings of Christ only part of morality. Not complete rule for our guidance 110. Low servile type of character.

Exclusive pretensions—just to infidels 110

Tendency of all opinions to become sectarian.

Recapitulate four grounds for freedom of expression (1) *True*—not infallible, (2) *Part truth*—silenced opinion may contain portion of truth, *Wholly true—(3)* importance of collision, even if whole truth (4) meaning of doctrine apt to be lost.

Finally impossibility of limiting because of manner of expression—sophisticated, bigoted, bad, immoral

---

DISCUSSION

Mill, Part 3 (*On Liberty*, Chapter II: Of the Liberty of Thought and Discussion)

Discussion Summary

Today we will continue our discussion of Mill's *On Liberty* by returning to our examination of chapter II.[1] As we saw last time in this chapter, Mill says he must take two contrary possibilities into account regarding opinions: that the suppressed opinion is right, where we assume the suppressed opinion to be true, or that the suppressed opinion is wrong, where we assume the received opinion to be true.

What does Mill set forth as his argument in chapter II? First, we shouldn't suppress an opinion if it is false, and we shouldn't suppress an opinion if it is true. Let us look at this from the point of view of the operational method. If we have an operational argument, how does it proceed? A characteristic of the operational method is that we operate on something with it. Let us begin at the beginning and assume that the suppressed opinion is true. We can't start by knowing the opinion is, in fact, true; for no one knows whether, by itself, it is true or false. We can't identify the true. The opinion may be true, but those who suppress it consider it false. So, operationally, we can't decide at the beginning; rather, you interpret as you go along. To begin with a list of the true opinions is to suppress the possibility of giving an operational argument for or of having a debate regarding the opinions. In other words, the position in the operational argument is that we cannot know whether opinion is right or wrong until it has been shown forth by means of argument. Notice, this is also seen in the case of Kant, where he lists categorical imperatives by examples of duties (see the discussion on Kant, part 2, and figs. 33, 36, and 37 above).

We begin on page 79 [in E; L:21].[2] The opinion that we attempt to suppress may be true, but we cannot at the beginning decide whether it is true or false. Remember, in the operational method, by itself any statement can be true or false. Only people who think they know the true can list the false; and

> [to] refuse a hearing to an opinion because they are sure that it is false is to assume that *their* certainty is the same thing as *absolute* certainty. All silencing of discussion is an assumption of infallibility. [E:79; L:21–22—italics in original]

Therefore, we cannot identify falsity simply from the mere statement of it; we must go into the operational argument. Note how we have translated the argument into our terms by way of the operational method. The operational method does this all the time: we start with two hypotheses that formally exhaust the possibilities, yet it is not easy to find the meaning of either hypothesis merely in itself. Here, one suppresses the false only when he thinks himself infallible. In short, characteristic of this approach is the perspective you take.

Mill explores his first hypothesis from three perspectives. The first view is the theoretic, namely, in the operational approach, what would happen if we do our analysis from the point of view of truth. The second view is the practical, that is, what actually happens in action. Most people, Mill argues, would grant their fallibility in theory; but they don't act upon that in their practical judgments, accepting, rather, their deeply held opinions as certain. Here, Mill uses the term *responsibility*, in the sense of the responsibility to act short of certainty, thereby acknowledging the necessity of taking action; yet he emphasizes that such action must grow out of a context in which there exists the complete freedom of dissenting opinions to be expressed. He also considers the frequent argument which says that in practice, we shouldn't take the argument for freedom of opinion too far. Refuting this argument, he says,

> Strange it is, that men should admit the validity of arguments for free discussion, but object to their being "pushed to an extreme"; not seeing that unless the reasons are good for an extreme case, they are not good for any case. [E:83; L:26]

Finally, the third perspective is that of utility [E:84; L:27]. He gives consideration to what the effect is on society as a whole of permitting such expression of diverse opinions and, in defense of that diversity, argues that we thereby avoid suppression of the better individuals and opinions.

The second main division of Mill's argument in chapter II begins on page 95 [in E; L:43].[3] What if the received opinion is true? The difficulty is that by itself, we can't know. We need to make a separate argument beyond the mere statement of the opinion: we can never be sure whether the opinion is false; and if even we were sure, it would still be an evil to strike it down. Designating something as false depends on a conviction of the truth; we know the false by means of someone else's argument. Truth is known only by argument; therefore, to be sure of your opinion, you must know both your argument as well as the argument of those you are contradicting. Unsupported by reasoning, an opinion can be false yet have no characteristic of being false; conversely, no characteristic can be found in an unsupported true proposition to mark it as true. Again, only contact with others will tell you the truth or falsity of a proposition.

Notice, these are not the same argument in both cases. Two different, though related, arguments are required, which can be seen, for instance, in his use of the common example of the Roman Catholic Church for each case [see E:83 and E:98; L:26 and L:47].[4] On these two pages, we see the same example, but one involving a different argument. In the first instance, Mill describes how the Catholic Church uses a "devil's advocate" when testing the case for someone being proposed posthumously for sainthood so that it can listen to all sorts of opinions that can be raised against the proposed individual's elevation, thereby assuring that the individual is truly a saint. In this case, the devil's advocate can be used to discover truth; but he can also be used to suppress opinion, namely, to identify the opinions that the church ultimately finds to be false. In the second use of the Catholic example, Mill observes that the church separates its believers into those who accept doctrine on conviction, knowing both the arguments for and those against a particular doctrine, and those believers who accept doctrine on trust without knowing the supportive reasoning. In both of these cases, the church's doctrinal position must be accepted as true, though on different grounds, namely, on conviction *versus* on trust. In order to get to a truth that is the clearest possible, to get conviction, the church recognizes that one must read heresy: you have to use false opinion to show that the church's (and your) opinion is true. Consequently, Mill's first use of the Catholic Church example looks at the possibility that the other's argument—the one presented by the devil's advocate—is true, and the received position—the one proposing that the individual should be viewed as a saint—is false. By contrast, in his second use, Mill shows how the received opinion of the church is held as true and alternatives to it are false, including the reasoning why the alternatives are false. Thus, in the operational method, we must supplement the true with the false, the one with the other.

On page 105 [in E; L:55],[5] Mill begins the third part of his argument. In repeating his language, he shows how he is not labeling either position as true or false in itself but is setting up the conditions for discussion. Notice, he is not now adding a third hypothesis; rather, each of the two hypotheses must be supplemented by a mixture of the other. This mixed position is given as a third possibility, namely, that each opinion is only partially true. Consequently, this is not an argument where, in method, we proceed deductively or dialectically or where we resolve problems. In Mill, the debate does not change the issues involved; consequently, it is not a dialectical method. Here he argues that this situation of mixed opinions is the "commoner case": it occurs

> when the conflicting doctrines, instead of being one true and the other false, share the truth between them; and the nonconforming opinion is needed to supply the remainder of the truth, of which the received doctrine embodies only a part. [E:105; L:56]

Remember, a debate indicates conflict, not the talking about higher truths which synthesize the apparent disagreement. Earlier on this point, Mill has appealed to Cicero; now he argues that the progress of science is also a consequence of this debate. Moreover, we can see that this is debate and not dialectic from the use of examples. What's the meaning of a partial truth? He gives the example of Rousseau's being partly right—art *has* hurt society—but the latter's defense of total primitivism is wrong. (Notice that Rousseau, like Mill, is working formally with a pair of contraries, in Rousseau's case, Art and Nature.) So, Mill is proving his own case by giving examples and giving meaning to words. In short, the operational method shows forth (the literal meaning of *demonstrate*) and gives meanings; thus, using instances is itself the proof.

At the end of chapter II, Mill gives a recapitulation of the grounds for the freedom of expression, the general topic of this chapter, which summarizes the four parts of his argument [E:111; L:64].[6] How does he get these four parts, that is, move from two hypotheses to three distinctions to four conclusions? From the beginning, we have been interested in distinguishing the false from the true opinion. He begins,

> First, if any opinion is compelled to silence, that opinion may, for aught we can certainly know, be true. To deny this is to assume our own infallibility.

So, the first of the grounds for the freedom of expression is that the suppressed opinion may be true. To this he adds,

> Secondly, though the silenced opinion be an error, it may, and very commonly does, contain a portion of truth; and since the general or prevailing opinion on any subject is rarely or never the whole truth, it is only by the collision of adverse opinions that the remainder of the truth has any chance of being supplied.

Here, neither the suppressed nor the received opinion is the whole truth, and so both must be placed in collision with each other through debate.

> Thirdly, even if the received opinion be not only true, but the whole truth; unless it is suffered to be, and actually is, vigorously and earnestly contested,

> it will, by most of those who receive it, be held in the manner of a prejudice, with little comprehension or feeling of its rational grounds. [E:111–12; L:64]

Thus, the received opinion may be the whole truth; but if it is not contested, it will not be held rationally. Finally, the fourth conclusion is that without debate,

> the meaning of the doctrine itself will be in danger of being lost, or enfeebled, and deprived of its vital effect on the character and conduct: the dogma becoming a mere formal profession, inefficacious for good, but cumbering the ground, and preventing the growth of any real and heartfelt conviction, from reason or personal experience. [E:112; L:64]

Here Mill raises the problem that the very meaning of truth may slip away, that the individual will lack the emotional conviction needed for action based on truth.

Notice in this fourth conclusion that operationally, the truth for Mill is not merely intellectual, and this is an important point of agreement with Kant. Such is the situation of debate: there, the received opinion is necessarily old opinion, and the old continually needs resuscitation. Therefore, we must set received opinion against anything else that might come up; and we can exhaust the possibilities of other opinions by means of our schematism, which shows all the possibilities which can occur. The movement of the argument has given us the reason why we can now say, "We have now recognized the necessity to the mental well-being of mankind (on which all their other well-being depends) of freedom of opinion, and freedom of the expression of opinion" [E:111; L:64]. The truth is not only what we mentally hold on to, but it also has meaning for the existential situation into which we are put. In other words, truth has significance and use in concrete situations of action. Remember, this was the sequence in the introduction to our argument in chapter I. There, "the appropriate region of human liberty" [E:75; L:16] entails, first, freedom of consciousness and expression, translated into the stance of the individual. Second comes taste, which is one's tendency, and pursuit, which is what one moves on to. At the end of chapter II, then, Mill is ready to make the transition to these individual tastes and pursuits. "Individuality, as One of the Elements of Well-Being," chapter III's title, reflects the way we are formed by our tastes and pursuits, which can now be addressed. So, chapter III will explore individuality as the translation of one's tastes and pursuits; and we thereby go on to issues of action and move beyond the earlier ones of freedom of thought as revealed in expression.

But first, let us address why this is the operational method. We have seen the importance of aphorisms for Mill and his use of individual ex-

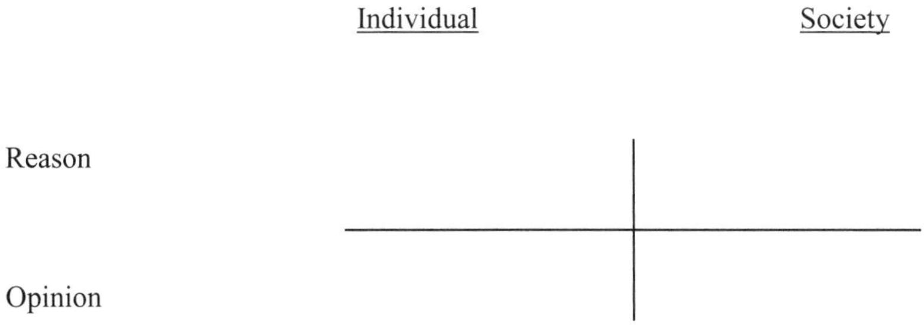

Fig. 44 *Mill's Schematism of True/False Opinion*

ample for inductive proof. However, the basic reason why this is an operational method can be seen in the similar schematisms used by Kant and Mill. Where Kant distinguished between self and other (see figs. 36 and 37 in the Kant discussions above), Mill talks of the individual and society (see fig. 44).[7] In addition, where, because of interpretation, Kant had imperfect and perfect duties, Mill has opinion and moves up to reason. By virtue of their differing interpretations, opinion is not a pejorative term for Mill, who is using a phenomenal, in particular an existentialist, one; whereas for Kant as well as for Plato, who both use an ontic interpretation, namely, an ontological one, opinion is pejorative. Similarly, reason is not absolute for Mill but, rather, the reason for an opinion; for Kant and Plato, however, reason itself is absolute. In short, any operational argument can be reduced to this same pattern, no matter the interpretation or principle involved.

How, then, does Mill deal with freedom of thought and expression? In the first statement of this division of the argument, he argues that freedom of thought is internal, and states that many think that the principle that governs freedom of expression differs from that which governs freedom of thought. However, for Mill, an unexpressed opinion is no opinion; therefore, he turns to possible expressions of it, both suppressed and received, and derives his hypotheses from the four squares of his schematism. Like Kant, he uses a negative form of argumentation. Where Kant dealt with the violation of duty, Mill considers freedom of thought in terms of an argument that one should not have freedom of thought, that is, of expressed opinions. He proceeds by dividing his argument into three exhaustive hypotheses. The first hypothesis is that the suppressed opinion may be considered false; but that happens when the received opinion is taken as absolutely true, a position which grows out of an assumption of infallibility and involves one in dogmatism (see fig. 45).[8] This hypothesis gets treated in a three-step argument from the perspectives of theory, practice, and utility. The second hypothesis is that

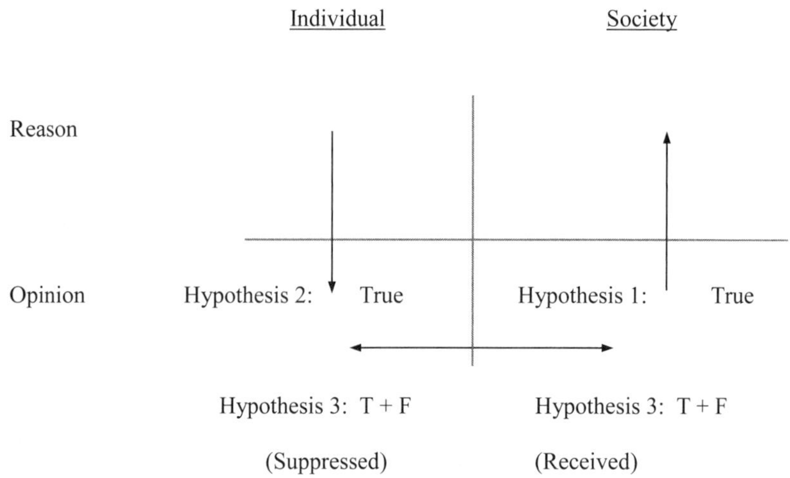

Fig. 45 *Mill's T/F Schematism and Three Hypotheses*

the suppressed opinion may be true, but Mill does not use the same argument as before, namely, that the received opinion is false; rather, one must go to the reason for holding the suppressed opinion. Here Mill examines three different areas of subject matter—mathematics, natural philosophy (science), and practical matters—from the viewpoint of the use of reason in them and introduces the example of Cicero. The third hypothesis, growing from the first two, is the much more common circumstance where both the received and the suppressed opinions are true and not true at once. In this instance, one must find the reason which will remove the false in the received opinion and make it true.

From these three hypotheses, Mill generates his recapitulation of four distinct grounds or conditions for the freedom of expression of opinion and, ultimately, for the freedom of thought; and these four conclusions directly reflect the fourfold character of his schematism. In the first place, we assume the suppressed opinion is true, and then assume it is false; in either case, we are interested in the reasons for, the truth of, the suppressed opinion (see *(a)* in fig. 46).[9] In the second *(b)*, we suppose that both suppressed and received opinions are true as well as false. In the third *(c)*, we suppose the received opinion is wholly true; but unless we have discussion, we won't know the reasons for the received opinion. In the fourth *(d)*, the possibility exists that the received opinion, although true, will lack vitality and lose meaning, thereby preventing the heartfelt conviction needed for action. So, four arguments are here because there are four boxes in the schematism. We began with two hypotheses because we started with the empirical opinions around us, and the three

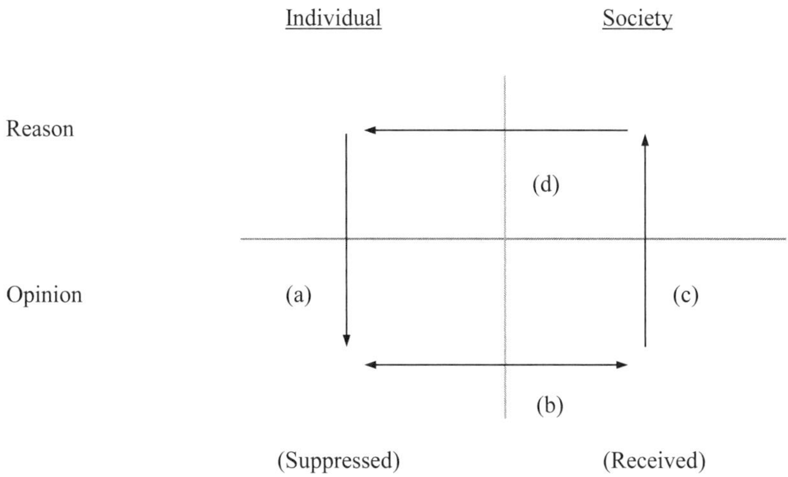

Fig. 46 *Mill's T/F Schematism and Four Conclusions*

divisions of our argument came out of the hypotheses because the truth is not wholly anywhere.

If we were to analyze chapter II in the form of a syllogism by means of the logistic method, we would have to make it an approximation. We would have imperfections; and if we did that, we would have to say that Mill was a little confused or that he did not see clearly what was involved. The same result would occur with other methods. The operational method does not make the analysis any truer, but it does give reasons for things Mill does, like the transition from two hypotheses to three arguments to four grounds for the freedom of thought and expression. The operational way of analysis gives a neat merry-go-round.

McKeon's Notes

Mill On Liberty 2.

Sequence of argument in Chapter 2. Operational method.

Schematism similar to that of Kant in the Fundamental Principles—individual and society instead of self and other in horizontal distinction; existential as opposed to ontological interpretation put emphasis on the empirical rather than the pure in perpendicular dimension—opinion to reason for opinion instead of perfect duties to imperfect duties.

Argument by filling in the possible squares: negative form again, as in Kant violation of duty. Silenced opinion and received opinion.

(1) Silenced opinion false—only if received opinion held dogmatically to be true: assumption of infallibility, silencing of discussion. (a) truth and discus-

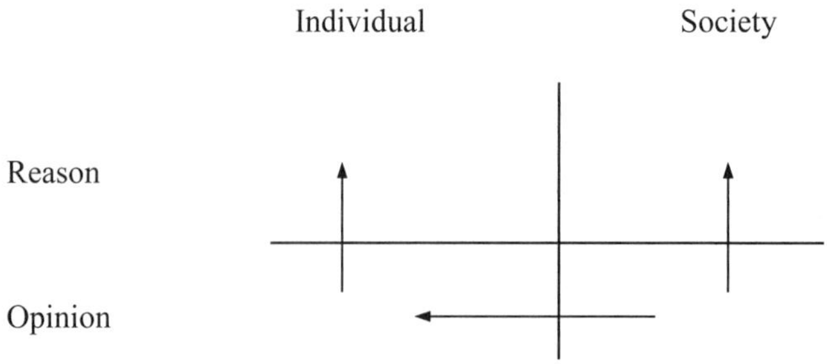

sion, (b) utility—usefulness of an opinion, condemnation of the best, (c) test of truth—truth and persecution.
(2) Opinion may be true. Do not use same argument—i.e. that received opinion false. Go rather to reason for holding it. Cicero and method
(3) The third possibility—usually the case—both are mixture of true and false.

Summary four distinct grounds — the form square of the diagram

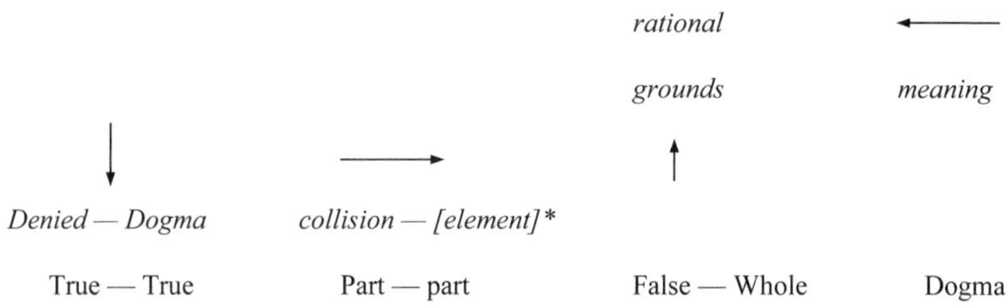

*** The editors are uncertain that this is the handwritten term McKeon uses here**

(1) silenced opinion true—deny this—infallibility
(2) silenced opinion in error, may contain a portion of the truth—received opinion seldom whole truth
(3) received opinion whole truth—unless contested little comprehension of rational ground.
(4) Meaning of doctrine lost—no heartfelt conviction.

Operational transformation of the second part of the outline given in the Introductory: (1) inward domain of consciousness—freedom of thought and sentiment. Liberty of expression and publishing opinions may seem to fall under a different principle—individual conduct which concerns other people; "but, being almost of as much importance as the liberty of thought itself and resting in great part on the same reasons, is practically inseparable from it."
(2) "the principle requires liberty of tastes and pursuits"—plan of life and doing what we like.

Becomes "Of Individuality, as one of the Elements of Well-Being."

DISCUSSION

Mill, Part 4
(*On Liberty*, Chapter III: Of Individuality, as One of the Elements of Well-Being; Chapter IV: Of the Limits to the Authority of Society over the Individual)

Discussion Summary

Chapter III is to be an examination of tastes and actions. Remember that in the introduction, the principle requires liberty not just of thought and expression but also of tastes and pursuits—a plan of life and doing as we like. This now appears in the chapter's title, "Of Individuality, as One of the Elements of Well-Being." Near the beginning of the chapter he says,

> As it is useful that while mankind are imperfect there should be different opinions, so it is that there should be different experiments of living; that free scope should be given to varieties of character, short of injury to others; and that the worth of different modes of life should be proved practically, when anyone thinks fit to try them. It is desirable, in short, that in things which do not primarily concern others, individuality should assert itself. [E:114–15; L:68][1]

Our individuality is the way we are formed by our tastes and pursuits, and testing our way of living "practically" is important in an operational method. So, we must talk of the reasons for action of both the individual and society, because humans act for reasons. Moreover, if we want to talk of individual action, we need to find out how individuality can be preserved in society. Why is individuality so important? Because it is essential to achieving the well-being of the individual.

What, then, is the argument of chapter III regarding the principle of the freedom of action? It has two parts. The first:

> In maintaining this principle, the greatest difficulty to be encountered does not lie in the appreciation of means toward an acknowledged end, but in the indifference of persons in general to the end itself. [E:115; L:68–69]

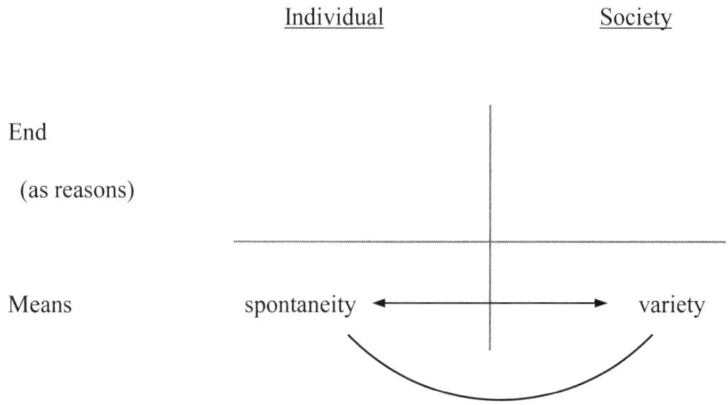

Fig. 47 *Mill on Individuality as Development*

So, the initial step of his argument is the treatment of the question of the general indifference to the end itself.[2] In the second step, Mill argues that since "individuality is the same thing with development" [E:121; L:77],[3] one must point out to those who do not desire liberty for themselves that they will be rewarded if they let others have it. So, the two parts of chapter III grow out of the fact that in any action a difference exists between the end, the reason for the action, and the means, and that you can either take the end into account or leave it out, just examining the means (see fig. 47).[4] In other words, Mill first assumes we want to persuade those indifferent to liberty as an end that liberty is an important end. However, he next assumes that this first argument is lost and that given the existential interpretation, he can then attempt to persuade his opponents that even solely as a means, liberty, letting others be spontaneous, is better for the opponents. Again, notice how the operational method tends to prove something by assuming the contrary.

Let us examine this in more detail. How does Mill treat the first half of his argument? As we have noted, he argues from the perspective of the negative, from the position opposed to the one he holds, namely, that liberty is not an end. For Mill, the liberty of an individual is seen in spontaneity; but he recognizes that most people do not think of spontaneity as an end. So, he needs to give meaning to spontaneity, which he does by quoting Wilhelm von Humboldt, who said that spontaneity in the individual does not make sense in isolation; rather, spontaneity means something only in relation to society. It is when we put spontaneity in relation to society, though, that we might get into difficulty because of the variety of circumstances possible. However, he argues that spontaneity actually develops when confronted with a variety of circumstances, and the individual can thereby develop his own individuality. Mill says Humboldt adds a further point:

> Human nature is not a machine to be built after a model, and set to do exactly the work prescribed for it, but a tree, which requires to grow and develop itself on all sides, according to the tendency of the inward forces which make it a living thing. [E:117; L:72]

So, the individual is not a mechanistic model merely acting according to its design; rather, humans follow impulses of their own. It is on this basis that Mill looks at individuality as spontaneity. He goes on to show the way in which freedom as spontaneity in a variety of circumstances will give rise to self-development if it occurs in a situation of self-protection. He sees this in primitive society where, contrary to the normal cliché about it and its supposed constraints upon the individual, the reality is that individuality, spontaneity, is in excess. By contrast, in our time everyone lives under censorship. At this point, Mill uses his reflexive principle to explore how others have gone about trying to straighten the issue out. The Calvinists may have held that self-will is an offense; yet if we look at the rest of history as well—from the Pagan self-assertion through the Greek idea of self-development and the Christian one of self-denial to the Platonic and Christian conception of self-government—we can see a progress of individuality. In all of this, Mill has tried to show the way in which the freedom of spontaneity in a variety of circumstances will give self-development if in circumstances of self-protection—this, of course, being held in balance with the liberty of others. Such is his argument.

Then we come to a sentence where it might seem that Mill is saying that we have done all we have to.

> Having said that the individuality is the same thing with development, and that it is only the cultivation of individuality which produces, or can produce, well-developed human beings, I might here close the argument: . . .

However, he proceeds to show that if this idea of liberty as an end is rejected, one can still argue for it as a means:

> Doubtless, however, these considerations will not suffice to convince those who most need convincing; and it is necessary further to show, that these developed human beings are of some use to the undeveloped—to point out to those who do not desire liberty, and would not avail themselves of it, that they may be in some intelligible manner rewarded for allowing other people to make use of it without hindrance. [E:121–22; L:77–78]

He wants to demonstrate to the people who do not desire liberty for themselves that doing so would be an advantage for them, and that

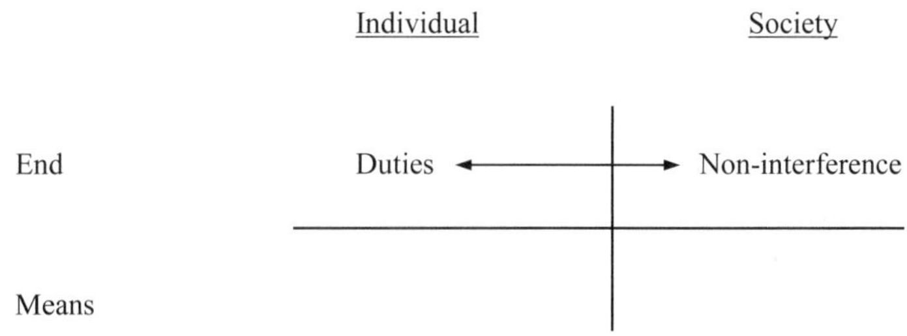

Fig. 48 *Mill on Limits of Social Authority*

therefore, they should allow such liberty for others. This gives rise to three points. In the first place, the alternative to allowing liberty to others is that society would have collective mediocrity—not something we would want. Second, there is no reason that the pattern of lives should conform to just one model. There is no single best pattern—one's own is what is best. Third, diversity of character leads to improvement. As Mill states, "The only unfailing and permanent source of improvement is liberty" [E:128; L:86]. To summarize, then: we want to keep what we have but don't thereby want mediocrity; there is no reason that all men should be the same; and improvement is possible. This analysis ties the idea of liberty for others to the argument that liberty is the end of action. Now we can say that the argument is exhaustive of all possibilities. Our reasons lie in the end which we seek. If we engage in action, reason leads to the selection of means.

In chapter IV, "Of the Limits to the Authority of Society over the Individual," Mill turns to the third region of human liberty laid out in his introduction (see chapter I [E:75; L:16]), namely, that we should have freedom to form associations. Why this? What is the relation to chapter III? Now we need look up to the top half of our diagram (see fig. 48)[5] to find our argument, and it has two parts in its treatment of the individual and society. As Mill expresses the proper balance between the two:

> How much of human life should be assigned to individuality, and how much to society?
>
> Each will receive its proper share, if each has that which more particularly concerns it. To individuality should belong the part of life in which it is chiefly the individual that is interested; to society, that part which chiefly interests society. [E:131–32; L:91]

Consequently, the first part of the argument in this chapter looks at the situation where social interests are primary; there, the influence of society over the individual leads to duty. Conversely, the second part of the argument looks at where individual interests are primary; there, he finds non-interference by society is best, even though one may still owe duties.

This second part, Mill believes, is crucial:

> The strongest of all the arguments against the interference of the public with purely personal conduct is that, when it does interfere, the odds are that it interferes wrongly, and in the wrong place. [E:140; L:102][6]

This is similar to Kant and, as we shall see, to Machiavelli, who both set up two different domains—the personal and the social.[7] To these domains Mill applies the operational method and makes arguments for two differences. In regard to social morality, the majority is usually right, and he notes that the majority tends to invest their own prejudices with the character of law. Conversely, from the perspective of personal or individual morality, he says "the odds are" that the public is wrong—note the operational character of this proposition in its expression in terms of probabilities—and goes on to give seven examples. As we have seen before, this is the way an operational method works.

Turning to chapter V, "Applications," Mill gathers all his conclusions together into two maxims in the second paragraph.

> The maxims are, first, that the individual is not accountable to society for his actions in so far as these concern the interests of no person but himself. . . . Secondly, that for such actions as are prejudicial to the interests of others, the individual is accountable, and may be subjected either to social or to legal punishment, if society is of opinion that the one or the other is requisite for its protection. [E:149–50; L114]

Consequently, the rest of the chapter is an examination of the way you can use these two formulations in detailed applications. Note that there are no general laws; rather, we always need to consider the detailed application of the maxims in specific circumstances.

[At this point in the discussion, one student's notes introduce two unelaborated notations, one a ratio and one a diagram:

"Ratio — Right : Law :: Nature : Transcendence";

and

The first is a ratio McKeon uses in lecture 8 when discussing the character of the existentialist interpretation, which is common to both Mill and Machiavelli. The second is a pair of terms joined by arrows in the manner McKeon uses in the basic knowledge matrix, clearly referring to the operational method, one that, again, both Mill and Machiavelli use, as well as Kant. Presumably, in both instances McKeon is connecting the particular Mill text to the former's formulation of Mill's schematism in order to exemplify how the text reflects that formulation.]

Begin reading Machiavelli's *The Prince*. The final exam will have two parts. The purpose is to deal not only with texts but also with items from memory. Half of the exam will treat texts which we have read. The other half will involve analysis of a text not addressed in class, namely, from the first forty-nine pages of Hegel's *Reason in History*; and the purpose there will be to see the manner of your interpretation.[8]

McKeon's Notes

Mill On Liberty 3.

Interpretation

Chapter 3. Of Individuality, as one of the elements of well-being. 114.

No one pretends that actions should be as free as opinions. Even opinions lose immunity when they become act.

Liberty *limited—not nuisance* to others.

Different experiments of living 115. In things that do not primarily concern others, individuality should assert itself.

(1) End

|| Difficulty in maintaining this principle, not in *means* but in *indifference to end*. Individuality coordinate as element with *civilization, instruction, education, culture*. *Spontaneity* not part of the ideal of most moral and social reformers. *Wilhelm von Humboldt*—end of man development of his powers to a complete and consistent whole. "Individuality of power and development." "Freedom and variety of situations." "*originality*." 116

Question of degree—not copy others, nor act as if nothing previously known. Find out what part of experience applicable to circumstances and character.

Faculties of perception, judgment, discriminative feeling, mental activity and moral preference exercised only in making *choice*. Mental and moral as well as muscular power improved only by being used.

Human being not built after model. 117.

Understanding, desires and impulses our own. 118

Strong impulses—energy.

Early society—element of *spontaneity* in excess.

In *our times everyone lives under* eye of dreaded censorship. 119 What suited to my position.

Calvinistic theory—self-will an offense. 119

Pagan self-assertion—Christian self-denial;

Greek ideal—self-development; Platonic and Christian ideal of self-government. 120. John Knox, Alcibiades, Pericles.

Human being as noble and *beautiful object* of contemplation. Individual bond to *race*; despotism and individuality. 121

> *individual = development.*

2. Argument for those who do not desire freedom, desirable to allow it to others.
122 *Means*
[1] Custom
Learn something from them. *Originality*. Genius breathes freely only in atmosphere of freedom.
Indifference of most to genius—get along without. 123
Individual lost in the crowd today—not a *power* as formerly. 123. Collective mediocrity. Government of mediocrity, mediocre government. Not hero-worship but power of individual vs. opinions of masses as dominant power—*eccentricity* a service. 125.
[2] The freest scope to uncustomary to determine which fit to be *converted into customs*. 125. No reason that all human existence should be constructed on one pattern.
Individual moved
Luxury of doing as one likes 126
Public opinion—general *average moderate* in intellect and in inclinations—discouragement of excesses. 127.
Result weak *feelings* and weak *energies*. Despotism of custom—hindrance to human advancement.
[3] The spirit of liberty and spirit of improvement—only unfailing source of *improvement liberty*. Liberty vs custom. Progress in Europe (inventions, politics, education, morals) vs. China—stationary. Modern regime of public opinion 129. Europe thus far preserved by diversity of character and culture.
But tendency toward Chinese ideal of making all people alike. De Tocqueville. Humboldt—*freedom and variety of situations* 130. Latter condition diminishing—political changes, extension of education, improvement of communication, increase of commerce and manufactures, and ascendancy of public opinion. Disappearance of social support for nonconformity.
One hope—value seen by the intelligent part of mankind.[9]

Concepts + Methods 202

Principles	*Methods*	*Interpretations*
How is it conceivable?	*How is it known?*	*What is it?*
possible?	*acquired?*	*What things are it?*

Mill | On Liberty | 4.

Chapter 4. Of the Limits of the authority of Society over the individual. 131.
Principle
(1) Distinctive Duties—Punishment Imperative
Individual and society—*each rules the part* of life that chiefly interests it. 132.
Society not based on contract, but one who receives benefit from it owes

return: (1) not injuring others. (2) bearing share of labors and sacrifices. *(3)* Also penalties by opinion as well as law. 132.

Not doctrine of *selfish* indifference. *Self*-regarding and *social* virtues. Education—*distinction between* better and worse. But respect for *individual spontaneity*.

Regard also for his *self*-regarding qualities or deficiencies. 133–34. Folly, lowness, or depravation. Right to act on unfavorable opinion not in oppression of his individuality but exercise of ours. 134.

Duty to self (prudence) = self-respect self-development

Inconveniences strictly inseparable from unfavorable judgment of others only one to which person should be subjected for portion of his conduct and character which concerns his own good. 135. *Acts injurious* to others totally *different treatment*. Cruelty of disposition, love of domineering, pleonexia. *Duties to ourselves* not *socially obligatory*.

Importance of the distinction. 136.

Many refuse to admit the distinction. 136.

Add the cause of children and those under age. 137.

Admit what a person does to himself affects others in sympathies and interests. But control for breach of duty—by law and opinion. 138. Drunkenness—and police or soldier.

> Contingent or constructive injury—society has absolute power when young—education, opinion, natural penalties. Cannot coerce to prudence or temperance—reaction to puritan regime. Example of *self*-harm salutary. 140.

(2) No interference with purely personal conduct—Interferes wrongly

Strongest of all arguments against public interference in purely personal conduct—odds that it *interferes wrongly*

In *social morality—majority oftener right.*

In *self-regarding conduct as likely to be wrong* as right. 140. Consider only own preference. Person's taste as much his own as his purse. No parity between feeling of a person for his own opinion and the feeling of another who is offended by his holding it.

Religion and philosophy—teaching things are right because they are right—we feel them to be so. 141.

Public of this age and country improperly invests its own *preferences* with the *character of moral laws*. 141.

Countrymen

Examples. First—Mohammedans and pork. 141.

Second, Spaniards and Catholicism. 142

Third, puritans and amusements, 143.

Fourth—democratic and socialist opinions. 143–4.

Pass beyond suppositious cases.

Fifth—intemperance and prohibition. 144–6.

Sixth Sabbatarian legislation.

Finally, Mormonism. 147.

LECTURE NINE

Power: Method (Part 2)

At our last meeting we went further into the aspects of the definition of power. We had talked about selection and interpretation; and as I told you, I wanted to give you some notion of how method cooperates with these, and therefore told you about the dialectical method, pausing at least briefly to indicate that the meaning of power yielded by the dialectical method could combine with any of the four interpretations of power. I will now review what we did on dialectic and then move to the other three methods.

Let me recall to you the interpretations which are answers to the question, What has power to do what? First, the ontic interpretations (see table 14). We had, for the ontological interpretation, the power to perfect; therefore, it is the wise man who has a power insofar as he has a freedom. The entitative interpretation is the power to move unassistedly; therefore, a body unrestricted has power. Now the two phenomenal interpretations. The existentialist is the power to initiate; therefore, animate things have power if they can start something. Finally, the essentialist: the power to develop. These we connected, then, with the four conceptions of freedom, that is, the freedom of self-perfection, the freedom of self-determination, the freedom of self-initiation or spontaneity, and finally the freedom of self-development. Next, with respect to method, beginning now with the universal methods, we said that the dialectical method was one of the two methods in which the use of knowledge to achieve power was direct and that consequently, there was the doubling of meaning that I told you that Hegel and Plato have, in which you have power either because you have knowledge and act according to it or because a structure has been set up in which you act according to knowledge without yourself having it. In other words, you can either act *by* knowledge or act *according to* knowledge, to modify the Kantian formula that has its operational equivalent. Therefore, since the process is a process of using reason to order and to organize—this is what I closed on—you could obviously use the dialectical method to order a situation in which wisdom was operative, or to order a situation in which you kept things moving on the assumption that if you keep things going, you have a chance even of moving up (see table 16). You notice, the organization would be totally different. You could also organize your community in order to preserve a maximum of diversified initiation, and obviously not all of the initiation would be wise, and not all of the initiation would get everything moving together. Or you could organize things in order to permit a maximum self-realization and self-development on the part of the members of the state. All of these would be uses of the dialectical method.

Let me make one final point which I didn't emphasize so much. You have two meanings and a characteristic degradation. First, you have the meaning of the dialectical method in which the ordering is an ordering set up by those who are wise in accordance with wisdom, in which, therefore, you need no law except the law of reason. You have, second, the ordering that it has in actual states where you have an ordering of law which you hope might be wise—it need not be, sometimes it is. Most of the men of experience, Plato says again and again, the men like Pericles and Themistocles and all of the great statesmen, will then have right opinion but not wisdom; and their experience would get them so that they could, without doing the dialectical job that the philosopher-king would do, set up an organization within which the operation approximated closely to reason. Then, finally, there are the degradations of the state. Books VIII and IX of the *Republic* run through five degradations of the state, and they are, in the terms that we've just been using, states in which power is exercised without wisdom or even right opinion. Properly organized, they can keep going for a long time; but there is a kind of disequilibrium by which the state, when it begins to get bad, continuously gets worse.

Let's turn now to the other of the universal method, the operational method (see table 15). You will recall, these are merely specifications of the more general terms that we have used before. We have talked about the method in which the dependence was on a rationality in the nature of things. The operational method goes in the opposite direction. The operational method is one in which you assume that power initiates and originates, and that therefore, it is not an approximation to a good which is up above. The good and, likewise, knowledge are both results of the initiation of the agent or, since a knower is an agent, the kind of an agent who produces knowledge. Again, there are two meanings that you have. There is, first, either the power which is exercised directly by those who are—and the phrase is always—"the stronger," that is, it is the power of those who are stronger; or, second, the power of those who are weaker, that is to say, the power of those who, within the structure of a state, operate in a particular fashion.

Let me emphasize the way in which the two methods are radically different. The difference is between basing right on a transcendent good and approximating it in varying degrees—a hypothesis which would make perfect sense, particularly since it is assumed that no one quite knows what that good is except by approximating it—and, second, using one's power to impose rights or using it as advantageously as possible under conditions. You would have an identity of power of the state and of the individual now in that in the case of the state, you would look to those individuals in the state who exercise a sovereign power—and it was out of this method that the whole discussion of sovereignty assumed the importance that it did both in antiquity and in the Renaissance—whereas people of lesser power conform to the state, which is determined by the sovereign power. Therefore, in any given state, the structure of the state is itself a manifestation of power—this is the framework within which one acts—and the individual acting within that framework has his rights and his powers, which are set up. Notice that reason or knowledge has become something quite different from what it had been in the dialectical approach. Reason is a skill, a skill including the skill that the scientist or the wise man acquires in order to set up wisdom and science. You have, therefore, the skilled ruler in the first sense, the skilled agent in the second case.

Let me give you two examples. The first example, since we are reading Machiavelli, will facilitate your replies and will give you at least one possible answer to the question of method in Machiavelli. We will be reading two treatises of Machiavelli, *The Prince* and *The Discourses on the Decades of Livy*. In *The Prince*—and usually when you talk about Machiavellianism, you talk only about meaning *a* of power—Machiavelli investigates the initial sense of power as a containing unit of the state. *The Prince* ends with his discussion of what is necessary in order to unify Italy, and he's convinced that nothing much can happen unless you can stop the fragmentation of Italy into a series of principates and duchies and papal states and so on. Therefore, in the first treatise you seek the power that will bring Italy together, and it involves using power, power in the sense of arms, skill, deception, anything else. The second work is *The Discourses of Livy*, and in *The Discourses on the Decades of Livy* he examines the history of Rome in order to discover the uses of the division of power. His is one of the classic statements. There are ancient ones, and he's quite right in finding it in Livy. You have the power of the emperor, which was the continuation of the power of the consul,[1] which was the continuation of the power of the king, which is the kingly power; you also have the senate, which was a continuation of the aristocratic power; and, finally, you have the power of the tribunes of the people, which represents the power of the plebes. Therefore, if these three can balance each other, you have a better chance of restoring republican virtues; and it's quite clear that Machiavelli was anxious to get the unity of Italy and the republican virtues as two complements of each other.

A second example, which may either lend respectability to Machiavelli or degrade my example, is in *The Federalist Papers*.[2] *The Federalist Papers* have two objectives. One is to set up, to use their phrase, "a stronger union"; the existing confederacy was too weak. They want, therefore, this initial, constitutional strength, power in the sense of something that the federal government can do. But within the operation of this constitution you have the problem of factions. And the famous position that Madison takes in the tenth *Federalist* paper is that you can't abolish factions, you can't control them in any easy way. The way you treat the problem is to multiply them; and if you multiply them, they become a utility rather than a danger, because they then give a verve and a sequence and a manifestation of rights and powers that you wouldn't otherwise have. Again, therefore, for the operational method you have the two approaches: one, an enclosing unity strong enough to hold the country together; and, two, the interaction of the powers within that unity. With differences, the ideal of Machiavelli and the ideal of Madison are comparable. And you notice—let me repeat this—in the operational method, there is no appeal to a superior reason: there isn't any. That is, the important thing is to permit the large states and the small states to operate in their proper way, to let the agrarian and the mercantilist interests get going, to prevent a tyranny either of the majority or of the minority, to preserve the interaction that comes from all the interplay and yet have the union itself not be endangered by this interplay. Consequently, the operation of power is in initiating and in originating; it is not in imposing something that you know is wiser or appealing to the experts to find out what it is that would constitute the wiser.

What are the degradations of the operational method? Well, the degradation is usually in the amalgamation of the method with other principles and interpretations. You notice that in this sense that I've been expressing it, it is quite clear that justice is preserved, is defined, by the stronger. All you need to do to change that, to degrade it, is to say that justice is the interest of the stronger. That isn't what the operational method is saying. Rather, the difference between the stronger union and the operation of factions is that the stronger union isolates the public good, and the operation of factions gives a chance for the private interest to operate within. Make justice the interest of the stronger, and then the private interest is determining what the public good is: this is a degradation. And there are a whole series of phrases like it. "Might makes right." Well, might makes right in the important sense that if you can't vindicate your rights, you don't have them. But if it means that a man powerful enough to get anything will get it, then might does not make right; and it doesn't make any difference whether it is the might of the agreeing powers or the might of the minority group which will assert itself to the extent of throwing everything off the track. As soon as you begin to make might make right in the sense of getting your own way, you have a degradation of the method, which otherwise has an important contribution to make. Even the rule of the majority is degraded in the same way; and from Mill on, the tyranny of the majority is to be feared as much as the tyranny of the minority. Even before Mill, as a matter of fact, as in the debate in Philadelphia on the United States Constitution, this was one of the things that was constantly brought up in the discussion.

Let's look at the two methods together in terms of their degradations, because the degradations are quite different. The degradation of the dialectical method is a degradation in which you go from arguing that it would be better for the wisest to rule, if there was some way of knowing who was wisest—this is obviously true—to the assumption that the man who is in power and is ruling is the wisest, and that therefore, there is a presumption that what he decides is wisdom. Then you're in the normal state of dictatorship: that is, the dictator is the man who will pronounce not only on questions of politics but on questions of anthropology, agriculture, the distribution of resources, the occupations of people. This becomes wisdom by making it, since it's in his power, the mark of the man who is in power. The degradation of the operational method is somewhat different. You take on now the initial meaning, namely, that power is the source of rights and of justice, and make it into the assertion that anything that you are able to do is therefore right, which thereby neglects the danger of destroying the power to initiate on the part of others. The continuation of the operational method will depend in all cases on the possibility of the defeated party coming back and taking another chance, maybe getting power. If, on the other hand, the might that comes with the electoral defeat leads to the extermination of the opposition, might is no longer the basis of justice. Destroy the characteristic self-initiation, and you have no longer used the operational method.

Let me put the two together more generally for a moment, then go on to the particular methods. What is the relation of the two universal methods? The dialectical method emphasizes the importance of the unitary, uniting force of knowledge—or of some substitute for knowledge—ruling the interrelations of all subsidiary forms of power. The operational method emphasizes the importance of the continued functioning or operation of spontaneous, undetermined power in the individual in order to build up the unity and the functioning of the community. Stated as ideals, both are excellent. The knowledge involved in the two cases, as I pointed out, is quite different. Dialectical knowledge is knowledge of the good; operational knowledge is knowledge of how to secure consequences. The methods—and let me repeat this; I've said it a number of times—are not methods in the same sense. The dialectical method is a method of organization and systematization in which the total scheme comes prior to any operation of the parts. The operational method is a method of invention, discovery, innovation (see fig. 6).[3]

The particular methods, unlike the universal methods, are not methods of acquiring power; they are methods of releasing, using, or developing power. The logistic method is a method in the area of releasing or developing power where power is the cause of motion or the cause of the continuation of motion or the cause of the cessation of motion. The problems of power logistically are problems of impulsion and repulsion. There is a single, identical meaning of power throughout; this is why it is a particular method. Power logistically is related to natures, and the natures may be either individual or nature in general. According to Spinoza, to take one practitioner of the logistic method that you've read, the nature of a thing is its *conatus* (from Latin, meaning "effort," "exertion"); and a *conatus* is an endeavor that each thing has as an individual to persist in its own being, and the being that it persists in is to continue the motion that it has, the motion or the state of rest. It operates in a context of other powers which help or hinder it; consequently, the motions affect the thing moved. In man they produce passions—passions like fear, ignorance, superstition, which will affect the motions that man goes through. The knowledge of nature and of powers can be used to remove fears and superstitions and to permit the proper use of power, that is, power in accordance with one's own nature or power in the sense of freedom—freedom is action in accordance with the laws of one's own nature. The state is then a compact; but within the conventions of the state, the powers which operate can be either the irrational powers that come from the passions or the rational powers that come from the laws of one's own nature. It makes no difference: you've entered into a compact; therefore, the compact is what leads to the characteristic of the community or the state.

How does power operate? We don't have our *a* and *b*; we don't need to go through it, therefore. But how does power operate? If there are no tensions or no fears, then it is a simple, cooperative interrelationship. This never occurs. Actual power is a complex or a structure calculated from consideration of the natures of the individual and the groups that are combined, not in this pure sense—although this is the model on which the calculation goes—but in the sense in which tensions need to be lessened—tensions can be interpersonal, intergroup, or international—and the problems of releasing power for its proper productive use then come in.

What are the degradations of the logistic conception of power? Well, since in setting up the state there's no way of distinguishing between an agreement or a convention in which you just get what you want and one that is according to the laws of human nature, which is one of the favorite conceptions of the logistic notion, opportunism is the first degradation. You get what's in your own interest in the circumstances: that's fine, that's the end of it, that's where the state operates or the community. The only way you get around this—and it's always out of the logistic method that this arises—is to have an ideal of a technocratic state; that is, a state in which you put in charge the people who are engineers, who know how to do things—and usually how to do things not on the political level but on the level of building bridges or getting computers to work or getting the maximum number of students in the buildings you're putting on a given plot of land. The method, you notice, is not systematization or innovation. It is more nearly the practical equivalent of proof: it is an examination of the consequences of assumptions and tracing them through (see fig. 6).

The second of the particular methods is the problematic method. In the problematic method, power actualizes, power becomes a function. You see, in the case of the logistic method, power moves: if you want to know whether a thing has power or not, you examine whether it's moving. If it's not, there's no other meaning of power except that it is doing the moving, which is, as I've said, quite different from initiating. That is, in the case of initiation, a lot of things are moved that aren't initiating, and you look at different evidence in order to get an answer to one or the other; but in the case of problematic power, you must have a knowledge of what the potentialities are of that which is to undergo the actualization. You may remember that in the various treatises of Aristotle, I warned you about the way *dunamis,* or *power* or *potentiality*, came in at various points, sometimes in meanings that for the other three would be meaningless. For example, in the *Poetics*, in the opening line, the long opening sentence—it's more than a line—Aristotle says that what he wants to undertake in this treatise is to examine poetic in general and so forth and the potentiality of each form of poetry. What he says in the beginning of his psychology, the *De Anima*, is that you can't talk about what the soul is unless you specify what it is that the individual with a soul has; therefore, what you've got to do is to make a list of their potentialities from the activities of animate beings. The word is *dunamis* again, but in the *De Anima* this is translated "faculties." Therefore, since an ode does not have a faculty, the translation prevents you from relating the term to the fact that you examine poetry and the soul and physics and biology in the same way. That is to say, for any thing that is to engage in a motion, it is the *dunamis*, power, potentiality that you want.

In dealing with human potentialities, then, in politics and in ethics we would want to know what potentialities are actualized and the particular forms. The constitution, one of the words that Aristotle gave a technical meaning to, is a form which realizes the potentialities of the citizens. Virtues are forms; they are habits which realize the potentialities of individuals for action. Consequently, the various constitutions would be considered in terms of a distribution of *offices*—and that's the way the translation always runs—what Aristotle is saying in the Greek is, a distribution of powers. Offices is right, that is, powers in the state; but what makes a constitution is the provision concerning who does what properly within the organization that is set up in this community. And the poor and the rich are among those involved, the oppositions of quantity and quality, the power of numbers *versus*—I'm quoting from Aristotle—"the power of virtue, birth or money; these are among the four reasons why men claim the power to rule," the four being either because they represent more citizens; or because they are better able; or because they came from families that have been doing it so long that the presumption is that they, too, can do it by inheritance or the grace of God; or because of money—and Aristotle's remark here is that what you normally assume is that the man who got the money had to have some ability to get it and that this is an ability in an enterprise similar to ruling, and so oligarchies come from this. This is one of the reasons why it is very easy for a man to assume power and to say that anything which was good for General Motors would also be good for the state, because the enterprise is similar.[4] It is meant to be a virtuous statement, and the poor man was amazed when the citizens didn't take it this way.

How does power operate? Well, the state is not a convention; it's not a compact. It is natural, and what you need to do is to consider the varieties of constitutions that have been set up much as you would consider the variety of animals before you began doing biology. Aristotle had a research team go out and write 158 descriptions of constitutions, Greek and barbarian. We have only one of them, the one that he wrote himself, which is the Constitution of Athens, but it was one of the 158. So, before he wrote the *Politics*, he examined the way in which states had operated. This is the problematic method; that is, you find out what the problems have been in all kinds of states instead of setting up ideals, instead of showing what the nature of man would demand, or instead of showing what the operation of power could achieve.[5] You examine the problems of states, and then you come to the various objectives or ends that are achieved in these communities.

What's the degradation of the problematic method? Well, from what I've said, you can see what it would be. Again, there are two. Since you examine all these differences, one degradation is relativism: you do what comes naturally under the circumstances, and you let it go at that. The other degradation is abstract constitutionalism: you become so attached to the form of the constitution that you won't permit it to be interpreted, and amending it would be quite beyond the pale.[6]

I will not do it; but you can see that I could take any one of these methods, as I took the dialectical method, and the setting up of constitutions, for example, could be to protect man in his wisdom, could be primarily to set things going and keep them going, could be primarily to permit the great variety of initiatives under certain circumstances, and could be to set up the means by which all citizens would have their maximum development. The constitutions would be quite different, but the method would work as well for the one or the other. And this is the reason why I keep saying, keep your method separate from your interpretation: the utility of the method will spread over all of the varieties of meanings that you attach in your interpretation. This method, you will recognize, is like the method of inquiry in abstract, theoretical areas (see fig. 6).

Let me review now, briefly, the relation of the meanings of power to the meanings of freedom. The question of method, as I said in the beginning, is, How is power acquired and used? Just as, when we were talking about freedom, it was the question, How is freedom acquired and used? Since freedom is conceived as the ability to act in the absence of external circumstances, the questions seem closely related, because power can be internal and external, one's own power or the power of others. But that internal/external relation, as I've warned you repeatedly, becomes quite different in the different methods.[7] In the universal methods, power is acquired. There is a direct relevance of reason to action or to the use of power. Freedom is the ability to exercise the acquired power. The acquisition and the use of power and freedom, therefore, are the same for both universal methods.

The dialectical method: power orders according to the pattern of a rational whole. This is the mode of assimilation. Sometimes it is expressly said that there is an eternal model that it follows, and that one acquires power as one approximates the true form of one's own nature according to this model. One is free when one acts rationally according to the pattern of one's own perfect nature. Power, the power of anything, defines its being, the rationale of its nature. Freedom is the ability to act according to that nature, according to reason. Power is a question of being, but freedom is limited to beings who acquire power by reason. Power orders in accordance with reason; freedom orders by use of reason. Power and freedom become the same.

The operational method: there's a reverse relation between the knower and knowledge: power initiates. Instead of ordering according to knowledge, the knower establishes the order of knowledge. In Kant's terminology, he legislates. This is the mode of discrimination. One acquires power by art, by practice, by arrangement. One is free when one uses this power. What things *are* is determined by power, internal or external, but it's now the power that makes them. Therefore, the beginning is not with things or their natures; it's with the power that initiated them. Freedom is the exercise of that power of initiation. Power is a question of action or process, extending to any process, since they're all instances of power. Freedom is limited to the initiating of a process as opposed to participating in it and undergoing it. Freedom and power are the same.

Let's look at the particular methods now. In the particular methods, power is used or actualized, and there's an indirect, not a direct, relevance of reason to action or the use of power. Power is manifested in action or in motion, with only an indirect appeal to reason. Therefore, in the particular methods the acquisition and the use of power are different from the acquisition and the use of freedom. One can have power to act and lack freedom to act; one can have freedom to act and lack the power to act. How this operates is different in the two cases, but in both cases the two propositions are true.

The logistic method: power moves. It moves by being the continuation of motion in the thing or the beginning of motion in something else, something impelled to motion by it. You continue in motion by the logistic method unless you're hindered. The basic conception of inertia in physics carries over to inertia in ethics and politics, all of the sciences of the community. Freedom is an absence of hindrance. You can have power without freedom. Obviously, the moving thing is then hindered externally. I can have a powerful person contained, chained, stopped—stopped even indirectly by fears of various sorts. Then, if you remove the hindrance, that is, give the person freedom of motion, his power is sufficient. The motion immediately occurs once the hindrance is removed. You can have freedom without power: no hindrance to prevent the motion but the body is at rest, it's unable to give motion to itself, it cannot initiate the motion. Therefore, although it is free, it lacks the power to move.

The problematic method: again, the two propositions are true: that is to say, you can have freedom without power and power without freedom. Power actualizes now. The power is potentiality. Power couldn't actualize if it weren't power in the sense of potentiality. You have potentialities in inanimate things, animate things, and in rational things. In rational things and in some animate things, it is possible to form habits. Habits become, in the language of the problematic method, second natures. I have the potentiality to know, I go to a university, I learn a science. I've actualized my potentiality to know with respect to this science. I now have the potentiality of proceeding in inquiry in this science. I have the science; that's what the word *habit* (from Latin *habere*, "to have") means. If I didn't have the potential, I wouldn't have acquired that science; my nature in the beginning was a potentiality to the actualization of that potentiality in one science. When I get the science, it is a potentiality to the next step. It is a potentiality narrower in scope but higher. Therefore, as I do something, I form habits by virtue of the action of doing it, which facilitate my performing like actions in the future; this is what a habit is. And this is an essential part of the analysis of freedom, since freedom occurs, in this meaning of freedom, only in animals that can form habits. In this approach, you don't analyze the will; instead, you analyze the voluntary, because habits are possible only with respect to voluntary actions. Consequently, you raise the question of freedom relative to the voluntary as opposed to the compelled. This is one of the reasons why Aristotle raises the shipboard question. I want to bring my cargo into port to sell it. There's a storm. Do I voluntarily have my cargo thrown overboard? There's compulsion here, but within the region of this compulsion I either have it thrown overboard voluntarily or I don't; that is, if it goes overboard or not, it's an act of will. Therefore, it is this region of the voluntary which would be set up. How do you have power without freedom? Well, you could have the ability to achieve something, such as the possession of intellectual powers, but no freedom to actualize them, that is to say, no way of going to college. You may have freedom without power. I may, by virtue of my circumstances, go to any college that I want, I might even be able to get into any college that I want; but I may lack the preparation—these are habits—or lack the ability—these are natural powers—to develop myself in these circumstances. And unless I have influence of some kind, I will have been free to go to college, but I will not have the power to make use of that opportunity.

Well, now, these are the relations between method and interpretation on the one hand, freedom and power on the other. I've deliberately gone through in this last ten minutes the varieties of interrelation, because I think it is of extreme importance to recognize that if we are talking about the use of power to achieve rights, all of these methods are used, can be used well, will be opposed for good or for bad reasons; and for the achievement of freedom, since power must be used, it is well to seek the way it has been used in all of these ways. Anything less than this would be a return to an imposition which, by definition, is a limitation of power and a loss of some of the rights.[8]

I will go on next time to consider how principles come into the picture.

LECTURE TEN

Power: Principle; and History: Interpretation

We had completed last time the analysis of power except for principles, and today I would like to complete that part and to move on to history. I think that the rest of the lecture today and the lecture on next Wednesday, laying out the considerations of history, will be something of a preparation for what you propose to do with Hegel's *Reason in History*.[1]

First, then, the principles related to power. I will go rapidly, because I will make use of what I have said about principles before. Holoscopic principles are based on a coincidence between knowledge and the known (see figs. 13 and 18). Metaphysically, this means that principles would either be the assimilation of everything that is known to the structure of knowledge—these are the assimilative principles of Plato and others like him—or they are the resolution of knowledge into the structure of the known. But in both cases your beginning point, either for theory or for the nature of things, is in the introduction of intelligibility into the very conditions of being. Those are the holoscopic principles. Instead of beginning either with the whole of everything, the cosmos, or the whole of a particular branch of knowledge, the reflexive principles, the meroscopic principles work on the opposite assumption, namely, that the inquiring mind can get to knowledge only if it separates what the knower contributes from what is the known. The simple principles are principles which are a good beginning point, because nothing remains that the person who enters into the inquiry or knowledge has contributed; consequently, you can be sure that at least with these simples, which have no parts and therefore no admixture of human error, you are dealing with the nature of things. Conversely, the actional principles are principles in the sense that what you can do, you know; therefore, if you can make the thing you are talking about, you don't have to raise the extra question about whether in nature it was made that way. The fact that you can produce it *is* its nature; and this variety of model, the philosophy of the "as-if,"[2] takes its place.

When you apply these principles to power and to freedom, as we have already done, the crucial difference between them in practical philosophy is that for both of the holoscopic principles, there are normative elements in the exercise of power, just as there are normative elements in the exercise of freedom (see table 12). Freedom does not consist in doing what you want to, what pleases you; it consists in doing what you should, depending on the kind of principle you want. Similarly, power will not be reduced to the crude push of a body but will have additional traits. In the case of the meroscopic principles, on the contrary, in morals and in politics there is no natural base for normative distinctions. This does not mean that they're therefore relativistic in the bad sense or immoral—this is what is normally said—on the contrary, it means that you need power antecedent to determining what is good or bad, and that therefore, the exercise of power will lead to the increase of the available good and bad. In the holoscopic principles, the criteria of good and bad are prior; in the meroscopic principles, the criteria of good and bad are the product and posterior.

I want merely to run through the principles because, as I said, I want to get on to history. Somewhere hidden in your notes I've already done this for freedom,[3] so I shall assume that what I've said about the relation of freedom and power will give you a guidance to come over to principles; therefore, I'll limit myself to power. In the case of the comprehensive principles, the exercise of power on the part of the individual, or of the state for that matter, is in the large context of an intelligible universe. Consequently, if you have the contrast between the arbitrary exercise of crude power and the exercise of power in accordance with the structure of nature, with the justice of things, then obviously the latter is more powerful, because it will not run amuck, it will continue. The crude tyrant without justice will run into his destruction. In the long run, the pursuit of justice is preferable even in power terms, because the individual and the state will persist longer.

Reflexive principles do not rely on the whole universe, you don't need a cosmic reason; you suppose, rather, that there will be plural reflexive principles instead of a single comprehensive principle. In any given community, there is a relation between the ruler and the ruled. The true community is one in which the ruled rules: this is the reflexivity. Well, on the other hand, not all communities are of this sort; therefore, to achieve justice in a community, one needs to consider the structure or the constitution of that community. There are as many kinds of justice as there are kinds of community, and the man of wisdom in most actual communities would not be in the best position to be the ruler. In the oligarchic state, for example, it is wealth which is the production, which is the end; consequently, it would be wise to get the large entrepreneur in executive positions. The wise man would be limited to activities that might lead to the eventual improvement of the state, the modification of the constitution, and the occasional intrusion of wisdom within the state.

You will notice that in both of these principles, power has a relation either to knowledge in general or to knowledge of particular circumstances. Therefore, in the case of the comprehensive principle, the ideal would be the philosopher-king. In the case of the reflexive principle, let me do the reflexivity a little bit further. If you deal with morals with a reflexive principle, you begin with power in the sense of the individual's potentiality. When he acts in any way, theoretically or practically, he produces habits, which are second natures and give him more power. A virtue is a habit which increases his power, as opposed to the numerous forms of bad habit. If you go to politics, similarly, there are potentialities or powers in the conditions of the state, the abilities of the citizens, which become, like habits, formalized in institutions. An institution has the same continuing character that a habit has: once you begin to form a state in a particular way, an institution becomes its second nature. For both of these, then, it is correct to say that the state is natural, that justice is natural, and that the intrusion, therefore, into morals has a natural basis. In the case of the comprehensive principle, the movement is more direct; that is to say, man by his very nature and the universe as such have a rational basis, and therefore, the various states approximate to this rationality. You notice, both of the holoscopic principles are, in a sense, comprehensive and reflexive: comprehensive in the case of the comprehensive principle, in that there is a single comprehensive principle which is reflexive upon the entire universe; comprehensive and reflexive in the case of the reflexive principle, in that there are many comprehensive principles, each of which is reflexive on the activities of the individuals.

The meroscopic principles are either simple or actional. Both of them are varieties of hedonism; that is to say, the good is that which causes pleasure. But there are different kinds of hedonism, because in the case of the simple principles, there is still the possibility of distinguishing between the pleasures that are in accordance with the laws of your nature and the unnatural pleasures. There is therefore a kind of therapeutic treatment of both morals and politics: remove fear and superstition and repressions, and men will act naturally and therefore well; that is, they will pursue pleasures that are according to human nature. In the case of the actional principles, there is not this difference; that is to say, pleasure *qua* pleasure is good, it is a mere hedonic calculus. You have, then, the basis of a difference. Therefore, when we do the state for either of these principles—this, incidentally, was true all the way back in

Table 17. Definitions of *Power*.

Ambiguous Formula: "Power is the condition or possibility of originating rather than undergoing change."

Mode of Thought	Principle	Method	Interpretation	Selection
	Holoscopic	*Universal*	*Ontic*	
Assimilation	Wisdom	Orders	Energy/Being	Wise Man
Resolution	Realization	Initiates	Force	Things
	Meroscopic	*Particular*	*Phenomenal*	
Construction	Nature	Moves	Possibility	Animals (with Impulses)
Discrimination	Action	Actualizes	Potentiality	Humans (Reflective)

antiquity—the state is not natural, it is based on a contract. In both cases, it is based on a contract wherein what you seek is a means by which to guarantee the sources of your pleasures against the dangers of others; and therefore, the common good is the result of the contract. Once more, the contracts would differ, in that there would be a ground in the case of simple principles to set up a preference of contracts which realize the satisfaction of the wants and the needs of the individual. This is easy: human nature would enter into it; you would, therefore, try to get the knowable, that is, the nature of man, as the basis of your contract. In the case of the actional principles, the contract would merely be the exercise of power as such. To summarize, then: power undifferentiated in the case of actional principles, that is, power as the source of any action and therefore of theoretic, practical, artistic, or what you will; power as the expression of the nature of man, simple principles; power as the realization of the potentialities of the individual or of the group, reflexive principles; and power as the exercise of wisdom in the realization of self-perfection, comprehensive principles (see table 17).[4]

Let's turn rapidly, now, to our third term: *history*. History completes the pair we have been talking about, for obvious reasons. As I've tried to present them to you in these various meanings, freedom and power are the ingredients in action. History is the examination of the facts of what is the case, what has happened, what the occurrences are. I'm deliberately using *history* here in the broad sense, because it runs all the way from natural history, which is a mere formulation of the facts of the case moving through the animate and even into the inanimate realm, down to history in the more ordinary sense of political or social or intellectual history. There is a natural tendency to think that if there's any doubt about the nature of freedom or of power, you go to the facts and find

POWER LIBERTY

(Law) (Right)

1) *lex* | *ius*

2) *lex* ⟵⟶ *ius*

3) *lex* ⟵ *ius*

4) *lex* ⟶ *ius*

Fig. 49 *Relationships of* Lex *(Power) and* Ius *(Liberty)*

out what the case is, and the facts would resolve it. You would appeal to history if you want the evolution set forth. On examination, however, it turns out that history is subject to exactly the same differences of meaning as freedom and power are. Therefore, the apparent resolution of differences turns out to be the support of your position by a history from a genius with the philosophy of freedom and of power that you have: history always supports the theory. In the process, you will criticize the historicity of alleged alternatives to your history; but properly pursued, there is no way in which the appeal to historical fact will remove the basic differences that we have been exploring. Understand, this doesn't mean that the appeal to historical fact will not remove some errors of philosophic analysis. It will mean simply that the homogeneity will be apparent, and sometimes in ways that are at first sight a little shocking.

You remember in the beginning of the talk about power, I put on the board four possible relations between freedom and power, using *lex* and *ius* as a means of making them more precise (see figs. 40 and 41). Let me put them on the board again. Liberty is a right, or a *ius*; power is a *lex*, or a binding form. One possibility is that freedom and power are on the same level and are mutually exclusive—let's call that meaning "1" (see fig. 49).[5] The second possibility is that they are on the same level and imply each other, that any instance of freedom is an instance of power, and *vice versa*. The third possibility is that power is prior and determines liberty. The final one is, of course, the reverse, namely, that liberty or right is basic and power is the application of liberty and right. The four possibilities are exhaustive of all possibilities. Let's take a look at what happens when you begin to put history in, and I want to illustrate what I meant by saying it is sometimes a little shocking to see what the result is.

Take power as fundamental and liberty as derived from it (alternative 3 in fig. 49). Among the philosophers who have taken this position are Hegel and Croce. Both of them describe history as an account of the development of freedom. You notice, the normal cliché that would attach to this sequence would be that of the superposition of despotic power and therefore the suppression of liberty. Maybe they are playing tricks on us; but as I say, to such an extent that in the case of Croce, who was to this degree following Hegel,[6] Croce's book in the English translation is called *History as an Account of the Development of Freedom*—that isn't the title in Italian, but that idea is in the title.[7] That's the first possibility. Suppose we turn from this, the third relationship of freedom and power, to the fourth possibility. What's history on the fourth assumption, which is the one, you notice, in which freedom is prior to the determination of power? Well, there are a vast number of histories of this sort. The history in this case is an account of the successions and the concentrations of power; and this is how freedom was discovered, gotten, advanced, achieved, in the struggles for liberty. In accordance with the first relation, then, moving up (see fig. 49), what would history be? Well, history is an account of the fundamental oppositions of freedom and power—not the concentrations of power which were necessary to have the sequence but the struggle back and forth between the two. What's the second? Well, the second is a kind of subtle presentation of the interpenetrations of the two in which unexpected uses of freedom turn paradoxically into power concentrations; and in like fashion, fortunately, concentrations of power lay the foundations of freedom where you have least expected it.

Now, I've deliberately put the kinds of history in a way in which, like the kinds of freedom and power, they sound as though they were in contradiction. The general theme that I've been trying to bring out is that whenever you state the two, three, or four conceptions baldly, they *are* in contradiction; and then you get refutation. This is the normal enjoyment of philosophy: instead of solving any problems, you refute your opponents; and it always turns out that they are meaningless, absurd, asking false questions, because putting them in opposition makes the statement of what they are doing conform to the statement of what you are doing. What they are doing in these terms is, naturally, absurd; otherwise, you'd be doing what they were doing. But conversely, if you use the concepts in action or in thought, the results are very frequently supplementary and move on to progress. For example, if you want to know what the history of the development of freedom in fact has been, it would be a mistake to think that any one of these theses is correct. It has been an interplay between those who have put power on the top and those who have put liberty on top, those who have seen a radical disparity and those who have seen an interpenetration; and the pluralism of theories, far from running counter to the advancement of freedom or the increase of stability, security, and power, has contributed to it. An advance made by theorists or men of action in their terms can then be translated into terms that will permit the holder of other theories to advance. This is true in science, and it is true in political action.

It is in these terms that I would like to present the conceptions of history. You don't need to take what I have just said about the fruitful interplay of the pluralism of approaches until you see it going on; but what I wanted to do was to guard against the normal tendency, when any contrast is set up, to put it into controversial opposition so that you must choose one rather than the other. Let's consider, rather, what each is saying. When you start thinking and get to work, you will have to land in one: you can't talk all four languages at once, you will have to think and work in the terms of one. But there's no reason why the accumulation of results that are successful from the other language cannot be put into your language rather than losing your time in the process of slaying the speakers of the opposed language.

What are the three questions as applied to history? Well, the problem of interpretation is, What is history about? What is the process of history? What is in process? And what is the account of the process? The question of method is, What are the connections in these processes? What is the sequence set forth in the account of the processes? And the principles: What is the relation of history to what is the case? What provides the grounds and the initiation of the process? What sets the order of the narrative? You'll notice, half the time I've been talking the formal language of history as narrative; part of the time I've been talking the material language of history as process.

Let's begin with the word *history*. It's a good old Greek word, *istoria*, or in the Ionic, *istorie*. Its original meaning was "inquiry"; and in the case of Herodotus, who uses it a good deal, it's still frequently translated "inquiry," largely because of the snobbish attitude of the modern historians, who think that it isn't history, and therefore you may as well call it inquiry. In the intention of Herodotus, this is less a denigration than a recognition of what history is. It means, then, knowledge obtained by inquiry. We're not sure about its etymology, but it was probably derived from a verb meaning "to see," in the perfect tense. Consequently, history is "to know" in the sense of having seen. Even if this isn't the etymology—and it probably is—it explains what history is. It's information. It's a question, therefore, about what are facts or what are connections of facts. History is a process of things, and history is an account of happenings. But in addition to this relation—and this is the one which has become almost a cliché when we talk about history—there's another relation that is equally important, which is not normally looked at. What's the relation between history and argument? Well, history is a specification of the concrete and the particular with all the indices of particularity, including time and place, within what is the argument. Therefore, we will run into theories of history in which the history of what happened and the theory of the nature of the thing are exactly the same. Let's turn to interpretation first. I'm skipping selection, because that's a luxury at this time.

What is history about? What has a history? How does one determine and relate facts? These are the questions of an interpretation. It is the bearing of narratives of concrete events or occurrences involving concrete things on the subject matter of those narratives. You will remember, in the beginning I said that you could take a single formula which all of the answers would agree with ambiguously. The answer to the question that I've just given—I'm trying to put it in terms that will not get into concrete/theoretic differences—is that history is the account of happenings or sequences or structures past, present, or future. Happenings, sequences, structures—sometimes the temporal element almost disappears from your history; we'll run into a number of these.

There are two basic kinds of interpretation: the ontic interpretations and phenomenal interpretations. Ontic histories are accounts of happenings in which the process is related to some independently known reality. That independently known reality is the subject matter concerning which one has knowledge apart from your history. To take the ontological interpretation, the first of the ontic interpretations, the independently known reality is the transcendence of the events; therefore, the history is a history of forms, rational or necessary, and the assimilation of both, that is, the rational and the necessary, in human history. The intelligibility of the whole is what is of fundamental importance. Entitative history is a history of processes, not of forms, and these processes are known because of the underlying reality for which we normally have a science or scientific laws. Phenomenal interpretations are not concerned with anything underlying; they are limited to the phenomena or the occurrences themselves. Therefore, there are two possibilities: you're concerned either with occurrences or with data—both of these are meanings of phenomena—which are the ultimate character of what it is you are talking about.

History may be a history of acts; then it is primarily the agents who are the subject of the history. Or history may be a history of facts. Aristotle, for example, distinguishes three kinds of fact, and in each of them you have a history. In the theoretic sciences, there is natural history, which is a mere enumeration of the observances that you come upon in experience: the organisms, their functions, the objects, their movement. There are the practical sciences, the end of which is virtue and institutions; this is the history of the actions of men within communities. And finally, there are the poetic sciences; the history of the poetic sciences would have to do with the objects made and the sequence of their determination.

Let's summarize them briefly. The ontological interpretation is the assimilation of being and of knowing; therefore, there's a history of all forms, and conversely, all discourse is a kind of history. The entitative is the construction of compositions of knowledge and emotion, and therefore, you have a history of the doings of the composite. The existentialist is the discrimination of the perspectives and the powers; this is a history of makings and the resulting things made. The essentialist, finally, is a history of the facts and the organization of facts in sequences within subject matters.

Now, let's run through them one by one, and I'd like, as we go along, to try to emphasize the specificity of the differences. The ontological interpretation first. What I have just said about the ontological interpretation—which is in abstract and general terms; namely, it is concerned with forms, rational and necessary—would fit the conception of power as a unifying force and of freedom as a process of self-perfection. To recount history is to establish frameworks in which the forms in question have relation either to their perfect nature or to other forms; consequently, there are two kinds of history. Let me limit myself to Plato, since he does this excellently and is the source of a great many later ontological interpretations of history. One of the two kinds of history is the history of degradations, because if you know what the perfect form is, you know that the departure from that form has a force and a direction of its own. In the *Republic*, for example, having constructed the perfect state in the first seven books, Plato in books VIII and IX deals with the degradations of the state that has been constructed. There are five stages of degradation, and they're stated causally. They're not intended—well, even that is not quite the correct thing: one of the things you need to watch as you go along is the way in which history as it is presented is not necessarily merely the step-by-step sequence of occurrences. To set that down is impossible. You have at least a process of selection which will give you the means by which to pick the aspects, and in some of the theories of history you will find that you depart from the basic conception. The method makes that stronger than otherwise, and in terms of the method let me illustrate it from the reading you will be doing in Hegel.

Hegel starts out by schematizing three kinds of history (it's on page 3)[8] original history, reflective history, and philosophical history. Original history is the history that is reported by contemporaries or the people involved in the event; they put down what happened. Hegel claims that this isn't very good, that it really isn't history at all yet. Reflective history—and there are several different kinds of reflective history—is when writers then organize this into a narrative. But you don't really get to history until you get to philosophical history; and you'll notice, philosophical history is not the recording the observer makes. Even without defending the position in detail, this is obvious: that is, if you are taking into account what is happening in the broadest possible sense, the person at the scene of a particular event would not be well equipped to indicate what was going on. At most, he would be in touch with the wiggle of one small part of an enormous interrelated whole, and it is that interrelated whole that the method of Hegel is aimed at. I'm not talking about his interpretation now; I wanted to get it in with respect to what I've been just saying about the ontological interpretation. In other words, don't put down in your notes that he is or is not ontological. I'm merely using him here.[9]

The first kind of history, then, would be the way in which the cultural ideal is exemplified. The degradations of books VIII and IX may not strike you as very good history; but if you look in the *Protagoras*, in the *Laws*, and in others of the myths of Plato, you will find the beginnings of cultural history. In fact, he used exactly the same form a great deal: that is, the myth Protagoras tells in the dialogue called the *Protagoras* is of the beginning of man. When Prometheus and Epimetheus handed out all of the gifts, Epimetheus used up the physical powers and Prometheus had to rectify this, and therefore gave a second set of gifts. The animals were self-protected with their hair and their nails and their physical strength. He gave man two gifts: the gift of fire—technological art—and the other arts. But then, Zeus recognized that this wasn't enough; therefore, Zeus gave the gift of justice, and the distribution of justice is different from the distribution of the other arts. People, through the state, are more or less able in the technological arts, but in justice there must be uniformity. He goes through, then, an evolution with a distinction that, as I say, has been worked up again and again by historians. The myth of Cronos, which occurs twice in the dialogues, once in the *Laws*, is another one which has been played with a great deal in serious history—I won't tell you the myth of Cronos; I'll resist this temptation.[10] Second, there are histories or myths which explore the particularities of all of the generalities of dialectical argumentation. What is history on the ontological basis? History is basic knowledge. Since the facts are already arranged in their intelligibility, anything that is presented historically would be intellectually organized in character.

Let me drive that home a little bit further. The *Republic* is supposed to be one of the highest examples of Plato's dialectic. When you come to the beginning of the *Timaeus*, the dialogue which occurs on the next dramatic date—that is, it was written much later, but the date on which the conversation is said to occur is the day after that of the *Republic*; not having worn themselves out yet, they began talking about physics—it turns out, then, that the perfect state was merely a myth, it wasn't argumentation or dialectic. The cosmology that we are about to engage in is merely a myth, and both of them need to be given a firm foundation in knowledge. And where do you find the knowledge? In history; and that is the history which is told in the dialogue.

Let's go on to the entitative interpretation. In the entitative interpretation, you have a conception of history concerned with processes, real or apparent; and this is a conception which fits the idea of power as inertia or as propelling force and a conception of freedom as self-determination in accordance with the laws of one's own nature. What is it to recount history? It's to assemble the various forces that come into contact at various times and places and then trace the consequences of the interplay, either in terms of what really happened or in terms of what they become as a result of submission to external form. I don't know whether you recall in your reading of the first book of Thucydides when he begins looking for the causes. He looks for two sets of causes, and they're both very important. One is the underlying causes, the accumulations of power which made the clash inevitable, and the other was what men thought—and this is why the dialogues are included, he says. You need, in the latter case, the formulation of the motives; but in addition to and underlying it, there is the movement of forces. What is history now? Well, history is concerned with occurrences, occurrences in which you can get some lines of direction from the underlying laws.

Notice, then, that on the basis of both ontic interpretations, the empirical records of history are not final evidence; they must be interpreted. They must be interpreted either in the light of a more intelligible total interpretation which would account for the errors of the record, or in the light of a better formulation of the natures that are involved which would throw doubt on the record as an instance of action or passion to be accounted for—in the one case, a transcendental reality; in the other case, a physical reality. In both cases, history is an ongoing process. The myth is recounted in order to inspire people to exemplify the unifying principle or one like it. The equation, in the entitative, is applied in order to set the stage for a continuation of the motions that have been described thus far.

The phenomenal interpretations—first, the existentialist. This is a conception of history as act which fits the conception of power as action and freedom as spontaneity. What's history about now? Well, it's not about forms and their structure, it's not about the processes or occurrences; it's about exploits, about actions, preferably actions that have had important results. This is the history in which the place of the hero is of importance—the "hero" is a bad name by now, but the influential man whose ideas have influenced the thoughts of others, whose actions have influenced the actions of others. Finally, the essentialist interpretation—this conception of history as concerned with facts fits the conception of power as potentiality and freedom as self-development. History is an account of facts in their functional interrelations. And bear in mind, one of the big works of Aristotle we have is called the *History of Animals*: this is what he means by *history*. We have also his Constitution of Athens, which is a history of the legal institutions and political institutions of Athens from its foundation down to his time. For the phenomenal interpretations, unlike the ontological, the empirical evidence and the precisions that you can have with respect to them have an importance which they lack in the ontic interpretations. You can't tamper with them, but they can be subjected to questions, to uncertainties, which require verification and defense. Remember, fundamentally, neither of the ontic interpretations believe the phenomenal facts as such; they must be transmuted in order to deal with the characteristic formulations of history. The way in which you examine your empirical evidence in your phenomenal approach is either by the method of debate, reorientation, or readjustment, which is the existentialist approach, or by the methods of observation, experimental determination, in different functional contexts.

I'll go on next time and bring in the concept of method, because in the method it will be possible to deal with the interrelations that are set up. I tried carefully to limit myself in interpretation to the question, What is it about? Interpretation deals only with sentences, and therefore, I've been examining historical sentences thus far. When we get to method, I'll be able to tell you about historical narratives.

DISCUSSION

Machiavelli, Part 1
(*The Prince*)

Discussion Summary

Today we move on to Machiavelli's *The Prince*. Let's begin by broadly understanding what he is trying to do. Chapter I makes a series of divisions: in their form, states are either monarchies or republics, and he separates the former into old, new, or a mixture of the two; next, the acquisition of states is by force of arms either of others or of oneself; and, finally, that acquisition comes through either fortune or personal ability. Chapter II opens with him saying that he will speak only of monarchies here, not of republics, which are to be discussed in the *Discourses*. Notice, he is setting up the manner or procedure of the whole work; that is, he is making a series of dichotomous divisions in his argument and will then postpone three of the main arms of that argument for the *Discourses* (see fig. 50).[1] Thus, it is important to realize that these two works fit together in a fixed plan.

So, where do these divisions of the argument appear in his work? In chapter XV, he talks of the character of the prince, and this is the third dichotomy or main arm of his argument. Here, he postpones discussion of certain aspects of the prince's character to his later work, because now he is interested in what the prince appears to be to his people. He discusses five characteristics that are important to be known for. At this point, the reader might expect in the discussion something about the abilities and virtues of men; but what, in fact, these real, as opposed to apparent, virtues are is treated in the *Discourses*. By contrast, he now wants to treat the prince's appearance, his reputation among the people, all in the context of how a ruler can be successful. Notice that consequently, *The Prince* should not be separated from the *Discourses*, or else Machiavelli gets a bad name.

If chapter XV begins a discussion of the prince's character as it ap-

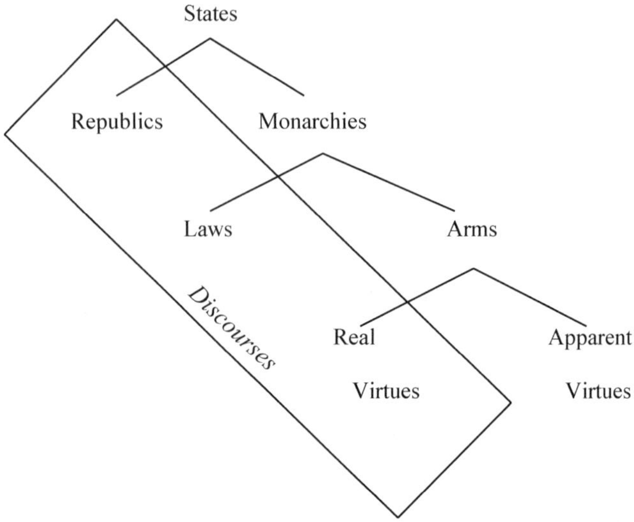

Fig. 50 *The Prince* vs. *The Discourses*

pears to others and chapter I starts the treatment of kinds of states and how they are acquired, chapter XII begins the second main line of argument by addressing the question of how the prince may retain control of his state once it has been acquired. What are the means and devices by which he can rule and the ways in which these can work? For Machiavelli, the foundations of a state rest upon good laws and good arms; but, not surprisingly, he says he will postpone the discussion regarding laws of the state, just as elsewhere he postpones treatment of both republics and real virtues, for the *Discourses*. To sum up broadly, then, this three-part structure of the work: (1) the first section (chapters II–XI), the kinds and acquisitions of states—monarchies, not republics—is concerned with *practice*; (2) the second section (chapters XII–XIV), arms—not laws—the means and devices available for ruling, are matters of *art*; and (3) the third section (chapters XV–XXIII), the appearance to the ruled—not the real character—of the ruler, addresses the prince's *nature* (see fig. 51).[2] In each section, then, Machiavelli repeatedly uses the self/other pair of contraries to help structure his argument.

With this as our outline, we can begin to understand what he is doing in more detail. An examination of chapters II through XI shows that he examines kinds of states and the methods of acquiring them—see the title to chapter I—in two parts: chapters II through V and VI through XI. Since he begins by saying that he will talk only about principates or monarchies, not republics, the line of his argument grows out of his method,

Practice	Chapters II - XI	Forms of Government: Monarchy	
		Others (People) (II – V)	Self (Prince) (VI – XI)
Art	Chapters XII – XIV	Means — Arms	
Nature	Chapters XV – XXIII	How Prince Appears	

Fig. 51 *Structure of* The Prince

which is going to leave a lot for the *Discourses*. The treatment of kinds of states arises from a natural beginning point and leads to a three-part division: states are either old, new, or of a mixed character (see fig. 52).[3] Moreover, talking about the forms of monarchies or principates gives rise to only two ways to do it. One can talk either in terms of the people being ruled by a ruler—others—which he does in chapters II through V, or in terms of the prince or ruler ruling them—self—which appears in chapters VI through XI. Notice, this reinforces the reason for omitting republics, where the ruled are in various ways the same as the ruler.

Consequently, Machiavelli begins with a brief treatment of hereditary monarchies, then turns to the new. Regarding the latter, when they are not completely new but mixed in character, he distinguishes a series of contrary possibilities and often provides historical examples. The mixed monarchies can have the ruler either ruling himself or ruling a group of barons. The people being ruled can either be the same in nationality and language or be other, differing in one or both of those two. Further, the people being ruled could have previously lived under another ruler, a prince, or not, that is, been free. Consequently, chapter V, the last in this first half of the section on forms of government and their acquisition, treats the question of the way in which a new ruler can handle ruling people that used to be free: he can either (1) ruin them, (2) live among them, or (3) let them keep their former laws.

With chapter VI, Machiavelli turns from differentiating the characteristics of states derived from the people living there to examining the state's character according to what the prince does with respect to ac-

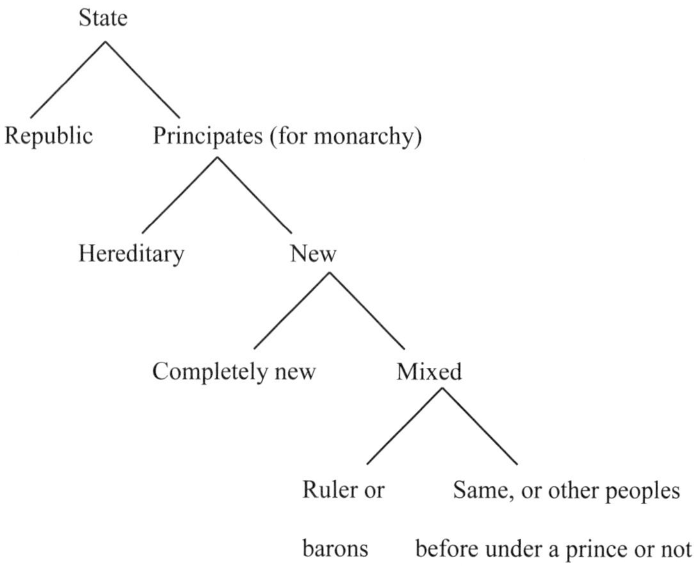

Fig. 52 *Machiavelli's Kinds of States*

quiring the state, to how it gets going through a series of actions. Notice how the operational method begins by considering the community—chapters II through V—and then turns to a discussion of a series of actions. Up to this point the prince has been looking to the people of the state; now he considers differing actions involved in acquiring the state. The main distinction among kinds of actions is between the actions of self (the prince) and those of others. Thus, chapter VI examines how the prince can acquire a new state by means of his own arms, distinguishing between ability and fortune. He discusses Moses, Cyrus, Romulus, and Theseus, and argues they are all great rulers, being good, not evil, kings of great ability. He also notes that one must distinguish getting power from holding power, for it is difficult to gain power but much easier to hold it. In all this, one can see that Machiavelli is using exemplary history.

If chapter VI treats how the prince can acquire a state by means of his own arms and ability, chapter VII presents principates that have been gotten through the military power of others or by fortune. Chapter VIII presents the issue of those who acquire princely power by means of evil deeds of themselves or of others. Here he treats the first with two examples, one ancient and one modern, of individuals engaged in criminal action; the latter he once more postpones for the *Discourses*. Chapter IX discusses the private citizen who becomes a prince through the favor of his fellow citizens, and Machiavelli holds that for this to happen, one

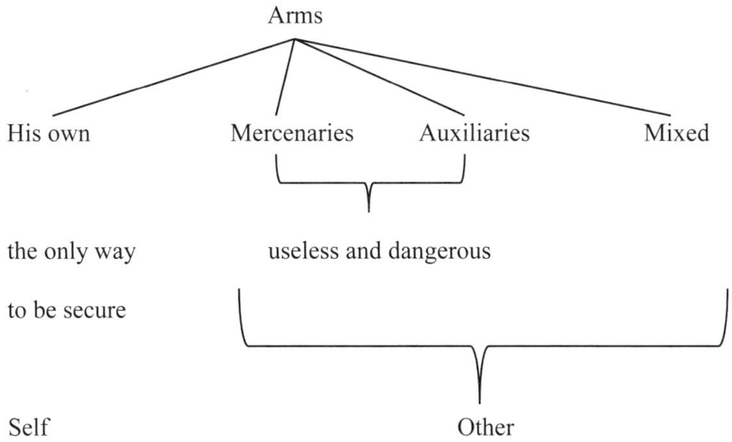

Fig. 53 *Machiavelli's Kinds of Arms*

needs a fortunate astuteness rather than pure ability or pure fortune. Chapter X argues that the proper way to estimate the strength of a state is to assess whether the prince has the ability to defend himself or needs the protection of others, the former being evidenced by his ability to field an army and the strength of his fortifications. Finally, chapter XI, "Of Ecclesiastical Principalities," explores the fact that such states are substantially different from those already discussed and are acquired through ability or fortune, though, once ruled, they can be held without either because, sustained by religious customs, they are maintained by God.

Chapter XII marks a major break in the argument which includes the following two chapters, XIII and XIV. The problem of the prince's acquisition of the state gives way to the problem of its foundations, which must be

> good, otherwise he is certain to be ruined. The chief foundations of all states, whether new, old, or mixed, are good laws and good arms. And as there cannot be good laws where there are not good arms, and where there are good arms there must be good laws, I will not now discuss the laws, but will speak of the arms. [ML:44][4]

The art concerned here, the art of arms, is once again explored through the customary dichotomy of self and other (see fig. 53).[5] First he deals with the other, the troops—and he even makes an opposition of self and other with respect to the army itself. Then, after treating the character of the troops, the other, he turns to the self and examines, as the title of chapter XIV states, "The Duties of a Prince with Regard to the Militia."

> A prince should therefore have no other aim or thought, nor take up any other thing for his study, but war and its organization and discipline, for that is the only art that is necessary to one who commands. [ML:53]

Even in peace, the prince should focus on this most important of arts, the art of war, for the "chief cause of the loss of states, is the contempt of this art" [ibid.].

As noted at the beginning of class, chapter XV introduces the third major line of the argument, the character or nature of the prince. The chapter's title—"Of the Things for Which Men, and Especially Princes, Are Praised or Blamed"—indicates how Machiavelli will approach his topic, namely, "the methods and rules for a prince as regards his subject and friends" [ML:56]. In examining the character of praise and blame, he again uses the pair of contraries, self and other. The question of reputation is central here, with what someone thinks of the prince being a question of the other, while what the prince truly is in himself is a question of self. Nevertheless, Machiavelli does not leave this question of reputation without nuance, for he raises the issue of even apparent virtues and vices being potentially injurious to the prince. For instance,

> he must not mind incurring the scandal of those vices, without which it would be difficult to save the state, for if one considers well, it will be found that some things which seem virtues would, if followed, lead to one's ruin, and some others which appear vices result in one's greater security and wellbeing. [ML:57]

Again, what is good in the operational method is that which leads to success, in this case, of the prince. So, complexity attaches to the five virtues that Machiavelli holds the prince should appear to have, namely, seeming to be compassionate, trustworthy, humane, honest, and religious.[6]

He concludes his work with three chapters (XXIV to XXVI) which deal with the contemporaneous situation in Italy.

Next time, we will go on to the *Discourses*.

McKeon's Notes

Machiavelli. The Prince.[7]

Op. Ref. Exist.

1. Organization of argument. Cf. Rhetoric. (a) kinds of *principalities* (b) *strength of prince devices* (c) *character of prince*. Comparable to three means of persuasion (a) audience, (b) speech (c) speaker.

> Preface to Lorenzo de' Medici. Lack of rhetorical ornamentation. He who wishes to understand nature of prince must be of people, and to understand nature of peoples must be prince. (93–94) *(4)*

(a) Kinds of principalities *and how established.*

Ruler	*Nature*	*Problem becomes*
Ruled	*Fortune*	*Acquire—Preserve*

Ch. 1. Division of principalities. (a) *republican* (b) *princely Principates* (i) *hereditary* or (ii) *new*. New (1) formerly *principates* or (2) *free*. Acquired (1) by *force* of others or (2) *one's own*—through (1) *fortune* or (2) *personal ability*. N.B. basis of division

> *(internal & external causes)*

(a) organic unites (b)[8]

Ch. 2. Omit republics *Hereditary principates*. (p. 96)
How governed & maintained.

Ch. 3. Mixed principates. (p. 97) *Part new.*
Language and region like or unlike; customs, laws.
Go to live in province; send colonies.
Romans 100. Louis 101. 5 errors 102.
Desire to acquire possessions natural.

Ch. 4. Alexander's Kingdom. 104.
Two kinds of principalities (1) one man prince, other officials slaves, (2) prince and barons. Turk as example of 1; France as 2. Alexander *conquering Darius* 1.

Ch. 5. States accustomed to living according to laws and liberty. *Three methods*. 107.
(1) ruin them (2) live among them (3) let them live according to own laws—organization of few to keep them friendly—tribute
> *Motion—generation*[?][9]

Ch. 6. New Principates gained by *own armies*. 109.
Ability or fortune.
→ Ability.—*Moses*, *Cyrus*, *Romulus*, *Theseus*. Cf. Ch. 26 *p. 177*.
Gain power with *difficulty*—hold it *easily*.
New laws and methods of government.

Ch. 7. New principates obtained through *military power of others* and *fortune*. 112.
Sforza and Cesare Borgia—Duke Valentino. esp, 117.

Ch. 8. Those who attain princely power through *evil deeds* p. 119.
(1) by *criminal and wicked* path (2) *private citizen* through favor of fellow citizens.
Latter reserved for work on *republics*—former treated by 2 examples—ancient and modern. Agathocles. Liverotto of Fermo.

Ch. 9. Civic principality. Method 2. p. 123. *Citizen to prince*
Fortunate astuteness needed rather than *pure ability* or pure *fortune*. People and upper classes—three results—*absolutism*, *liberty*, *license*.
Favor of people 124. Nabis and Spartans.

Ch. 10. Ways to estimate the strength of princely government. p. 127
Whether he has the power to defend self or needs protection of others. *(1) Ability to take field*—and (2) *fortifications*.
German cities. Prince who has strong city and is not hated.

Ch. 11. *Principalities of Churchmen*. 129.
Gained by *ability* or *fortune* but kept without either.
Do not defend territories.

| (b) Devices and means—laws and arms
Ch. 12. Kinds of soldiers. 131.
Have discussed kinds of princely government; also causes of their good and evil; also methods of gaining and holding them.
Now survey injuries *they can suffer and means of defense*.
Chief foundation of all states—*good laws and good arms*.
Own, *mercenary*, auxiliary.
Mercenaries

Ch. 13. *Auxiliaries*, *mixed* and *national* 137.
Mercenaries—danger laziness; auxiliaries efficiency. Charles VII, Louis XI.
National Armies.

Ch. 14. How Prince should act about military matters 139. No other object of thought than war.
First cause of loss of position neglect of art of war.
Peace as well as war. Philopoemen.

Machiavelli Prince 2.

(c) *Character of the Prince*. *Prince 2.*
Ch. 15. Things for which princes praised or censured. 141. How prince conducts self in dealing with friends.

Criticism of imaginary republics. 141 Difference between way men live and way they ought to live. Prince should learn how to be not good and use that ability or not.
Praise and blame external character. List of qualities.

Ch. 16. Liberality and parsimony. 143.
Good to be thought liberal. Not care if called stingy. If already prince, liberality dangerous; if becoming, necessary.

Ch. 17. Cruelty and pity. p. 145.
Is it better to be feared or loved?
Refrain from taking property. Since they love as they please and fear as the prince pleases, wise prince will rely on what is in his power.

Ch. 18. Dissimulation and keeping faith. p. 148
Two ways to fight—by laws and by force.
First man, second animals.
Advice bad if men were all good.

Not necessary to have all the virtues listed but is necessary to seem to have them. Seem *compassionate, trustworthy, humane, honest and religious*. p. 149. Be careful of statements contrary to these five qualities.
Everyone able to see few to understand.

Ch. 19. Avoiding contempt and hatred. 151.
Hatred from seizing property and women. Contempt.
Two kinds of fear—external and internal.
a. Conspiracies—not be hated by majority. People
b. Upper classes 153
c. Soldiers 154
Example of Roman emperors.

Ch. 20. Fortresses. 160 *Things*
Disarm subject or build fortresses. New prince never disarms subjects; acquisition of new state.
If prince more to fear from subjects than foreigners build fortresses; otherwise not. Not to be hated by people best fortress.

Ch. 21. The excellent prince. 164
Respect from undertakings and examples of ability
True friend and true enemy. Careful in alliances.

Ch. 22. Ministers 168.
Three types of brains.

Ch. 23. Flatterers. 170.
(a) If speak truth not offend (b) but lose respect (c) therefore third method.
Men always wicked at bottom—unless made good by compulsion.

(d) Application
Ch. 24. Why princes of Italy have lost authority. 172
Double glory—new princedom—and good law, good arms, and good examples.
Depend on *self* and vigor.

Ch. 25. Fortune 174.

Ch. 26. Redemption of Italy. 179.
Moses, Cyrus, Theseus.

2. Cf. with Aurelius—Social philosophy leads to aphorism concerning individual endurance; means of acquiring and maintaining without moral emphasis—leads to restitution of Italy.

3. Cf. with Aristotle—in perfect state good man and good citizen coincide. Machiavelli—prince—how achieve and hold power, and how achieve good of people.

4. What omitted.
Under (a) the republic.
(b) laws
(c) virtues like justice, courage, temperance, wisdom.

Instead, (a) kinds of government under prince—even those accustomed to be free.
(b) arms
(c) Seeming and real compassion, humanity, faith, honesty, religion.

5. What constitutes practical science?

Machiavelli The Prince 3.[10]

A. Organization of the work
1. Kinds of Principalities Ch. 1–11
Dichotomous division—Ch. 1. *Republics, monarchies*; (omitting republics) monarchies—hereditary *or new*; new—*entirely or mixed*. *New*—previously free or principalities; *annexed* either by force of arms of prince or others; fortune or ability.

Analysis therefore in terms of condition of ruled and attitude toward ruler under the circumstances in which he rules. Division between *ability* and *fortune*—internal and external cause.

Ch. 10 indicates the progress of the analysis through the various kinds of states—maintenance of self alone or need of protection by others. Self—abundance of men or money put together in sufficient army = ability to take field against enemy. Need of others those who cannot—remain in walls and on defensive.

Or Ch. 8—two ways of becoming prince which cannot be attributed to *fortune* or *ability*—villainy and favor of fellow-citizens (would be discussed in republic).

Or Chapter 6 on *ability*—distinction between ease of obtaining and retaining dominions

First part then classification of principalities in terms of problem of becoming and continuing to be prince—relative to nature of prince and nature of his circumstances

2. Foundations of all states—good laws and good arms (omission of good laws and discussion of good arms). Ch. 12–14.

Summary of what have been done thus far—treated qualities of principalities, causes of their prosperity or failure, methods by which many have sought to obtain such states.

Part 2 becomes therefore treatment of defense of possessions against external enemies.

3. "Methods and rules for prince as regards his subjects and friends." Character of prince 15–23.

Part 3 therefore relation of prince to persons *internal* to the kinds of state described in Part 1.

Conclusion about Italy 24–26

(1) Ability—fortune

(2) present fortunate situation for ability

B. Method—dichotomous division (cf. operational method)
Appearance of being empirical, practical, scientific.

C. Principles—internal and external (~~actional~~ *reflexive* principle)[11]

D. What happens to the objective or goals. Answered by observing the operation of the principles and the methods, in combination.

Two indirect sources of principles (1) *internal*—praise, i.e. the estimation that the prince possesses desirable or esteemed traits—i.e. those which will not impede his action. Cf. Ch. 3, p. 13: "The desire to acquire possessions is a very natural and ordinary thing, and when those men do it who can do so successfully, they are always praised and not blamed, but when they cannot and yet want to do so at all costs, they make a mistake deserving of great blame."

Likewise the prince should seem to possess the virtues listed, but he should be able without hesitation to act contrary to any of them.

(2) external—bearing on the same question of his virtues or abilities—the principle of *imitation*—he should *imitate the great princes of the past*. Cf. Ch. 14, p. 55: "But as to exercise for the mind, the prince ought to read history and study the actions of eminent men, see how they acted in warfare, examine the causes of their victories and defeats in order to imitate the former and avoid the latter, and above all, do as some men have done in the past, who have imitated some one, who has been much praised and glorified, and have always kept his deeds and actions before them, as they say Alexander the Great imitated Achilles, Caesar Alexander, and Scipio Cyrus. And whoever reads the life of Cyrus written [by] Xenophon will perceive in the life of Scipio how gloriously he imitated the former, and how in chastity, affability, humanity, and

liberality Scipio conformed to those qualities of Cyrus as described by Xenophon." For imitation cf. Ch. 6, p. 19; Ch. 7, pp. 27, 29; Ch. 8, p. 31; Ch. 19, p. 76.

E. Characteristic Machiavellian method apparent from these e.g. Ch. 12 (a) kinds of militia and then (b) kinds of captains—able or not; if able not rely on them (i) oppress you (ii) oppress others against your intentions. If not able ruin you.

Machiavelli Prince 4.

Nature = ability. If able captain of mercenaries should happen to be faithful that is fortune and therefore should properly be left out of calculation except as addition to what is legitimately expected. Ability—internal cause of action—usually in own interest and against others. Therefore consider possibilities—against you or against those you would not oppress or if not able dangerous.

Example from history for all of these

For the same reason prince has no other study than war—that his only art—ability against.

Yet objectives beyond found in the *dominion*—thus Ch. 17: cruelty of Cesare Borgia "had brought order to the Romagna, united it, and reduced it to peace and fealty."

So to questions of law in terms of proper action Ch. 18: "men love at their own free will, but fear at the will of the prince, and . . . a wise prince must rely on what *is in his power* and not *what is in the power of other* . . ."

Similarly statements and acts—statements should exemplify the five virtues—mercy, faith, integrity, humanity, and religion. p. 65.

Similar ground for the low estimation of men as whole Ch. 18: "the world consists only of the vulgar, and the few who are not vulgar are isolated when the many have a rallying point in the prince."

Prince has two kinds of fear Ch. 19—"one internal as regards his subjects, one external as regards foreign powers." Former—good arms and good friends, latter not being hated by the masses. (conspiracy).

Populace, soldiery, nobles.

Cf. judgment of men in general Ch. 17 p. 62:[12] "For it may be said of men in general that they are ungrateful, voluble, dissemblers, anxious to avoid danger, and covetous of gain; as long as you benefit them, they are entirely yours; they offer you their blood, their goods, their life, and their children, as I have before said, when the necessity is remote; but when it approaches, they revolt."

DISCUSSION

Machiavelli, Part 2 (*Discourses on the First Ten Books of Titus Livius*)

Discussion Summary

We now come to the second of Machiavelli's works, his *Discourses on the First Ten Books of Titus Livius*. Let's begin at the very beginning. You may remember that *The Prince* is dedicated to Lorenzo de' Medici, a ruling prince. The *Discourses*, by contrast, is dedicated to two men who are not princes but who, Machiavelli implies, ought to be. So, in the distinction between *The Prince* and the *Discourses*, he is indicating that the former is addressed to *apparent* power of a ruler, what others say and do, whereas the latter addresses the *real* virtue of true rulers; consequently, his emphasis now will be not on external action and consequences, as it was earlier, but on internal virtues and abilities.

When we turn to the introduction of the first book, we find him distinguishing two key points: first, he complains that despite "the general respect for antiquity" [ML:103],[1] many more things are admired than are imitated; and second, to address this issue, he intends "to open a new route" [ibid.]. He acknowledges that although "the discovery and introduction of any new principles and systems" [ibid.] are always dangerous, he nevertheless plans to introduce a new method or way of proceeding. Since he has distinguished two terms—*admire* and *imitate*—and related them in opposition, he can use them to show operationally how his method works. What is new about this method? And if it is indeed new and he wants to show that, what should he do? In the operational method, one has a problem to solve only when one lights up the relevant circumstances. Here he naturally wants to talk of the distinction between the theoretic—admiring—and the practical—doing (see fig. 54).[2] As he puts it, we admire antiquity and spend time and even money on looking at its works of art; but we ought to recognize that we need not just to talk about antiquity but actually to imitate it in social and political matters if

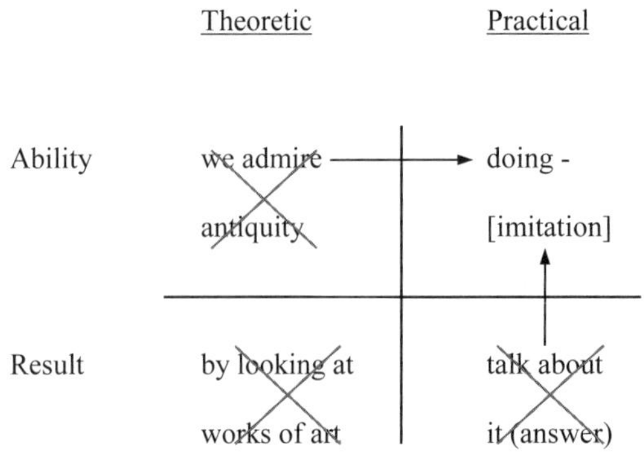

Fig. 54 *Admiration* vs. *Imitation*

we are not to be in error. Consequently, we need to translate dead history into a mode of action; and by our doing so, the new method and imitation can become the same thing. In short, what he is doing here is using his method on his method. Notice, he did not boast about using a new method in *The Prince*; but here he is boasting of his method, because the method is what is important. In *The Prince*, he merely talks about his selection of what to do in the circumstances addressed.

Given this orientation, where does Machiavelli make his beginning? In chapter I, whose title is "Of the Beginning of Cities in General, and Especially That of the City of Rome." Cities owe their origin to their genesis; and the beginning point, the principle, is how they got started in general. Here, the thing is what it is made to be. In other words, cities are given their natures. To treat this, Machiavelli introduces the self/other distinction to explore the process (see fig. 55).[3] This figure demonstrates the operational method at work. Here he begins with two different columns headed by symbols—natives and strangers—which have no meaning and can be rejected; but they can subsequently take on meaning as they are used. How does the argument run? The words do not even keep their meaning as he moves along. Here he uses free men and subjects, but elsewhere he can use other pairs, such as one's ability or chance.

Substantively, what are we working on? We are looking for an independent city, that is, one similar to a free man, a city independent of other cities—though he leaves open that it need not necessarily be founded by men who are free. He will end up, nevertheless, with a democratic form of the city, not a principate one. In considering the city's beginnings, he explores a series of contraries. In one set he asks, Is it better for the city to be founded on wisdom, that is, choice, or on chance? The answer is that sometimes one, sometimes the other is best: it all depends upon the

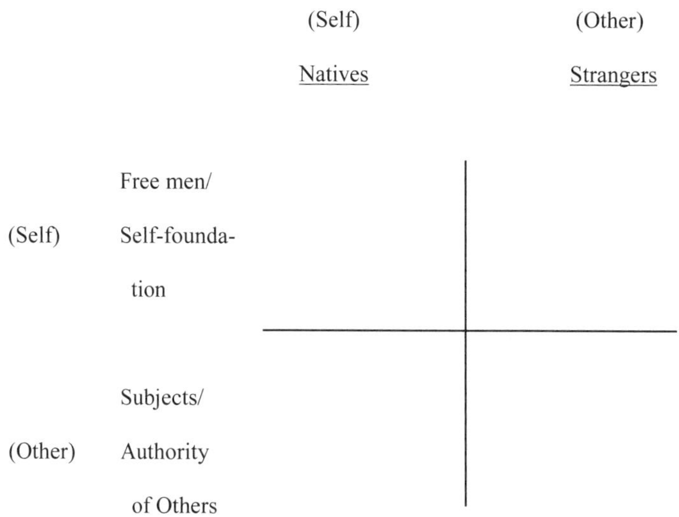

Fig. 55 *Beginnings of Cities*

circumstances. Similarly, regarding another set of contraries describing the region where the city is located, that is, whether the land is fertile or sterile, the answer also depends on circumstances. Sterility makes for industry, while fertility makes for laziness—but laws can change that. Either kind of region can go askew; yet generally, a fertile region leads to a powerful people, while a sterile one leads to a virtuous populace. These oppositions play out with relation to Rome in his treatment of the question of whether Aeneas or Romulus was the better founder of the city. Although both Aeneas, a stranger, or Romulus, a native, have been considered responsible for the origin of Rome, the city would in either case still have ended up free. Why? Notice, first, with regard to its origins, an independent city need not necessarily come from independent citizens; but if it is a colony, that is, ruled by another city, it is by nature not independent, and therefore not an instance of what we are examining. Turning to Romulus, Machiavelli argues that the native made laws for the city which constricted the freedom of its citizens; whereas Aeneas, the stranger, picked the site for the city and then, from that point on, had to make laws for it. Either way, Rome was free and independent from the beginning: free because the natives made the laws which made the tribe that made Rome, and independent because an outside prince came, picked a good site, and started a city. Unity, therefore, was achieved by means of laws or of external circumstances. From the perspective of the native, Romulus, the natives were joined together by the laws imposed, which took those who were the same in both place of origin and as a people and bound them together differently. From the perspective of the outsider, Aeneas and his band of Trojans were starting out anew in a new place. Either way, Rome ends up the same independent city.

As its title proclaims, chapter II explores the character "Of Different Kinds of Republics, and of What Kind the Roman Republic Was." Machiavelli distinguishes three kinds of state—monarchy, aristocracy, and democracy—and their respective degradations—tyranny, oligarchy, and licentiousness. He observes that chance and choice both enter into all, with each form leading into the others, and proceeds to give the story of how that happens (see ML:112). Chance was involved in which kind of state arose, but in "uniting themselves for defence," humans "chose the strongest and most courageous" to lead them and make laws. Out of such beginnings came the origin of justice and the choice of those individuals who were not necessarily "the strongest and bravest" but the "wisest and most just" to act as leader. With hereditary sovereignty and the succession of the children of the original leader, the city soon degraded into tyranny. In response, the people rose up, chose leaders to remove the tyrant, and when successful, encouraged the creation of an aristocracy. Next, over time, the aristocracy degenerated into an oligarchy, and once again the people rose up and removed the leadership. This time they instituted popular government; but that form over time underwent degradation when the passions of each individual led it into chaos. That unsustainable circumstance then gave rise to a new prince taking control, completing the circle. In short, Machiavelli has translated everything into a genetic sequence, a natural evolution, in which it does not matter what is put on the side of chance or what on the side of choice. As he says, "Such is the circle which all republics are destined to run through" [ML:114], though he immediately thereafter adds the caveat that republics "seldom . . . come back to the original form of government." Given the operational character of the method, notice that Machiavelli's argument that all kinds of government are defective is similar to Mill's position that all ideas are defective, neither entirely true nor false.

This examination of the different kinds of government leads Machiavelli to conclude that a mixed form of government, one combining the powers of prince, nobility, and people, would be "the most stable and solid" [ML:115]. Given these criteria, he can separate the differences between Sparta and Athens. Lycurgus, the founder of the former, organized the government by "giving to the king, the nobles, and the people each their portion of authority and duties" [ibid.], a structure which endured for hundreds of years. By contrast, Solon created for Athens a constitution which "established only a popular government" [ibid.], which proved quite unstable. This leads him to Rome, which began like neither Sparta nor Athens, that is, with a government neither mixed nor popular. Nevertheless, "chance did for her what the laws had failed to do" [ML:116]. As he gives the history, Romulus did provide good laws, but their intent was to support the monarchy. When the kings were removed, only consuls and the senate, the monarchic and aristocratic elements, remained. Ultimately, the absence of power for the people was corrected with creation of the people's tribunes. Machiavelli concludes that he will use Rome, with this tripartite form of government, as his model, because the combination of these three powers "rendered the constitution perfect" [ibid.]. Thus, by the end of chapter II, Machiavelli has indicated how he will pursue his new route to the good state through an analysis of imitation of the internal operation of that state, Rome.

McKeon's Notes

Machiavelli. The Discourses 1.[4]

Dedication. Contrast to Prince—not dedicated to prince (Prince dedicated to Lorenzo) but to one worthy by his infinite good qualities to be prince.

Not those who can be generous but those who are.

I.e., emphasis to be not on external action and consequences but on internal virtues and abilities.

Book I. Introduction. Plan to open up a new route and use a new method. (103)

Example of antiquity imitated in art—but not ancient virtues and institutions. "More admired than imitated."

"The civil laws are in fact nothing but decisions given by their jurisconsults, and which, reduced to a system, direct our modern jurists in their decisions. What is the science of medicine, but the experience of ancient physicians, which their successors have taken for their guide?" [ML:105] Similar—found republic.

Undertake comparison of ancient and modern events.

Ch. I. Beginnings of cities in general and particularly of Rome.

Those who know beginnings of Rome not surprised that so much virtue maintained so many centuries. (105)

Dichotomous division of kinds of origin—

Natives—*strangers*. *Natives* build cities for mutual security—own accord—advice of someone with authority among them. (Athens—Theseus; Venice—tribes without prince.)

Second case—*strangers*: freemen—subjects; subject of republic or prince; *colonies* to relieve excessive population or to defend new territory; prince to live there or as monuments. (Latter deprived of liberty, little progress, not great powers—Florence in empire)

Independent cities—prince or people themselves—seek new home. *Inhabit cities* (Moses) or build *new* ones (Aeneas)

Selection of place and the nature of laws.

Necessity and *Choice* (107) *Virtue* has more sway where labor is the result of necessity rather than choice.

Sterile region—to make men industrious (avoid idleness and discord) (Ragusa). Wise is men content with what they possess.

People cannot make themselves secure unless powerful; therefore avoid sterile country (sterile—fertile)

Rely on laws to avoid idleness. Egypt. Alexandria.

Rome. If *Aeneas*—built by strangers; if *Romulus*—by natives. Either way—free and independent from the first. Privations to which the laws subjected inhabitants.

Great things of Rome—work of *government* or private *individuals*: *interior* or *exterior* affairs. *Begin with internal* operations.

Ch. II. *Different kinds of republics* and the kind Roman was.

Dichotomous divisions again. Subject to *foreign power*—*independent*: *republics* or *principalities* in origin.

Some had *legislator* (Lycurgus), others owed laws to *chance* or events (Rome). Good fortune to have *legislator*. Misfortune—republic without wise legislator; obliged to *reform laws*. More—diverged from *good laws*. Most—*vicious institutions*.

Contrasted—republics which without perfect constitution made fair beginning—improvement; Majority not willing to change constitution unless need clearly demonstrated.

Division into *six kinds of government*. (111) Degradation of three good into three bad.

Chance origin of these different kinds of government.

Chose strongest—made laws, origin of justice (112)

Thereafter no longer chose strongest and bravest, but *wisest* and most *just*.

Prince—became tyranny through hatred and fear. Liberation—civil *equality*. (113) *Aristocratic* government degenerate into oligarchic tyranny.

Origin of *popular government* (114) *Degradation*—each individual consult only his own passions—return to princely government.

This the circle which all governments destined to run through (114). Seldom go back to original form.

All kinds of government defective—good and bad (114) good because short-lived. *Mixed government*—checks of three *powers*.

Lycurgus—Sparta—*kings*, *nobles*, *people*. vs. policy of Solon—people. *800* years vs. 100 years.

Rome—no legislator like Lycurgus (115) to insure

liberty for a length of time. *Chance* did for her what laws failed to.

Romulus and other kings—good laws—but to found monarchy. On becoming *free* lacked all institutions most essential to *liberty*.

Consuls and *Senate*—monarchic and aristocratic. Popular power missing—*Tribunes*—combination formed of the three powers which rendered the constitution perfect.

Ch. III. (117) Events leading to creation of the Tribunes. Whoever desires to found a state and give it laws, must begin with the *assumption that all men are bad*.

Nobility after expulsion of the Tarquins from fear of Tarquins treated people well—lest they side with them

Assumption—men act right only upon compulsion. From the moment they have the option and liberty to commit wrong with impunity, they carry confusion and disorder everywhere.

Poverty and hunger make men industrious; *law makes men good*. If fortunate circumstances cause good to be done without constraint, the law may be dispensed with. But when such happy influence is lacking, the law immediately becomes necessary.

Ch. IV. Disunion of senate and people renders Rome ***[powerful]*** and ***[free]***.

Good fortune and military discipline supplied defects of constitution. Where good discipline prevails good order prevails.

Quarrels of Senate and people origin of ***[liberty]***.

Laws favorable to liberty resulted from oppression.

Yet differences caused few exiles or loss of blood.

[Good education]—[good example]—[good laws].

Every ***[good republic]*** ought to give people opportunity to give vent to their ambition.

Cicero—people appreciate truth though ignorant.

Ch. V. (121) Guardianship of ***[liberty]***—people or nobles? Which have more cause for creating disturbances—those who wish to ***[acquire]*** or to ***[conserve]***?

Guarding and preserving freedom. Lacedaemonians and Venetians—nobles; Romans—people. Incline to nobles. *Endured longer*. Objects—nobles to dominate; people not to be dominated. Argument for people—not likely to encroach on liberty.

Argument for nobility (122) Sparta and Venice. 2 advantages. (1) those in power satisfied by administration (2) restrain restless spirit of masses.

Balance of two arguments. Distinguish between republic which extends self—Rome—or confines self to own preservation.

Which more dangerous: those who wish to acquire power or those who fear to lose that which they possess?

Most frequently occasioned by those who possess.

N.B. Chs. 4 and 5 Concerned with the *acquisition and preservation, respectively, of power* and freedom. Power and freedom discussed together. Power and freedom of the *whole state*—and the *interactions of the "powers" of the three parts and their freedom*.

Ch. 6. Whether it was possible to establish government putting to end enmity between nobles and people.

Example of republics without such enmities—Sparta and Venice—latter chance rather than foresight.

Sparta—equality in fortunes and inequality in conditions. Two principal causes cementing union—few people—no strangers.

Rome had to do one of two things—not employ people in army, not admit strangers. (Venice first, Sparta second). Then remove cause of expansion.

If expansion—organize like Rome (128); if confine organize like Sparta or Venice. Sparta internal organization; Venice—strong location.

Two motives for making war on a republic—desire to subjugate her, or apprehension of being subjugated.

Above two methods of removing these causes.

If republic could maintain this equilibrium—best political existence. But every thing human in perpetual movement, necessity compels them to many acts to which reason does not influence them. Might have to expand.

Since equilibrium impossible—take constitution of Rome as model. Rather than other two.

N.B. organization of first six chapters. 1–3 introduction in terms of origins: 1. of all cities, 2. of republics (both origins giving kinds) 3. of republic with power of *people*

Machiavelli Discourses 3.

Chs. 4–6 likewise three steps of organization of model republic, with respect to power and freedom: 4. acquisition, 5. guardianship, 6. enmity of parts.

Consideration of last three gives scheme of organization; problem in terms of change, its causes and causes of its cessation, internal and external.

4. Causes of power and liberty—internal interplay of two classes. 5. Preservation of power and liberty—action of one or the other of two classes—relative to each other (internal) static or expanding (external). 6. Opposition of two—result in endurance (internal) and effective expansion (external).

Two powers: (4) in cooperation to establish
(5) in respective sovereign action to preserve
(6) in opposition to move or change.

Look back at the first three introductory chapters which reduced all states to Roman state as model.
(1) all states—among the internal external principles—people (self) prince (other); Independent cities.
(2) leave out principalities, series of divisions—foreign powers, independent, laws, chance. Athens and Sparta—lawgivers; Rome chance (internal in sense of no rationally imposed laws)—monarchic and aristocratic principles—no laws for freedom.
(3) Rome—institution of Tribunes—operation and opposition of senate and people. Men act right only under compulsion. Law makes men good—fear of people restrains senate.

Ch. 7 (130) Taking Rome as model—proceed to the specific function of Tribunes—accusing.

Showing how necessary the faculty of accusation is in a republic for the maintenance of liberty.

Two advantages: (1) apprehension of being accused prevents citizens from attempting anything against the state, (2) gives those with evil disposition vent,—ex. Coriolanus; Florence: bring charges against ambitions of powerful citizens.

Whenever aid of foreign powers called in, result of defects of constitution—particularly want of means to enable people to exhaust malign humors (133)

Ch. 8. (134) In proportion as accusations are useful calumnies are pernicious.

No more effective way of putting end to calumnies than by instituting system of legal accusations. (135)

Calumnies require neither witnesses nor confrontings nor particulars to prove them; accusations require positive proof and circumstances.

Well-organized in Rome—badly in Florence (136)

Ch. 9. To found a New Republic or to reform institutions of existing republic entirely, must be work of one man.

Romulus—killing brother. Never or rarely happens that a republic or monarchy is well constituted or its old institutions entirely reformed, except by one individual. (138) All authority in self.

On other hand it will not long endure if the authority remains on the shoulders of one individual.

Rome became free after the expulsion of the Tarquins.

Corroborated by examples of <u>Moses</u>, <u>Lycurgus</u>, <u>Solon</u>.

Ch. 10 (141) As founders of monarchy deserve praise, founders of a tyranny deserve execration.

Eulogy—<u>first</u> founders of religions, <u>second</u> founders of republics and kingdoms; next commanders of armies; literary men; then arts and professions.
Infamy destroyers of religions and republics.

Caesar (142) good and bad emperors (145)

Study of emperors—way to glory or infamy. Also lesson in how to hold empire—inheritance and adoption.
Caesar vs. Romulus (145)

Discourses[6]

1. Republics (rather than principalities)

2. Emphasis on freedom

3. (Chance—vs. ability)

4. Internal organization
(a) Balance of power for liberty
(b) Princes—accusations and religion
(arms law religion)
(c) Character of people

Outline same as Prince
1. Internal organization
2. External expansion
3. Renewal of principates (character of prince)

New Route: Imitation—Internal

1. Beginnings of city

2. Kinds of republics—circle
Rome chance
Aristocratic monarchies
Balance of 3 powers

3. Tribunes

4. Senate and people—freedom

5. Liberty—nobles or people
Expanding or stationary

6. Possible to end enmity
Sparta—Venice
means of [?][7] *p. 129*

7. Accusation—Liberty

8. Calumnies are against people pernicious

—

9. One man

10. Tyranny

11. Religion—Numa or Romulus

12. Italy

—

13. Romans

14. Auspices

15. Samnites

Machiavelli *Discourses* [1][8]

1st [Book]

1. Origin.

Natives — Strangers

Free subject

excessive population defend

Founders — independent.

new old city

place laws

sterile rich

Laws to make men work and rich
First internal

2. Kinds of Republic 110
Majority of men conservative 111
Leave aside subject cities only independent cities 110
First governed by own laws 111
Six kinds of government—chance.
Right and good dependent
Rome chance—combination of three powers
Monarchy and Aristocracy

3. Tribunes—people
Right—compulsion

4. Disunion people and senate—made Rome free.

5. Which best guardian of freedom.
Two objects — dominate—nobles
not be dominated—people.
Extend or not extend boundaries
Rome Sparta Venice
Which more dangerous—those seeking power or those fearing to lose power
Fear to lose

6. Possible to establish Rome with dissension between nobles and people?
Sparta Venice
End of state 129.
Expansion

———

7. Accusation—private free against state
Apprehension—venting

8. Calumnies—pernicious.

9. Found or reform republic—one man.

10. Tyranny.

———

11. Religion—oath and laws. 146
lawgiver and divine authority

Religion—good laws—good fortune. |||
Successors 148
All men 149. 216

12. Prince and religion—Roman
Church and Italy

13. Romans and religion—difficulties

14. Auspices.

15. Samnites.

Machiavelli *Discourses* [2]

> *People*
16. People under prince—when free.

17. Corrupt People 164
Laws no avail unless with superior power. 166

18. Corrupt state maintain free government
Habits—laws. 168
good and bad princes. 171.

>

19. Feeble prince after strong.

20. Two successive good princes.

21. National Army

22. Horatii: (a) agreement where observance doubtful

23. (b) whole fortune part of force

24. (c) Well ordered state—merits and crimes.

>

25. Reform—preserve semblance of old forms.

26. New Prince—everything new.
Entirely good—bad—middle course

27. Men rarely entirely good or bad.

28. Rome less ungrateful

< *29. Which most ungrateful people or prince*
Purpose free city—aggrandize self—protect freedom

30. Prince and ingratitude

31. Roman generals.

>

32. Will of people.

33. Evil in state—temporize

34. Dictatorship—never pernicious

35. Decemvirs

>

36. Citizen higher and lower offices.

37. Retrospective laws
Nature and fortune 208
Republic rich Citizens poor.
Riches—honors. 210

38. Feeble republics irresolute

Machiavelli. The Prince. The Discourses. 1.[9]

1. Use of commonplaces in dedications.
Prince—to Lorenzo di Medici. Subject—prince. Have long pondered and scrutinized the actions of the great. Receive it with favor, not in power to offer greater gift. (3)
Necessary to be prince to know thoroughly the nature of the people, and one of the populace to know the nature of princes.
Lofty position—humble spot. Unmerited sufferings of cruel fate: [generous actions of considerate ability or power]. Ruler-ruled. Standpoint of ruled.
Discourses. Book I. Introduction. Envious nature of men slow to praise. Praise:blame::merit:defect.
Discovery and introduction of new principles and systems dangerous. Proposes to open new route.

Poor talents, little experience of present and insufficient study of past. Show way to others. Greater ability, eloquence, and judgment [Commonplace—action, statement, thought—for the treatment of things]. (103)

Respect for antiquity and other examples.

Art—ancient art for adornment and imitation.

History of ancient kingdoms and republics—prodigies of virtue and wisdom—kings, captains, citizens and legislators—who have sacrificed themselves for their country.

More admired than imitated. [Feeling: action].

Ancient civil laws and jurisconsults (decisions)

Reduced to systems direct modern jurists in their decisions.

Medicine and politics.

Found a republic, maintain states, govern a kingdom, organize an army, conduct a war, dispense justice, and extend empires [actions], Prince, republic, captain, citizen [agents] do not consider examples of antiquity.

Vice of our education. History used for pleasure in variety of events—not imitating noble actions

As if motions and powers of universe changed from antiquity

[Nature and powers of universe: nature and powers of state]

A phenomenal interpretation. What rulers and ruleds do.

Not based on transcendent ideas, underlying nature, or the structure of virtues and institutions. Existential.

A universal method—differentiation of kinds of states and kinds of powers. *Operational*.

A symbolic interpretation—prominence of common-place praise and blame in the determination of actions and attitudes, thoughts and things. Propose to show the way, a new way, invention. Cf. rhetoric—nature (of agent, his ability or power), practice (imitation of successful agents), and art (system of rules based on consideration of successful actions).[10]

From the basic commonplace the relation of the two works and the introduction of their aims or normative statements. Successful action of rulers: virtue and wisdom of agents. Dominion: sacrifice. Power: freedom.

Ch. 1. Prince—(1) kinds of governments and ways in which they are established. Republics, monarchies, hereditary, new—entirely new, new added to hereditary.

(2) Division of dominions—previously prince, free

(3) Division of action—force of arms, of prince or others, good fortune or special ability.

[Use of common places to distinguish three questions and sub questions of each. Kinds of states, previous condition of people, action of ruler.

Old, new; subjugated, free; self, other—ability, fortune]

Ch. 1. Discourses—beginnings of cities—in general and Rome. (105)

[Focus now on the government and virtue, rather than governor and power]

Beginnings or principles. Origin, lawgivers, and organization of Rome [action, lawgivers, organization]—one change, division of populaces in Prince, or lawgivers in Discourses.

Dichotomous division of all cities—founded by natives, strangers.

Natives—for security; on own accord or advice. Athens, Venice.

Strangers—freemen, or subjects (republic or prince) relieve overpopulation or defend new acquisitions. Ex. Romans. Cities sometimes built for glory, Alexandria. Such cities deprived of liberty, no progress (107)

Founders of cities are independent when, under prince or by themselves, they have been obliged to fly from pestilence, war, or famine and seek new homes.

Either inhabit cities already built or build new ones. Ex. of first Moses, second Aeneas. Appreciate talents of founder and success of his work, as he displays more or less wisdom and skill. (107) Both

---

Machiavelli The Prince. The Discourses 2.

recognized by selection of place and the nature of laws established.

Men work by necessity or choice, and virtue more sway when labor the result of necessity rather than choice, therefore choice of sterile region might be better—more industrious, less discord. Would be more useful and wise, if men content with what they possess and not desire command over others. (108)

To be secure must be powerful, avoid sterile country.

Choose fertility for strength.

Resulting idleness; laws to compel men to labor. Ex. Egyptians.

Alexander—Mount Athos (what will the inhabitants live on). Alexandria, richness of country.

Use of dichotomous division on the founding of Rome. (109)

Romulus—natives; Aeneas, strangers. Either way Rome free and independent.

Privations of laws of Romulus and Numa.

Great things achieved by Rome—work of government or individuals; interior or exterior affairs.

[*Operational* method—symbolic verbal characteristics: dichotomous divisions used as topics—terms which acquire significance, by use of examples. The method opens up meanings—frequently by paradoxical combination or merging of terms which seem opposed; it is heuristic and persuasive.

Difference from problematic method, which might use the same topics and examine relevant history: but the topics are given an interpretation in which kinds of government are recognized from their properties and are conditioned by circumstances—virtue is a habit not a power, and states are actualizations of potentialities, not products of power. Inductive rather than heuristic.

Difference from dialectical method, which might use the same topics and consult history—differentiation rather than assimilation, and virtue and government are knowledge rather than virtue and government being products as is knowledge of the exercise of power. Method assimilation.

Difference from the logistic method, which might use the same topics and consult history—virtue and government emotive as in operational but on the basis of nature and human nature which can be grasped cognitively and provide a criterion for distinguishing good and bad. Method deductive.]

LECTURE ELEVEN

History: Method and Principle; and Conclusion

I want today to finish our analysis of history, and then to say a few words in conclusion about what we have been doing in general with our analysis of freedom, power, and history. Since we did interpretation in history last time, let me begin with method now, and run quickly through the four kinds of history as seen from that aspect.

The dialectical is the first of the universal methods, and that method leads to a conception of history as epochal (see table 18).[1] As you would expect from its dialectical character, such an approach treats history as a series of wholes, of ages or epochs, in which everything reflects to a greater or lesser extent the ideal which characterizes that age or epoch. All events and occurrences more or less approximate to this ideal form: you can have histories of degradation or histories which lead to a golden age—that is, you begin high and you come down, or you begin low and go up—but more frequently the histories are cyclical. When they are cyclical, you usually have some natural figure of speech: the ages of man is a favorite one. In fact, a good part of medieval history was written that way; and as the Middle Ages moved on, one moved from five to six to seven ages of man, ranging about birth and growth, maturity and full development, and decline. Your cycles would be such that you could have a succession of new growths following declines of the previous ages. Another favorite form is the seasons of the year. That is frequently like Spengler's *Decline of the West*.[2] There are four seasons of the year, four ages. We are living in winter, and the coming of spring is rather far away. *The Decline of the West* has been answered by *The Rise of the West* by William H. McNeill:[3] there are similar sequences that are involved. Obviously, there are also the dialectical sequences of Hegelian history and the dialectical sequences of the history of dialectical materialism.[4] These are all epochal. But you will notice that in general, the characteristic of the epochal is that you are able to characterize a large whole; and since

Table 18. Definitions of *History*.

Ambiguous Formula: "History is the account of happenings or sequences or structures past, present, or future."

Modes of Thought	Principle What are grounds of process? What sets order of narrative?	Method What are the connections in processes? How set forth?	Interpretation What is (in) process? What is account of the process?	Selection What am I talking about?
	Holoscopic	*Universal*	*Ontic*	
Assimilation	Whole (Inclusive)	Rational Connections (Epochal History)	Forms (Rational, Necessary)	Rational Beings
Resolution	Cause (Self-)	Technical Connections (Exemplary History)	Processes (of Composition)	Things
	Meroscopic	*Particular*	*Phenomenal*	
Construction	Motion (of Object)	Mechanical Connections (Causal History)	Acts (of Making)	Animals (with Impulses)
Discrimination	Agent (of Action)	Essential Connections (Disciplinary History)	Facts (of Subject Matters)	Humans (Habits, Institutions)

you're dealing with history, it is an age that you characterize, then you characterize the sequence of ages, and you have your history.

Let me say a word more about it, because one of the striking things about dialectical history is that there is a strict equivalence between argument and myth, using myth in the nonpejorative sense in which the Greeks used it. That is to say, if you tell the complete history of anything, you give the complete analysis; and if you give the complete analysis, you've given the history. Hegel was fond of saying this: that is, he will frequently pause to indicate the strict equivalence between the developmental aspect viewed historically and the developmental aspect viewed argumentatively, because dialectic is a development; therefore, there is a relation. Short of doing it completely, you can give an argument and then illustrate it by a myth, and then you can discover that your argument was a myth and your myth was an argument. Plato does this several times. I have mentioned this before, and therefore, I will not go back to it.[5]

Second under universal methods is the operational method, discrimination. History is the account of the operations of an agent and the effects of his actions and innovations. In general for the operational approach, thought and action are the same, not as we've just been talking about with the processes of becoming and the nature of being in the dialectical, but rather in the sense that anything which is thought is the result of a thinker doing it, and therefore, the process enters in. If you put an admirable action—and an admirable action is merely an effective action, one which has consequences; the operational method gets its normative terms later—if you put an effective action in its context, you will have both the sequence of history set forth and material for imitation. This operational history is therefore exemplary history. The great thinker, the great actor, did the things which ought to be recounted, and from the way he did them you will be able to find a solution to the problems you face. You have had your experience with exemplary history: the argument of Machiavelli was based on history, both in *The Prince* and in *The Discourses on the Decades of Livy*. In both cases, he gives you the examples to be imitated. In the one it is the examples of the admirable rulers, ranging from Moses, Cyrus, and the great rulers to the rulers who were effective for particular things. In *The Discourses* you have, as a result of chance, the evolution of the mixed form of government in which three powers are balanced one against the other; and out of this he hopes that he can set up again a republic in which virtue will be ground out by the operation of the three powers found, each limiting the other two. Exemplary history makes the person, makes his values, and makes him available for imitation.

The particular methods differ from these. First the logistic method, the mode of construction. What happens? A sequence of causes and events. How do you account for what happens? Find a cause. History is therefore a thin line of causal sequences, of action and reaction, rather than organizing forces or innovating actions, which were our other two possibilities. In causal history, you usually either implicitly or explicitly go to what you take to be the basic science. This is the reason why for a long time there was so much political history, economic history, and military history, because what you do is to take the sequence of political events as the underlying cause and then reduce all of the events to that, and equally easily you can take the economic foundation and reduce the political, the moral, the cultural and aesthetic to the economic form. This is done in other forms than the form that it takes in its dialectical counterpart, namely, materialistic interpretation. Beard's interpretation of the [United States] Constitution, for example, is an interpretation in which you account for the provisions of the Constitution by examining one by one the economic backgrounds of the people who participated in the Constitutional Convention. He does a very nice job of it. It doesn't account for some of the things that I'm interested in, but it accounts for all the things he's interested in. Consequently, as I warned you, the history is always adapted to the method of argument; therefore, to introduce into the picture what I'm interested in is irrelevant, because if we were doing the other part of the analysis, the analysis of power and freedom, what I'm interested in doesn't exist logistically.

You have in causal history, therefore, one result which is rather striking: it is usually the causal histories that yield progress. Let me warn you at once that this does not mean that if you read in a philosopher of history or in a historian the word *progress*, he has, therefore, used it causally. This is progress in the sense that there are certain processes which are cumulative, and there are other processes which are not. Your historian usually chooses one of the cumulative processes. For example, Buckle wrote a history which used to be very popular—I don't suppose anyone reads it anymore—four volumes on the Constitution of England. He was going to do the constitution of the whole world; but he discovered that the data was not available—and for causal history you rely on data much more than you do in dialectical history—and so he reduced it to England. The point that he makes is that the increase of knowledge is cumulative; that is to say, as you get more knowledge, you are able to go on further. This is a dogma of logistic history; it's the regular way in which you contrast the humanities and the social sciences and science. That is, science is cumulative because scientists in their history are men who forget only their mistakes and remember all of their advances; whereas if you have a great poet, that doesn't mean that the next poet is going to be better, it usually means he's going to be worse—a discouraging situation—likewise a great philosopher, and so on. Consequently, Buckle argues, in England there had been an increase of knowledge, and one of the indirect effects of the increase of knowledge is that it is applied technologically; therefore, progress in the sense of a level of production and a level of living is an inevitable process based on the previous process of history. This Buckle history is logistic in the sense that I've been using it.

Then, finally, there is the problematic method, the mode of resolution. Problematic history is disciplinary history. The sequence that you deal with is the sequence of problems and their solutions; therefore, you can ask how problems change and what is the reservoir of knowledge that is relevant to the solution of problems. The result is that in disciplinary history, you get the history of the arts and of sciences. Aristotle, one of our great problematic writers, did several such histories. His pupil, Theophrastus, did a history of biology which includes one of the first histories of psychology; and one by one the Peripatetics for several hundred years wrote histories of mathematics, histories of art. They were the librarians of the library of Pergamum, and there dealt with the evolution and direction of progress.

Let me, before I leave the problem of history, give a concrete illustration which may bring it closer to home in the sense of indicating what the relation is between these various parts or kinds of history. Philosophy has its history, and one of the reasons why I want to tag this on is that you might get the notion that all histories of philosophy are disciplinary and therefore problematic. There are relatively few disciplinary histories of philosophy. There are epochal histories of philosophy. They are extremely numerous. Hegel is one of the greatest, but they exist even before and after Hegel. They are the ones that will give you the characteristics of philosophy at different times and in different places. They will assemble, therefore, the sharp differences between modern and ancient, the sharp differences between the Roman and the Greek varieties of philosophy. There are exemplary histories. Exemplary histories are the ones that tell you primarily about the achievements of the philosopher: the biography, the details, what he did, what his achievement was—these would be set forth in considerable detail. And the effect of exemplary history should be to inspire the reader to go out and do likewise, just as the effect of the epochal history should be to encourage the reader to recognize two things: you recognize the character of your own time, and you also recognize that for philosophers, your own time combines everything that went before it. Therefore, there's no sense going back to Plato and Aristotle—Plato and Aristotle are thesis and antithesis amalgamated by Plotinus—and there's no sense going to Plotinus, because he's a thesis to which an antithesis and a synthesis resulted—you should do your own synthesis. Consequently, Hegel was convinced, without undue pride, that the philosophy he was expounding assimilated everything that went before.

There are causal histories of philosophy. The causal histories of philosophy are probably the most popular in America. They're easy to write, because what you do is to lay down an account of the times, and then you've laid down what the philosophy is—and you can criticize any other history, because it does the history of philosophy *in vacuo*. One of the recent masterpieces of this kind of history is Bertrand Russell's *History of Western Philosophy*. It is an account of the historical background, which is fairly inaccurate: it's a good account of what happened, on the basis of which an account of what the philosophers are saying is laid—and it isn't what the philosophers said—but it does have the advantage that the account of the times explains precisely what Bertrand Russell says the philosophers meant. Therefore, it hangs together perfectly. This is causal history.

Finally, there is disciplinary history. There are relatively few of those. The best is a French history, which hasn't been translated and is out of date now, by Janet and Séailles,[6] which takes up particular problems. If, for example, you wanted to go to a history of philosophy to find out what the philosophers said about power and freedom, which you might have wanted to do in order to shine in this class, you wouldn't find many. You'd be apt to find in the histories of philosophy that Protagoras talked about power; and then, in the same history of philosophy, that Plato and Aristotle didn't; and then, that Saint Augustine did—or *vice versa*. It's a matter of accident what problem happens to come in. But to carry through and give a sequential account of any problem, any concept, any approach, would be the characteristic of a disciplinary history.

There is no way sensibly to ask, Which is the correct history of philosophy? If you wanted to know what the ways are by which category mistakes are made, you would want the disciplinary history; but you'd want a disciplinary history only if you had a problematic interest. If you're interested in the contributions of great philosophers, you'd go to an exemplary history: there's no point going into the niceties of particular problems and how they are resolved. Consequently, it is no great damage that there are all these various histories of philosophy. The damage is that there are so few good ones in any one of the categories.[7]

Let me leave history, because I want now to save approximately half of our time to say a word about what we have been doing. We've been analyzing, as you know, three concepts—freedom, power, and history—and we have tried to do it in a way which would bring out the philosophic problems, both in the sense of the philosophic problems that philosophers talk about and the philosophic problems that are encountered in the nature of things. It would be easy to approach this on the supposition that these three concepts—freedom, power, and history—are concepts which everyone understands, and that therefore, our only problem is to find out which philosophers treated them best. This is not only natural; it's even more than natural, it's normal. This is the way the question is normally asked. But the disturbing thing is that if you read with an eye even half open, it's quite apparent that they're not talking about the same thing when they talk about freedom, power, and history. There's no great interest, of course, in discovering that three words have many meanings; this is a pushover for anyone who has looked into the dictionary. But there is a significance if one begins to ask, What is power when it operates in these ways? You'll notice, you're immediately in the frame in which the operation of power is not determined monolithically: everyone who used power did not have the same philosophy, and the way they used power is dependent upon how they conceived of power. Therefore, it begins to be important to recognize—leave the meanings of words out—the different ways in which power has been exercised, the

Table 19. Semantic Profiles of Authors Read.

Author	Principle	Method	Interpretation	Selection
Hobbes —	Actional	Logistic	Entitative	Thing
Spinoza —	Reflexive	Logistic	Ontological	Thing
Kant —	Reflexive	Operational	Ontological	Thought
Mill —	Reflexive	Operational	Existential	Thought
Machiavelli —	Reflexive	Operational	Existential	Word, Action

different ways in which freedom has been achieved and used. And once you get this far, you're immediately involved in the question of how the history proceeds. If this is the case, as I have said repeatedly, it's important to get the formal aspect and the material aspect going together; that is to say, the meanings of the terms are of no great interest unless what is signified by the meaning has a force and a push.

Therefore, we have been using a schematism. You may have noticed it—I'm sure that you have, though I haven't warned you about it. Instead of going in on the supposition that all of our men will mean the same thing, suppose we see if we can get our variables going so that we can separate them in varying ways. Any old writer on power and freedom would not do, so we began by taking two writers who used the same method. Moreover, we began with the logistic method, because there's a kind of superstition that the logistic method is the way we think. If you ask a student suddenly what thinking is, he always gives the logistic response; he very seldom uses the logistic method, but he always talks the logistic method. But then—and we kept our authors apart—one had actional principles, the other had reflexive principles. One had an entitative interpretation; the other had an ontological interpretation. They were contemporaries; therefore, their selection was the same. We began, consequently, with these two, namely, Hobbes and Spinoza (see table 19).[8]

We turned, then, to another pair of writers. We shifted the method, but both of our writers had an operational method, both used reflexive principles; therefore, there was a coincidence in two parts of the definition. But they used different interpretations: one used an ontological interpretation, the other used an existential interpretation. This was a good exercise, because at first sight it might not look as if Kant and Mill had anything much in common. If they had a method and principles in common, we could look into why it was that the difference of interpretation led to the striking difference. Bear in mind, again, what would be of importance would not be that we would have a way of tagging something as *Kant* and something else as *Mill* but, rather, that we would have two conceptions of freedom, power, and history which have importance and can be understood better if we see the similarities and the differences.

Then, we put a final reading on our sequence. It was by a man named Machiavelli, who had reflexive principles, operational method, and existential interpretation, exactly the same assortment as Mill. This could almost be the experimental *crucis*:[9] if this made sense, if this contributed to our understanding of Mill and Machiavelli and saved us from the simple labels by which we say "Machiavellianism" and feel bad and say "Mill" and think of the progress of freedom, then we would have done something. This is the point where selection comes in: the selection of Machiavelli was in terms of words and actions; the selection of Mill and Kant was in terms of the thought.

Well, now, what I would like to do by way of review is to go through and ask in the substantive sense, What is it we've discovered? Let's begin with our middle pair, since they are the ones which, in many respects, will give us a toehold into our method. What is it that Kant and Mill have in common? Well, they have the operational method. The operational method is a way of discovery and making. Notice, I've used two words, that is, the operational method is one of discovery and making. What would the logistic method begin with? Well, the logistic method is a method of proof and doing. I suspect the difference between the proof and the discovery is clearer to you than the difference between making and doing. There is, in the one case, the axiomatic, mathematical, deductive method which both Hobbes and Spinoza shared; but there's also the fact that in the case of the operational method, for both Kant and Mill we constructed our system of duties, and we constructed our conception of the individual, his relations to society, and what the accountability of the individual was. Kant begins with the facts of ordinary human behavior, and in the very first section he tries to discover value, to discover what is good in itself, by isolating from the facts the principles that make duty possible and that regulate duty. One of his favorite approaches is to deal first with what makes a thing possible and then go into what you do in order to make the possible actual. The emphasis on duty is a characteristic aspect of the selection, thought; therefore, we shall have duty in Mill as well. Every once in a while, I will attack the concept of duty on the ground that it is out of date, that we, out of our present selection, ought not to be talking about the nineteenth-century concepts of morality. Oddly enough, I think that outside the academic circle this is recognized, not explicitly but in fact; but in the academic circle we're still talking of the nineteenth century, and therefore, I don't get very far in my diatribes against duty. It's a concept one doesn't attack with impunity.

The characteristic of the operational method, the relation between knower and knowledge, is that one does not begin with the prior definition. We've seen that by seeing the way in which, from the diagrams we've drawn on the board, meanings were acquired by trying them out.

One first establishes relations, and one interprets experience in terms of the relations. Therefore, for practical purposes, that is, for ethics, in Kant and Mill the basic distinction is the self and the other. We've seen how that worked out in our diagram to set up the more refined conception. Kant has an ontological interpretation; that is, freedom is self-perfection. The distinction between self and other yields four possibilities by distinguishing duties to self, duties to other, perfect duties, imperfect duties. Previously, you had separated duties as categorical imperatives from hypothetical or technical imperatives in which the end is externally set up. Mill had the same method but an existentialist interpretation. Freedom now is spontaneity, not self-perfection. The top that Spinoza put on is removed, and a new separation or top is put on. By selection Mill is concerned with duty as well.

Since so far I've merely been sketching to recall to your mind what we have done in class, let me now try to describe what we've been doing. Mill lived later than Kant, and Mill, consequently, talks about Kant fairly frequently, particularly in the essay on utilitarianism.[10] What would Mill say about the conception of duty in Kant? It would seem to me that what we would expect him to say—and bear in mind, this is not fair: I've already read it, and I know what the answer is—what we would expect him to say is that Kant was pretty good, but that the only thing wrong about him is that he doesn't realize that the only way in which you set up his distinctions is by examining consequences. Put the consequences in—the consequence is the utilitarian method—and Kant is right. Does he say that? Well, this is from chapter V of *Utilitarianism*—and notice, incidentally, this is the way in which the self and the other come in, because the other for Mill must always be literally an external other; whereas for Kant, the other in a perfect duty is not external. Says Mill:

> It is a part of the notion of Duty in every one of its forms, that a person may rightly be compelled to fulfill it. Duty is a thing which may be *exacted* from a person as one exacts a debt. Unless we think it may be exacted from him we do not call it his duty.[11]

Chapter V is concerned with how justice is connected with utility, and morality in general is marked off from the remaining provinces of Expediency and Worthiness. You must, therefore, recognize that anyone who makes a distinction into perfect and imperfect obligations has made a mistake. "Justice implies something which it is not only right to do, and wrong not to do, but which some individual person can claim from us as his moral right." There's a similar distinction between the individual and society in *On Liberty*.

Let's take a look now at the reflexive principles and see what they do to this analysis. I'll come back to Mill on Kant in a moment, but I need the principles in before I complete what we have to say about his reflections. They both have reflexive principles. Reflexive principles in this context would be the individual operating with respect to himself. For Kant, reflexivity involves the self in an ontological sense. It's self-legislation: it's self-legislation as a synthetic judgment which is made possible by liberty in which the self is both the agent and the object of the law. For Mill, it is the active self in relation to others that is the mark of reflexivity. The reflexive principle operates positively as self-legislation in the case of Kant to achieve self-perfection; it operates negatively in the case of Mill to prevent harm to self and others, it becomes self-defense or self-protection. If you have self-defense and self-protection, then you can achieve spontaneity in the variety of circumstances or—and this is the same thing—indetermination with respect to others.

What does Mill say about Kant that brings this in? Well, in the first part of *Utilitarianism*, which is called "On General Remarks," he says, "That to all those *a priori* moralists who deem it necessary to argue at all, utilitarian arguments are indispensable." He refers to the *Metaphysics of Ethics* of Kant and says:

> This remarkable man, whose system of thought will long remain one of the landmarks in the history of philosophical speculation, does, in the treatise in question, lay down a universal first principle as the origin and ground of moral obligation; it is this:—"so act, that the rule on which thou actest would admit of being adopted as a law by all rational beings." But when he begins to deduce from this precept any of the actual duties of morality, he fails, almost grotesquely, to show that there would be any contradiction, any logical (not to say physical) impossibility, in the adoption of the most outrageously immoral rules of conduct. All he shows is that the *consequences* of their universal adoption would be such as some one would choose to incur.

In chapter V, Mill is discussing the principle of utility and justice, and he comes to the question of how justice is related to the benefit of others. Kant comes into the picture again.

> If he is not feeling this—if he is regarding the act solely as it affects him individually—he is not consciously just; he is not concerning his self about the justice of his actions. This is admitted even by anti-utilitarian moralists. When Kant (as before remarked) propounds as the fundamental principle of morals, "So act, that thy rule of conduct might be adopted as a law by all rational beings," he virtually acknowledges that the interest of mankind collectively, or at least mankind indiscriminately, must be in the mind of the agent when conscientiously deciding on the morality of the act. Otherwise he uses words

> without a meaning; for, that a rule even of utter selfishness could not *possibly* be adopted by all rational beings—that there is any insuperable obstacle in the nature of things to its adoption—cannot be even plausibly maintained. To give any meaning to Kant's principle, the sense put upon it must be, that we ought to shape our conduct by a rule which all rational beings might adopt *with benefit to their collective interest.*

Well, notice what has been happening here. As you saw, there's nothing that Mill has to object to in Kant's method. The reflexivity of the principle he doesn't object to, but the ontological twist to the reflexive principle is what gets him every time. Therefore, he needs to remove the transcendental reference and the examination of intention. Instead, examine the consequences; and for the consequences on the level of becoming, Kant is all right.

Let's turn to Machiavelli, since we don't have much time. As I said, the only difference between Machiavelli and the other two involves the same argument: namely, Machiavelli's schematism is Mill's schematism, and therefore, it's easy to see how he would differ from Kant; but why does he seem to differ so much from Mill? One of the reasons for the difference is that he is working in terms of the selection in which the basic terms come from a process of action and of significance of discourse; whereas Mill is working in a tradition of thought. There is some importance to this. The existentialist interpretation, as a result, is not simply a concern with the actions of individuals and of society; but it becomes a distinction among kinds of society, for example, principalities and republics, in which you treat the actions that come up and, in the schematism, move constantly back and forth looking at the action.

Let me try to make this a little more emphatic. In a period of action and of discourse—and Machiavelli's Renaissance and our twentieth century are the same here—there is a case for concreteness, a case for fact, a case for specificity. The period is not necessarily less abstract, but the specificity is what is emphasized; whereas, in a period in which thought is fundamental, what you need is the method by which you can get objectivity, so that any time you want it you can get it—but you don't need to fill any baskets full of facts in order to be sure that they're available. It is this, then, that would characterize the difference of Machiavelli from both Kant and Mill, who are very much concerned to make philosophy objective but don't need to go into the examination of what particular men did when in order to get this objectivity specified. The actions of princes to secure the unity of Italy, the actions of the parts of the state in the case of Rome, these secured the objectives that are necessary. I think that a further comparison would be interesting if you would like to see the differences in selection worked out a little bit more. Montesquieu, who is in, let us say, the transition from the metaphysical to the thought variety, did a job very much like Machiavelli in dealing with the different kinds of states and of individuals; but the formulation is totally different, and it's this difference that I wanted to deal with.

What does the reflexive principle mean for Machiavelli? Well, it's neither self-legislation nor self-protection. It's self-rule: self-rule by the Prince if he is able to in good circumstances or if he can take care of some other aspect; or self-rule by the citizens cooperating in a mixed interaction of the three centers of power. But, you notice, once you get the selection out of the way, the formulation is quite similar. That is, much of the so-called Machiavellianism comes from reading *The Prince* alone. Put *The Prince* and *The Discourses* together and see the way in which by action one can achieve power and liberty and virtues; then, what Machiavelli is saying is not unlike what Madison is saying when he deals with the oppositions of power and the need for a stronger union as a defense for the American Constitution.

We don't have much time for the logistic method. Let me merely say a word for Hobbes and Spinoza, about their common use of the logistic method. In the part of Hobbes that you didn't read, he says that thinking is calculation, and it is calculation in which you go by composition from the least part to a whole. Consequently, since composition is of this sort and if the method determines the interpretation, you would expect that his composition would have to be of least parts like elements. In point of fact, neither of these men have least parts in this sense. It's a little puzzling if you read the *De Homine* or the logic of Hobbes and then go on to his treatment of substance. In the sequence of his writings, Hobbes wrote one part on body, *De Corpore*, one part on man, *De Homine*, and one part on the citizen, *De Cive*.[12] There is, therefore, by virtue of the composition, a reductive process: that is, when you get to the state, the state is merely an artificial man, and it is the actions of the parts on one another that you proceed with. But how is it that you discover what the parts are? Well, you have actional principles and entitative interpretation. The actional principles mean that you begin by assuming anything could be the case, and the calculations that Hobbes talks about are of this sort. They are not principles imposed by the nature of things; but in the composition of such principles you can by the method build wholes that are governed by the laws of nature, of human nature, of the nature of society.

How do you go about it when you move to Spinoza? There is immediately a striking difference between them. That is to say, the reflexive principles of Spinoza make it possible for him to argue that what is, is good:

there are normative elements, therefore, in the nature of things. By contrast, the actional principles of Hobbes make it possible for him to argue that good and evil, like just and unjust, right and wrong, are all results of the will of the sovereign: they are arbitrary. The difference of principles means, therefore, that for the one, the normative element is prior, and that for the other, the normative element is posterior. What does it mean for what they are talking about? Well, the individual man for Spinoza is a mode of an attribute of God; therefore, you have both the consideration of what he is in himself, which is identity with God under the aspect of the mode of either of the attributes, and what he is relative to other people—these are the inadequate ideas which come from bustling back and forth towards nature. What's man entitatively? He's his body and all the things that body can do, including having knowledge—that's the motion of bodies—and having emotions. Therefore, in the emotions, you have both the danger to the state and a basis for values, and you have the possibility of calculating the nature of man and of the state by dealing with the interrelations of the motions of all these bodies.

Well, this is what we have been doing. And the reason I have schematized it this way is so that you'll observe I have not been asking, How do these fellows use their words differently? I've been trying to tell you what these philosophers say freedom is, power is, history is. They're good philosophers; consequently, you can't find any who will say it better. I could have told you which one is right, but that would have been merely my opinion, and my opinion isn't as good as the five on the board.

McKeon's Notes for History: Principles.[13]

Concepts and Methods 202 (VI) Cf. (V) History 11.1

. . .

Principles

What is the basis of the historical sequences and what [is] use to which historical narrative put.

Relation of the historian to historical events.

Holoscopic principles. (Being, truth, values)

1. Comprehensive principles. Assimilation

History the processes exemplifying unifying forces.

History imitation of ideas.

Forces bring together in direction which has place for aspiration to objective values.

Histories of decline and return to the ideal

Cycles. Sages and impediments.

2. Reflexive principles.
History the processes consequent on nature, prudence, or art.
Reflexive causes in nature; present when prudence operates but substituted by other forms of self-rule; present in art but also other forms of self-expression or unification of art object.

Meroscopic principles. (Causes of history causes of action but prior to discriminations of values.)
3. Actional principles. Historical sequences the result of actions—consideration only of operation of power in its various forms and consequences on the accumulation of power. Action influencing action.
4. Logistic principles. Historical sequences the result of the interactions of things. Separate out the varieties of kinds of things or parts and the possible influences they can have on the motions of other in different schemata.

Concepts and Methods 202 (VIII) History Methods 10.1

. . .
Principles
Comprehensive—Reason—whole: inclusive whole.
Reflexive—Actuality—cause: self-cause.
Simple—motion—object.
Actional—Agent—action.

DISCUSSION

Review

Discussion Summary[1]

The point of this class will be to address aspects of our treatment of the social sciences that have given you particular difficulty, so we will use this review discussion to answer questions you have about what we have been doing this quarter.

A number of you have asked me about the double character of our analysis which I have emphasized, namely, What is the difference between the formal and material aspects? In interpretation, a sentence is the formal character of what we are dealing with, whereas the fact referred to by the sentence is the material aspect and can be whatever you say it is. Another way of expressing it is to say that the *way* that you say something is the formal, while *what* you say, the basis for your statement regarding the fact, is the material. It is in your method, then, that you can both nail down what you are saying and show the connections among your facts.

Turning to history, since I did not have a chance to cover the question of principles when dealing with history in the last lecture, let me briefly run through them to complete our schematism for history. If you want to deal with the processes in history, you need to have a beginning point. In other words, you must ask, How is history possible? Let's begin with the holoscopic principles (see table 18). If you argue that a thing can have development and change only as part of an inclusive, organic whole, then you are using a comprehensive principle as the principle of your epochal history. Note, this occurs in the context of a singular unity. By contrast, if you have plural unities, you are working with reflexive principles. So, if you say that a thing can have a history, not as part of an organized whole but as it*self* a whole, then any thing which you can isolate as an organized whole would have a history, and you then have plural histories. It's important to remember that you can only isolate a whole if you can examine its form, say, its form of philosophy; if you can do that, then you have a beginning point, a reflexive principle, for your disciplinary history. Notice, here you end up with plural comprehensive principles; that is, the reflexivity is found in many unities. Turning to the other pair of principles, the meroscopic, now, we find that if the history is possible only when individual things have diverse relations with other things, entering into a variety of combinations, then we are dealing with simple principles. Here, *simple* means you can have as many simples as have a unity. What you need is a criterion of what the parts, the objects selected are, which is the characteristic of simple history; and you get a line, such as a line of force in Newtonian physics, which provides the linear relations of causal history. Finally, if you have a history in which anything which happens, any action, can be history, you find out what the happening does in action, and you will have an actional principle guiding an exemplary history.

On a broader issue, a number of questions have come up related to the basic distinctions of our schematism, namely, interpretation, method, and principle. Let's start with interpretation. Interpretation is a matter of what you can say in one sentence; it is a question of fact, say, the fact of freedom. Remember our ambiguous sentence for freedom (see table 10): "Freedom is the power to act without external hindrance." So, the only question is whether freedom does or does not have an external impediment; and the different interpretations will provide diverse answers to that question, dividing into ontic and phenomenal interpretations as to what they mean by *external*. Next, in method, we are dealing with a series of sentences, not just single sentences. If speaking of human freedom, you would want a series of statements in which the important thing is how the rationale that made it a series came to be there, either because the rational pattern is already in it and is recognized by reason—universal methods—or because that rational pattern has been put into it—particular methods (see table 12). Finally, principle deals with the question of system, with two of the principles, the meroscopic, being antisystematic. In principle, you are taking more than a series of sentences, series which in themselves are not merely compendent, and you can get from one series to another in a variety of ways. The key question here is whether any of the norms that are talked about are within the system itself—holoscopic—or are stuck into it—meroscopic.

Maybe this will become clearer if we briefly review the authors we have read this quarter (see table 19).[2] Let's start with Machiavelli. His principle is reflexive. In *The Prince*, Machiavelli is telling the prince how to form himself: "On the basis of what your natural powers and the circumstances make possible, do this . . ." This is reflexivity as self-rule (see table 10): the prince should form himself in terms of nature and circumstance. In the *Discourses*, the question is, How is it possible for a state to have the virtues of republican Rome? His answer: only if the state has the balance and separation of powers. He is saying that the operations of the aristocratic, monarchical, and democratic principles are defined relative to one another, not purely each in itself. Thus, they are self-balancing, they are operating reflexively. Now, what the balance of powers means depends primarily on whether one is looking at interpretation, method, or principle. And since Machiavelli and Mill have the same interpretation, method, and principle yet still have some significant differences, one also needs to examine the question of selection, which, in their case, reveals a difference between a period of word and action on Machiavelli's part and a period of thought on Mill's.[3]

As I have said before, our schematisms of terms are structures of commonplaces, and one can see relations that authors have with one another when they use certain terms in common. Let me expand on that with an example. In Plato's *Laches*, Socrates' advice is sought by two generals who are concerned about the military education of their sons. They focus on the virtue of courage, an *action*, but find that they have only the *word* itself in common. To help clarify their positions, they give examples of courage, or *things*. Finally, they end up having to turn to *ideas* and try to define their term, giving numerous definitions but never able to agree on one. Notice, this is frequently the experience of a group of people who meet together: they refer to a common term but soon find that they are dealing with different things, are using words differently, and end up attempting to agree on the words in question by giving examples. Another Platonic dialogue where this occurs is the *Philebus*. It explores the idea of the indeterminate, with many names being used to explain it, from the *infinite* to *pleasure*. This dialogue, too, runs along the same lines as the *Laches* by first getting merely the name, then trying to identify it by giving examples, and finally attempting to give the idea behind them all.

We can see a similar issue arise in another author we read, namely, Kant. The meaning of the terms *synthetic* and *analytic* are slippery. The issues cannot be resolved by looking at selection, because selection deals with unity; no breaking up or putting together[4] takes place there. So, let's turn to issues involved in the other parts of our schematism, and look at how, say, Kant and Hume differ in their use of the two terms. Kant, for example, argues that Hume gets it all wrong in his treatment of synthetic and analytic judgments. Our schematism would indicate some important disagreement, both with respect to aspects of interpretation as well as with respect to those of principle (see table 20).[5] With regard to

Table 20. Semantic Profiles of Selected Authors.

Author	Principle	Method	Interpretation	Selection
Aristotle —	Reflexive	Problematic	Essentialist	Thing
Descartes —	Reflexive	Logistic	Existentialist	Thing
Kant —	Reflexive	Operational	Ontological	Thought
Hume —	Simple	Operational	Entitative	Thing
Newton —	Comprehensive	Logistic	Entitative	Thing

principle, although Hume says that he gets his knowledge *a priori*, Kant argues, rather, that Hume's principle is unknown without reference to experience and is, consequently, *a posteriori* and not *a priori*. Kant goes on to state that he will be working with an *a priori* synthetic judgment, by which he is indicating two different points. First, since he is dealing with the *a priori*, he is dealing with what is not derived from experience and is therefore a matter of principle. Second, since he is dealing with the synthetic, he is treating as significant those sentences where the predicate adds meaning to the subject; as a result, he is dealing with a matter of interpretation. On the other hand, in his *Critiques*[6] Kant runs through a doctrine of method, and part of that method is analytic, though used in a different sense here; and since they are both using the same method, the operational, Kant does not there have objection to Hume's treatment of the analytic, although he did so with respect to principle and interpretation.

Turning to the first two of our authors (see table 19), we can ask the question: If one put into effect the meaning of *freedom* that Spinoza uses, how would it differ from doing the same thing with Hobbes's meaning of *freedom*? Let's first take a look at method by using an example. If one were a primitive Christian in Rome and a Roman came around demanding sacrifice to an idol, both our authors would agree that all one has to do is to go up to an image of the goddess Diana and make the appropriate sacrifice. Spinoza says that for such external action, the sovereign of the state decides what religious practice is; the important thing, though, is what the individual's thought is, and here the state cannot compel the individual. Thus, the sovereign can compel one to perform the act, but one can have at the back of one's mind the possibility, if one were to have the chance, of changing the constitution. Hobbes would agree: it is the business of the sovereign to decide what subjects should do, and they must do it. So, the action is the same for both. However, if we bring in principle, for Spinoza, the sovereign can make a mistake according to the law of nature; but not for Hobbes.

What is at issue between Spinoza and Hobbes, then, in connection to freedom? If we look at interpretation, Hobbes argues that everything with a body can be free; whereas for Spinoza, only a wise man can be free (see tables 19 and 10). What things are free in a human's individual and social life does not, however, necessarily lead to difference. What would decide the debate between the two? The issue arises, because general statements can be used to deal with two different purposes: (1) as a way of dealing with what is the case, or (2) as a way of uniting people who are prepared or could be persuaded to undertake a common course of action. In the second case, the two philosophers might have followers who were united on one or the other's principles, and each group would, therefore, act differently. But this can lead to a second issue: differences in statement need not prevent cooperative action as time goes on, and Hobbes's and Spinoza's followers are not radically different in this regard. Cooperative action is possible. Instead of having controversial opposition, the possibility exists of cooperation since the views in purity, though not in degradations, can conform one with the other. Therefore, it's possible to have a common action even for change of the constitutional law, for opening up the situation in a peaceful way.

Let me end on another example. In the seventeenth century, a great debate sprang up between the followers of Descartes and Newton regarding the nature of physical motion. Newton argued that Descartes and others before him, such as Aristotle in the ancient world and Ramus in the early modern period, for example, had fundamentally wrong notions of science. Yet the different approaches are partly based upon differences in the conception of analysis, the term we have been following here, which have continually led to further scientific inquiry.[7]

McKeon's Notes[8]

Concepts and Methods 212 Conclusion; see 202 (VII) 11.1[9]

Purpose of the course to separate formal from substantive aspects of questions. Many of the relations between aspects of any subject under consideration can be determined in advance. Illustrated by two uses made of statistics in the social sciences: (1) "use" statistics on inquiries already made to determine whether the differences and relations are "significant," or (2) set up variables significantly related and frame questions in accord with them. For the most part the facts that you have before you know what questions to ask are useless: they may have led to the investigations, but at that point new facts must be acquired.

If this is the case there are two ways to review what we have done this quarter.

(1) To ask what light the techniques we have employed throw on problems of moral and political philosophy, problems of action, problems of freedom, power, and history. Either the problems themselves or the problems discussed by the philosophers we have read. Limit ourselves to the latter form—do the

problems emerge more clearly from your readings by the use of considerations of principles, methods, interpretations, selections?

(2) what is the pattern that has been employed to separate formal from substantive questions.

The two questions go together, but since the second is the technical device to be used to answer the first (unless the answer is to be subjective impressions) begin with the second.

1. Two philosophers who were contemporary and use the same selection—Hobbes and Spinoza. Chosen among contemporary 17 century because their use of the same method—logistic has frequently led to the comparison of their basic doctrines of political philosophy in spite of striking differences. Use of the devices of principles and interpretation to supplement method and selection to see what the respects of likeness and difference were that could be specified.

Hobbes—Actional, logistic, entitative.

Spinoza—Reflexive, logistic, ontological.

2. Machiavelli—chosen in part because the obvious clichés attached to his name require reinterpretation and also because his works present contrasts to the works already read plus points of comparison.

Different selection—instead of metaphysical concern with principles of things and interpretive concerned with facts of experience and action.

Reflexive, operational, existential.

A universal instead of a particular method—first experience of class with operational method.

A phenomenal instead of an ontic interpretation.

But a use like Spinoza's of a reflexive principle. Question: does the likeness of the two philosophers justify this reading?

3. Kant and Mill. Agree in selection—epistemological or methodological—revolution from the metaphysics of the 17th and early 18th century.

Kant—Reflexive, operational, ontological.

Mill—Reflexive, operational, existential.

Two schematic reasons for the choice

(1) What emerges from the conclusion that two philosophers as radically different as Kant and Mill differ only in interpretation?

(2) What is the significance of the fact that we give exactly the same analysis of Mill and Machiavelli—except that they differ in selection?

The question of schematisms in this way focuses on the question of substance.

3. Begin with the third stage of analysis—Kant and Mill and work back.

Their common use of the operational method. A method (a) of discovery and (b) ~~action~~ *making. (Logistic (a) proof (b) doing.)*

Kant begins with the facts of ordinary human behavior—discover value—what is good in itself by isolating from the facts the principles that make duty possible and that regulate duty. (Emphasis on duty a characteristic of selection of "thought.")

Mill: agreement concerning intellectual formulation but no examination of *problems of practice*.

Discover the relations between individual and society that make freedom possible and guide its attainment.

Characteristic of the operational *method* (knower—knowledge) that one does not begin with prior definitions—one establishes relations and interprets experience in terms of them. For practical problems—self and other at the basis of the

---

Concepts and Methods 212 Conclusion 11.2

variables.

Kant—ontological *interpretation*. Freedom is self-perfection. Distinction of self-other yields four possibilities by distinction of perfect and imperfect duties. (Previously, duties as categorical imperatives have been distinguished from hypothetical imperatives in which the end is externally determined.)

Mill—existentialist interpretation. Freedom is spontaneity. By selection concerned as Kant is with duty. But definition of duty (*Utilitarianism*, V, p. 45) "It is a part of the notion of Duty in every one of its forms, that a person may rightly be compelled to fulfill it. Duty is a thing which may be exacted from a person as one exacts a debt. Unless we think it may be *exacted* from him, we do not call it his duty."

Chapter V how justice is connected with utility.

Morality in general marked off from the remaining provinces of Expediency and Worthiness. (p. 46) Criticism of distinction into Perfect and Imperfect obligation.

"Justice implies something which is not only right to do, and wrong not to do, but which some individual person can claim from us as his moral right."

Similar distinction between individual and society in *On Liberty*.

Both *Reflexive principles*. But for Kant the reflexivity must involve the self in an ontological sense—it is self-legislation, a synthetic judgment made possible by liberty, in which the self is agent and object of the law.

For Mill it must be the active self in relation to others. The reflexive principle operates positively as self-legislation to achieve self-perfection; it operates negatively to prevent harm to self and others as self-protection or self-defense (*Utilitarianism*) to achieve spontaneity (in a variety of circumstances) or indetermination by others.

This difference reflected in Mill's remarks about Kant. *Utilitarianism*. I. General Remarks, p. 3. Says, "that to all those a priori moralists who deem it necessary to argue at all, utilitarian arguments are indispensable." Refers to the *Metaphysics of Ethics* of Kant. "This remarkable man, whose system of thought will long remain one of the landmarks in the history of philosophical speculation, does, in the treatise in question, lay down a universal first principle as the origin and ground of moral obligation; it is this:—'So act, that the rule of which thou actest would admit of being adopted as a law by all rational beings.' But when he begins to deduce from this precept any of the actual duties of morality, he fails, almost grotesquely, to show that there would be any contradiction, any legal (not to say physical) impossibility, in the adoption of the most outrageously immoral rules of conduct. All he shows is that the consequences of their universal adoption would be so much as some one would choose to incur."

In chapter V in the discussion of the connection between utility and justice.

Sentiment of justice related to the benefit of other. (pp. 48–49)

"If he is not feeling this—if he is regarding the act solely as it affects him individually—he is not consciously just; he is not concerning himself about the justice of his actions. This is admitted even by anti-utilitarian moralists. When Kant (as before remarked) propounds as the fundamental principle of morals, 'So act that thy rule of conduct might be adopted as a law by all rational beings,' he virtually acknowledges that the interest of mankind collectively, or at least mankind indiscriminately, must be in the mind of the agent when consciously deciding on the morality of the act. Otherwise he uses words without a meaning: for, that a rule even of utter selfishness could not possibly be adopted by all rational beings—that there is any insupportable obstacle in the nature of things to its adoption—cannot be even plausibly maintained. To give any meaning to Kant's principle, the sense put upon it must be, that we ought to shape our conduct by a rule which all rational beings might adopt with benefit to their collective interest."

2. Machiavelli. Different selection—facts of experience or action rather than thought and rational rules of action.

But operational method alike both for Kant and Mill and reflexive principles alike for both and existentialist interpretation like Mill.

Importance of the factual selection.

As a result, the existentialist interpretation is not simply a concern with the actions of individuals and society but becomes a distinction between two kinds of societies—principalities and republics which he treats in two different works—the schematism in each indicating

---

Concepts and Methods 212 Conclusion 11.3

the part omitted.

Action of princes to secure the unity of Italy; action of the parts of the state on the example of Rome to secure the republic virtues and the endurance of the state.

Reputation of princes and virtues of citizens as substitution for the distinction of society and the individual, with rearrangement of the distinctions made.

Reflexive principle—neither self-legislation nor self-protection, but self-rule—by the prince if he is able, in good circumstances or if he can take advantage of some other aspect—by the citizens, operating in the mixed interaction of three centers of power.

1. Hobbes and Spinoza—different selection—metaphysical, and different method—logistic.

But Spinoza—reflexive principle like other three and ontological interpretation like Kant. Difference from Kant the difference between operational and logistic methods.

Hobbes—logistic method like Spinoza; but only instance of actional principle or entitative interpretation.

Concepts and Methods 202 (VII) Conclusion. 11.1

What have we been doing in our examination of principles, methods, and interpretations? Has it been a verbal semantics in which we have merely determined that there are many meanings for important terms like freedom, power, and history and that one is as good, consistent, and defensible as another? Has it been the establishment of a moral and cultural relativism in which we have argued that one course of action, one mode of life, one system of values is as good, just, and right as another?

Negative answer to both of these questions. Beginning of the affirmative answer lies in recognition that there are two dimensions in what we have done—problems of the social sciences, problems of action, therefore one dimension of the answer [is] in how to conceive the relevant knowledge and other dimension lies in how to conceive the desirable action. But the first stage of the reply is that there is no single true relation between "theory" and "practice" and no single true answer to the question of how we use knowledge to improve individual and associated action. According to the universal methods there is no basic difference between theoretic and practical action—for the dialectical method true practice is theory; for the operational method true theory is practice. According to the particular methods it is a basic mistake to identify theoretic and practical methods—for the problematic method there is a science of the practical which is not a simple application of theories; for the logistic method there is a science only of the theoretic, while the practical and the aesthetic employ methods of preference or emotion. Since the meanings of each of the terms are different, there is no univocal meaning to the question of which of these is correct.

On the theoretic side we have not engaged in a simple verbal semantics because we have been concerned not only with the words "power," "freedom," "history," but with the terms or the words with the assigned meanings. Therefore we have examined both the formal and the material aspects of the meanings determined by each of the modes of thought. There have been systems of meant things as well as systems of meaningful words, and the relations among them therefore involve questions of the relations of objective organizations as well as systematic expressions.

The conclusion that there is no a priori reason a complete and satisfactory analysis might not be achieved in accordance with each of the modes of thought therefore implies not only (a) that the alternative philosophies require and deserve analysis in their own right and according to their specified meanings, but also (b) that each is susceptible to its characteristic errors in formulation and degradations in application, and (c) that the solution of practical problems (if one is to avoid the degradations) requires a means of mutual understanding and cooperation among people holding different views.

On the practical side we have examined not the simple imposition of ideologies but rather the structures of institutions and actions consequent on policies formulated according to the different modes.

The conclusion that there is no a priori reason why any one of them must be labeled *a priori* as immoral or ineffectual therefore implies not only (a) that the alternative policies must be conceived and judged relative to their own criteria, but also (b) that those criteria may be applied poorly unless there is an intelligible relation to the criteria conceived by others in accordance to other modes of analysis, and (c) that common action in the community is possible only if the common course of action and the institutions to ensure its execution are the center of inquiry rather than motivations imputed to agents or groups.

Our procedure has been to consider, first, the concepts of freedom, power, and history in philosophers who used different modes of thought throughout, that is, who differed in principles, methods, and interpretation—Plato, Aristotle, Democritus, and the Sophists.

Second we chose two philosophers who made a similar selection, that is, sought metaphysical bases for their analyses and who shared a method but differed in principles and interpretations—Hobbes and Spinoza with the logistic methods; but Hobbes actional principles and existentialist interpretation,[10] Spinoza with reflexive principles and ontological interpretation.

Third we chose two philosophers who made a different selection, that is, sought the philosophic bases of their analysis in modes of thought rather than in the nature of things and who shared principles and methods but not interpretations—Kant and Mill with reflexive principles and

---

Concepts and Methods 202 (VII) 11.2

operational methods, but Kant with ontological and Mill with existential interpretations. A further element for comparison is the fact that Kant shares with Spinoza the ontological interpretation and Mill shares with Hobbes the existential interpretation.

Examine the effect of differences in one element of meaning on the operation of the others.

Mill—interpretation, freedom as spontaneity, existential.

Kant—interpretation, freedom as self-perfection, ontological. The only thing good without qualification is the good will; the characteristic of moral as opposed to hypothetical prescriptions is that they are good in themselves, not means to other ends—not according to duty but for duty.

Mill and Kant operational methods. Kant—differentiation or discriminations of duties perfect and imperfect, self and others; Mill—since the interpretation removes the distinction between perfect and imperfect duties, the discrimination of duties relative to self and others, therefore the whole method of the essay *On Liberty* is the relation of man and society, the discrimination of the two kinds of accountability.

Mill and Kant—principles, reflexive, a principle with the knower and known, or the applier and the object applied to, are the same. What is involved in the process of reflexive identification assumes a different meaning as the result of the difference of interpretation. For Kant, freedom the principle because it makes possible self-legislation or the autonomy of the will—the interpretation led to the discrimination of noumenal self and phenomenal nature, the principle relates the two varieties of laws. For Mill, the principle is self-protection because it relates the individual and society—the interpretation led to the discrimination of individuals and their perspectives, duties to self and to others, self-protection of individual and of the public ends.

With respect to principles, therefore, the will emerges as basic in Kant's self-legislation, and the consequences are calculated in Mill's self-protection in utilitarianism.

Hobbes and Spinoza—logistic method, deductive examination of the nature of man separated from the political consideration of the state set up artificially by social contract with the underlying law of nature. Similarities in use of social contract and law of nature.

Differences in principle—Hobbes actional: differences of right and wrong, mine and thine, good and evil, dependent on the will of the sovereign; Spinoza reflexive: natural basis for the differences of right and wrong and good and bad (yet according to method, good is that which one wishes—perfection of man).

Differences in interpretation—Hobbes freedom of spontaneity—method brings in limitations of obligation, so that freedom and obligation mutually exclusive, free when not bound by law; Spinoza ontological, freedom of self-perfection—wise man the free man in the *Ethics*; but good state permits freedom of thought and speech as consequence of the method.

>

Turn from these applications to consider the elements of meanings contributed by principles, method and interpretation in the philosophical generality.

Principles—holoscopic and meroscopic, problem of the whole and the part. Holoscopic principles the part in relation to an organic whole—it means that the basis of values is nature. Comprehensive principles—values perceived by reason; reflexive principles—ethics and politics part of a single science—ethics virtues of habituation, politics ruler-ruled—needs and institutions determining natural basis.

Meroscopic principles found in the part—it means values are not determined by nature—by convention or power. Action—what one is able to do, simple what pleases, with the addition of nature as element to discriminate among pleasures.

That is, two varieties of natural basis and two varieties of conventional basis. Methods—universal and particular—problems of the universal and particular. Universal methods—all virtues one and identical with knowledge. Dialectic—knowledge is virtue and two levels, perfect and actual; Operational—all virtues are one—knowledge is operation—two levels—the controlling stronger and the subservient weaker.

Particular methods—virtues different and different from knowledge. Problematic—theoretic and practical science; logistic—sciences are cognitive—practical is preferential and agreement.

Concepts and Methods 202 (VII) 11.3

Interpretations—ontic and phenomenal—problems of reality and appearance.

Ontic interpretations—doubling of levels (as in case of holoscopic principles and universal methods), real and apparent principles. Ontological—freedom self-perfection—freedom and freedom of judgment; entitative—freedom of self-determination—self-determination in accordance with one's nature and self-determination according to emotions.

Phenomenal—single concepts. Existential—freedom of spontaneity determined simply by self; essentialist—freedom of self-development—freedom relative to potentialities and circumstances.

Uses of the analysis—both theoretical and practical.

Problems of our times formulated for the most part in selection characterized as semantic or pragmatic, i.e. words or actions. Prominence given, therefore, to facts, existences, decisions.

- Ontological—Freedom of self-perfection (*libertas* and *liberum arbitrium*); power is energy, knowledge, or [is] joined to persuasion; History epochal—cultural growth and decay of times. *forms*
- Entitative—Freedom of self-determination (nature or emotion); power is force (actual operation or potential due to changed circumstances); History is causal—of basic processes.
- Existential—freedom of spontaneity or indetermination; power is action relative to wishes; history is exemplary—history of acts (use to make person and his values).
- Essentialist—freedom of self-determination; power as potentiality; history as disciplinary (history of fact, present status of problems and relation to past proposals).

Is there any meaning to asking which of these is the true nature of freedom, power, and history? Consider history relative to institutions to bring out issues between them.

- Essentialist—histories of constitutions (Aristotle, Maitland): one set of problems and the devices used in constitutions and institutions. Criticized as imperfect history from viewpoint of other interpretations

Existentialist—histories of what men have done within constitutions and without: given the man and power, constitution no effective interference. Center therefore on devices and uses of power rather than on formal institutions.

Logistic—history of the basic process, such as economic change. Economic interpretation of the constitution gives its real meaning and the processes determining changes in its operation and interpretation. *Human nature.*

Dialectical—history of applications of basic values in any institutional framework, history and myth of interpretation—equivalence of history of proof.

Use of one or the other—use of others to supplement or correct emphases.

Compare on practical side—oppositions of policy or policy for different reasons.

Insert 202 (II) 9.1–3 on Method—advantages and errors

Consider use of duties in Cicero (comprehensive, operational, existential), *Kant* (reflexive, operational, ontological), and *Mill* (reflexive, operational, existential)

Cicero—is duty not to lie to be followed always? Book III: contradictions between perfect and median duties—circumstances which make it improper *not* to lie (existential). Kant—perfect duty never modified by imperfect (ontological); therefore rule not to lie universal in application without exception.

Two questions—possible to use different principles and interpretations in negotiation for common course of action? Relation of different moralities for individual action or action and cooperation?

For *first*, pluralism in negotiation to concentrate on consequences without consideration of principles.

For *second*, principles of individual action—and joint consideration of mutual effects not in individual ethics but social negotiation.

Hobbes[11]

Actional, logistic, existentialist

Spinoza

Reflexive, logistic, ontological

Kant

Reflexive, operational, ontological

Mill

Reflexive, operational, existential

Hegel[12]

Reflexive, dialectical, entitative

Concepts and Methods. Conclusion (II) 9.1

Dealt in last lecture with the relations of the different conceptions of history. History as the ascertainment and statement of facts concerning the past—have found close relation between conception of such historical facts and conception of freedom. In *dialectical* mode, history as account of the development of freedom and like approximation in the other modes. Have seen that this relation does not carry with it the consequences that each set of concepts involves fundamental assumptions which affect the conception of both history and freedom and therefore determine the "facts" so that they fit the theory.

Rather different regions of interest or historical problems—not directly relevant to each other: historical theory [is] means of resolving the problem, and historical account [is] assemblage and treatment of the relevant facts.

Regions of interplay.

Thus in the case of the history of philosophy:

(1) dialectical history—each age has its philosophy; succession of ages and what appropriate to one cannot be anticipated in earlier—occurrence and resolution of contradictions. *History of Philosophy Philosophy of History*

(2) operational history—accounts of the systems or achievements of the great philosophers: formation of system and success in securing such acceptance as it received.[13]

(3) logistic history—evolution of knowledge—beginning with superstition; honorable place of philosophy—in beginning all knowledge was philosophic, successive separation of each of the sciences; philosophy the unscientific remainder, now on the edge of being made scientific. *Science Freedom*

(4) problematic history—the problems of philosophy and the variety of methods employed in their resolution. *Idea in Theory and Practice*

Few points of direct contact—thus the philosophy of the age or the climate of opinion of the dialectical method does not appear in other histories—and in apparent contradiction with the problematic, where each age characterized by the variety of philosophies formed in solution of more or less widely recognized common problems.

Points of contact by generalizing the interest of each—thus problematic: is this in fact the question treated by a given philosopher and is this in fact the position he took; or the dialectic: is this in fact the difference that separated two ages in attitude and interest; logistic: is this in fact the nature of scientific method and its bearing on philosophic problems; operational: is this in fact the doctrine and the program of a given exemplar philosopher?

Problem of common action another form of the application of different principles in different circumstances or instances. Not particulars of past fact but of projected action and future fact. Freedom and power as the source of the principles of such action. Our problem common action (which has different and characteristic relations to the problem of individual moral action). Common action suggests the form of the solution—action in which expectations based on each of the principles in relation justified and realized. (What is expected in each instance not necessarily the same but involved in what is expected by others.) (Each of the approaches has its characteristic distortion and perversion which would be corrected by the same considerations.)

1. Dialectical approach. Freedom is wisdom or grace—rightness perceived intellectually or by non-intellectual agency. Power (in true sense, as contrasted to delusive use of power which is self-destructive) depends on knowledge of right or other awareness applied in action.

Distortion and perversion of dialectical method—identification of those in power with the wise or the good; difficulty in any actual situation to be sure which is the case.

Peculiarity of the dialectical method—calculation in terms of ideal specification, and recognition that no actual situation is the ideal. (Socrates—the republic a city in the skies that never did or will exist—utility is in its guidance in actual situation.) Mathematical analogy—to point at infinity to which finite instances approximate.

In Plato's dialectic actual instance treated in second-best state of the *Laws*: based on the virtues of Athens and Persia—three principles (*Laws*, III. 693 D)—friendship, freedom, and wisdom. Different virtues of Persia and Athens, but identity of results of corruption: slavery. Use of laws—persuasion and force.

Basic error—identifying ideal with any actual situation—misuse of power; education and persuasion.

Concepts and Methods. II Conclusion 9.2

Basic insight—importance of "right"—perceived by knowledge in wisdom or felt by grace; danger of intolerance as a result of conviction of possession of right. As an ideal to be approximated, requisite recognition that one may be mistaken in that conviction however intense, and search, therefore, to adjust action based on it to other convictions without abandoning adherence to the right or effort to convince others.

2. ~~Logistic~~ *Operational* approach. Freedom the exercise of power—right the interest of the stronger. Values consequent on pronouncement of the stronger *or exemplary* rather than criteria affecting their action. Good is that which is desired—good because desired, not desired because good. Adjustment of interests.

Two *strains* in traditional statement of the operational approach: use of power to unify (as Machiavelli and Italy)—any prince will do, but important that someone be induced to seek that concentration of power *Marx*; within that unity, cultivation of the rights and interests of others—republican virtues of Machiavelli's *Discourses*.

Classical example of the contribution of the ancient kings of Rome.

Madison's device of multiplication of factions—no one sufficient to impose its will on the others.

Peculiarity of the operational conception of the practical in common action—the interplay of powers. Dominance by one power leads to situation indistinguishable from the misuse of the dialectical approach.

Protection from that tendency not by appeal to right but by safeguard of interests in the multiplication of power concentrations to prevent any unique power concentration.

Mark of the tradition—emphasis on *Revolution* rather than *Utopia*, but expectation that use of violence one device by which to improve situation by removing from power those who prevent the realization of the will of people. Jefferson's justification of revolution—whenever government does not represent the will of people and no other means available to those who suffer from this usurpation.

Double basic error—corresponding to the two stages of the application of the method in Machiavelli—(1) anarchy—oppositions of power without needed unification for common life; (2) domination by a single power without representation of the other groups which possess some power but no effective means of employing it.

Basic insight—power essential to the preservation of rights and freedoms; without vigilance, freedoms lost. Ultimately any improvement or social good dependent on active use of power to achieve and continue it. Need therefore for effective organization of power structure to preserve the peace and to secure the benefits possible during peace.

3. Logistic approach. Freedom is action according to the principles of one's own nature. Power internal and external. As in the dialectical method, need of knowledge to know what the principles of one's own nature are and it is therefore the expert rather than the individual or group who knows what is better for one. Application of science in individual and group action tends to be therapeutic—remove the causes of disorder or confusion or tension and possible then to act without interference according to natural principles.

Distortion or perversion of logistic method different from distortions of dialectical or operational. Not a danger of tyranny, but a dilemma—in the form of who will bell the cat. Thus if all rulers or all politicians were psycho-analyzed or given intelligence tests or submitted to proper examination of their social and political pasts and attitudes, most political problems would be solved. But who will achieve this? If Hitler were controlled sufficiently to be subjected to psycho-analysis, the people would already possess the insight necessary to prevent him from attaining power; but if psychological tests applied to politicians, who will guard the guardians—how to prevent corruption in the administration of tests? What would become of our democratic processes?

Russell—the use of mass psychology to induce people to desire what they should—how will that be decided and who ultimately will decide what they should desire?

Tendency in the logistic method to decide that preferences (although they can be examined scientifically) are not themselves a result of cognitive processes—avoidance of the distortion therefore in recognition that the politics itself is a means of determining courses of action (including the manner of employing and applying

---

Concepts and Methods II Conclusion 9.3

science, which is itself noncognitive and nonscientific).

Basic error (similar to the dialectical)—conviction that power should be employed to achieve what is known (scientifically); need to supplement by consideration of values.

Basic insight—the tremendous advance in instruments by which to satisfy needs and desires as the result of the advance of science—new problems resulting from the impact of science on society; science can make its contribution to the solution of those problems, but they are not characteristically scientific in character.

4. Problematic approach.

Freedom is in the region of interplay of individual and group—region in which results of action do not interfere with the freedoms of others. Power in the sense of political power is distribution of offices and functions in the government.

Distortion or perversion of problematic method—relativisms—to circumstances and to actual situation. Comparable to operationalism in which structures of power balanced; instead the consideration is of structures of government suited to different circumstances and characters of peoples. Difference between operational and problematic—Aristotle's four senses of "best" as typical of the reference to criteria in variety of ways: best absolutely, best in general, best under the circumstances, best in process of change (revolution and counterrevolution). Peculiarity of the problematic method—consideration of what the problem is and effort to consider variety of possible solutions; therefore consider (say) the best absolutely only under conditions in which some possibility of achieving it.

Basic error—tendency to relativism and definition of the good as simply that which is accepted as the good, differing from place to place and time to time.

Basic insight—importance of considering what is in fact practicable and what is in fact, under the circumstances, the problem and the need.

Adjustment of each of the methods takes them to same point but approached differently in terms of orientation of that method; and the discussion of adjustments has even the outward marks of consideration of the other possible approaches. (This is most obvious in the case of the problematic method, in which the four kinds of best might be taken as descriptions of the four methods viewed from the problematic stand-point.)

Adjustments: (1) in view of dialectical orientation to perfect instance, adjustment to actual situation by use of force and persuasion to ideals of freedom, friendship, wisdom.

(N.B. four methods: the dialectic of wisdom (d[ialectical]), force (o[perational]), friendship (l[ogistic]), and freedom (p[roblematic]).

(2) in view of operational orientation to power, adjustment to balance and distribution of power, in accordance with a variety of interests and to prevent unjust concentration.

(3) in view of logistic orientation to technical applications[,] adjustment to considerations of values and their realization (criticism of lowering of stan-

dards in mass culture, and opportunism in use of science—as opposed to basic research).

(4) in view of problematic orientation to problematic situation and therefore apparent relativism, adjustment to framework of discussion for the resolution of problems.

This latter solution corresponds in (4) to the best in general; it provides for resolution of problems by other than scientific processes and provides thus for the political in (3); it is the framework for the opposition of powers in (2); and the dialectic of the resolution of questions by discussion short of technical philosophy [1].

Or in like fashion it can be identified in the schematism of the other three and equivalent places be sought in the alternative analyses.

In practical terms, this is an examination of the possibility of coming to agreement in common courses of action for different reasons. Differentiation of three loci: (1) principles (different), (2) statements of belief examined in historical semantics directly or in relation to their principles in philosophic semantics; (3) actions consequent on statements which may be the same although differently described in different philosophies and narrated in different contexts in different histories.[14]

APPENDIX A

Class Schedule,[1] Ideas and Methods 212
Concepts and Methods: The Social Sciences

Professor Richard P. McKeon — Winter Quarter, 1965

Mon. Jan. 4	Lecture 1	Philosophic Problems in the Social Sciences
Wed. Jan. 6	Lecture 2	Freedom: Method
Fri. Jan. 8	Discussion	Hobbes, *Leviathan*
Mon. Jan. 11	No Class	
Wed. Jan. 13	Lecture 3	Freedom: Interpretation
Fri. Jan. 15	Discussion	Hobbes, *Leviathan*; *Philosophical Rudiments Concerning Government and Society*
Mon. Jan. 18	Discussion	Spinoza, *Ethics*
Wed. Jan. 20	Lecture 4	Freedom: Principle
Fri. Jan. 22	Discussion	Spinoza, *Ethics*
Mon. Jan. 25	Discussion	Spinoza, *Tractatus Theologico-Politicus*
Wed. Jan. 27	Lecture 5	Freedom: Selection
Fri. Jan. 29	Discussion	Spinoza, *Tractatus Theologico-Politicus*
Mon. Feb. 1	Discussion	Kant, *Fundamental Principles of the Metaphysics of Morals*
Wed. Feb. 3	Lecture 6	Freedom: Selection (Part 2)
Fri. Feb. 5	Discussion	Kant, *Fundamental Principles*
Mon. Feb. 8	Discussion	Kant, *Fundamental Principles*
Wed. Feb. 10	Lecture 7	Power: Selection
Fri. Feb. 12	No Class	
Mon. Feb. 15	Discussion	Kant, *Fundamental Principles*
Wed. Feb. 17	Lecture 8	Power: Interpretation
Fri. Feb. 19	Discussion	Mill, *On Liberty*

Mon. Feb. 22	Discussion	Mill, *On Liberty*
Wed. Feb. 24	Lecture 9	Power: Method
Fri. Feb. 26	Discussion	Mill, *On Liberty*
Mon. Mar. 1	Discussion	Mill, *On Liberty*
Wed. Mar. 3	Lecture 10	Power: Principle; and History
Fri. Mar. 5	Discussion	Machiavelli, *The Prince*
Mon. Mar. 8	Discussion	Machiavelli, *The Discourses*
Wed. Mar. 10	Lecture 11	History (Part 2)
Fri. Mar. 12	Discussion	Review
Tue. Mar. 16	Final Examination	

APPENDIX B

List of Names

Aeneas, a Greco-Roman mythological hero, was the offspring of Aphrodite, the goddess of love, and Anchises, a Trojan prince. He appears in Homer's *Iliad*, the Greek epic poem about the fall of Troy, and is the chief character in Virgil's *Aeneid*, first escaping the fall of Troy and then traveling to Italy, where he becomes the founder of ancient Rome.

Aristophanes (~446–386 BCE), an Athenian comic playwright, is considered the father of comedy. His surviving plays give one of the best recreations of ancient Athens, and his satire of individuals was popular. Plato (*s.v.*) viewed *The Clouds* as a slanderous attack on his mentor, Socrates (*s.v.*), creating one of the reasons for the latter's condemnation and death sentence at his trial in 399 BCE.

Aristotle (384–322 BCE), a philosopher and scientist from northern Greece, was a student of Plato (*s.v.*) at the Academy and a tutor of Alexander the Great. Considered one of the greatest of Western philosophers, he wrote on a number of subjects, including physics, biology, zoology, ethics, politics, aesthetics, poetry, theater, music, rhetoric, logic, and metaphysics. His influence has endured for two and a half millennia.

Augustine of Hippo (354–430), a North African Roman Catholic bishop and philosopher, is one of the fathers of the Catholic Church, a saint whose writings greatly influenced the development of the church up to the Middle Ages. Much of his work was influenced by Plato (*s.v.*) via the Neoplatonism of Plotinus (*s.v.*).

Bacon, Francis (1561–1626), an English statesman, scientist, and philosopher, is often viewed as a key proponent of an inductive scientific method, as philosophically described in the *Novum Organum* (1620), literally, the "New Instrument."

Beard, Charles A[ustin] (1874–1948), a leading American historian before World War II, is best known for *An Economic Interpretation of the Constitution of the United States*, published in 1913, which argued that the economic interests of those who wrote the Constitution were more important in determining the character of that document than their political philosophies.

Bentham, Jeremy (1748–1832), an English philosopher, jurist, and social reformer, taught both James Mill and his son, John Stuart Mill (*s.v.*). He espoused a utilitarianism which took as its fundamental moral maxim that the measure of good was the greatest happiness, namely, pleasure, of the greatest number.

Bohr, Neils (1885–1962), a Danish physicist, studied atomic structure and quantum mechanics. This work earned him a Nobel Prize in Physics in 1922.

Bridgman, Percy (1882–1961), an American physicist, won the Nobel Prize in Physics in 1946 for his work on high pressures. He wrote extensively on the philosophy of science, including the pluralistic nature of scientific methodologies.

Buckle, Henry Thomas (1821–1862), an English historian, planned an unfinished historical work entitled *History of Civilization in England*, of which he published two of a proposed fourteen volumes in 1857 and 1861. He is most remembered for helping found a modern historiographical analysis based on a scientific method.

Cassirer, Ernst (1874–1945), a German philosopher, began his career as a follower of Kant and eventually developed his own influential approach to phenomenology, which included a philosophy of science, of symbolic forms, and of culture.

Cicero (106–43 BCE), a Roman philosopher, orator, and politician, was highly influential in the spread of Greek philosophy in Rome. He has had a great influence on subsequent Western culture. For instance, the cause of the Renaissance has often been attributed to a revival of the works of Cicero, and his Latin prose style has been reflected through the centuries, even being emulated in modern European languages.

Comte, Auguste (1798–1857), a French philosopher, is often cited as a founder of modern sociology and the first modern philosopher of science, arguing for a positivism which distinguishes natural philosophy from empirical science.

Copernicus, Nicolaus (1473–1543), a Polish astronomer and mathematician, developed the heliocentric model of the solar system, which was influential in the scientific revolution and was later condemned by the Catholic Church.

Cornford, Francis Macdonald (1874–1943), an English classical scholar, is a well-known translator of Plato (*s.v.*).

Croce, Benedetto (1866–1952), an Italian philosopher and politician, is known for his contributions to liberal political theory and his criticisms of fascism.

Cyrus "the Great" (576–530 BCE), the Persian founder of the Achaemenid Empire, oversaw its expansion from the Hellespont and the Mediterranean Sea to include most of southwest and central Asia up to the Indus in northwest India. His rule was considered, both at the time and subsequently, one of the most enlightened in the ancient world, and has had great influence both East and West.

Darwin, Charles (1809–1882), an English naturalist, is the founder of the theory of biological evolution by natural selection. In 1859, he published his foundational *On the Origin of Species*, which set forth his scientific conception of evolution by natural selection.

Democritus (460–370 BCE), a Greek philosopher, is best known for his atomic theory of the universe. His work has survived only in fragments and secondhand reports, which are frequently conflicting or of doubtful authenticity.

Descartes, René (1596–1650), a French philosopher and mathematician, emphasized the role of reason and the limitations of the senses in his philosophical work. He is considered the father of analytical geometry and the developer of the Cartesian coordinate system. He is also viewed as having formulated the modern version of the fundamental distinction between mind, whose essence is thought, and body, whose character is extension.

Dewey, John (1859–1952), an American philosopher and educator, is best known for his philosophy advocating democracy and holding the pragmatic view that philosophy is the general theory of education.

Dilthey, Wilhelm (1833–1911), a German philosopher, wrote on scientific method and its relation to the method of history. His empiricism was in sharp contrast to the idealism then prevalent in Germany.

Durkheim, Émile (1858–1917), a French sociologist, is frequently credited as being a founder of modern sociology and of the social sciences.

Einstein, Albert (1879–1955), a German physicist, is the developer of the general theory of relativity and recipient of the Nobel Prize in Physics in 1921. He is considered equal to Newton in his influence on both physics and the philosophy of science.

Epicurus (341–270 BCE), a Greek philosopher, held that the world consisted of only the atoms and the void, and that the purpose of philosophy was to increase the pleasures and decrease the pains of life. His ideas led to a school of philosophy called Epicureanism, conventionally thought to focus on seeking pleasure.

Epimetheus (lit., "after-thinker," "hindsight"), a Greek mythological figure, was a Titan and the twin brother of Prometheus (*s.v.*; lit., "fore-thinker," "foresight"). In various myths, Epimetheus is customarily the foolish one, while Prometheus is depicted as clever. In subsequent interpretation of the myths, however, the relationship of the two brothers has been more varied: for instance, Epimetheus has been seen to represent materialism, where thought follows after natural action, while Prometheus is viewed as the opposite, thought preceding nature.

Euclid (fl. 300 BCE), a Greek mathematician in Alexandria, is considered the founder of geometry. His *Elements* is one of the most influential mathematical works in history: it was used up to the early twentieth century as the main text for teaching mathematics, especially geometry.

Fermat, Pierre de (~1607–1667), a French mathematician and lawyer, made contributions in number theory, analytic geometry, probability, and what was to become differential calculus.

Freud, Sigmund (1856–1939), an Austrian neurologist, is known as the founder of psychoanalysis. His influence on psychology, across the humanities, and in culture in general has been both broad and highly controversial.

Galileo Galilei (1564–1642), an Italian scientist, mathematician, engineer, astronomer, and philosopher, advanced telescope design, supported the heliocentric theory of Copernicus (*q.v.*), and was highly influential in the scientific revolution. His work on the pendulum and the use of idealization to account for natural phenomena has caused him to be considered a founder of modern science.

Hegel, Georg Wilhelm Friedrich (1770–1831), a German philosopher, is most noteworthy for his work in absolute idealism and dialectic. He was highly influential in continental European philosophy.

Heisenberg, Werner (1901–1976), a German physicist, is best known for his work on quantum mechanics and his uncertainty principle. He was awarded the Nobel Prize in Physics in 1932.

Helmholtz, Herman von (1821–1894), a German, was trained originally in medicine and physiology. He pursued research in the areas of vision and the eye, sound, thermodynamics, electrodynamics, and the conservation of energy. His philosophical work focused on the philosophy of science, aesthetics, and the relationship between laws of perception and laws of nature.

Herodotus (~484–425 BCE), a Greek historian, has been viewed as the "Father of History," a characterization first made by Cicero (*q.v.*). His *Histories* (lit., "Inquiries") is a systematic inquiry into the wars between the Greeks and the Persians. The work investigated a wide range of circumstances surrounding these wars and has been interpreted as the first exploration of the conflict between Eastern and Western civilizations. His holistic approach to telling history is opposed to Thucydides' (*s.v.*) examination of the causes of the Peloponnesian War.

Hobbes, Thomas (1588–1679), an English philosopher, is most remembered today for his political philosophy, especially the idea of the social contract, as developed in his *Leviathan; or, The Matter, Forme, and Power of a Common Wealth, Ecclesiasticall and Civil*, which was published in 1651. He is considered one of the founders of modern political philosophy and political science.

Holmes, Oliver Wendell, Jr. (1841–1935), an American Supreme Court associate justice (1902–32), was known for his skeptical stance regarding legal formal-ism, the idea that individual decisions should be logically deduced from the system of legal rules. Also noteworthy is his advocacy of the conception of society and, consequently, law evolving over time; cases being decided not so much upon logic as upon the results of the defendant's actions; and the balance of injury between the two parties involved being the central issue.

Hume, David (1711–1776), a Scottish philosopher known for philosophical empiricism and skepticism, asserted that desire governed human behavior (as opposed to reason, as Descartes [*q.v.*], for instance, had argued) and advanced a theory of free will that was influential on moral philosophy thereafter.

Isocrates (436–338 BCE), a Greek rhetorician and educator, was one of the most famous of the rhetoricians of his time. Because of his educational encouragement of a broad range of knowledge and virtue in his students, Plato's (*s.v.*) well-known refutations of the rhetorical approach of the Sophists (*s.v.*) apparently did not extend to him.

Janet, Paul (1823–1899), a French philosopher, published a two-volume history of political science and its relation to morality in 1872 (*Histoire de la science politique dans ses rapports avec la morale*). A later edition coauthored with Gabriel Séailles (s.v.) appeared in 1887 and focused on the history of philosophy as revealed in its problems and schools of thought (*Histoire de la philosophie: Les problèmes et les écoles*).

Jowett, Benjamin (1817–1893), an English theologian and classicist, was a famous Oxford tutor who translated a number of Plato's (*s.v.*) and Thucydides' (*s.v.*) works. The translations and introductions of Plato were frequently and widely reprinted.

Kant, Immanuel (1724–1804), a German philosopher, has had a major influence on epistemology, ethics, metaphysics, political philosophy, and aesthetics. The idealism in his work emphasizes the central importance of reason in human experience.

Leibniz, Gottfried Wilhelm von (1646–1716), a German mathematician and philosopher, was influential in the development of calculus, which he developed independently of Newton (*s.v.*), and of mechanical calculators. His philosophical work is, along with that of Descartes (*q.v.*) and Spinoza (*s.v.*), one of the three major defenses of rationalism in the seventeenth century.

Livy, or Titus Livius Patavinus (64 or 59 BCE–17 CE), a Roman historian, wrote a monumental history of Rome and the Roman people from earliest times up to his lifetime.

Locke, John (1632–1704), an English philosopher and physician known as the "Father of Classical Liberalism," was an empiricist who contributed to social contract theory. Locke's work was highly influential in both political philosophy and epistemology. He proposed that the mind is a *tabula rasa*, a "blank slate," and that knowledge is composed of experiences which have made impressions on the mind.

Lucretius (~99–55 BCE), a Roman poet and philosopher, founded Epicureanism, which is known for atomic materialism. His single known work, *On the Nature of Things*, explores atomism, sensation, thought, and the development of the world.

Lycurgus (fl. 8th century BCE?), the legendary/possibly real leader of Sparta in Greece, is credited with having given Sparta its constitution, a set of laws based on equality of all citizens, communal dining for male citizens, and extensive requirements for military service.

Machiavelli, Niccolò (1469–1527), an Italian philosopher, historian, and politician, lived in Florence. He is considered a founder of political science and is known for his work on political ethics. Machiavellianism is a widely used epithet to describe an unscrupulous and wholly untrustworthy politician such as the one described in *The Prince* (published 1532).

Madison, James (1751–1836), an American political theorist and statesman, was president of the United States from 1809 to 1817. With Alexander Hamilton and John Jay he wrote *The Federalist Papers*, a series of essays encouraging the ratification of the Constitution based on its careful multiplying and balancing of factions, designed to encourage democracy and prevent tyranny.

Maitland, Frederic William (1850–1906), an English jurist and historian of English law, published, among numerous other works, his *The Constitutional History of England* (1908), which argues that one should interpret English history—and by extension, history in general—not in terms of the historian's contemporary society but, rather, in terms of the circumstances and problems contemporaneous with the society about which the history is being written.

Marx, Karl (1818–1883), a German philosopher, economist, and sociologist, was a revolutionary socialist who had a major influence on the development of sociology and of socialism. His most famous works are *The Communist Manifesto* (1848), coauthored with Friedrich Engels, and *Das Kapital* (*Capital*) (1867–94).

Maxwell, James Clerk (1831–1879), a Scottish physicist, made important contributions to our understanding of electromagnetism, wave properties of light, and electric and magnetic fields, which laid the groundwork for special relativity and quantum mechanics.

McNeill, William Hardy (1917–), a Canadian-born American professor of history at the University of Chicago, published his world history, *The Rise of the West: A History of the Human Community*, in 1963. In it, he argues for the growth in importance of Western culture in its influence on other cultures over the last five hundred years.

Mill, John Stuart (1806–1873), a British philosopher and political economist, was a proponent of utilitarianism. His work *On Liberty* (1859) explores individual freedom and its relation to others.

Montesquieu, Baron de (1689–1755), a French writer and political philosopher, published his most famous work, *De l'Esprit des Lois* (*The Spirit of the Laws*), in 1748. It became influential outside France (where it was banned), especially in the English-speaking world.

Moore, George Edward (1873–1958), an English philosopher and professor of philosophy at Cambridge University, was one of the founders of analytic philosophy.

Moses, a Hebrew prophet and leader, is considered the author of the Torah and the most important prophet in Judaism. He led the Israelites out of captivity in Egypt and received the Ten Commandments from God on Mount Sinai. He is also considered an important prophet in Christianity and Islam.

Newton, Isaac (1642–1727), an English physicist and mathematician, invented calculus (independently of Leibniz [*q.v.*]) and conducted famous experiments on light and optics. His *Principia* (*Philosophiae Naturalis Principia Mathematica*, or "Mathematical Principles of Natural Philosophy") is the foundation of classical mechanics and supported a heliocentric view of the solar system, providing evidence that laws of nature can be applied beyond earth.

Nietzsche, Friedrich Wilhelm (1844–1900), a German philosopher, addressed moral philosophy and nihilism. He published criticisms of utilitarianism, Kantianism, and institutionalized Christianity, and is known for bold statements that incited controversy, such as "God is dead."

Pascal, Blaise (1623–1662), a French philosopher, mathematician, physicist, inventor, and writer, advanced our understanding of fluids and pressure, projective geometry, and probability theory, and he is one of the developers of a mechanical calculator. In philosophy, he defended Christianity, argued against Descartes's (*q.v.*) rationalism, and emphasized the limits of empiricism in treating ultimate questions.

Pericles (495–429 BCE), a Greek orator, general, and statesman, was the most prominent public figure of the Athenian Golden Age, between roughly the Persian and Peloponnesian Wars (respectively, 499–449 and 431–404 BCE). His dominance in political and cultural affairs was such that this high point of ancient Greek civilization has frequently been denoted as "the Age of Pericles."

Peripatetic (from the Greek words for "colonnades" and for "walking") was a school of philosophy in ancient Greece founded by Aristotle (*q.v.*) around 335 BCE and, after his death, led first by Theophrastus (*s.v.*) and then by Strato (*s.v.*). Not being a citizen of Athens, Aristotle was not permitted to own land; consequently, he had to hold his school informally in a public space, the Lyceum, where legend held that he lectured while walking around. Although the school died out in the third century BCE, much of its work influenced early Islamic philosophy and helped preserve the Aristotelian tradition that was reintroduced into the West through Roman Catholicism in the Middle Ages, most notably by Thomas Aquinas (*s.v.*).

Plato (~427–348 BCE), from a wealthy Athenian family, was a Greek philosopher and mathematician, a student of Socrates (*s.v.*), and teacher of Aristotle (*q.v.*). His work has survived almost wholly intact and is considered the foundation of Western philosophy. The *Republic* and *Socratic Dialogues* address issues of politics, logic, ethics, rhetoric, religion, science, and education. Plato argues that ideas, forms, are what ultimately exist and are beyond the range of empirical experience, to be conceived only through reason. This view of the ideal as being undiscoverable through investigation of the natural world distinguished him from his most famous student, Aristotle.

Plotinus (~205–270), a Greek philosopher, is the founder of Neoplatonism. He viewed the existence of a transcendent One that is not divisible and is identified with the concepts of the Good and Beauty. Even the cosmos is a consequence of the existence of the overarching One.

Prichard (also spelled Pritchard), Harold Arthur (1871–1947), an English moral philosopher, was an Oxford Fellow who refuted utilitarianism and helped found the approach called ethical intuitionism, which holds that intuition, not reasoning, is the basis of moral obligations.

Prometheus, a Greek mythological figure and twin Titan brother of Epimetheus (*q.v.*), sided with Zeus and the Olympian gods to defeat Cronos and the other Titans. In the myths, Prometheus is depicted as clever: the one who stole fire from the Greek gods, brought it to humans against the will of Zeus (*s.v.*), and was consequently punished by Zeus for that act by being tied to a rock and having his liver eaten out each day by an eagle, only to have it regrow at night, since he was an immortal.

Protagoras (ca. 490–420 BCE), a pre-Socratic philosopher, was known as a Sophist (*s.v.*) and for his views on virtue, politics, and rhetoric. The title character of one of Plato's (*q.v.*) dialogues, he is known for the famous saying "Man is the measure of all things." (McKeon often argued that a better translation is "Man is the maker of all things," since he represents the mode of thought discrimination.)

Ramus, Peter (1515–1572), a French logician, humanist, and educational reformer, early in his life distinguished himself by his rejection of Aristotle's (*q.v.*) philosophy and of Scholasticism, and by his advocacy of dialectic as central to logic. His philosophy was attacked for undermining Christian religion, and his conversion to Protestantism led to his death in the Saint Bartholomew's Day massacre.

Romulus and Remus, twin brothers in Roman mythology, are central to the legend of the founding of Rome. Romulus kills Remus over an argument about which hill to locate the city on, and subsequently names the city for himself.

Rousseau, Jean-Jacques (1712–1778), a Swiss philosopher from Geneva, influenced the French Revolution and modern political, sociological, and educational thought. He viewed humans as born essentially good and developing to maturity in stages; moreover, since morality is innate, society is what creates unnatural desires and thereby degrades humans.

Russell, Bertrand (1872–1970), a British philosopher, mathematician, logician, and social critic, is considered one of the founders of analytic philosophy. His wide-ranging philosophic and logical contributions (he was a student of A. N. Whitehead [*s.v.*]) included *History of Western Philosophy and Its Connection with Political and Social Circumstances from the Earliest Times to the Present Day* in 1945. Besides his research, he was active in pacifist and nuclear disarmament movements.

Sartre, Jean-Paul (1905–1980), a French philosopher, writer, and political activist, was a major proponent of existentialism and Marxism, though he never joined the Communist Party.

Schrödinger, Erwin (1887–1961), an Austrian physicist and philosopher, advanced quantum mechanics and was awarded the Nobel Prize in Physics in 1933. His *What Is Life?* explored issues of consciousness, mind, and matter.

Séailles, Gabriel Jean Raymond (1852–1922), a French philosopher, was a professor at the Sorbonne in Paris. In 1887 he coauthored with Paul Janet (*q.v.*) *Histoire de la philosophie: Les problèmes et les écoles*, which explored philosophic problems in history.

Socrates (460–399 BCE), an Athenian stonemason, is customarily considered the father of Western philosophy. Since he left behind no written works, interpretation of his thought is problematic. Plato (*q.v.*), his student, uses a character called Socrates in a number of his dialogues who may or may not be close to the real individual. From these and other contemporaneous accounts, Socrates is assumed to have frequently questioned his fellow citizens closely regarding the conduct of their lives, arguing that "the unexamined life is not worth living." For this "gadfly" behavior, troubling the rich and powerful, he is thought to have been tried and executed by the Athenian state. In general, Socrates is thought of less in terms of advocating a particular doctrine than of encouraging the rigorous practice of philosophic inquiry.

Solon (638–558 BCE), a Greek statesman from Athens, is known for his efforts to pass legislation to reduce the economic, political, and moral decline of early Athens. Though initially unsuccessful, his reforms formed the basis of the democracy achieved in Athens in the following century.

Sophists (5th century BCE), a group of teachers in ancient Greece, particularly Athens, taught virtue and higher skills such as rhetoric and oratory to those of high social standing who could afford to pay for their teachings and who often wanted to be political leaders. The Sophists were criticized by Plato (*q.v.*) and Aristophanes (*q.v.*), particularly for their high fees and the influence that making a profit had on their teachings. For instance, Protagoras (*q.v.*) was a Sophist.

Spengler, Oswald (1880–1936), an independent scholar of German history and philosophy of history, published the two volumes of his most famous work, *Der Untergang des Abendlandes: Umrisse einer Morphologie der Weltgeschichte*, in 1918–22. It was translated into English almost immediately as *The Decline of the West*, which traces eight main civilizations in world history and argues that Western culture is coming to its end because it is in the winter of its development.

Spinoza, Benedict de (1632–1677), a Dutch philosopher, was a rationalist and determinist who refuted Descartes's (*q.v.*) dualism of mind/body in his *Ethics*. His work is considered to have laid the groundwork for the Enlightenment in the eighteenth century. Spinoza was expelled from the Jewish community in which he was raised, and his work was banned by the Catholic Church. His work continues to be influential in the twenty-first century.

Stoics (third century BCE—sixth century AD), a tradition of philosophers who argued that the key to a successful life was controlling the emotions by reason, a discipline which would allow one to bear the vicissitudes of life and to achieve virtuous well-being. Their position was widely praised in the Roman world and was famously adopted by the emperor Marcus Aurelius (161–180).

Strato of Lampsacus (335–269 BCE), a Greek philosopher, was the third director of Aristotle's (*q.v.*) Lyceum after Theophrastus's (*s.v.*) death. A Peripatetic (*q.v.*), his research focused on the natural sciences.

Themistocles (~524–459 BCE), a Greek general and statesman, fought at the critical Battle of Marathon (490 BCE), which turned back the first Persian invasion of Greece. He led the Greek fleet that won the Battle of Salamis (480 BCE), which was the turning point in defeating the second Persian invasion.

Theophrastus (371–287 BCE), a Greek philosopher, was a student first of Plato (*q.v.*) and then of Aristotle (*q.v.*), and upon Aristotle's death was appointed his successor as Lyceum director. As a Peripatetic (*q.v.*), Theophrastus investigated a wide range of fields, and although much of his work has not survived, the fragments which were preserved had influence in the Roman and medieval periods.

Theseus, a Greek mythological figure, founded and ruled Athens, thereby unifying Attica. He is also known for numerous heroic acts, including slaying the Minotaur, a half-man, half-bull monster confined in a labyrinth on the island of Crete.

Thomas Aquinas (1225–1274), an Italian Dominican priest and philosopher and a saint of the Roman Catholic Church, is the founder of Thomism and a proponent of natural theology. Much of his work was influenced by Aristotle (*q.v.*), and he is considered one of the greatest theologians of the church for synthesizing Aristotelian philosophy with the principles of Catholicism, thereby supplanting Augustine's (q.v.) earlier Platonic formulations of Catholicism.

Thrasymachus (459–400 BCE), a Sophist of ancient Greece, appears as a character in Plato's (*q.v.*) *Republic* and is also mentioned in Aristotle's (*q.v.*) *Rhetoric*.

Thucydides (460–ca. 395 BCE), a Greek general and historian, is considered one of the founders of the discipline of history for *The History of the Peloponnesian War* (431–404 BCE), an account of the destructive war between Sparta and Athens, which the latter ultimately lost. His account has been called the first "scientific" history, because of his strict criteria of evidence and his focus on human causes which omitted intervention by the gods. Compare his approach with Herodotus's (*q.v.*) encyclopedic one.

Vaihinger, Hans (1852–1933), a German professor of philosophy at the Universities of Strasbourg and Halle, was a Kant (*q.v.*) scholar. In 1911, he published his *Philosophie des Als-Ob* (the English version, *Philosophy of the "As-If,"* appeared in 1924), in which he argued that we cannot really know the external world, so we construct models of it, treating these "as if" they were reality.

von Humboldt, Wilhelm (1767–1835), a German philosopher, diplomat, and educator, was a vigorous advocate of individual liberty. His *The Spheres and Duties of Government* (English translation of original, 1854) was an important influence on John Stuart Mill (*q.v.*).

Whitehead, Alfred North (1861–1947), an English mathematician and philosopher, published his *Process and Reality* in 1929, helping found process philosophy. With Bertrand Russell (*q.v.*), his former student, he had earlier coauthored the *Principia Mathematica*, published in 1910–13; it was an attempt to ground mathematics on logic and led to twentieth-century analytic philosophy.

Wittgenstein, Ludwig (1889–1951), an Austrian philosopher who lived the latter half of his life in England, was extraordinarily influential in twentieth-century logic as well as in the philosophies of mathematics, mind, and language. He published little during his lifetime, but posthumous publication of his manuscripts greatly increased his reputation, even though they often contradicted his earlier work.

Wolff, Christian (1679–1754), a German philosopher, has been considered the most important philosopher between Leibniz (*q.v.*) and Kant (*q.v.*). He created a rationalist system based on a mathematical, deductive method that encompassed the full range of philosophic inquiries.

Zeus, a Greek mythological figure, is the sky and thunder god, being frequently depicted as brandishing a thunderbolt. As the leader/king of the gods, he rules from Mount Olympus in northeastern Greece with his sister and wife Hera.

APPENDIX C

One Alternate Introduction to the Course[1]

Concepts and Methods *(202)* (VII) (1962) (cf. VI 1,1.) *(VIII)* 1.1

Nature of Introduction to philosophy.

Second quarter independent of other two quarters, although concerned with similar philosophic problems and approached by similar philosophic analysis.

Beginnings of philosophy in discussion of fundamental problems. Autumn quarter problems taken from the physical sciences—problems of motion become philosophical when different theories are encountered[;] resolution of problems presented by these differences or the elaboration of one position and the related problems in the nature of time, space, and cause are philosophical. The results of the positions can be ascertained and traced in experience; but the grounds of the choice are not imposed on us—relating of the means by which we determine them and the means employed in science itself [are] a philosophical question.

Our manner of treating these problems was to differentiate four places of their occurrences—principles, methods, interpretations, and selection. Problems which are sometimes stated in relation to the nature of things and sometimes formally with relation to the manner of formulation.

To differentiate these problems we made use of distinction of four modes of thinking about basic problems—assimilation, discrimination, construction and resolution.

Use these same distinctions with respect to problems arising in the social sciences. Set of basic concepts to be analyzed—freedom, power, history. Explain to those who have not yet had that explanation the ways in which problems of principle, method, interpretation, and selection occur with respect to them, and how the four modes of thought can be discovered or used.

The social sciences treat various aspects of man's behavior in communities or relative to other men. Philosophic problems involved in the determination of what that knowledge consists in. These questions spread thru the four headings of our interest. Indicate them briefly with special emphasis on what is involved for the question of Freedom. Then in later lectures, go into the problems in more detail for Power and History as well.

1. Principles.

The starting points of the social sciences. From one philosophic point of view (assimilation and resolution) a question of what passes for knowledge is to be tied in with what is the case or what is known. Other ways of stating the function of principles, but they are all ways of tying down the science to its proper material.

In the case of the Social Sciences this often takes the form of a problem of the relation of values to facts—a question of whether the social sciences should be normative or whether they will be sciences only if they are non-normative.

Thus, two basic positions concerning the nature of moral and political principles—stated in varying terms from antiquity to the present—nature and convention.

a. Morals and law have a natural basis, and the difference between good and evil, merit and demerit (or virtue and sin), and right and wrong can be found in the nature of man and of things.

b. Morals and law have only a conventional basis—differences between good and evil, merit and demerit, right and wrong depend on customs of the community and preferences of the individual.

Natural law and social contract. Question of whether we desire what is good or call good what we desire.

Problem (a) of how to discover the good and how to motivate men to seek it[;] as opposed to problem (b) of how, since the good is simply what one desires, to acquire it or get other men to seek it too.

Usually in the statement of these problems an agreement on an ambiguous statement of definition—as Freedom is action in absence of external restraint (ambiguity in determination of what constitutes "external" and "restraint"). In respect to questions of principle the division is between those who hold (a) external restraint is overcome only by "rational choice" and therefore only men are free, and (b) external restraint is overcome only by adequate power and therefore non-rational objects, like bodies, may move freely.

2. Methods.

The problems of method in the social sciences are forms of the problem of the relation of knowledge or

---

Concepts and Methods 202 (VII) 1.2

what passes for knowledge to action. Method in the practical—stated in varying ways since antiquity—method to guide action distinguished from or identified with the method of acquiring knowledge and finding it warranted.

Two basic answers have been given:

a. Knowledge and virtue are the same (identification of theoretic method with practical or practical method with theoretic).

b. Knowledge and virtue are different. It is possible (Plato to the contrary notwithstanding) to know the better and do the worse. Importance of habit and emotion, and their operation distinct from knowledge.

From one philosophic point of view (assimilation and discrimination), questions of method are questions of the relation of knowledge to the knower—the discovery or increase of knowledge in its various operations and functions.

Basic question of the relation of theory and practice. Question of whether wise action is action guided by knowledge or knowledge is action in accordance with rules agreed to by consensus (of all or of the experts who know how to operate).

Freedom—in respect to methods the divisions are between those who hold (a) that freedom is dependent on law—that is, that the external restraint can be internalized to the passions, and freedom is therefore individual, and (b) those who hold that freedom is the opposite of law—that is, that the external restraint is always imposed by others, and freedom is therefore social.

3. Interpretation.

The problems of interpretation are problems of fact, data, or conclusions (as opposed to assumptions and inference). They are questions of what we are talking about.

Two basic positions—(a) we are talking about basic realities like structures of values or human nature, or (b) about experience and phenomenal relations which have no fixed or enduring structure. The same difference occurs in the natural sciences.

(a) In both cases we seek beyond direct empirical experience fixed relations in fields or ultimate particles or elements underlying phenomena, experience or observations.

(b) We seek projections from or generalizations of phenomena relations—habits, skills, desires, customs, communities, constitutions, institutions.

Freedom—in respect to interpretations the division is between (a) those who hold that freedom consists in doing as one should, whether or not one pleases, and (b) those who hold that it consists in doing as one pleases, whether or not one should (i.e., Plato, Stoics, Spinoza, Hegel, Marx vs. Aristotle, Locke, Hume, Mill, Dewey).

From one philosophical point of view (assimilation and construction) questions of interpretation are questions of the relation of what passes for knowledge to its applications in the knowable or the objects of knowledge. Other ways of stating interpretation—differs from questions of principles which are concerned with reasons for the assumption that what one says corresponds to what must be the case—question of how what is said is put in operation on particular subjects in particular circumstances.

4. Selection

Choice of the terms which enter into discussion of any subject matter or choice of the aspect under which any subject matter is to be considered. Infinite possible terms or aspects. Finite choices.

Selection governed by determination to make principles, methods or interpretations fundamental. Tendency to follow historical sequence—Kant's Copernican revolution, and Dewey's second Copernican revolution.

Being	Reason	Experience (Acts)
Becoming	Impressions	Language (Words)
Things	Thoughts	Words, Deeds
Metaphysics	Epistemology	Semantics Pragmatics

APPENDIX D

Schema of Philosophic Semantics[1]

Modes of Thought	*Principles*	*Methods*	*Interpretations*	*Selections*
	Holoscopic	*Universal*	*Ontic*	
ASSIMILATION	Comprehensive	Dialectical	Ontological	Hierarchies (transcendental)
RESOLUTION	Reflexive	Operational	Entitative	Matters (reductive)
	Meroscopic	*Particular*	*Phenomenal*	
CONSTRUCTION	Simple	Logistic	Existentialist	Types (perspective)
DISCRIMINATION	Actional	Problematic	Essentialist	Kinds (functional)

APPENDIX E

Reading Selections from Hobbes[1]

LEVIATHAN *by Thomas Hobbes, in*
THE ENGLISH WORKS, *Edited by Wm. Molesworth*

PART I, CHAPTER XIV (VOL. 3, PP. 116–20)

[1] The ***[Right]*** of Nature, which writers commonly call ***[jus]*** naturale, is the ***[liberty]*** each man hath, *(1)* to use his own *power*, as he will himself, for the preservation of his own *nature*; that is to say, of his own life; and *(2)* consequently, of doing any thing, which *in his own judgment*, and reason, he shall conceive to be the aptest means thereunto.
[2] By Liberty, is understood, according to the proper signification of the word, *(1)* the absence of *external* impediments: which impediments, may oft take away part of a man's *power to do what he would; (2)* but cannot hinder him from using the *power* left him, according as his *judgment*, and *reason* shall dictate to him.
[3] A ***[Law]*** of Nature, ***[lex]*** naturalis, is a ***[precept]*** or general rule, found out by reason, by which a man is *forbidden (1)* to do that, which is *destructive of his life*, or taketh away the means of preserving the same; and *(2)* to omit that, by which he *thinketh* it may be best preserved. ***[4]*** For though they that speak of this subject, use to confound jus, and lex, right and law: yet they ought to be distinguished; because RIGHT, consisteth in liberty to do, or to forbear; whereas LAW, determineth, and *bindeth* to one of them: so that law, and right, differ as much, as *obligation*, and *liberty*; *which in one and the same matter are inconsistent.*

[5] And because the condition of man, as hath been declared in the precedent chapter, is a condition of war of every one against every one; in which case everyone is *governed by his own reason*; and there is nothing he can make use of, that may not be a help unto him, in preserving his life against his enemies, it *followeth*, that in such a condition, every man has a *right to every thing*; even to another's body. And therefore, as long as this natural right of every man to every thing endureth, there can be no *security* to any man, how strong or wise soever he be, of living out the time, which nature ordinarily alloweth men to live. And consequently it is a *precept*, or *general rule of reason*, *(1)* that every man, ought to endeavor peace, as far as he has hope of obtaining it; and when *(2)* he cannot obtain it, that he may seek, and use, all helps, and advantages of war. The first branch of which rule, containeth the *first, and fundamental* ***[law]*** *of nature*; which is, to seek peace, and follow it. The second, the sum of the ***[right]*** of nature; which is, by all means we can, to defend ourselves.

[6] *From* this ***[fundamental law of nature]***, by which men are commanded to endeavour peace, is *derived* this ***[second law]***; *(1)* that a man be willing, when others are so too, as far-forth, as for peace, and defence of himself he shall think it necessary, to lay down this right to all things; *(2)* and be contented with so much liberty against other men, as he would allow other men against himself. For as long as every man holdeth this *right*, of *doing any thing he liketh*; so long are all men in the condition of *war*. But if other men will not *lay down their right*, as well as he; then there is no reason for any one, to divest himself of his: for that were to expose himself to prey, which no man is bound to, rather than to dispose himself to peace. This is that *law* of the Gospel; whatsoever you require that others should do to you, that do ye to them. And that law of all men, quod tibi fieri non vis, alteri ne feceris [trans.: what you do not want to be done to you, do not do to others].

[7] To lay down a man's ***[right]*** to any thing, is to *divest* himself of the ***[liberty]***, of ***[hindering]*** another of the benefit of his own right to the same. For he that renounceth, or passeth away his right, *giveth not to any other man* a right which he had not before; because this is nothing to which every man had not right by nature: but only *standeth out of his way*, that he may enjoy his own original right, without hindrance from him; not without hindrance from another. So that the effect which redoundeth to one man, by another man's defect of right, is but so much diminution of impediments to the use of his own right original.

[8] Right is laid aside, either by simply *renouncing* it; or by *transferring* it to another. By simply RENOUNCING; when he cares not to whom the benefit thereof redoundeth. By TRANSFERRING; when he intendeth the benefit thereof to some certain person, or persons. And when a man hath in *either manner abandoned*, or granted away his right; then is he said to be *OBLIGED*, or *BOUND*, not to hinder those, to whom such right is granted, or abandoned, from the benefit of it; and that he *ought*, and it is his *DUTY*, not to make void that voluntary act of his OWN: and that such hindrance is *INJUSTICE*, and *INJURY*, as being sine jure; the right being before renounced, or transferred. So that injury, or injustice, in the controversies of the world, is somewhat like to that, which in the disputations of scholars is called ***[absurdity]***. For as it is there called an absurdity to contradict what one maintained in the beginning: so in the world, it is called injustice, and injury, voluntarily to undo that, which from the beginning he had voluntarily done. The way in which a man either simply renounceth, or transferreth his right, is a declaration, or signification, by some voluntary and sufficient *sign*, or *signs*, that he doth so renounce, or transfer; or hath so renounced, or transferred the same, to him that accepteth it. And these signs are either words only, or actions only; or, as it happeneth most often, both words, and actions. And the same are the *BONDS*, by which men are *bound* and *obliged*: bonds, that have their strength, not from their own nature, for nothing is more easily broken than a man's word, but from fear of some evil consequence upon the rupture.

[9] Whensoever a man transferreth his right, or renounceth it; it is either in *consideration of some right reciprocally transferred* to himself; or for some other good he hopeth for thereby. For it is a *voluntary* act: and of the voluntary acts of every man, the object is some good to himself. And therefore there be *some rights*, which *no man* can be understood by any words, or other signs, to have *abandoned*, or *transferred*. *(1)* As ***[first]*** a man cannot lay down the right of resisting them, that assault him by force, to take away his life; because he cannot be understood to aim thereby, at *any good* to himself. *(2)* The ***[same]*** may be said of *wounds*, and *chains*, and *imprisonment*; both because there is no benefit consequent to such patience; as there is to the patience of suffering another to be wounded, or imprisoned: as also because a man cannot tell, when he seeth men proceed against him by violence, whether they intend his *death* or not. *(3)* And ***[lastly]*** the motive, and end for which this renouncing, and transferring of right is introduced, is nothing else but the *security of a man's person*, in his life, and in the means of so preserving life, as not to be weary of it. And therefore if a man by words, or other signs, seem to despoil himself of the end, for which those signs were intended; he is not to be understood as if he mean it, or that it was his will; but that he was ignorant of how such words and actions were to be interpreted.

[10] The *mutual transferring* of right, is that which men call *CONTRACT*.

PART II, CHAPTER XXI (VOL. 3, PP. 196–201)

[1] Liberty, or Freedom, signifieth, properly, the absence of opposition; by opposition, I mean external impediments of motion; and may be *applied no less to irrational, and inanimate creatures*, than to *rational*. For whatsoever is so tied, or environed, as it cannot move but within a certain space, which space is determined by the opposition of some external body, we say it hath not liberty to go further. And so of all living creatures, whilst they are imprisoned, or restrained, with walls, or chains; and of the water whilst it is kept in by banks, or vessels, that otherwise would spread itself into a larger space, we use to say, they are not at liberty, to move in such manner, as without those external impediments they would. But when the *impediment of motion*, is in the constitution of the thing itself, we use not to say; it wants the *liberty*; but the *power* to move; as when a stone lieth still, or a man is fastened to his bed by sickness.

[2] And according to this proper, and generally received the meaning of the word, a ***[FREEMAN]***, is he, that in those things, which by his strength and wit he is able to do, is not hindered to do what he has a will to. But when the words free, and liberty, are applied to any thing but ***[bodies]***, they are abused; for that which is not subject to motion, is not subject to impediment: and therefore, when it is said, for example, the ***[way]*** is free, no liberty of the way is signified, but of those that walk in it without stop. And when we say a ***[gift]*** is free, there is not meant any liberty of the gift, but of the giver, that was not bound by any law or covenant to give it. So when we ***[speak]*** freely, it is not the liberty of voice or pronunciation, but of the man, whom no law hath obliged to speak otherwise than he did.

Lastly, from the use of the word ***[free-will]***, no liberty can be inferred of the will, desire, or inclination, but the liberty of the man; which consisteth in this, that he finds no stop, in doing what he has the will, desire, or inclination to do.
[3] ***[Fear]*** and ***[liberty]*** are consistent; as when a man throweth his goods into the sea for fear the ship will sink, he doth it nevertheless very willingly, and may refuse to do it if he will: it is therefore the action of one that was free: so a man sometimes pays his debt, only for fear of imprisonment, which because nobody hindered him from detaining, was the action of a man at liberty. And generally, all actions which men do in commonwealths, for fear of the law, are actions, which the doers had liberty to omit.
[4] ***[Liberty]*** and ***[necessity]*** are consistent: as in the water, that hath not only liberty, but a necessity of descending by a channel; so likewise in the actions which men voluntarily do: which because they *proceed from their will*, proceed from liberty; and yet, because every act of a man's *will*, and every *desire*, and *inclination* proceedeth *from some cause*, and that from another cause, in a continual chain, whose first link is in the hand of God the first of all causes, proceed from necessity. So that to him that could see the connection of those causes, the necessity of all men's voluntary actions, would appear manifest. And therefore God, that seeth, and disposeth all things, seeth also that the liberty of man in *doing what he will*, is accompanied with *the necessity of doing that which God will*, and no more, nor less. For though men may do many things, which God does not command, nor is therefore author of them; yet they can have no passion nor appetite to anything, of which appetite God's will is not the cause. And did not his will assure the necessity of man's will, and consequently of all that on man's will dependeth, the liberty of ***[men]*** would be a contradiction, and impediment to the omnipotence and liberty of ***[God]***. And this shall suffice, as to the matter in hand, of that *natural* liberty, *which only is properly called* liberty. <

[1] But as men, for the attaining of peace, and conservation of themselves thereby, have made an *artificial man*, which we call a commonwealth; so also have they made *artificial chains*, called *civil laws*, which they themselves, by mutual covenants, have fastened at one end, to the lips of that man, or assembly, to whom they have given the sovereign ***[power]***; and at the other end to their own ears. These bonds, in their own nature but weak, may nevertheless be made to hold, by the danger, though not by the difficulty of breaking them.
[2] *a)* In *relation to these bonds* only it is, that I am to speak now of the liberty of subjects. For seeing there is no commonwealth in the world, wherein there be rules enough set down, for the regulating of all the actions, and words of men; as being a thing impossible: it followeth necessarily, that in all kinds of *actions by the laws praetermitted*, men have the *liberty*, of doing what their own reasons shall suggest, for the most profitable to themselves. *(1)* For *if we take liberty in the proper sense, for corporal liberty*; that is to say, freedom from chains and prison; it were very *absurd* for men to clamour as they do, for the liberty they so manifestly enjoy. *(2)* Again, *if we take liberty, for an exemption from laws*, it is no less *absurd*, for men to demand as they do, that liberty, by which all other men may be masters of their lives. And yet, as absurd as it is, this is it they demand; not know-

ing that the laws are no *[power]* to protect them, without a sword in the hands of a man, or men, to cause those laws to be put in execution. *The liberty of a subject*, lieth therefore only in those things, which in regulating their actions, the *sovereign* hath praetermitted: such as is the liberty to buy, and sell, and otherwise contract with one another; to choose their own abode, their own diet, their own trade of life, and institute their children as they themselves think fit; and the like. ***[3]*** Nevertheless we are not to understand, that by such liberty, the *sovereign power* of life and death, is either abolished, or limited. For it has been already shown, that *nothing the sovereign representative can do to a subject, on what pretence soever, can properly be called injustice, or injury*; because every subject is author of every act the sovereign doth; so that he never wanteth ***[right]*** to anything, otherwise, than as he himself is the subject of God, and *bound thereby to observe the laws of nature*. And therefore it may, and doth often happen in commonwealths, that a *subject may be put to death*, by the command of the sovereign power; and *yet neither do the other wrong*: as when Jephtha caused his daughter to be sacrificed: in which, and the like cases, he that so dieth, had liberty to do the action, for which he is nevertheless, without injury put to death. And the *same* holdeth also in a *sovereign* prince, that putteth to death an *innocent subject. For though the action be against the law of nature, as being contrary to equity*, as was the killing of Uriah, by David; yet it was *not an injury* to Uriah, but to God. Not to Uriah, because *the right to do what he pleased* was given him by Uriah himself: and yet to God, because David was God's subject and prohibited all iniquity by the law of nature: which distinction, David himself, when he repented the fact, evidently confirmed, saying, To thee only have I sinned. In the same manner, the people of Athens, when they banished the most potent of their commonwealth for ten years, thought they committed no injustice; and yet they never questioned what crime he had done; but what hurt he would do: nay they commanded the banishment of they knew not whom; and every citizen bringing his oystershell into the marketplace, written with the name of him he desired should be banished, without actually accusing him, sometimes banished an Aristides, for his reputation of justice; and sometimes a scurrilous jester, as Hyperbolus, to make a jest of it. And yet a man cannot say, the *sovereign* people of Athens wanted *right to banish* them; or an *Athenian* the *liberty* to jest or to be just.

* * * * *

PHILOSOPHICAL RUDIMENTS CONCERNING GOVERNMENT AND SOCIETY, *Chapter XIV, by Thomas Hobbes, in* THE ENGLISH WORKS, *Edited by Wm. Molesworth,*

VOL. 2, PP. 185–86

They confound ***[laws]*** with ***[right]***, who continue still to do what is permitted by *divine right*, notwithstanding it be forbidden by the ***[civil law]***. That which is *prohibited* by the ***[divine law]***, cannot be *permitted* by the ***[civil]***; neither can that which is commanded by the divine law, be *prohibited* by the civil. Notwithstanding, that which is permitted by the divine right, that is to say, that which may be done by divine right, doth no whit hinder why the same may not be forbidden by the civil laws; for inferior laws may restrain the liberty allowed by the superior, although they cannot enlarge them. Now natural liberty is a right *not constituted*, but *allowed* by the laws. For the laws being removed, our liberty is absolute. This is first restrained by the natural and divine laws; the residue is bounded by the civil law: what remains, may again be restrained by the constitutions of particular towns and societies. There is great difference therefore between law and right. For law is a fetter, right is freedom; and they differ like *contraries*.

APPENDIX F

Kant, *Fundamental Principles*
Three Editions with Major Sections' Pagination[1]

		McKeon Notes		
Section	Subsection	Typed Page #s	Pencil Page #s	Beck's Edition
Preface		1–8	4–8	50–55
First Section:	Common Rational Knowledge of Morality to Philosophical	9–24	9–22	55–66
	Part 1: Nothing good except good will	9–14	9–12	55–58
	Part 2: 3 Propositions—tested by 4 duties	14–22	13–20	58–64
	Part 3: Principle—duty	22–24	20–22	64–66
Second Section:	Popular Moral Philosophy to Metaphysics of Morals	24–73	22–64	66–101
	Part 1: Moral principle <— pure reason	24–38	22–34	66–76
	a) Duty <— practical reason, not empirical	24–32	22–30	66–72
	b) 3 kinds of imperatives	33–38	30–34	72–76
	Part 2: How possible?	38–66	34–59	76–97
	Introduction: Difficulties involved	38–43	34–38	76–80
	a) CI: Maxim as universal law (form)	43–52	38–46	80–87
	b) CI: Rational being end in itself (matter)	52–57	46–51	87–90
	c) Autonomy *vs.* heteronomy: Realm of ends			
	Part 3: Autonomy of will supreme principle of morality	57–66	51–57	90–97
Third Section:	Metaphysics of Morals to Critique of Pure Practical Reason	73–93	64–79	101–17
Total Pages:		93	76	67

APPENDIX G

Mill, *On Liberty*
Four Editions with Major Sections' Pagination[1]

Chapter	Subsection	McKeon's Everyman Edition	McKeon's Library of Liberal Arts	Betz's Edition	Gould's Appleton-Century-Crofts
I	Introductory	65–67	2–19		1–
	Part 1: Historical struggle between liberty and authority	65–	3–		1–
	Part 2: Purpose of essay—principle of self-protection	73–	13–	95	9–
	Part 3: Sphere of human liberty	75–	15–	99	12–
II	Of the Liberty of Thought and Discussion	78–113	19–67	102	15–
	Part 1: Assume suppressed opinion true	79–	21–	104	17–
	a) Perspective of theory		21–		17–
	b) Perspective of practice		22–		18–
	Example of Catholic Church	83	26		20
	c) Perspective of utility	84–	27–		21–
	Part 2: Assume received opinion true	95–	43–	126	34–
	Example of Catholic Church	98	47		38
	Part 3: Assume conflicting opinions share truth	105–	55–	140	45–
	Part 4: Recapitulation—4 grounds for freedom of expression	111–	64–	148	52–

Chapter	Subsection	McKeon's Everyman Edition	McKeon's Library of Liberal Arts	Betz's Edition	Gould's Appleton-Century-Crofts
III	Of Individuality, As One of the Elements of Well-Being	114–30	67–90		55–
	Part 1: Indifference to end itself	115–	68–	153	56–
	Part 2: Unfree should allow freedom for others	122–	77–	162–	63–
	a) Unfree can learn from free	122–	78–		64–
	b) Uncustomary can become customary	125–	82–		67–
	c) Liberty true source of improvement	127–	85–		70–
IV	Of the Limits of the Authority of Society over the Individual	131–48	91–113		75–
	Part 1: Interests of society and duties	131–	91–		75–
	Part 2: Interests of the individual and noninterference	140–	102–		84–
V	Applications	149–70	114–41		95–118
	2 maxims	149	114		95

APPENDIX H

McKeon Notes on *Freedom and History*[1]

Review of Freedom and History

1. Occasion of the Book. Discussion of problems of international understanding at UNESCO.[2] Moral and intellectual considerations in relation to action; education, science and culture.
   a. Apparent difficulties of communication (apart from possible intention to mislead or deceive) in differences of basic assumptions and basic methods of thinking and expressing thoughts.
   b. Relation of this practical tendency to the theoretic fashions of philosophy. History of subject matters—things, thoughts, and actions-words.
      Combination of practical and theoretic emphases on pragmatism—semantics in present time.

Three related ideas at the basis of the difficulties of communication.
   a. Basis of action in the nature of man—concept of freedom expressive of that nature as manifested in action.
   b. Examination of the nature of human action in the history of human actions.
         Tendency to go from facts of history to conception of freedom which explains them; or from doctrine of freedom to the facts of history for verification.
      But becomes immediately apparent that there is an intimate relation between freedom and history, that each is used in a variety of senses which corresponds to a sense of the other, and therefore the facts always fit the theory, and the opposed doctrines never meet.
   c. Consequently necessary to consider the variety of senses in which "semantics" is used.
         First distinguish three main kinds—philological, philosophic and historical. Historical as comparison of the meanings historically given to terms in philosophic systems, explicit or implicit.

Discover three main kinds, which many subdivisions—dialectical, logistic, and problematic.[3]

Expound three senses of history and freedom.
Dominance of the dialectical in Europe and the East; dominance of problematic and logistic in USA.

Practical results to be anticipated from semantic analysis:

(1) mutual understanding and establishment of possibility of cooperation on basis of different reasons, principles and religions without uncertainties which come from suspicion of doctrine.

(2) possibility of differentiation [of] the proper and improper uses of conceptions—thus degradation of dialectic, logistic, problematic. Latter problem to be treated locally.

Institution of self-review—state intentions and imperfections. Practical intention—consequent difficulty, need of longer exposition and fuller explanation. Do that tonight in expectation that further difficulties may be indicated in question period and removed.[4]

APPENDIX I

Final Examination

Tuesday, March 16, 1965

Final Examination

Ideas and Methods 212

Note: The three questions are of equal importance: you should spend forty minutes on each. Please return this question sheet with your examination book.

1. Compare and contrast the conception of Freedom in Machiavelli, Kant, and Mill in the respects in which their methods of defining and establishing freedom influence the meaning they give to it.

2. What is the place of Power in the moral philosophies of Hobbes, Spinoza, and Kant?

3. Comment on Hegel's conception of history and philosophy—of data and ideas—and indicate briefly the ways in which he removes the apparent contradiction between history and philosophy set forth in the following passage from Reason in History:

"In history, thinking is subordinate to the data of reality, which latter serve as guide and basis for historians. Philosophy, on the other hand, allegedly produces its own ideas out of speculation, without regard to given data. If philosophy approached history with such ideas, it may be held, it would treat history as its raw material and not leave it as it is, but shape it in accordance with these ideas, and hence construct it, so to speak, a priori. But since history is supposed to understand events and actions merely for what they are and have been, and is the truer, the more factual it is, it seems that the method of philosophy would be in contradiction to the function of history. This contradiction and the charge consequently brought against philosophy shall here be explained and refuted. But we shall not, for that matter, attempt to correct the innumerable specific misrepresentations which are current and continuously recur about the aims, interests, and methods of history, and its relations to philosophy."

APPENDIX J

Semantic Profiles of Selected Western Thinkers[1]

1. Arranged Alphabetically

Name	DOB*	Principle	Method	Interpretation
Academy	–347	Actional	Dialectical	Existentialist
Academy, New	–213	Comprehensive	Operational	Existentialist
Adams, John[†]	1735	Simple	Operational	Ontological
Addison, Joseph	1672	Actional	Logistic	Essentialist
Albertus Magnus	1200	Actional	Problematic	Ontological
Anselm	1033	Reflexive	Operational	Ontological
Aristotle	–384	Reflexive	Problematic	Essentialist
Arnold, Matthew	1822	Comprehensive	Problematic	Existentialist
Augustine	354	Actional	Dialectical	Ontological
Austin, John L.	1911	Actional	Operational	Essentialist
Ayer, Alfred J.	1910	Actional	Logistic	Entitative
Bacon, Francis	1561	Reflexive	Operational	Ontological
Bacon, Roger	1220	Comprehensive	Operational	Essentialist
Baier[‡]	1929	Actional	Dialectical	Entitative
Baumgarten, Alexander	1714	Comprehensive	Operational	Existentialist
Beard, Charles A.	1874	Reflexive	Operational	Entitative
Bergson, Henri	1859	Reflexive	Dialectical	Entitative
Berkeley, George[†]	1685	Comprehensive	Operational	Existentialist
Bernard of Clairvaux	1090	Reflexive	Dialectical	Entitative
Bonaventura	1217	Reflexive	Dialectical	Ontological
Booth, Wayne	1921	Reflexive	Operational	Ontological
Bosanquet, Bernard[†]	1848	Comprehensive	Dialectical	Existentialist
Bossuet, Jacques	1627	Reflexive	Operational	Ontological
Boyle, Robert	1627	Simple	Logistic	Existentialist
Brentano, Franz	1838	Comprehensive	Operational	Essentialist
Bridgman, Percy	1882	Reflexive	Operational	Entitative
Buckle, Henry	1821	Comprehensive	Logistic	Essentialist
Burke, Kenneth[†]	1897	Comprehensive	Operational	Entitative
Cardozo, Benjamin	1870	Reflexive	Logistic	Existentialist

Name	DOB*	Principle	Method	Interpretation
Carnap, Rudolf	1891	Actional	Logistic	Existentialist
Cassirer, Ernst	1874	Actional	Operational	Essentialist
Cicero, Marcus Tullius	–106	Comprehensive	Operational	Existentialist
Coleridge, Samuel T.	1772	Reflexive	Operational	Ontological
Collingwood, Robin G.†	1889	Reflexive	Dialectical	Existentialist
Comte, Auguste	1798	Comprehensive	Problematic	Entitative
Condorcet, Marquis de	1743	Reflexive	Operational	Entitative
Cournot, Antoine A.	1801	Reflexive	Operational	Entitative
Crane, Ronald S.	1886	Reflexive	Operational	Entitative
Croce, Benedetto	1866	Actional	Dialectical	Existentialist
D'Alembert, Jean	1717	Reflexive	Logistic	Existentialist
Darwin, Charles	1809	Reflexive	Operational	Entitative
Demetrius Phalereus§	–317	Reflexive	Operational	Entitative
Democritus	–460	Simple	Logistic	Entitative
Descartes, René	1596	Reflexive	Logistic	Existentialist
Dewey, John†	1859	Actional	Problematic	Entitative
Einstein, Albert	1879	Comprehensive	Dialectical	Entitative
Empson, William	1906	Reflexive	Operational	Existentialist
Epicurus†	–341	Reflexive	Logistic	Entitative
Erigena, John Scotus	810	Actional	Operational	Entitative
Euclid	–300	Actional	Logistic	Ontological
Feuerbach, Ludwig	1804	Comprehensive	Operational	Entitative
Fichte, Johann	1762	Actional	Dialectical	Essentialist
Foucault, Michel	1926	Comprehensive	Operational	Entitative
Frege, Gottlob	1848	Reflexive	Operational	Ontological
Freud, Sigmund†	1856	Actional	Logistic	Ontological
Frye, Northrop	1912	Comprehensive	Operational	Essentialist
Galen	129	Comprehensive	Logistic	Existentialist
Galileo Galilei	1564	Reflexive	Operational	Entitative
Grosseteste, Robert	1168	Reflexive	Operational	Ontological
Hanslick, Eduard**	1825	Reflexive	Dialectical	Entitative
Hare, Richard M.	1919	Actional	Dialectical	Existentialist
Harris, James††	1709	Comprehensive	Logistic	Essentialist
Hegel, Georg W. F.	1770	Reflexive	Dialectical	Entitative
Heidegger, Martin†	1889	Comprehensive	Operational	Entitative
Heller, Joseph	1923	Simple	Operational	Existentialist
Heraclitus	–540	Actional	Dialectical	Entitative
Hobbes, Thomas†	1588	Actional	Logistic	Entitative
Horace	–65	Reflexive	Operational	Entitative
Hugh of St. Victor	1100	Comprehensive	Operational	Essentialist
Hume, David	1711	Simple	Operational	Entitative
Husserl, Edmund	1859	Reflexive	Operational	Ontological
James, William	1842	Actional	Problematic	Existentialist
Jaspers, Karl	1883	Comprehensive	Operational	Existentialist
Jefferson, Thomas†	1743	Reflexive	Operational	Entitative
John of Salisbury	1115	Reflexive	Operational	Ontological
Johnson, Samuel	1709	Comprehensive	Operational	Essentialist
Kant, Immanuel	1724	Reflexive	Operational	Ontological
Kubler, George A.	1912	Comprehensive	Dialectical	Essentialist

Name	DOB*	Principle	Method	Interpretation
La Bruyere, Jean de	1645	Comprehensive	Operational	Essentialist
Langer, Susanne	1895	Actional	Problematic	Ontological
Leibniz, Gottfried W.	1646	Comprehensive	Logistic	Essentialist
Leonardo da Vinci	1452	Comprehensive	Operational	Existentialist
Lewis, C. I.	1883	Reflexive	Operational	Entitative
Locke, John	1632	Actional	Logistic	Essentialist
Longinus	1	Simple	Operational	Ontological
Lorentz, Hendrick A.[‡‡]	1853	Comprehensive	Operational	Entitative
Lucretius	–96	Simple	Operational	Essentialist
Lully, Raymond	1232	Comprehensive	Operational	Essentialist
Machiavelli, Niccolò	1469	Reflexive	Operational	Existentialist
Malebranche, Nicolas de	1638	Actional	Dialectical	Entitative
Mandeville, Bernard de	1670	Reflexive	Operational	Entitative
Marx, Karl	1818	Actional	Dialectical	Entitative
Maxwell, James Clerk	1831	Actional	Operational	Entitative
Merleau-Ponty, Maurice	1908	Actional	Operational	Essentialist
Mill, John Stuart	1806	Reflexive	Operational	Existentialist
Milton, John	1608	Reflexive	Operational	Existentialist
Montaigne, Michel E. de	1533	Reflexive	Operational	Entitative
Montesquieu, Baron de	1689	Actional	Problematic	Essentialist
Moore, George E.	1873	Reflexive	Operational	Ontological
Newton, Isaac	1642	Comprehensive	Logistic	Entitative
Nicholas of Cusa	1401	Simple	Operational	Ontological
Niebuhr, Barthold Georg	1776	Actional	Logistic	Essentialist
Nietzsche, Friedrich Wilhelm	1844	Comprehensive	Operational	Entitative
Ogden, Charles Kay[§§]	1889	Reflexive	Problematic	Entitative
Panofsky, Irwin	1892	Comprehensive	Operational	Entitative
Parmenides	–515	Simple	Dialectical	Existentialist
Peirce, Charles Sanders[†]	1839	Reflexive	Operational	Ontological
Philo	–20	Actional	Dialectical	Essentialist
Piaget, Jean	1896	Comprehensive	Problematic	Essentialist
Plato	–428	Comprehensive	Dialectical	Ontological
Plotinus	205	Simple	Dialectical	Essentialist
Poincaré, Henri	1854	Reflexive	Operational	Entitative
Polanyi, Michael	1891	Comprehensive	Problematic	Existentialist
Protagoras	–490	Actional	Operational	Existentialist
Rameau, Jean-Philippe	1683	Comprehensive	Operational	Entitative
Richards, Ivor Armstrong	1893	Actional	Logistic	Existentialist
Ricoeur, Paul	1913	Reflexive	Operational	Ontological
Robinson, James Harvey	1863	Comprehensive	Logistic	Essentialist
Rousseau, Jean-Jacques	1712	Comprehensive	Operational	Essentialist
Russell, Bertrand[†***]	1872	Reflexive	Operational	Entitative
Ryle, Gilbert	1900	Actional	Logistic	Existentialist
Santayana, George[†]	1863	Reflexive	Logistic	Existentialist
Sartre, Jean-Paul	1905	Comprehensive	Operational	Existentialist
Schelling, Friedrich	1775	Actional	Dialectical	Ontological
Schopenhauer, Arthur	1788	Reflexive	Operational	Ontological
Schrodinger, Erwin	1887	Actional	Operational	Entitative
Shelley, Percy Bysshe	1792	Comprehensive	Problematic	Essentialist

Name	DOB*	Principle	Method	Interpretation
Spinoza, Baruch	1632	Reflexive	Logistic	Ontological
Stevens, Wallace†††	1879	Comprehensive	Operational	Entitative
Stoics	–300	Comprehensive	Problematic	Entitative
Teilhard du Chardin, Pierre	1881	Reflexive	Dialectical	Entitative
Theophrastus†	–371	Reflexive	Dialectical	Entitative
Thomas Aquinas	1224	Reflexive	Problematic	Ontological
Thucydides	–460	Reflexive	Operational	Entitative
Tolstoi, Leo	1828	Comprehensive	Operational	Essentialist
Vico, Giovan Battista	1668	Comprehensive	Operational	Essentialist
Voltaire	1694	Comprehensive	Operational	Entitative
Whitehead, Alfred North†	1861	Simple	Dialectical	Existentialist
Wilkins, John‡‡‡	1614	Comprehensive	Problematic	Entitative
Wittgenstein, Ludwig§§§	1889	Comprehensive	Operational	Entitative
Wordsworth, William†	1770	Comprehensive	Operational	Entitative

*DOB = Date Of Birth.
† McKeon made changes to the cards of the following individuals. The original profiles are provided in the following table.

Name	DOB	Principle	Method	Interpretation
Adams, John	1735	Reflexive	Operational	Entitative
Berkeley, George	1685	Comprehensive	Operational	Entitative?
Bosanquet, Bernard	1848	Comprehensive	Dialectical	Existentialist (?)
Burke, Kenneth	1897	Comprehensive	Operational	Existentialist
Collingwood, Robin G.	1889	Reflexive	Dialectical	Ontological?
Dewey, John	1859	Actional	Problematic	Essentialist
Epicurus	341	Reflexive	Dialectical	Entitative
Freud, Sigmund	1856	Actional	Problematic	Entitative?
Heidegger, Martin	1889	Comprehensive	Dialectical	Entitative
Hobbes, Thomas	1588	Actional	Logistic	Existentialist
Jefferson, Thomas	1743	Reflexive	Problematic	Entitative
Peirce, Charles Sanders	1839	Reflexive	Logistic (dialectical?)	Existentialist
Russell, Bertrand	1872	Reflexive	Logistic	Entitative
Santayana, George	1863	Actional	Logistic	Existentialist
Theophrastus	–371	Actional	Problematic	Entitative
Whitehead, Alfred North	1861	Simple	Dialectical	Ontological
Wordsworth, William	1770	Comprehensive	Operational	Existentialist

‡ "Baier" may refer to either Annette Baier (b. 1929) or Karl Baier (b. 1917).
§ McKeon occasionally provided the name of the writer's work on which he is assumed to have based his profiles. This card lists "*Peri Hermeneias*."
**McKeon adds the note "*The Beautiful in Music*," which was written by Hanslick and published in 1854.
†† McKeon adds the note "*Hermes*," the full title of which is *Hermes: A Philosophical Inquiry Concerning Universal Grammar*, written by Harris and published in 1751.
‡‡ The card for Hendrick A. Lorentz also included Galileo, Newton, and Maxwell. McKeon is clearly focusing his attention on distinctions in how important physicists think about their work.
§§ Charles Kay Ogden is filed under "Ogden and Richards." This profile was likely created from the 1923 joint work of C. K. Ogden and I. A. Richards, entitled *The Making of Meaning: A Study of the Influence of Language upon Thought and of the Science of Symbolism*. A separate profile card exists for I. A. Richards, taken from works authored solely by Richards, such as *A Philosophy of Rhetoric* (1936), a topic central to McKeon's own philosophizing.
***McKeon notes that Russell's "earlier position" had a logistic method, based on *Principia Mathematica*, a work coauthored with Alfred North Whitehead and first published in 1910.
††† A second card exists for Wallace Stevens, and states: "Methods—logistic; interpretation—existentialistic; selection—perspectival."
‡‡‡ McKeon wrote "Real Character of Lang.," referring to *An Essay towards a Real Character and a Philosophical Language*, published in 1668 by John Wilkins.

§§§ McKeon notes, "(Tractatus). Method—logistic; interpretation—existentialist (Philosophical Investigations)." The *Tractatus Logico-Philosophicus* was completed by Wittgenstein in 1918, and *Philosophical Investigations* was published in 1953.

2. Grouped by Date of Birth

Name	DOB	Principle	Method	Interpretation
Heraclitus	–540	Actional	Dialectical	Entitative
Parmenides	–515	Simple	Dialectical	Existentialist
Protagoras	–490	Actional	Operational	Existentialist
Democritus	–460	Simple	Logistic	Entitative
Thucydides	–460	Reflexive	Operational	Entitative
Plato	–428	Comprehensive	Dialectical	Ontological
Aristotle	–384	Reflexive	Problematic	Essentialist
Theophrastus	–371	Reflexive	Dialectical	Entitative
Academy	–347	Actional	Dialectical	Existentialist
Epicurus	–341	Reflexive	Logistic	Entitative
Demetrius Phalereus	–317	Reflexive	Operational	Entitative
Euclid	–300	Actional	Logistic	Ontological
Stoics	–300	Comprehensive	Problematic	Entitative
Academy, New	–213	Comprehensive	Operational	Existentialist
Cicero, Marcus Tullius	–106	Comprehensive	Operational	Existentialist
Lucretius	–96	Simple	Operational	Essentialist
Horace	–65	Reflexive	Operational	Entitative
Philo	–20	Actional	Dialectical	Essentialist
Longinus	1	Simple	Operational	Ontological
Galen	129	Comprehensive	Logistic	Existentialist
Plotinus	205	Simple	Dialectical	Essentialist
Augustine	354	Actional	Dialectical	Ontological
Erigena, John Scotus	810	Actional	Operational	Entitative
Anselm	1033	Reflexive	Operational	Ontological
Bernard of Clairvaux	1090	Reflexive	Dialectical	Entitative
Hugh of St. Victor	1100	Comprehensive	Operational	Essentialist
John of Salisbury	1115	Reflexive	Operational	Ontological
Grosseteste, Robert	1168	Reflexive	Operational	Ontological
Albertus Magnus	1200	Actional	Problematic	Ontological
Bonaventura	1217	Reflexive	Dialectical	Ontological
Bacon, Roger	1220	Comprehensive	Operational	Essentialist
Thomas Aquinas	1224	Reflexive	Problematic	Ontological
Lully, Raymond	1232	Comprehensive	Operational	Essentialist
Nicholas of Cusa	1401	Simple	Operational	Ontological
Leonardo da Vinci	1452	Comprehensive	Operational	Existentialist
Machiavelli, Niccolò	1469	Reflexive	Operational	Existentialist
Montaigne, Michel E. de	1533	Reflexive	Operational	Entitative
Bacon, Francis	1561	Reflexive	Operational	Ontological
Galileo Galilei	1564	Reflexive	Operational	Entitative
Hobbes, Thomas	1588	Actional	Logistic	Entitative
Descartes, René	1596	Reflexive	Logistic	Existentialist
Milton, John	1608	Reflexive	Operational	Existentialist
Wilkins, John	1614	Comprehensive	Problematic	Entitative

Name	DOB	Principle	Method	Interpretation
Bossuet, Jacques	1627	Reflexive	Operational	Ontological
Boyle, Robert	1627	Simple	Logistic	Existentialist
Locke, John	1632	Actional	Logistic	Essentialist
Spinoza, Baruch	1632	Reflexive	Logistic	Ontological
Malebranche, Nicolas de	1638	Actional	Dialectical	Entitative
Newton, Isaac	1642	Comprehensive	Logistic	Entitative
La Bruyere, Jean de	1645	Comprehensive	Operational	Essentialist
Leibniz, Gottfried W.	1646	Comprehensive	Logistic	Essentialist
Vico, Giovan Battista	1668	Comprehensive	Operational	Essentialist
Mandeville, Bernard de	1670	Reflexive	Operational	Entitative
Addison, Joseph	1672	Actional	Logistic	Essentialist
Rameau, Jean-Philippe	1683	Comprehensive	Operational	Entitative
Berkeley, George	1685	Comprehensive	Operational	Existentialist
Montesquieu, Baron de	1689	Actional	Problematic	Essentialist
Voltaire	1694	Comprehensive	Operational	Entitative
Harris, James	1709	Comprehensive	Logistic	Essentialist
Johnson, Samuel	1709	Comprehensive	Operational	Essentialist
Hume, David	1711	Simple	Operational	Entitative
Rousseau, Jean-Jacques	1712	Comprehensive	Operational	Essentialist
Baumgarten, Alexander	1714	Comprehensive	Operational	Existentialist
D'Alembert, Jean	1717	Reflexive	Logistic	Existentialist
Kant, Immanuel	1724	Reflexive	Operational	Ontological
Adams, John	1735	Simple	Operational	Ontological
Condorcet, Marquis de	1743	Reflexive	Operational	Entitative
Jefferson, Thomas	1743	Reflexive	Operational	Entitative
Fichte, Johann	1762	Actional	Dialectical	Essentialist
Hegel, Georg W. F.	1770	Reflexive	Dialectical	Entitative
Wordsworth, William	1770	Comprehensive	Operational	Entitative
Coleridge, Samuel T.	1772	Reflexive	Operational	Ontological
Schelling, Friedrich	1775	Actional	Dialectical	Ontological
Niebuhr, Barthold Georg	1776	Actional	Logistic	Essentialist
Schopenhauer, Arthur	1788	Reflexive	Operational	Ontological
Shelley, Percy Bysshe	1792	Comprehensive	Problematic	Essentialist
Comte, Auguste	1798	Comprehensive	Problematic	Entitative
Cournot, Antoine A.	1801	Reflexive	Operational	Entitative
Feuerbach, Ludwig	1804	Comprehensive	Operational	Entitative
Mill, John Stuart	1806	Reflexive	Operational	Existentialist
Darwin, Charles	1809	Reflexive	Operational	Entitative
Marx, Karl	1818	Actional	Dialectical	Entitative
Buckle, Henry	1821	Comprehensive	Logistic	Essentialist
Arnold, Matthew	1822	Comprehensive	Problematic	Existentialist
Hanslick, Eduard	1825	Reflexive	Dialectical	Entitative
Tolstoi, Leo	1828	Comprehensive	Operational	Essentialist
Maxwell, James Clerk	1831	Actional	Operational	Entitative
Brentano, Franz	1838	Comprehensive	Operational	Essentialist
Peirce, Charles Sanders	1839	Reflexive	Operational	Ontological
James, William	1842	Actional	Problematic	Existentialist
Nietzsche, Friedrich W.	1844	Comprehensive	Operational	Entitative
Bosanquet, Bernard	1848	Comprehensive	Dialectical	Existentialist
Fregc, Gottlob	1848	Reflexive	Operational	Ontological

Name	DOB	Principle	Method	Interpretation
Lorentz, Hendrick A.	1853	Comprehensive	Operational	Entitative
Poincaré, Henri	1854	Reflexive	Operational	Entitative
Freud, Sigmund	1856	Actional	Logistic	Ontological
Bergson, Henri	1859	Reflexive	Dialectical	Entitative
Dewey, John	1859	Actional	Problematic	Entitative
Husserl, Edmund	1859	Reflexive	Operational	Ontological
Whitehead, Alfred North	1861	Simple	Dialectical	Existentialist
Robinson, James Harvey	1863	Comprehensive	Logistic	Essentialist
Santayana, George	1863	Reflexive	Logistic	Existentialist
Croce, Benedetto	1866	Actional	Dialectical	Existentialist
Cardozo, Benjamin	1870	Reflexive	Logistic	Existentialist
Russell, Bertrand	1872	Reflexive	Operational	Entitative
Moore, George E.	1873	Reflexive	Operational	Ontological
Beard, Charles A.	1874	Reflexive	Operational	Entitative
Cassirer, Ernst	1874	Actional	Operational	Essentialist
Einstein, Albert	1879	Comprehensive	Dialectical	Entitative
Stevens, Wallace	1879	Comprehensive	Operational	Entitative
Teilhard du Chardin, Pierre	1881	Reflexive	Dialectical	Entitative
Bridgman, Percy	1882	Reflexive	Operational	Entitative
Jaspers, Karl	1883	Comprehensive	Operational	Existentialist
Lewis, C. I.	1883	Reflexive	Operational	Entitative
Crane, Ronald S.	1886	Reflexive	Operational	Entitative
Schrodinger, Erwin	1887	Actional	Operational	Entitative
Collingwood, Robin G.	1889	Reflexive	Dialectical	Existentialist
Heidegger, Martin	1889	Comprehensive	Operational	Entitative
Ogden, Charles Kay	1889	Reflexive	Problematic	Entitative
Wittgenstein, Ludwig	1889	Comprehensive	Operational	Entitative
Carnap, Rudolf	1891	Actional	Logistic	Existentialist
Polanyi, Michael	1891	Comprehensive	Problematic	Existentialist
Panofsky, Irwin	1892	Comprehensive	Operational	Entitative
Richards, Ivor Armstrong	1893	Actional	Logistic	Existentialist
Langer, Susanne	1895	Actional	Problematic	Ontological
Piaget, Jean	1896	Comprehensive	Problematic	Essentialist
Burke, Kenneth	1897	Comprehensive	Operational	Entitative
Ryle, Gilbert	1900	Actional	Logistic	Existentialist
Sartre, Jean-Paul	1905	Comprehensive	Operational	Existentialist
Empson, William	1906	Reflexive	Operational	Existentialist
Merleau-Ponty, Maurice	1908	Actional	Operational	Essentialist
Ayer, Alfred J.	1910	Actional	Logistic	Entitative
Austin, John L.	1911	Actional	Operational	Essentialist
Frye, Northrop	1912	Comprehensive	Operational	Essentialist
Kubler, George A.	1912	Comprehensive	Dialectical	Essentialist
Ricoeur, Paul	1913	Reflexive	Operational	Ontological
Hare, Richard M.	1919	Actional	Dialectical	Existentialist
Booth, Wayne	1921	Reflexive	Operational	Ontological
Heller, Joseph	1923	Simple	Operational	Existentialist
Foucault, Michel	1926	Comprehensive	Operational	Entitative
Baier	1929	Actional	Dialectical	Entitative

3. Grouped by Principle and Method

Name	DOB	Principle	Method	Interpretation
Plato	–428	Comprehensive	Dialectical	Ontological
Einstein, Albert	1879	Comprehensive	Dialectical	Entitative
Bosanquet, Bernard	1848	Comprehensive	Dialectical	Existentialist
Kubler, George A.	1912	Comprehensive	Dialectical	Essentialist
Rameau, Jean-Philippe	1683	Comprehensive	Operational	Entitative
Voltaire	1694	Comprehensive	Operational	Entitative
Wordsworth, William	1770	Comprehensive	Operational	Entitative
Feuerbach, Ludwig	1804	Comprehensive	Operational	Entitative
Nietzsche, Friedrich W.	1844	Comprehensive	Operational	Entitative
Lorentz, Hendrick A.	1853	Comprehensive	Operational	Entitative
Stevens, Wallace	1879	Comprehensive	Operational	Entitative
Heidegger, Martin	1889	Comprehensive	Operational	Entitative
Wittgenstein, Ludwig	1889	Comprehensive	Operational	Entitative
Panofsky, Irwin	1892	Comprehensive	Operational	Entitative
Burke, Kenneth	1897	Comprehensive	Operational	Entitative
Foucault, Michel	1926	Comprehensive	Operational	Entitative
Academy, New	–213	Comprehensive	Operational	Existentialist
Cicero, Marcus Tullius	–106	Comprehensive	Operational	Existentialist
Leonardo da Vinci	1452	Comprehensive	Operational	Existentialist
Berkeley, George	1685	Comprehensive	Operational	Existentialist
Baumgarten, Alexander	1714	Comprehensive	Operational	Existentialist
Jaspers, Karl	1883	Comprehensive	Operational	Existentialist
Sartre, Jean-Paul	1905	Comprehensive	Operational	Existentialist
Hugh of St. Victor	1100	Comprehensive	Operational	Essentialist
Bacon, Roger	1220	Comprehensive	Operational	Essentialist
Lully, Raymond	1232	Comprehensive	Operational	Essentialist
La Bruyere, Jean de	1645	Comprehensive	Operational	Essentialist
Vico, Giovan Battista	1668	Comprehensive	Operational	Essentialist
Johnson, Samuel	1709	Comprehensive	Operational	Essentialist
Rousseau, Jean-Jacques	1712	Comprehensive	Operational	Essentialist
Tolstoi, Leo	1828	Comprehensive	Operational	Essentialist
Brentano, Franz	1838	Comprehensive	Operational	Essentialist
Frye, Northrop	1912	Comprehensive	Operational	Essentialist
Newton, Isaac	1642	Comprehensive	Logistic	Entitative
Galen	129	Comprehensive	Logistic	Existentialist
Leibniz, Gottfried W.	1646	Comprehensive	Logistic	Essentialist
Harris, James	1709	Comprehensive	Logistic	Essentialist
Buckle, Henry	1821	Comprehensive	Logistic	Essentialist
Robinson, James Harvey	1863	Comprehensive	Logistic	Essentialist
Stoics	–300	Comprehensive	Problematic	Entitative
Wilkins, John	1614	Comprehensive	Problematic	Entitative
Comte, Auguste	1798	Comprehensive	Problematic	Entitative
Arnold, Matthew	1822	Comprehensive	Problematic	Existentialist
Polanyi, Michael	1891	Comprehensive	Problematic	Existentialist
Shelley, Percy Bysshe	1792	Comprehensive	Problematic	Essentialist
Piaget, Jean	1896	Comprehensive	Problematic	Essentialist

Name	DOB	Principle	Method	Interpretation
Bonaventura	1217	Reflexive	Dialectical	Ontological
Theophrastus	–371	Reflexive	Dialectical	Entitative
Bernard of Clairvaux	1090	Reflexive	Dialectical	Entitative
Hegel, Georg W. F.	1770	Reflexive	Dialectical	Entitative
Hanslick, Eduard	1825	Reflexive	Dialectical	Entitative
Bergson, Henri	1859	Reflexive	Dialectical	Entitative
Teilhard du Chardin, Pierre	1881	Reflexive	Dialectical	Entitative
Collingwood, Robin G.	1889	Reflexive	Dialectical	Existentialist
Anselm	1033	Reflexive	Operational	Ontological
John of Salisbury	1115	Reflexive	Operational	Ontological
Grosseteste, Robert	1168	Reflexive	Operational	Ontological
Bacon, Francis	1561	Reflexive	Operational	Ontological
Bossuet, Jacques	1627	Reflexive	Operational	Ontological
Kant, Immanuel	1724	Reflexive	Operational	Ontological
Coleridge, Samuel T.	1772	Reflexive	Operational	Ontological
Schopenhauer, Arthur	1788	Reflexive	Operational	Ontological
Peirce, Charles Sanders	1839	Reflexive	Operational	Ontological
Frege, Gottlob	1848	Reflexive	Operational	Ontological
Husserl, Edmund	1859	Reflexive	Operational	Ontological
Moore, George E.	1873	Reflexive	Operational	Ontological
Ricoeur, Paul	1913	Reflexive	Operational	Ontological
Booth, Wayne	1921	Reflexive	Operational	Ontological
Thucydides	–460	Reflexive	Operational	Entitative
Demetrius Phalereus	–317	Reflexive	Operational	Entitative
Horace	–65	Reflexive	Operational	Entitative
Montaigne, Michel E. de	1533	Reflexive	Operational	Entitative
Galileo Galilei	1564	Reflexive	Operational	Entitative
Mandeville, Bernard de	1670	Reflexive	Operational	Entitative
Condorcet, Marquis de	1743	Reflexive	Operational	Entitative
Jefferson, Thomas	1743	Reflexive	Operational	Entitative
Cournot, Antoine A.	1801	Reflexive	Operational	Entitative
Darwin, Charles	1809	Reflexive	Operational	Entitative
Poincaré, Henri	1854	Reflexive	Operational	Entitative
Russell, Bertrand	1872	Reflexive	Operational	Entitative
Beard, Charles A.	1874	Reflexive	Operational	Entitative
Bridgman, Percy	1882	Reflexive	Operational	Entitative
Lewis, C. I.	1883	Reflexive	Operational	Entitative
Crane, Ronald S.	1886	Reflexive	Operational	Entitative
Machiavelli, Niccolò	1469	Reflexive	Operational	Existentialist
Milton, John	1608	Reflexive	Operational	Existentialist
Mill, John Stuart	1806	Reflexive	Operational	Existentialist
Empson, William	1906	Reflexive	Operational	Existentialist
Spinoza, Baruch	1632	Reflexive	Logistic	Ontological
Epicurus	–341	Reflexive	Logistic	Entitative
Descartes, René	1596	Reflexive	Logistic	Existentialist
D'Alembert, Jean	1717	Reflexive	Logistic	Existentialist
Santayana, George	1863	Reflexive	Logistic	Existentialist
Cardozo, Benjamin	1870	Reflexive	Logistic	Existentialist
Thomas Aquinas	1224	Reflexive	Problematic	Ontological

Name	DOB	Principle	Method	Interpretation
Ogden, Charles Kay	1889	Reflexive	Problematic	Entitative
Aristotle	–384	Reflexive	Problematic	Essentialist
Parmenides	–515	Simple	Dialectical	Existentialist
Whitehead, Alfred North	1861	Simple	Dialectical	Existentialist
Plotinus	205	Simple	Dialectical	Essentialist
Longinus	1	Simple	Operational	Ontological
Nicholas of Cusa	1401	Simple	Operational	Ontological
Adams, John	1735	Simple	Operational	Ontological
Hume, David	1711	Simple	Operational	Entitative
Heller, Joseph	1923	Simple	Operational	Existentialist
Lucretius	–96	Simple	Operational	Essentialist
Boyle, Robert	1627	Simple	Logistic	Existentialist
Democritus	–460	Simple	Logistic	Entitative
Augustine	354	Actional	Dialectical	Ontological
Schelling, Friedrich	1775	Actional	Dialectical	Ontological
Heraclitus	–540	Actional	Dialectical	Entitative
Malebranche, Nicolas de	1638	Actional	Dialectical	Entitative
Marx, Karl	1818	Actional	Dialectical	Entitative
Baier	1929	Actional	Dialectical	Entitative
Academy	–347	Actional	Dialectical	Existentialist
Croce, Benedetto	1866	Actional	Dialectical	Existentialist
Hare, Richard M.	1919	Actional	Dialectical	Existentialist
Philo	–20	Actional	Dialectical	Essentialist
Fichte, Johann	1762	Actional	Dialectical	Essentialist
Erigena, John Scotus	810	Actional	Operational	Entitative
Maxwell, James Clerk	1831	Actional	Operational	Entitative
Schrodinger, Erwin	1887	Actional	Operational	Entitative
Protagoras	–490	Actional	Operational	Existentialist
Cassirer, Ernst	1874	Actional	Operational	Essentialist
Merleau-Ponty, Maurice	1908	Actional	Operational	Essentialist
Austin, John L.	1911	Actional	Operational	Essentialist
Euclid	–300	Actional	Logistic	Ontological
Freud, Sigmund	1856	Actional	Logistic	Ontological
Hobbes, Thomas	1588	Actional	Logistic	Entitative
Ayer, Alfred J.	1910	Actional	Logistic	Entitative
Carnap, Rudolf	1891	Actional	Logistic	Existentialist
Richards, Ivor Armstrong	1893	Actional	Logistic	Existentialist
Ryle, Gilbert	1900	Actional	Logistic	Existentialist
Locke, John	1632	Actional	Logistic	Essentialist
Addison, Joseph	1672	Actional	Logistic	Essentialist
Niebuhr, Barthold Georg	1776	Actional	Logistic	Essentialist
Albertus Magnus	1200	Actional	Problematic	Ontological
Langer, Susanne	1895	Actional	Problematic	Ontological
Dewey, John	1859	Actional	Problematic	Entitative
James, William	1842	Actional	Problematic	Existentialist
Montesquieu, Baron de	1689	Actional	Problematic	Essentialist

4. Grouped by Principle and Interpretation

Name	DOB	Principle	Interpretation	Method
Plato	–428	Comprehensive	Ontological	Dialectical
Einstein, Albert	1879	Comprehensive	Entitative	Dialectical
Rameau, Jean-Philippe	1683	Comprehensive	Entitative	Operational
Voltaire	1694	Comprehensive	Entitative	Operational
Wordsworth, William	1770	Comprehensive	Entitative	Operational
Feuerbach, Ludwig	1804	Comprehensive	Entitative	Operational
Nietzsche, Friedrich Wilhelm	1844	Comprehensive	Entitative	Operational
Lorentz, Hendrick A.	1853	Comprehensive	Entitative	Operational
Stevens, Wallace	1879	Comprehensive	Entitative	Operational
Heidegger, Martin	1889	Comprehensive	Entitative	Operational
Wittgenstein, Ludwig	1889	Comprehensive	Entitative	Operational
Panofsky, Irwin	1892	Comprehensive	Entitative	Operational
Burke, Kenneth	1897	Comprehensive	Entitative	Operational
Foucault, Michel	1926	Comprehensive	Entitative	Operational
Newton, Isaac	1642	Comprehensive	Entitative	Logistic
Stoics	–300	Comprehensive	Entitative	Problematic
Wilkins, John	1614	Comprehensive	Entitative	Problematic
Comte, Auguste	1798	Comprehensive	Entitative	Problematic
Bosanquet, Bernard	1848	Comprehensive	Existentialist	Dialectical
Academy, New	–213	Comprehensive	Existentialist	Operational
Cicero, Marcus Tullius	–106	Comprehensive	Existentialist	Operational
Leonardo da Vinci	1452	Comprehensive	Existentialist	Operational
Berkeley, George	1685	Comprehensive	Existentialist	Operational
Baumgarten, Alexander	1714	Comprehensive	Existentialist	Operational
Jaspers, Karl	1883	Comprehensive	Existentialist	Operational
Sartre, Jean-Paul	1905	Comprehensive	Existentialist	Operational
Galen	129	Comprehensive	Existentialist	Logistic
Arnold, Matthew	1822	Comprehensive	Existentialist	Problematic
Polanyi, Michael	1891	Comprehensive	Existentialist	Problematic
Kubler, George A.	1912	Comprehensive	Essentialist	Dialectical
Hugh of St. Victor	1100	Comprehensive	Essentialist	Operational
Bacon, Roger	1220	Comprehensive	Essentialist	Operational
Lully, Raymond	1232	Comprehensive	Essentialist	Operational
La Bruyere, Jean de	1645	Comprehensive	Essentialist	Operational
Vico, Giovan Battista	1668	Comprehensive	Essentialist	Operational
Johnson, Samuel	1709	Comprehensive	Essentialist	Operational
Rousseau, Jean-Jacques	1712	Comprehensive	Essentialist	Operational
Tolstoi, Leo	1828	Comprehensive	Essentialist	Operational
Brentano, Franz	1838	Comprehensive	Essentialist	Operational
Frye, Northrop	1912	Comprehensive	Essentialist	Operational
Leibniz, Gottfried W.	1646	Comprehensive	Essentialist	Logistic
Harris, James	1709	Comprehensive	Essentialist	Logistic
Buckle, Henry	1821	Comprehensive	Essentialist	Logistic
Robinson, James Harvey	1863	Comprehensive	Essentialist	Logistic
Shelley, Percy Bysshe	1792	Comprehensive	Essentialist	Problematic
Piaget, Jean	1896	Comprehensive	Essentialist	Problematic

Name	DOB	Principle	Interpretation	Method
Bonaventura	1217	Reflexive	Ontological	Dialectical
Anselm	1033	Reflexive	Ontological	Operational
John of Salisbury	1115	Reflexive	Ontological	Operational
Grosseteste, Robert	1168	Reflexive	Ontological	Operational
Bacon, Francis	1561	Reflexive	Ontological	Operational
Bossuet, Jacques	1627	Reflexive	Ontological	Operational
Kant, Immanuel	1724	Reflexive	Ontological	Operational
Coleridge, Samuel T.	1772	Reflexive	Ontological	Operational
Schopenhauer, Arthur	1788	Reflexive	Ontological	Operational
Peirce, Charles Sanders	1839	Reflexive	Ontological	Operational
Frege, Gottlob	1848	Reflexive	Ontological	Operational
Husserl, Edmund	1859	Reflexive	Ontological	Operational
Moore, George E.	1873	Reflexive	Ontological	Operational
Ricoeur, Paul	1913	Reflexive	Ontological	Operational
Booth, Wayne	1921	Reflexive	Ontological	Operational
Spinoza, Baruch	1632	Reflexive	Ontological	Logistic
Thomas Aquinas	1224	Reflexive	Ontological	Problematic
Theophrastus	–371	Reflexive	Entitative	Dialectical
Bernard of Clairvaux	1090	Reflexive	Entitative	Dialectical
Hegel, Georg W. F.	1770	Reflexive	Entitative	Dialectical
Hanslick, Eduard	1825	Reflexive	Entitative	Dialectical
Bergson, Henri	1859	Reflexive	Entitative	Dialectical
Teilhard du Chardin, Pierre	1881	Reflexive	Entitative	Dialectical
Thucydides	–460	Reflexive	Entitative	Operational
Demetrius Phalereus	–317	Reflexive	Entitative	Operational
Horace	–65	Reflexive	Entitative	Operational
Montaigne, Michel E. de	1533	Reflexive	Entitative	Operational
Galileo Galilei	1564	Reflexive	Entitative	Operational
Mandeville, Bernard de	1670	Reflexive	Entitative	Operational
Condorcet, Marquis de	1743	Reflexive	Entitative	Operational
Jefferson, Thomas	1743	Reflexive	Entitative	Operational
Cournot, Antoine A.	1801	Reflexive	Entitative	Operational
Darwin, Charles	1809	Reflexive	Entitative	Operational
Poincaré, Henri	1854	Reflexive	Entitative	Operational
Russell, Bertrand	1872	Reflexive	Entitative	Operational
Beard, Charles A.	1874	Reflexive	Entitative	Operational
Bridgman, Percy	1882	Reflexive	Entitative	Operational
Lewis, C. I.	1883	Reflexive	Entitative	Operational
Crane, Ronald S.	1886	Reflexive	Entitative	Operational
Epicurus	–341	Reflexive	Entitative	Logistic
Ogden, Charles Kay	1889	Reflexive	Entitative	Problematic
Collingwood, Robin G.	1889	Reflexive	Existentialist	Dialectical
Machiavelli, Niccolò	1469	Reflexive	Existentialist	Operational
Milton, John	1608	Reflexive	Existentialist	Operational
Mill, John Stuart	1806	Reflexive	Existentialist	Operational
Empson, William	1906	Reflexive	Existentialist	Operational
Descartes, René	1596	Reflexive	Existentialist	Logistic
D'Alembert, Jean	1717	Reflexive	Existentialist	Logistic
Santayana, George	1863	Reflexive	Existentialist	Logistic

Name	DOB	Principle	Interpretation	Method
Cardozo, Benjamin	1870	Reflexive	Existentialist	Logistic
Aristotle	–384	Reflexive	Essentialist	Problematic
Longinus	1	Simple	Ontological	Operational
Nicholas of Cusa	1401	Simple	Ontological	Operational
Adams, John	1735	Simple	Ontological	Operational
Hume, David	1711	Simple	Entitative	Operational
Democritus	–460	Simple	Entitative	Logistic
Parmenides	–515	Simple	Existentialist	Dialectical
Whitehead, Alfred North	1861	Simple	Existentialist	Dialectical
Heller, Joseph	1923	Simple	Existentialist	Operational
Boyle, Robert	1627	Simple	Existentialist	Logistic
Plotinus	205	Simple	Essentialist	Dialectical
Lucretius	–96	Simple	Essentialist	Operational
Augustine	354	Actional	Ontological	Dialectical
Schelling, Friedrich	1775	Actional	Ontological	Dialectical
Euclid	–300	Actional	Ontological	Logistic
Freud, Sigmund	1856	Actional	Ontological	Logistic
Albertus Magnus	1200	Actional	Ontological	Problematic
Langer, Susanne	1895	Actional	Ontological	Problematic
Heraclitus	–540	Actional	Entitative	Dialectical
Malebranche, Nicolas de	1638	Actional	Entitative	Dialectical
Marx, Karl	1818	Actional	Entitative	Dialectical
Baier	1929	Actional	Entitative	Dialectical
Erigena, John Scotus	810	Actional	Entitative	Operational
Maxwell, James Clerk	1831	Actional	Entitative	Operational
Schrodinger, Erwin	1887	Actional	Entitative	Operational
Hobbes, Thomas	1588	Actional	Entitative	Logistic
Ayer, Alfred J.	1910	Actional	Entitative	Logistic
Dewey, John	1859	Actional	Entitative	Problematic
Academy	–347	Actional	Existentialist	Dialectical
Croce, Benedetto	1866	Actional	Existentialist	Dialectical
Hare, Richard M.	1919	Actional	Existentialist	Dialectical
Protagoras	–490	Actional	Existentialist	Operational
Carnap, Rudolf	1891	Actional	Existentialist	Logistic
Richards, Ivor Armstrong	1893	Actional	Existentialist	Logistic
Ryle, Gilbert	1900	Actional	Existentialist	Logistic
James, William	1842	Actional	Existentialist	Problematic
Philo	–20	Actional	Essentialist	Dialectical
Fichte, Johann	1762	Actional	Essentialist	Dialectical
Cassirer, Ernst	1874	Actional	Essentialist	Operational
Merleau-Ponty, Maurice	1908	Actional	Essentialist	Operational
Austin, John L.	1911	Actional	Essentialist	Operational
Locke, John	1632	Actional	Essentialist	Logistic
Addison, Joseph	1672	Actional	Essentialist	Logistic
Niebuhr, Barthold Georg	1776	Actional	Essentialist	Logistic
Montesquieu, Baron de	1689	Actional	Essentialist	Problematic

5. Grouped by Method and Interpretation

Name	DOB	Method	Interpretation	Principle
Plato	–428	Dialectical	Ontological	Comprehensive
Bonaventura	1217	Dialectical	Ontological	Reflexive
Augustine	354	Dialectical	Ontological	Actional
Schelling, Friedrich	1775	Dialectical	Ontological	Actional
Einstein, Albert	1879	Dialectical	Entitative	Comprehensive
Theophrastus	–371	Dialectical	Entitative	Reflexive
Bernard of Clairvaux	1090	Dialectical	Entitative	Reflexive
Hegel, Georg W. F.	1770	Dialectical	Entitative	Reflexive
Hanslick, Eduard	1825	Dialectical	Entitative	Reflexive
Bergson, Henri	1859	Dialectical	Entitative	Reflexive
Teilhard du Chardin, Pierre	1881	Dialectical	Entitative	Reflexive
Heraclitus	–540	Dialectical	Entitative	Actional
Malebranche, Nicolas de	1638	Dialectical	Entitative	Actional
Marx, Karl	1818	Dialectical	Entitative	Actional
Baier	1929	Dialectical	Entitative	Actional
Bosanquet, Bernard	1848	Dialectical	Existentialist	Comprehensive
Collingwood, Robin G.	1889	Dialectical	Existentialist	Reflexive
Parmenides	–515	Dialectical	Existentialist	Simple
Whitehead, Alfred North	1861	Dialectical	Existentialist	Simple
Academy	–347	Dialectical	Existentialist	Actional
Croce, Benedetto	1866	Dialectical	Existentialist	Actional
Hare, Richard M.	1919	Dialectical	Existentialist	Actional
Kubler, George A.	1912	Dialectical	Essentialist	Comprehensive
Plotinus	205	Dialectical	Essentialist	Simple
Philo	–20	Dialectical	Essentialist	Actional
Fichte, Johann	1762	Dialectical	Essentialist	Actional
Anselm	1033	Operational	Ontological	Reflexive
John of Salisbury	1115	Operational	Ontological	Reflexive
Grosseteste, Robert	1168	Operational	Ontological	Reflexive
Bacon, Francis	1561	Operational	Ontological	Reflexive
Bossuet, Jacques	1627	Operational	Ontological	Reflexive
Kant, Immanuel	1724	Operational	Ontological	Reflexive
Coleridge, Samuel T.	1772	Operational	Ontological	Reflexive
Schopenhauer, Arthur	1788	Operational	Ontological	Reflexive
Peirce, Charles Sanders	1839	Operational	Ontological	Reflexive
Frege, Gottlob	1848	Operational	Ontological	Reflexive
Husserl, Edmund	1859	Operational	Ontological	Reflexive
Moore, George E.	1873	Operational	Ontological	Reflexive
Ricoeur, Paul	1913	Operational	Ontological	Reflexive
Booth, Wayne	1921	Operational	Ontological	Reflexive
Longinus	1	Operational	Ontological	Simple
Nicholas of Cusa	1401	Operational	Ontological	Simple
Adams, John	1735	Operational	Ontological	Simple
Rameau, Jean-Philippe	1683	Operational	Entitative	Comprehensive
Voltaire	1694	Operational	Entitative	Comprehensive
Wordsworth, William	1770	Operational	Entitative	Comprehensive

Name	DOB	Method	Interpretation	Principle
Feuerbach, Ludwig	1804	Operational	Entitative	Comprehensive
Nietzsche, Friedrich W.	1844	Operational	Entitative	Comprehensive
Lorentz, Hendrick A.	1853	Operational	Entitative	Comprehensive
Stevens, Wallace	1879	Operational	Entitative	Comprehensive
Heidegger, Martin	1889	Operational	Entitative	Comprehensive
Wittgenstein, Ludwig	1889	Operational	Entitative	Comprehensive
Panofsky, Irwin	1892	Operational	Entitative	Comprehensive
Burke, Kenneth	1897	Operational	Entitative	Comprehensive
Foucault, Michel	1926	Operational	Entitative	Comprehensive
Thucydides	–460	Operational	Entitative	Reflexive
Demetrius Phalereus	–317	Operational	Entitative	Reflexive
Horace	–65	Operational	Entitative	Reflexive
Montaigne, Michel E. de	1533	Operational	Entitative	Reflexive
Galileo Galilei	1564	Operational	Entitative	Reflexive
Mandeville, Bernard de	1670	Operational	Entitative	Reflexive
Condorcet, Marquis de	1743	Operational	Entitative	Reflexive
Jefferson, Thomas	1743	Operational	Entitative	Reflexive
Cournot, Antoine A.	1801	Operational	Entitative	Reflexive
Darwin, Charles	1809	Operational	Entitative	Reflexive
Poincaré, Henri	1854	Operational	Entitative	Reflexive
Russell, Bertrand	1872	Operational	Entitative	Reflexive
Beard, Charles A.	1874	Operational	Entitative	Reflexive
Bridgman, Percy	1882	Operational	Entitative	Reflexive
Lewis, C. I.	1883	Operational	Entitative	Reflexive
Crane, Ronald S.	1886	Operational	Entitative	Reflexive
Hume, David	1711	Operational	Entitative	Simple
Erigena, John Scotus	810	Operational	Entitative	Actional
Maxwell, James Clerk	1831	Operational	Entitative	Actional
Schrodinger, Erwin	1887	Operational	Entitative	Actional
Academy, New	–213	Operational	Existentialist	Comprehensive
Cicero, Marcus Tullius	–106	Operational	Existentialist	Comprehensive
Leonardo da Vinci	1452	Operational	Existentialist	Comprehensive
Berkeley, George	1685	Operational	Existentialist	Comprehensive
Baumgarten, Alexander	1714	Operational	Existentialist	Comprehensive
Jaspers, Karl	1883	Operational	Existentialist	Comprehensive
Sartre, Jean-Paul	1905	Operational	Existentialist	Comprehensive
Machiavelli, Niccolò	1469	Operational	Existentialist	Reflexive
Milton, John	1608	Operational	Existentialist	Reflexive
Mill, John Stuart	1806	Operational	Existentialist	Reflexive
Empson, William	1906	Operational	Existentialist	Reflexive
Heller, Joseph	1923	Operational	Existentialist	Simple
Protagoras	–490	Operational	Existentialist	Actional
Hugh of St. Victor	1100	Operational	Essentialist	Comprehensive
Bacon, Roger	1220	Operational	Essentialist	Comprehensive
Lully, Raymond	1232	Operational	Essentialist	Comprehensive
La Bruyere, Jean de	1645	Operational	Essentialist	Comprehensive
Vico, Giovan Battista	1668	Operational	Essentialist	Comprehensive
Johnson, Samuel	1709	Operational	Essentialist	Comprehensive
Rousseau, Jean-Jacques	1712	Operational	Essentialist	Comprehensive

Name	DOB	Method	Interpretation	Principle
Tolstoi, Leo	1828	Operational	Essentialist	Comprehensive
Brentano, Franz	1838	Operational	Essentialist	Comprehensive
Frye, Northrop	1912	Operational	Essentialist	Comprehensive
Lucretius	–96	Operational	Essentialist	Simple
Cassirer, Ernst	1874	Operational	Essentialist	Actional
Merleau-Ponty, Maurice	1908	Operational	Essentialist	Actional
Austin, John L.	1911	Operational	Essentialist	Actional
Spinoza, Baruch	1632	Logistic	Ontological	Reflexive
Euclid	–300	Logistic	Ontological	Actional
Freud, Sigmund	1856	Logistic	Ontological	Actional
Newton, Isaac	1642	Logistic	Entitative	Comprehensive
Epicurus	–341	Logistic	Entitative	Reflexive
Democritus	–460	Logistic	Entitative	Simple
Hobbes, Thomas	1588	Logistic	Entitative	Actional
Ayer, Alfred J.	1910	Logistic	Entitative	Actional
Galen	129	Logistic	Existentialist	Comprehensive
Descartes, Rene	1596	Logistic	Existentialist	Reflexive
D'Alembert, Jean	1717	Logistic	Existentialist	Reflexive
Santayana, George	1863	Logistic	Existentialist	Reflexive
Cardozo, Benjamin	1870	Logistic	Existentialist	Reflexive
Boyle, Robert	1627	Logistic	Existentialist	Simple
Carnap, Rudolf	1891	Logistic	Existentialist	Actional
Richards, Ivor Armstrong	1893	Logistic	Existentialist	Actional
Ryle, Gilbert	1900	Logistic	Existentialist	Actional
Leibniz, Gottfried W.	1646	Logistic	Essentialist	Comprehensive
Harris, James	1709	Logistic	Essentialist	Comprehensive
Buckle, Henry	1821	Logistic	Essentialist	Comprehensive
Robinson, James Harvey	1863	Logistic	Essentialist	Comprehensive
Locke, John	1632	Logistic	Essentialist	Actional
Addison, Joseph	1672	Logistic	Essentialist	Actional
Niebuhr, Barthold Georg	1776	Logistic	Essentialist	Actional
Thomas Aquinas	1224	Problematic	Ontological	Reflexive
Albertus Magnus	1200	Problematic	Ontological	Actional
Langer, Susanne	1895	Problematic	Ontological	Actional
Stoics	–300	Problematic	Entitative	Comprehensive
Wilkins, John	1614	Problematic	Entitative	Comprehensive
Comte, Auguste	1798	Problematic	Entitative	Comprehensive
Ogden, Charles Kay	1889	Problematic	Entitative	Reflexive
Dewey, John	1859	Problematic	Entitative	Actional
Arnold, Matthew	1822	Problematic	Existentialist	Comprehensive
Polanyi, Michael	1891	Problematic	Existentialist	Comprehensive
James, William	1842	Problematic	Existentialist	Actional
Shelley, Percy Bysshe	1792	Problematic	Essentialist	Comprehensive
Piaget, Jean	1896	Problematic	Essentialist	Comprehensive
Aristotle	–384	Problematic	Essentialist	Reflexive
Montesquieu, Baron de	1689	Problematic	Essentialist	Actional

6. Grouped by Method and Principle

Name	DOB	Method	Principle	Interpretation
Plato	–428	Dialectical	Comprehensive	Ontological
Einstein, Albert	1879	Dialectical	Comprehensive	Entitative
Bosanquet, Bernard	1848	Dialectical	Comprehensive	Existentialist
Kubler, George A.	1912	Dialectical	Comprehensive	Essentialist
Bonaventura	1217	Dialectical	Reflexive	Ontological
Theophrastus	–371	Dialectical	Reflexive	Entitative
Bernard of Clairvaux	1090	Dialectical	Reflexive	Entitative
Hegel, Georg W. F.	1770	Dialectical	Reflexive	Entitative
Hanslick, Eduard	1825	Dialectical	Reflexive	Entitative
Bergson, Henri	1859	Dialectical	Reflexive	Entitative
Teilhard du Chardin, Pierre	1881	Dialectical	Reflexive	Entitative
Collingwood, Robin G.	1889	Dialectical	Reflexive	Existentialist
Parmenides	–515	Dialectical	Simple	Existentialist
Whitehead, Alfred North	1861	Dialectical	Simple	Existentialist
Plotinus	205	Dialectical	Simple	Essentialist
Augustine	354	Dialectical	Actional	Ontological
Schelling, Friedrich	1775	Dialectical	Actional	Ontological
Heraclitus	–540	Dialectical	Actional	Entitative
Malebranche, Nicolas de	1638	Dialectical	Actional	Entitative
Marx, Karl	1818	Dialectical	Actional	Entitative
Baier	1929	Dialectical	Actional	Entitative
Academy	–347	Dialectical	Actional	Existentialist
Croce, Benedetto	1866	Dialectical	Actional	Existentialist
Hare, Richard M.	1919	Dialectical	Actional	Existentialist
Philo	–20	Dialectical	Actional	Essentialist
Fichte, Johann	1762	Dialectical	Actional	Essentialist
Rameau, Jean-Philippe	1683	Operational	Comprehensive	Entitative
Voltaire	1694	Operational	Comprehensive	Entitative
Wordsworth, William	1770	Operational	Comprehensive	Entitative
Feuerbach, Ludwig	1804	Operational	Comprehensive	Entitative
Nietzsche, Friedrich W.	1844	Operational	Comprehensive	Entitative
Lorentz, Hendrick A.	1853	Operational	Comprehensive	Entitative
Stevens, Wallace	1879	Operational	Comprehensive	Entitative
Heidegger, Martin	1889	Operational	Comprehensive	Entitative
Wittgenstein, Ludwig	1889	Operational	Comprehensive	Entitative
Panofsky, Irwin	1892	Operational	Comprehensive	Entitative
Burke, Kenneth	1897	Operational	Comprehensive	Entitative
Foucault, Michel	1926	Operational	Comprehensive	Entitative
Academy, New	–213	Operational	Comprehensive	Existentialist
Cicero, Marcus Tullius	–106	Operational	Comprehensive	Existentialist
Leonardo da Vinci	1452	Operational	Comprehensive	Existentialist
Berkeley, George	1685	Operational	Comprehensive	Existentialist
Baumgarten, Alexander	1714	Operational	Comprehensive	Existentialist
Jaspers, Karl	1883	Operational	Comprehensive	Existentialist
Sartre, Jean-Paul	1905	Operational	Comprehensive	Existentialist
Hugh of St. Victor	1100	Operational	Comprehensive	Essentialist

Name	DOB	Method	Principle	Interpretation
Bacon, Roger	1220	Operational	Comprehensive	Essentialist
Lully, Raymond	1232	Operational	Comprehensive	Essentialist
La Bruyere, Jean de	1645	Operational	Comprehensive	Essentialist
Vico, Giovan Battista	1668	Operational	Comprehensive	Essentialist
Johnson, Samuel	1709	Operational	Comprehensive	Essentialist
Rousseau, Jean-Jacques	1712	Operational	Comprehensive	Essentialist
Tolstoi, Leo	1828	Operational	Comprehensive	Essentialist
Brentano, Franz	1838	Operational	Comprehensive	Essentialist
Frye, Northrop	1912	Operational	Comprehensive	Essentialist
Anselm	1033	Operational	Reflexive	Ontological
John of Salisbury	1115	Operational	Reflexive	Ontological
Grosseteste, Robert	1168	Operational	Reflexive	Ontological
Bacon, Francis	1561	Operational	Reflexive	Ontological
Bossuet, Jacques	1627	Operational	Reflexive	Ontological
Kant, Immanuel	1724	Operational	Reflexive	Ontological
Coleridge, Samuel T.	1772	Operational	Reflexive	Ontological
Schopenhauer, Arthur	1788	Operational	Reflexive	Ontological
Peirce, Charles Sanders	1839	Operational	Reflexive	Ontological
Frege, Gottlob	1848	Operational	Reflexive	Ontological
Husserl, Edmund	1859	Operational	Reflexive	Ontological
Moore, George E.	1873	Operational	Reflexive	Ontological
Ricoeur, Paul	1913	Operational	Reflexive	Ontological
Booth, Wayne	1921	Operational	Reflexive	Ontological
Thucydides	–460	Operational	Reflexive	Entitative
Demetrius Phalereus	–317	Operational	Reflexive	Entitative
Horace	–65	Operational	Reflexive	Entitative
Montaigne, Michel E. de	1533	Operational	Reflexive	Entitative
Galileo Galilei	1564	Operational	Reflexive	Entitative
Mandeville, Bernard de	1670	Operational	Reflexive	Entitative
Condorcet, Marquis de	1743	Operational	Reflexive	Entitative
Jefferson, Thomas	1743	Operational	Reflexive	Entitative
Cournot, Antoine A.	1801	Operational	Reflexive	Entitative
Darwin, Charles	1809	Operational	Reflexive	Entitative
Poincaré, Henri	1854	Operational	Reflexive	Entitative
Russell, Bertrand	1872	Operational	Reflexive	Entitative
Beard, Charles A.	1874	Operational	Reflexive	Entitative
Bridgman, Percy	1882	Operational	Reflexive	Entitative
Lewis, C. I.	1883	Operational	Reflexive	Entitative
Crane, Ronald S.	1886	Operational	Reflexive	Entitative
Machiavelli, Niccolò	1469	Operational	Reflexive	Existentialist
Milton, John	1608	Operational	Reflexive	Existentialist
Mill, John Stuart	1806	Operational	Reflexive	Existentialist
Empson, William	1906	Operational	Reflexive	Existentialist
Longinus	1	Operational	Simple	Ontological
Nicholas of Cusa	1401	Operational	Simple	Ontological
Adams, John	1735	Operational	Simple	Ontological
Hume, David	1711	Operational	Simple	Entitative
Heller, Joseph	1923	Operational	Simple	Existentialist
Lucretius	–96	Operational	Simple	Essentialist

Name	DOB	Method	Principle	Interpretation
Erigena, John Scotus	810	Operational	Actional	Entitative
Maxwell, James Clerk	1831	Operational	Actional	Entitative
Schrodinger, Erwin	1887	Operational	Actional	Entitative
Protagoras	–490	Operational	Actional	Existentialist
Cassirer, Ernst	1874	Operational	Actional	Essentialist
Merleau-Ponty, Maurice	1908	Operational	Actional	Essentialist
Austin, John L.	1911	Operational	Actional	Essentialist
Newton, Isaac	1642	Logistic	Comprehensive	Entitative
Galen	129	Logistic	Comprehensive	Existentialist
Leibniz, Gottfried W.	1646	Logistic	Comprehensive	Essentialist
Harris, James	1709	Logistic	Comprehensive	Essentialist
Buckle, Henry	1821	Logistic	Comprehensive	Essentialist
Robinson, James Harvey	1863	Logistic	Comprehensive	Essentialist
Spinoza, Baruch	1632	Logistic	Reflexive	Ontological
Epicurus	–341	Logistic	Reflexive	Entitative
Descartes, René	1596	Logistic	Reflexive	Existentialist
D'Alembert, Jean	1717	Logistic	Reflexive	Existentialist
Santayana, George	1863	Logistic	Reflexive	Existentialist
Cardozo, Benjamin	1870	Logistic	Reflexive	Existentialist
Democritus	–460	Logistic	Simple	Entitative
Boyle, Robert	1627	Logistic	Simple	Existentialist
Euclid	–300	Logistic	Actional	Ontological
Freud, Sigmund	1856	Logistic	Actional	Ontological
Hobbes, Thomas	1588	Logistic	Actional	Entitative
Ayer, Alfred J.	1910	Logistic	Actional	Entitative
Carnap, Rudolf	1891	Logistic	Actional	Existentialist
Richards, Ivor Armstrong	1893	Logistic	Actional	Existentialist
Ryle, Gilbert	1900	Logistic	Actional	Existentialist
Locke, John	1632	Logistic	Actional	Essentialist
Addison, Joseph	1672	Logistic	Actional	Essentialist
Niebuhr, Barthold Georg	1776	Logistic	Actional	Essentialist
Stoics	–300	Problematic	Comprehensive	Entitative
Wilkins, John	1614	Problematic	Comprehensive	Entitative
Comte, Auguste	1798	Problematic	Comprehensive	Entitative
Arnold, Matthew	1822	Problematic	Comprehensive	Existentialist
Polanyi, Michael	1891	Problematic	Comprehensive	Existentialist
Shelley, Percy Bysshe	1792	Problematic	Comprehensive	Essentialist
Piaget, Jean	1896	Problematic	Comprehensive	Essentialist
Thomas Aquinas	1224	Problematic	Reflexive	Ontological
Ogden, Charles Kay	1889	Problematic	Reflexive	Entitative
Aristotle	–384	Problematic	Reflexive	Essentialist
Albertus Magnus	1200	Problematic	Actional	Ontological
Langer, Susanne	1895	Problematic	Actional	Ontological
Dewey, John	1859	Problematic	Actional	Entitative
James, William	1842	Problematic	Actional	Existentialist
Montesquieu, Baron de	1689	Problematic	Actional	Essentialist

7. Grouped by Interpretation and Method

Name	DOB	Interpretation	Method	Principle
Plato	–428	Ontological	Dialectical	Comprehensive
Bonaventura	1217	Ontological	Dialectical	Reflexive
Augustine	354	Ontological	Dialectical	Actional
Schelling, Friedrich	1775	Ontological	Dialectical	Actional
Anselm	1033	Ontological	Operational	Reflexive
John of Salisbury	1115	Ontological	Operational	Reflexive
Grosseteste, Robert	1168	Ontological	Operational	Reflexive
Bacon, Francis	1561	Ontological	Operational	Reflexive
Bossuet, Jacques	1627	Ontological	Operational	Reflexive
Kant, Immanuel	1724	Ontological	Operational	Reflexive
Coleridge, Samuel T.	1772	Ontological	Operational	Reflexive
Schopenhauer, Arthur	1788	Ontological	Operational	Reflexive
Peirce, Charles Sanders	1839	Ontological	Operational	Reflexive
Frege, Gottlob	1848	Ontological	Operational	Reflexive
Husserl, Edmund	1859	Ontological	Operational	Reflexive
Moore, George E.	1873	Ontological	Operational	Reflexive
Ricoeur, Paul	1913	Ontological	Operational	Reflexive
Booth, Wayne	1921	Ontological	Operational	Reflexive
Longinus	1	Ontological	Operational	Simple
Nicholas of Cusa	1401	Ontological	Operational	Simple
Adams, John	1735	Ontological	Operational	Simple
Spinoza, Baruch	1632	Ontological	Logistic	Reflexive
Euclid	–300	Ontological	Logistic	Actional
Freud, Sigmund	1856	Ontological	Logistic	Actional
Thomas Aquinas	1224	Ontological	Problematic	Reflexive
Albertus Magnus	1200	Ontological	Problematic	Actional
Langer, Susanne	1895	Ontological	Problematic	Actional
Einstein, Albert	1879	Entitative	Dialectical	Comprehensive
Theophrastus	–371	Entitative	Dialectical	Reflexive
Bernard of Clairvaux	1090	Entitative	Dialectical	Reflexive
Hegel, Georg W. F.	1770	Entitative	Dialectical	Reflexive
Hanslick, Eduard	1825	Entitative	Dialectical	Reflexive
Bergson, Henri	1859	Entitative	Dialectical	Reflexive
Teilhard du Chardin, Pierre	1881	Entitative	Dialectical	Reflexive
Heraclitus	–540	Entitative	Dialectical	Actional
Malebranche, Nicolas de	1638	Entitative	Dialectical	Actional
Marx, Karl	1818	Entitative	Dialectical	Actional
Baier	1929	Entitative	Dialectical	Actional
Rameau, Jean-Philippe	1683	Entitative	Operational	Comprehensive
Voltaire	1694	Entitative	Operational	Comprehensive
Wordsworth, William	1770	Entitative	Operational	Comprehensive
Feuerbach, Ludwig	1804	Entitative	Operational	Comprehensive
Nietzsche, Friedrich W.	1844	Entitative	Operational	Comprehensive
Lorentz, Hendrick A.	1853	Entitative	Operational	Comprehensive
Stevens, Wallace	1879	Entitative	Operational	Comprehensive
Heidegger, Martin	1889	Entitative	Operational	Comprehensive

Name	DOB	Interpretation	Method	Principle
Wittgenstein, Ludwig	1889	Entitative	Operational	Comprehensive
Panofsky, Irwin	1892	Entitative	Operational	Comprehensive
Burke, Kenneth	1897	Entitative	Operational	Comprehensive
Foucault, Michel	1926	Entitative	Operational	Comprehensive
Thucydides	–460	Entitative	Operational	Reflexive
Demetrius Phalereus	–317	Entitative	Operational	Reflexive
Horace	–65	Entitative	Operational	Reflexive
Montaigne, Michel E. de	1533	Entitative	Operational	Reflexive
Galileo Galilei	1564	Entitative	Operational	Reflexive
Mandeville, Bernard de	1670	Entitative	Operational	Reflexive
Condorcet, Marquis de	1743	Entitative	Operational	Reflexive
Jefferson, Thomas	1743	Entitative	Operational	Reflexive
Cournot, Antoine A.	1801	Entitative	Operational	Reflexive
Darwin, Charles	1809	Entitative	Operational	Reflexive
Poincaré, Henri	1854	Entitative	Operational	Reflexive
Russell, Bertrand	1872	Entitative	Operational	Reflexive
Beard, Charles A.	1874	Entitative	Operational	Reflexive
Bridgman, Percy	1882	Entitative	Operational	Reflexive
Lewis, C. I.	1883	Entitative	Operational	Reflexive
Crane, Ronald S.	1886	Entitative	Operational	Reflexive
Hume, David	1711	Entitative	Operational	Simple
Erigena, John Scotus	810	Entitative	Operational	Actional
Maxwell, James Clerk	1831	Entitative	Operational	Actional
Schrodinger, Erwin	1887	Entitative	Operational	Actional
Newton, Isaac	1642	Entitative	Logistic	Comprehensive
Epicurus	–341	Entitative	Logistic	Reflexive
Democritus	–460	Entitative	Logistic	Simple
Hobbes, Thomas	1588	Entitative	Logistic	Actional
Ayer, Alfred J.	1910	Entitative	Logistic	Actional
Stoics	–300	Entitative	Problematic	Comprehensive
Wilkins, John	1614	Entitative	Problematic	Comprehensive
Comte, Auguste	1798	Entitative	Problematic	Comprehensive
Ogden, Charles Kay	1889	Entitative	Problematic	Reflexive
Dewey, John	1859	Entitative	Problematic	Actional
Bosanquet, Bernard	1848	Existentialist	Dialectical	Comprehensive
Collingwood, Robin G.	1889	Existentialist	Dialectical	Reflexive
Parmenides	–515	Existentialist	Dialectical	Simple
Whitehead, Alfred North	1861	Existentialist	Dialectical	Simple
Academy	–347	Existentialist	Dialectical	Actional
Croce, Benedetto	1866	Existentialist	Dialectical	Actional
Hare, Richard M.	1919	Existentialist	Dialectical	Actional
Academy, New	–213	Existentialist	Operational	Comprehensive
Cicero, Marcus Tullius	–106	Existentialist	Operational	Comprehensive
Leonardo da Vinci	1452	Existentialist	Operational	Comprehensive
Berkeley, George	1685	Existentialist	Operational	Comprehensive
Baumgarten, Alexander	1714	Existentialist	Operational	Comprehensive
Jaspers, Karl	1883	Existentialist	Operational	Comprehensive
Sartre, Jean-Paul	1905	Existentialist	Operational	Comprehensive
Machiavelli, Niccolò	1469	Existentialist	Operational	Reflexive

Name	DOB	Interpretation	Method	Principle
Milton, John	1608	Existentialist	Operational	Reflexive
Mill, John Stuart	1806	Existentialist	Operational	Reflexive
Empson, William	1906	Existentialist	Operational	Reflexive
Heller, Joseph	1923	Existentialist	Operational	Simple
Protagoras	–490	Existentialist	Operational	Actional
Galen	129	Existentialist	Logistic	Comprehensive
Descartes, René	1596	Existentialist	Logistic	Reflexive
D'Alembert, Jean	1717	Existentialist	Logistic	Reflexive
Santayana, George	1863	Existentialist	Logistic	Reflexive
Cardozo, Benjamin	1870	Existentialist	Logistic	Reflexive
Boyle, Robert	1627	Existentialist	Logistic	Simple
Carnap, Rudolf	1891	Existentialist	Logistic	Actional
Richards, Ivor Armstrong	1893	Existentialist	Logistic	Actional
Ryle, Gilbert	1900	Existentialist	Logistic	Actional
Arnold, Matthew	1822	Existentialist	Problematic	Comprehensive
Polanyi, Michael	1891	Existentialist	Problematic	Comprehensive
James, William	1842	Existentialist	Problematic	Actional
Kubler, George A.	1912	Essentialist	Dialectical	Comprehensive
Plotinus	205	Essentialist	Dialectical	Simple
Philo	–20	Essentialist	Dialectical	Actional
Fichte, Johann	1762	Essentialist	Dialectical	Actional
Hugh of St. Victor	1100	Essentialist	Operational	Comprehensive
Bacon, Roger	1220	Essentialist	Operational	Comprehensive
Lully, Raymond	1232	Essentialist	Operational	Comprehensive
La Bruyere, Jean de	1645	Essentialist	Operational	Comprehensive
Vico, Giovan Battista	1668	Essentialist	Operational	Comprehensive
Johnson, Samuel	1709	Essentialist	Operational	Comprehensive
Rousseau, Jean-Jacques	1712	Essentialist	Operational	Comprehensive
Tolstoi, Leo	1828	Essentialist	Operational	Comprehensive
Brentano, Franz	1838	Essentialist	Operational	Comprehensive
Frye, Northrop	1912	Essentialist	Operational	Comprehensive
Lucretius	–96	Essentialist	Operational	Simple
Cassirer, Ernst	1874	Essentialist	Operational	Actional
Merleau-Ponty, Maurice	1908	Essentialist	Operational	Actional
Austin, John L.	1911	Essentialist	Operational	Actional
Leibniz, Gottfried W.	1646	Essentialist	Logistic	Comprehensive
Harris, James	1709	Essentialist	Logistic	Comprehensive
Buckle, Henry	1821	Essentialist	Logistic	Comprehensive
Robinson, James Harvey	1863	Essentialist	Logistic	Comprehensive
Locke, John	1632	Essentialist	Logistic	Actional
Addison, Joseph	1672	Essentialist	Logistic	Actional
Niebuhr, Barthold Georg	1776	Essentialist	Logistic	Actional
Shelley, Percy Bysshe	1792	Essentialist	Problematic	Comprehensive
Piaget, Jean	1896	Essentialist	Problematic	Comprehensive
Aristotle	–384	Essentialist	Problematic	Reflexive
Montesquieu, Baron de	1689	Essentialist	Problematic	Actional

8. Grouped by Interpretation and Principle

Name	DOB	Interpretation	Principle	Method
Plato	−428	Ontological	Comprehensive	Dialectical
Bonaventura	1217	Ontological	Reflexive	Dialectical
Anselm	1033	Ontological	Reflexive	Operational
John of Salisbury	1115	Ontological	Reflexive	Operational
Grosseteste, Robert	1168	Ontological	Reflexive	Operational
Bacon, Francis	1561	Ontological	Reflexive	Operational
Bossuet, Jacques	1627	Ontological	Reflexive	Operational
Kant, Immanuel	1724	Ontological	Reflexive	Operational
Coleridge, Samuel T.	1772	Ontological	Reflexive	Operational
Schopenhauer, Arthur	1788	Ontological	Reflexive	Operational
Peirce, Charles Sanders	1839	Ontological	Reflexive	Operational
Frege, Gottlob	1848	Ontological	Reflexive	Operational
Husserl, Edmund	1859	Ontological	Reflexive	Operational
Moore, George E.	1873	Ontological	Reflexive	Operational
Ricoeur, Paul	1913	Ontological	Reflexive	Operational
Booth, Wayne	1921	Ontological	Reflexive	Operational
Spinoza, Baruch	1632	Ontological	Reflexive	Logistic
Thomas Aquinas	1224	Ontological	Reflexive	Problematic
Longinus	1	Ontological	Simple	Operational
Nicholas of Cusa	1401	Ontological	Simple	Operational
Adams, John	1735	Ontological	Simple	Operational
Augustine	354	Ontological	Actional	Dialectical
Schelling, Friedrich	1775	Ontological	Actional	Dialectical
Euclid	−300	Ontological	Actional	Logistic
Freud, Sigmund	1856	Ontological	Actional	Logistic
Albertus Magnus	1200	Ontological	Actional	Problematic
Langer, Susanne	1895	Ontological	Actional	Problematic
Einstein, Albert	1879	Entitative	Comprehensive	Dialectical
Rameau, Jean-Philippe	1683	Entitative	Comprehensive	Operational
Voltaire	1694	Entitative	Comprehensive	Operational
Wordsworth, William	1770	Entitative	Comprehensive	Operational
Feuerbach, Ludwig	1804	Entitative	Comprehensive	Operational
Nietzsche, Friedrich W.	1844	Entitative	Comprehensive	Operational
Lorentz, Hendrick A.	1853	Entitative	Comprehensive	Operational
Stevens, Wallace	1879	Entitative	Comprehensive	Operational
Heidegger, Martin	1889	Entitative	Comprehensive	Operational
Wittgenstein, Ludwig	1889	Entitative	Comprehensive	Operational
Panofsky, Irwin	1892	Entitative	Comprehensive	Operational
Burke, Kenneth	1897	Entitative	Comprehensive	Operational
Foucault, Michel	1926	Entitative	Comprehensive	Operational
Newton, Isaac	1642	Entitative	Comprehensive	Logistic
Stoics	−300	Entitative	Comprehensive	Problematic
Wilkins, John	1614	Entitative	Comprehensive	Problematic
Comte, Auguste	1798	Entitative	Comprehensive	Problematic
Theophrastus	−371	Entitative	Reflexive	Dialectical
Bernard of Clairvaux	1090	Entitative	Reflexive	Dialectical

Name	DOB	Interpretation	Principle	Method
Hegel, Georg W. F.	1770	Entitative	Reflexive	Dialectical
Hanslick, Eduard	1825	Entitative	Reflexive	Dialectical
Bergson, Henri	1859	Entitative	Reflexive	Dialectical
Teilhard du Chardin, Pierre	1881	Entitative	Reflexive	Dialectical
Thucydides	–460	Entitative	Reflexive	Operational
Demetrius Phalereus	–317	Entitative	Reflexive	Operational
Horace	–65	Entitative	Reflexive	Operational
Montaigne, Michel E. de	1533	Entitative	Reflexive	Operational
Galileo Galilei	1564	Entitative	Reflexive	Operational
Mandeville, Bernard de	1670	Entitative	Reflexive	Operational
Condorcet, Marquis de	1743	Entitative	Reflexive	Operational
Jefferson, Thomas	1743	Entitative	Reflexive	Operational
Cournot, Antoine A.	1801	Entitative	Reflexive	Operational
Darwin, Charles	1809	Entitative	Reflexive	Operational
Poincaré, Henri	1854	Entitative	Reflexive	Operational
Russell, Bertrand	1872	Entitative	Reflexive	Operational
Beard, Charles A.	1874	Entitative	Reflexive	Operational
Bridgman, Percy	1882	Entitative	Reflexive	Operational
Lewis, C. I.	1883	Entitative	Reflexive	Operational
Crane, Ronald S.	1886	Entitative	Reflexive	Operational
Epicurus	–341	Entitative	Reflexive	Logistic
Ogden, Charles Kay	1889	Entitative	Reflexive	Problematic
Hume, David	1711	Entitative	Simple	Operational
Democritus	–460	Entitative	Simple	Logistic
Heraclitus	–540	Entitative	Actional	Dialectical
Malebranche, Nicolas de	1638	Entitative	Actional	Dialectical
Marx, Karl	1818	Entitative	Actional	Dialectical
Baier	1929	Entitative	Actional	Dialectical
Erigena, John Scotus	810	Entitative	Actional	Operational
Maxwell, James Clerk	1831	Entitative	Actional	Operational
Schrodinger, Erwin	1887	Entitative	Actional	Operational
Hobbes, Thomas	1588	Entitative	Actional	Logistic
Ayer, Alfred J.	1910	Entitative	Actional	Logistic
Dewey, John	1859	Entitative	Actional	Problematic
Bosanquet, Bernard	1848	Existentialist	Comprehensive	Dialectical
Academy, New	–213	Existentialist	Comprehensive	Operational
Cicero, Marcus Tullius	–106	Existentialist	Comprehensive	Operational
Leonardo da Vinci	1452	Existentialist	Comprehensive	Operational
Berkeley, George	1685	Existentialist	Comprehensive	Operational
Baumgarten, Alexander	1714	Existentialist	Comprehensive	Operational
Jaspers, Karl	1883	Existentialist	Comprehensive	Operational
Sartre, Jean-Paul	1905	Existentialist	Comprehensive	Operational
Galen	129	Existentialist	Comprehensive	Logistic
Arnold, Matthew	1822	Existentialist	Comprehensive	Problematic
Polanyi, Michael	1891	Existentialist	Comprehensive	Problematic
Collingwood, Robin G.	1889	Existentialist	Reflexive	Dialectical
Machiavelli, Niccolò	1469	Existentialist	Reflexive	Operational
Milton, John	1608	Existentialist	Reflexive	Operational
Mill, John Stuart	1806	Existentialist	Reflexive	Operational

Name	DOB	Interpretation	Principle	Method
Empson, William	1906	Existentialist	Reflexive	Operational
Descartes, René	1596	Existentialist	Reflexive	Logistic
D'Alembert, Jean	1717	Existentialist	Reflexive	Logistic
Santayana, George	1863	Existentialist	Reflexive	Logistic
Cardozo, Benjamin	1870	Existentialist	Reflexive	Logistic
Parmenides	–515	Existentialist	Simple	Dialectical
Whitehead, Alfred North	1861	Existentialist	Simple	Dialectical
Heller, Joseph	1923	Existentialist	Simple	Operational
Boyle, Robert	1627	Existentialist	Simple	Logistic
Academy	–347	Existentialist	Actional	Dialectical
Croce, Benedetto	1866	Existentialist	Actional	Dialectical
Hare, Richard M.	1919	Existentialist	Actional	Dialectical
Protagoras	–490	Existentialist	Actional	Operational
Carnap, Rudolf	1891	Existentialist	Actional	Logistic
Richards, Ivor Armstrong	1893	Existentialist	Actional	Logistic
Ryle, Gilbert	1900	Existentialist	Actional	Logistic
James, William	1842	Existentialist	Actional	Problematic
Kubler, George A.	1912	Essentialist	Comprehensive	Dialectical
Hugh of St. Victor	1100	Essentialist	Comprehensive	Operational
Bacon, Roger	1220	Essentialist	Comprehensive	Operational
Lully, Raymond	1232	Essentialist	Comprehensive	Operational
La Bruyere, Jean de	1645	Essentialist	Comprehensive	Operational
Vico, Giovan Battista	1668	Essentialist	Comprehensive	Operational
Johnson, Samuel	1709	Essentialist	Comprehensive	Operational
Rousseau, Jean-Jacques	1712	Essentialist	Comprehensive	Operational
Tolstoi, Leo	1828	Essentialist	Comprehensive	Operational
Brentano, Franz	1838	Essentialist	Comprehensive	Operational
Frye, Northrop	1912	Essentialist	Comprehensive	Operational
Leibniz, Gottfried W.	1646	Essentialist	Comprehensive	Logistic
Harris, James	1709	Essentialist	Comprehensive	Logistic
Buckle, Henry	1821	Essentialist	Comprehensive	Logistic
Robinson, James Harvey	1863	Essentialist	Comprehensive	Logistic
Shelley, Percy Bysshe	1792	Essentialist	Comprehensive	Problematic
Piaget, Jean	1896	Essentialist	Comprehensive	Problematic
Aristotle	–384	Essentialist	Reflexive	Problematic
Plotinus	205	Essentialist	Simple	Dialectical
Lucretius	–96	Essentialist	Simple	Operational
Philo	–20	Essentialist	Actional	Dialectical
Fichte, Johann	1762	Essentialist	Actional	Dialectical
Cassirer, Ernst	1874	Essentialist	Actional	Operational
Merleau-Ponty, Maurice	1908	Essentialist	Actional	Operational
Austin, John L.	1911	Essentialist	Actional	Operational
Locke, John	1632	Essentialist	Actional	Logistic
Addison, Joseph	1672	Essentialist	Actional	Logistic
Niebuhr, Barthold Georg	1776	Essentialist	Actional	Logistic
Montesquieu, Baron de	1689	Essentialist	Actional	Problematic

APPENDIX K

Alternative Definitions of *Freedom, Power,* and *History*[1]

Ambiguous Definition: "Freedom is the power to act without external hindrance."
Ambiguous Definition: "Power is the condition or possibility of originating rather than undergoing change."
Ambiguous Definition: "History is the account of happenings or sequences or structures past, present, or future."

Possible specifications of what freedom, power, and history mean:

Mode of Thought	Term	Principle	sets conditions to	Method	which results in	Interpretation	of Selection
Assimilation	Freedom:	Autonomy	. . .	choose rightly	. . .	wisdom	. . . rational beings
	Power:	Wisdom	. . .	order	. . .	energy/Being	
	History:	Wholeness	. . .	connect rationally (epochal history)	. . .	forms	
Resolution	Freedom:	Self-Rule	. . .	deliberate	. . .	voluntary action	. . . humans
	Power:	Realization	. . .	actualize	. . .	potentiality	
	History:	Self-Causation	. . .	connect essentially (disciplinary history)	. . .	facts	
Construction	Freedom:	Nature	. . .	act naturally	. . .	unimpeded motion	. . . things
	Power:	Nature	. . .	move	. . .	force	
	History:	Motion	. . .	connect mechanically (causal history)	. . .	processes	
Discrimination	Freedom:	Power	. . .	choose	. . .	spontaneous behavior	. . . animals
	Power:	Action	. . .	initiate	. . .	possibility	
	History:	Agency	. . .	connect technically (exemplary history)	. . .	acts	

NOTES

Foreword

1. New York: Longmans, Green, 1928.

2. Alan Gewirth, "Richard Peter McKeon (1900–1985)," *Proceedings of the American Philosophical Association* 58, no. 5 (June 1985): 751–52.

3. For an extended introduction to the full range of McKeon's work, see the website www.richardmckeon.org.

4. Gewirth, "Richard Peter McKeon," 752. For sources regarding the sketch of Chicago's curriculum history that follows, see the following:

Bell, Daniel. *The Reforming of General Education: The Columbia College Experience in Its National Setting*. Garden City, NY: Anchor Books, 1968. Orig. pub. 1966.

Callahan, John F. "Richard Peter McKeon (1900–1985)." *Journal of the History of Ideas* 47, no. 4 (October–December 1986): 653–62.

Conley, Thomas M. "The Virtues of Controversy: In Memoriam R. P. McKeon." *Quarterly Journal of Speech* 71, no. 4 (November 1985): 470–75.

Gewirth, Alan. "Richard Peter McKeon (1900–1985)." *Proceedings of the American Philosophical Association* 58, no. 5 (June 1985): 751–52.

Hauser, Gerard. "Richard P. McKeon." In *Thinkers of the Twentieth Century: A Biographical, Bibliographical and Critical Dictionary*, edited by Elizabeth Devine, Michael Held, James Vinson, and George Walsh, 376–77. London: Macmillan, 1983.

Present and Former Members of the Faculty, University of Chicago. *The Idea and Practice of General Education: An Account of the College of the University of Chicago*. Chicago: University of Chicago Press, 1950.

Press, Jacques Cattell, ed. *Directory of American Scholars*. Vol. 4, *Philosophy, Religion, and Law*. New York: R. R. Bowker, 1982.

5. Richard McKeon, *On Knowing—The Natural Sciences*, ed. David B. Owen and Zahava K. McKeon (Chicago: University of Chicago Press, 1994). See the beginning of the first lecture for McKeon's account both of the relations among

the three courses (especially endnote 1) and of the approach he is making to philosophic controversies.

Ultimately, this cycle of three courses will act as an introduction to the full range of McKeon's philosophy. Planning is also under way to publish a second group of courses given close to the end of his teaching career that provides an advanced overview of his whole philosophy. Given in 1972 and 1973, those latter courses treat issues, respectively, of topics, hypotheses, themes, and inquiry. Together, the two sets of courses will provide a thorough guide to understanding the roughly 160 articles he published, a number of which have been republished in *The Selected Writings of Richard McKeon*, ed. Zahava K. McKeon and William G. Swenson, vol. 1, *Philosophy, Science, and Culture* (Chicago: University of Chicago Press, 1998); vol. 2, *Culture, Education, and the Arts* (Chicago: University of Chicago Press, 2005); and vol. 3 (forthcoming).

6. The notes prepared for both the lectures and the discussions of the different readings in the numerous versions of each of the three courses still exist, and are preserved in the University of Chicago Archives at Regenstein Library as part of McKeon's Collection of Papers. A general listing of them can be located on the Internet at http://www.lib.uchicago.edu/e/scrc/findingaids/view.php?eadid=ICU.SPCL.RPMCKEON&q=richard%20mckeon%20papers.

To suggest something of his "extraordinary energy and creativity" just mentioned, one of the editors (Owen) would like to report that in the early 1990s, in preparation for this project, he was granted permission by McKeon's widow, Zahava McKeon, to examine the note files in his library at McKeon's house. In the filing drawers filled with notes prepared for classes from the 1930s onward, he found roughly fourteen thousand pages of single-spaced, typed sheets of paper. These were only the materials prepared for teaching and did not include McKeon's reading notes, his correspondence, or his manuscripts, which were stored in other, equally massive filing drawers. In addition, it should be added that at the graduate level, he virtually never taught the same course twice.

7. In the 1960s and 1970s, tape recordings were made of numerous McKeon courses, independent lectures, and miscellaneous discussions by quite a few students, undergraduate and graduate, and were shared among students, usually those in I&M. During that period, one of the editors (Owen) collected copies of a number of these tape recordings, and has had them in his possession since. (Ultimately, they will be given to the McKeon Archives in Regenstein Library at the University of Chicago.) Unfortunately, the recordings used here for this class were originally made by an unknown student.

McKeon permitted students to use portable tape recorders to record his remarks in a variety of public presentations. These devices included those using 3-inch-diameter, 5-inch, and 7-inch reels of tape that varied in thickness and quality. Print-through of magnetic fields recording the sound could be a serious problem on the thinner thicknesses of tape when it was wound up upon itself, and inexpensive tape would frequently become brittle and could even break over time. Fortunately, the recordings for this course were made on quality tape and a good machine. Consequently, the transfer to digital sound allowed for a good recording from which to make these transcripts. Yet because the original recording was not a professional one, made in a sound-controlled environment—one can frequently hear a truck passing or steam heat knocking in a radiator!—and because the microphone was not always ideally placed, in a number of instances it is difficult to hear what McKeon is saying, especially when he turns away from the students to write on the blackboard at the front of the class, or to hear what students are saying during discussions, given that they are frequently behind the microphone or on the other side of the classroom from it.

8. For a brief description of these changes in the complete introductory Ideas and Methods sequence, see the foreword and lecture 1, endnote 1, in McKeon, *On Knowing—The Natural Sciences*.

9. For a number of possible individual profiles, the editors have created appendix J.

LECTURE 1. Philosophic Problems in the Social Sciences

1. Since the first meeting of this class was in a room other than the one specified in the University's official *Time Schedule*, which listed the initial time and location for each course, a number of students missed the first lecture. A result of the confusion is that apparently, no one made a tape recording of this introductory lecture. Consequently, what follows in this lecture is based on McKeon's own typed notes for the lecture found in his files. These notes are identified as "Concepts and Methods 202 (VIII)" and were originally prepared for the 1963 version of the course, version VIII being chronologically the last set of notes found in his files prepared for this introductory lecture; to them, the editors have made minor, stylistic changes for ease in reading. These notes have been supplemented by class notes kept by students, and those student notes conform closely to those McKeon prepared for class, both in structure and in content, with the single exception described in endnote 10 below. For a general description of McKeon's and students' class notes and how the editors have used them, see the foreword.

2. These four problems—motion, space, time, and cause—are the focus of the lectures and discussions in McKeon's *On Knowing—The Natural Sciences, ed. David B. Owen and Zahava K. McKeon (Chicago: University of Chicago Press, 1994)*. For a brief description of the individuals McKeon mentions both here and throughout in these lectures and discussions, see appendix B.

3. Though McKeon does not mention it in the lecture, he views "data" the same way he views "fact," which he discusses in the next paragraph. He would frequently remind students that "data" is the plural form of the past participle, *datum*, from the Latin verb *do*, "to give." Data, therefore, are particulars one human selects or creates out of the infinite variety of possibilities to give to others; they are not simply what nature self-evidently reveals to us.

4. "Fact" comes from the Latin *factum*, the past participle of the verb *facio*, "to make."

5. Classic syllogistic reasoning is based on the work of Aristotle, who first formulated this kind of logic. A famous example of a syllogism is: "All men are

mortal; Socrates is a man; therefore, Socrates is mortal." In this syllogism, two terms, one general (*mortality*) and one particular (*Socrates*), are bound together by a middle term (*man*), which joins them in a necessary relationship.

6. The adjective "compendent" is derived from the Latin *cum* + *pendere*, meaning literally "to hang with" or "to hang together," and by extension, "to be weighed or valued together."

7. To summarize the previous five paragraphs, the editors have constructed table 1, which does not appear in student notes. For another brief discussion of this approach to definition, see McKeon, *On Knowing—The Natural Sciences*, pp. 66–67.

8. The editors have constructed table 2 from the paragraph. It is not in student notes.

9. McKeon never treated selection as the beginning question in the set of courses introductory to the natural sciences, social sciences, and humanities because it is unusually difficult to deal with. As he says later, in the opening of lecture 5, selection is a matter of single terms; therefore, anything one says about selection immediately involves one in a proposition, that is, in interpretation, and any clarification of that proposition necessarily involves method and eventually leads to principle. Given this inherent difficulty of treating selection in isolation, McKeon always introduces selection last in these introductory courses, after the other three questions have been elaborated.

10. Here begins a brief treatment of modes of thought, a key concept in McKeon's semantic analysis. In the next lecture—which, unlike this, has been recorded on tape—he states that he has already treated these modes in this first lecture; but student notes for this first lecture give no indication of any such exposition, though they do identify the respective mode of thought, using that phrase, related to each of the four methods. Here, then, McKeon may not have followed his own notes exactly. Consequently, the editors have inserted this and the following three paragraphs directly from the second page of the version VIII notes used for this introductory lecture (see endnote 1 for a description of those lecture notes).

11. Figure 1, the "knowledge matrix," appears in student notes for lecture 2 (at the beginning), though not for lecture 1. The editors have introduced it here to help the reader see the basic structure on which is based the ensuing discussion of the four modes of thought. This matrix of cognate terms of knowing is at the heart of McKeon's semantic analysis, both here and in his many courses and writings from the 1950s onward. In the matrix, the terms function as empty variables which have no value, no meaning, until they are put into relation with other terms. This idea of terms as variables or distinctions which are meaningless until employed is a fundamental reason for McKeon's use of matrices. As he says in the preceding paragraph in the text, the matrix is intended to be a "pre-philosophic set of distinctions"; and out of each matrix—from the Latin *mater*, "mother"—can be born a semantic analysis which treats all positions descriptively, equivalently, and without prejudgment. (For an extended discussion of antecedent matrices in the development of McKeon's thought, see George Kimball Plochmann, *Richard McKeon: A Study* [Chicago: University of Chicago Press, 1990]).

This *Ur*-matrix represented by figure 1 will appear in a variety of transformations throughout the following lectures, each transformation reflecting the application of new sets of distinctions to generate new terms while simultaneously retaining the same structure of relations among the terms thereby distinguished. As an example, the editors have constructed figure 2 to summarize the characteristic orientation of each position in the matrix as it was stated earlier in this paragraph in the text. In addition, figure 2's relation to the text should not only alert the reader to the precise parallelism with which McKeon constructs his arguments but also suggest how he should be read. The careful reader can very often find some transformation of the knowledge matrix underlying a series of expressions, whether that series be composed of single terms, phrases, clauses, sentences, paragraphs, or even groups of paragraphs. This is because McKeon expresses his meaning by laying down an arbitrary set of distinctions—frequently ones derived from the knowledge matrix—and then making a disciplined exploration of relations among them, not by laying down unambiguous definitions at the beginning and thereafter deducing consequences from them. As he will explain below, this is the difference between, respectively, the operational and the logistic methods (see endnote 15 below).

12. The editors have constructed figures 3 and 4 to show, respectively, the relationships among the four modes of thought and the relationship between each mode of thought and its typical form of expression, all set forth according to their respective locations in the knowledge matrix (fig. 1).

13. In effect, McKeon has constructed a simple 4 × 4 table or schematism—four questions, each of which independently permits four variants derived from the modes of thought—which gives rise to 256 (4^4) different lines of possible philosophic argumentation (for the full table of distinctions, see appendix D). This complexity is useful in providing not only a subtle refinement in the semantic analysis of existing arguments from the past but also a heuristic guidance in the creation of new arguments to deal with problems encountered in the present and future. This latter aspect—the prospective, creative character, as distinct from the retrospective, analytic one—has been frequently overlooked in responses to McKeon's work.

With the conclusion of this paragraph, the text returns to the 1965 lecture as recorded in student notes while at the same time continuing uninterruptedly in the sequence of McKeon's own notes from version VIII.

14. As he mentioned earlier, instead of beginning the philosophic analysis with the formal issues of method and the material issues of the "closely related" modes of *thought*, one could begin the analysis formally with principles and materially with modes of *being* or, alternatively, begin formally with interpretation and materially with modes of *fact*. For a highly concentrated overview of the relations between, on the one hand, principle, method, interpretation, and selection and, on the other, respectively, the modes of being, thought, fact, and simplicity, see McKeon's 1966 paper entitled, "Philosophic Semantics and Philosophic Inquiry," first published posthumously in Richard McKeon, *Freedom and History and Other Essays: An Introduction to the Thought of Richard McKeon*, ed. Zahava K. McKeon (Chicago: University of Chicago Press, 1990), 242–56. For the schematism based on the modes of thought, see appendix D.

15. The preceding description of the operational method, particularly the concluding sentence, shows that McKeon is himself using the operational method and the mode of thought discrimination (he is explicit about this at the end of lecture 2). He is thereby able to develop his philosophic semantics in such a way as to keep clear the intellectual distinctions at the heart of debates in the history of ideas.

16. Figure 5 is based on student notes for the beginning of lecture 2, which include the basic knowledge matrix, the terms *universal* and *particular* appropriately placed, and the connecting lines. For clarity, the editors have emphasized the appropriate method terms with capitals and put the associated knowledge matrix terms in parentheses. In this and all subsequent figures, the arrowheads point *toward* the basic term.

17. McKeon is presumably referring in the *Elements* to the discussion following proposition 18 at the end of book XIII, where Euclid demonstrates that only five solid figures can be composed of "equilateral and equiangular figures equal to each other." He does that by building up from the simplest examples to the most complex. In the preceding books, he has already constructed complex plane and solid figures out of their simplest forms, which are themselves constructed out of various kinds of lines, which, in turn, as he states in his definitions at the beginning of book I, are themselves constructed out of points, the ultimate "elements." Continuing that method here at the end of book XIII, he begins with the equilateral triangle—the three lines of the triangle are the minimum needed to make a two-dimensional figure—and builds up from three triangles—the minimum needed to make a three-dimensional figure—to four, then to five, at which point he reaches the most complex possible construction, showing that solids composed of equilateral triangles are not possible beyond. Next, he applies the same process to squares, then to pentagons. At this point, he can demonstrate that equiangular, equilateral polygons with more than five sides cannot be used to create solid figures. This method, which McKeon calls logistic, is commonly described as the deductive, reductive, or analytic method.

18. A transliteration of the Greek word, which means a blocked path or passage.

19. This grouping of methods into two pairs, the universal and the particular (see fig. 5), points to the fact that McKeon is himself using the operational method throughout these lectures, as he acknowledges in a brief discussion with students at the end of lecture 2. Briefly, the method works as follows: among the four arbitrary variables of the original knowledge matrix (which could just as easily be four letters—A, B, C, D—or four numbers—1, 2, 3, 4—as four terms), three sets of pairings logically exhaust the possible relationships, allowing each term to be related both once to every other term and once within every set. In the next three lectures, consequently, McKeon explores each possible set of relations (see fig. 1); that is, lecture 2 examines the set of pairs devoted to method (knowledge/knower; knowable/known), lecture 3 examines the set devoted to interpretation (knowledge/knowable; knower/known), and lecture 4 examines the set devoted to principle (knowledge/known; knower/knowable). As is typical of the operational method, a method of arbitrary

distinction permits each of the terms or variables to take on meaning as, first, each is grouped together with one other term and that pair is explored as a whole in its relation to the remaining pair of terms in that particular set of two pairs; and then, second, each term or variable within each pair is explored in its relation to the other member of that pair, each of these activities examining both similarities and differences. As McKeon will note later on, the test of such a method's value lies in its utility, in whether it allows one to see something more clearly than before, to discover simplicity where previously complexity existed, to resolve a problem that up to that time was insolvable, or to comprehend something that was apparently contradictory.

20. The editors have constructed figure 6.

21. For an alternative to the present formal and topical approach to beginning an introduction to the social sciences, see the material orientation McKeon took in the immediately earlier versions of this course sketched out in appendix C.

22. For the specific readings chosen from Hobbes's *Leviathan*, see the discussion of Hobbes, part 1, endnote 1, as well as appendix E.

LECTURE 2. Freedom: Method

1. For the confusion over where the course was meeting, see lecture 1, endnote 1.

2. The University's *Time Schedule*, published each academic quarter, listed course titles plus the times and location(s) of class meetings. Thus, at this point in his lecture, McKeon briefly repeats the mechanics of the sequence of class meetings.

McKEON: The course will meet three times a week, not two times a week. The place for discussion will be Swift [Hall] 201 on Monday and Friday; Wednesday I will lecture in this room [*i.e.*, Swift Hall 200]. My lectures will be open freely to visitors.

3. Instead of *freedom*, McKeon here says the word *liberty*, the term he used for "freedom" in the previous versions of this course.

4. Not being immediately able to find chalk for the blackboard, McKeon interrupts himself at this point to comment to the class, "I have to write with my finger!"

5. Table 3 is not in student notes. The editors have created it to clarify McKeon's distinctions in method.

6. References, respectively, to Nietzsche and Wittgenstein.

7. For McKeon's approach to Plato's *Timaeus*, see his discussions and comments on it in the previous volume, *On Knowing—The Natural Sciences., ed. David B. Owen and Zahava K. McKeon (Chicago: University of Chicago Press, 1994).* }

8. Figure 7 is in one student's notes.

9. This may well be an allusion to the nationwide student movement which, already quite active by 1965, frequently used the term *dialogue* to describe

their attempts to get university administrations to redefine the proper role of the university in supporting social justice in the larger society. Only a few years later, in 1968, McKeon's own university was to be shut down by such student protests.

10. McKeon also briefly discusses Bridgman's views at several points in the previous volume, McKeon, *On Knowing—The Natural Sciences*.

11. A reference to Freud.

12. For example, Lucretius presented his philosophic ideas in poetic form.

13. The locations and periods of these men's lives is central to McKeon's point here. See his discussions of these individuals in McKeon, *On Knowing—The Natural Sciences*.

14. Pressed for time, McKeon does not discuss here how the particular methods' plurality applies to the problematic approach. In his notes for the 1963 version (VIII) of this course, however, he did. There he states that for the problematic method, because the problems encountered are different in *kind*, they require different modes of solution. As a result, three broad, fundamentally different, scientific fields must be distinguished: namely, the theoretic, practical, and productive sciences, each having its own characteristic kind of method. McKeon often remarked that this threefold problematic distinction, originally made by Aristotle, is broadly reflected in the modern university's conventional division of knowledge into the natural sciences, social sciences, and humanities, though that division has tended to collapse in the latter half of the twentieth century into a division between science and humanities, reflecting a logistic conception of method.

15. Table 3 summarizes the consequences that the differences of method have on the definition of *freedom*. As a result, the reader may see more clearly that from the perspective of method, as is noted in the middle of this paragraph, freedom can increase or decrease the scope of its reference, moving between a very broad conception—acting according to nature—through more restrictive ones—first choice, and then deliberation—until reaching its narrowest base—right use of choice. McKeon often characterized these shifts in the breadth of meaning of a term as being like a handheld fan fully open, partially open, or fully closed. This issue of varying breadth is treated more extensively in lecture 3, on interpretation.

16. In 1965, bells were rung in classrooms to signal the beginning and ending of classes.

17. Students' names have been changed in this and the discussions which follow, but each pseudonym has been used consistently throughout the discussions. Where it is not clear from the tape recording which student is speaking, the speaker is identified generically as "Student."

18. Presumably, McKeon is referring to the Greek *logos*, a key philosophic term more customarily translated as "speech" or "reason." Given McKeon's use of Greek, in which he was fluent—he once mentioned in class that he had read the entire corpus of Aristotle in Greek fifty times [*sic*] over the course of his lifetime—it is significant that etymologically, *logos* is also the source of the English "logic," a term which, in his view, like *freedom*, *power*, and *history*, also reflects a plurality of methods and meanings.

DISCUSSION. Hobbes (Part 1)

1. As noted in the foreword, the editors have found no tape recordings for the discussion classes on the readings in this Winter Quarter 1965 course, except for two discussions of Kant (see below). What appears here, therefore, is a compilation of three students' notebooks—fortunately, two of these students went on to become professional academic philosophers—which describes what was discussed in class, although without the benefit of McKeon's customary question-and-answer dialectic. During class, McKeon handed out to students a typed, mimeographed copy of selected passages from Hobbes's *Leviathan* as it appeared in the nineteenth-century collection of *The English Works of Thomas Hobbes*, vol. III, ed. William Molesworth (London: Bohn, 1839–45; reprint, Aalen, Germany: Scientia Verlag, 1966). The handout contained four typewritten pages covering part I, chapter XIV (pp. 116–20) and part II, chapter XXI (pp. 196–201). The handout also contained a fifth page, which was a brief excerpt from chapter XIV of *Philosophical Rudiments Concerning Government and Society*, which appears in *The English Works*, vol. II, pp. 185–86 (see appendix E).

2. This first paragraph does not appear in student notes but does reflect McKeon's typical introduction to a course's series of discussions of readings. It has here been modeled on his introduction to the first of the discussions in *On Knowing—The Natural Sciences*, ed. David B. Owen and Zahava K. McKeon (Chicago: University of Chicago Press, 1994) (see p. 25), which was on Plato.

3. Figure 8 is in students' notes.

4. In appendix E, see chapter XIV, the end of paragraph 3.

5. Figure 9 is in one student's notes.

6. What follows are the notes McKeon prepared for discussing Hobbes's *Leviathan* in a number of versions of the course. Because they do not have the customary "I&M 202" or "I&M 212" in the upper right-hand corner of the first page but instead have "Liberty 1," it cannot be determined whether they were originally prepared for use with the 1965 version of this course (though, in the editors' judgment, they were not). Nevertheless, this and the following notes were found filed with those that were clearly prepared for this version of his social sciences introduction, and in most cases follow closely with student notebooks from class. Here, as in all such notes which follow lectures and discussions below, the notes are reproduced as McKeon typed them, with the exception that *italics* indicate penciled additions to the typewritten material, and italic *underline* represents typed words that McKeon later underlined in pencil.

7. The following series of italicized, underlined, bracketed, bold numbers, such as ***[1]***, at the beginning of each section reflect additions to his typed notes which McKeon subsequently added in pencil and then circled. They correspond to specific passages similarly numbered in his own copy of the mimeographed Hobbes texts used in class (see appendix E). The editors encourage readers to trace out in detail the relation between the typewritten notes reproduced here and the Hobbes passages, including McKeon's penciled additions, in appendix E. It offers a unique opportunity to observe line by line his approach to engag-

ing a philosophic position. More important, even, than the conclusions drawn is the exemplification of a way of carefully reading and revealing the structure of an argument.

8. These two examples of McKeon crossing out a typed term and replacing it with another in pencil indicate how his view of an author could change over time. First, it indicates his engaging afresh with a text. Second, and more important, it should remind readers that the characterization of an author's profile in this course is not the only one possible, is not an absolute, definitive statement, but only one which reflects what was his latest orientation toward the work at the time of this course. The same applies, of course, to the intellectual profiles in appendix J.

DISCUSSION. Hobbes (Part 2)

1. For a brief description of the origin of this summary of the second Hobbes discussion, which is based on students' and McKeon's notes, see endnote 1 of the previous discussion.

2. Both figures 10 and 11 are in students' notes.

3. What follows are the next three in the sequence of McKeon note cards prepared for his discussion of Hobbes's *Leviathan* and *Philosophical Rudiments Concerning Government and Society*. The reader can review the conclusion of endnote 6 in the discussion of Hobbes, part 1, for the rules used here in transcribing McKeon's notes.

4. The following series of italicized, underlined, bracketed, bold numbers, such as ***[1]***, at the beginning of each section reflect additions to his typed notes which McKeon subsequently added in pencil and then circled. They correspond to specific passages similarly numbered in his own copy of the mimeographed Hobbes texts used in class (see appendix E). For a more complete description of the relation between McKeon's notes and the Hobbes text, see endnote 1 in appendix E or endnote 7 in the discussion of Hobbes, part 1.

5. In what follows, McKeon concludes his series of four typed note cards on Hobbes with a summary of the structure of argument represented in the three mimeographed selections (see appendix E) from *Leviathan* and *Philosophical Rudiments*.

6. The note cards just reproduced all present McKeon's analysis of the topic of freedom as developed by Hobbes in *Leviathan* and in the *Philosophical Rudiments*. However, he also prepared one card, which follows, that summarizes in *Leviathan* his treatment of power, the second of the organizing topics of this course. This is reproduced below exactly as prepared for class, and the reader is encouraged to refer to it when the topic of power is introduced in the lectures and analyzed in the authors discussed hereafter.

It is important to note, however, that this card was prepared for a class in some prior year, which is shown by his characterization of Hobbes as using the *existential* interpretation instead of the current course's *entitative* interpretation. The fact that here, as well as elsewhere, he changed his view on various authors' principle, method, and/or interpretation should alert the reader to the fact that

McKeon is not claiming that his semantic profiles of individuals are absolute and unchanging. Rather, the profiles are attempts to bring clarity to the interpretation of authors in the context of their intellectual relations to others, not attempts to locate each one definitively and unequivocally in the universe of discourse. This tentativeness or circumstantiality, an important feature of McKeon's own operational or rhetorical method (see the end of lecture 2), is something to be kept very much in mind when working with the profiles in appendix J.

Hobbes Power 1.

Leviathan ch. 14.
Power used to define right or liberty—man's own power. Law defined as a precept or general rule, recognized by reason—which binds or obliges.
Rights and impediments to use of rights.
Laying down, transferring, and renouncing rights.

ch. 21. Liberty as absence of opposition. Difference between want of liberty and want of power to move. (p. 2)

In the state or the artificial man establishment of sovereign power. (p. 3)
Laws no power to protect them without the sword. (p. 4)
Sovereign power of life and death.

Three observations—power related to one's own nature. Logistic method. Single meaning of power—ability to move—related to possible impediments to movement.

Need of principle—institution of state by covenant, artificial man with locus of power in the sovereign. Actional principle.

Meaning or interpretation of power. Oriented to the sovereign—unlimited except by law of nature. Oriented to the individual—silence of law with minimum exception of life, imprisonment and security. Existential interpretation.

LECTURE 3. Freedom: Interpretation

1. In figure 12, the knowledge matrix, the connecting lines and the general terms *ontic* and *phenomenal* are in student notes for this lecture. The editors have put the terms of the knowledge matrix in parentheses, however, because McKeon spends the rest of this lecture focusing in detail on their respective interpretations, the names of which have been added in capitals for emphasis.
2. See Plato's *Republic*, 509a–511e.

3. A key phrase from Protagoras. For McKeon's rationale in translating *metron* as "maker" rather than the more customary "measure," see the following lecture. Also see McKeon's *On Knowing—The Natural Sciences*, ed. David B. Owen and Zahava K. McKeon (Chicago: University of Chicago Press, 1994), p. 69.

4. Though it does not appear in student notes of this lecture, the reader may want to refer to figure 3, which shows the relation between the basic knowledge matrix and the four modes of thought. Where formerly it was used as the basis for generating distinctions in method, here McKeon has used it as the basis for generating distinctions in interpretation.

5. This discussion occurs at 425d–e in Plato's *Republic*, shortly after the statement at 423e that education is the one essential factor in the perfect state.

6. Table 4 appears in student notes.

7. McKeon is creating table 4 one row at a time as he discusses each interpretation. He does not start with the completed table as it appears here in the text.

8. McKeon is emphasizing that in the knowledge matrix, when one node, here the knowable, is chosen as basic, all the other nodes shift as a consequence whatever meanings they formerly had.

9. McKeon's use of *nature* here is clearly equivalent to the knowable.

10. McKeon is referring to the column of table 4 which lists "What things are free?"

11. Because McKeon did not have time to give more than a short introduction to the essentialist interpretation, the editors are here providing the description of this interpretation from the notes he used as the basis of this lecture, which were found in his files. The sheet is entitled "Concepts and Methods 202 (VII) 4,3.," but the course and version numbers have been crossed out and replaced in light pencil by "212." It is laid out and reproduced as typed, with any editorial changes being noted in square brackets, except for a few regularizations of spelling, which are not noted. McKeon's own penciled additions are added in *italics*

4. Essentialist interpretation—resolution—Freedom of self-realization. *self-development*
Resolution of response of knower in known—the known [is] the accustomed through habit and thought, the knower as such appears on encounter of problematic situation. [Thereafter,] beginning of thought, development of knowledge, exploration of the knowable: prior to that habitual or automatic reaction. Exemplified in the interpretation of Aristotle, Cassirer, Dewey.

> Thus in Aristotle formation of man in his biological and social contexts. Politics, [is] the architectonic science of his activities. On the basis of his nature he forms habits and institutions, virtues and laws. Ethics is part of the architectonic science of politics. Deliberation and choice [occur] within the region of things within one's own power. Free acts, [are] voluntary acts. Freedom as one objective of [one] state—namely, the democratic, but in varying degrees [it is] present in all states[,] at least for some [individuals].

Freedom therefore [is] where choice occurs and action follows on choice and since the further developments on nature are habits and institutions, these are free insofar as they [lead to] development [of] human potentialities for further action [that is] self-originated, that is, the freedom of self-development as distinct from external influences[,] whether they develop or repress potentialities.

What things are free? Men in society. Deliberate action.

LECTURE 4. Freedom: Principle

1. The English *principle* derives from the Latin *princeps*, meaning "first" or "foremost."

2. In figure 13, the knowledge matrix, the connecting lines, and the general terms *holoscopic* and *meroscopic* are in student notes of this lecture. The editors have put the terms of the knowledge matrix in parentheses, however, because McKeon spends the rest of this lecture focusing in detail on their respective principles, the names of which have been added in capitals for emphasis.

3. These last two sentences are an elaboration of a point made succinctly in McKeon's notes from the previous version of the course but used for this lecture ("Concepts and Methods 202 [VIII] Principles 3,1."). The relevant sentence is as follows (the editors' additions are in square brackets): "Even on the level of knowledge, the distinction [between opinion and knowledge, becoming and being] [is] needed in that discursive proofs of reason are assimilated into the simple ideas of understanding."

4. In his notes for this lecture (see the preceding endnote), McKeon adds that not only the doctrine of reminiscence but also "love" can "trace the path of such assimilation" in Plato.

5. Table 5 appears neither in students' nor in McKeon's notes for this lecture. The editors have constructed it in parallel with tables 3 and 4 to suggest for principle, as McKeon previously has for method and interpretation, something of the structure of the distinctions he is making. The terms *autonomy* and *self-rule* do not appear in the text as they are used in this table. *Autonomy*, literally, "law given to self," reflects Plato's orientation to knowledge, to the rational recognition of universal law to which one chooses to submit oneself; and the term has an extended history throughout philosophy of similar use. *Self-rule*, which McKeon has already introduced in the discussion of Plato, may fit better in the table under the reflexive principle because, as his subsequent discussion of Aristotle indicates, the term readily applies both to the ruler-ruled principle of politics as well as to the voluntary, self-willed, quality of free individual action. The terms *power* and *nature* follow more directly from the exposition McKeon gives in lecture 4 and in his notes (see below, endnote 15).

6. The Latin sentence means "I think; therefore, I am" or "I exist."

7. The Latin phrase (literally, "cause of self") is customarily translated as "cause of Himself."

8. In McKeon's notes for this lecture ("Concepts and Methods 202 [VIII] 3,2."), he gives a succinct formulation of the ancient Greek distinction between

holoscopic and meroscopic principles: "In antiquity the relation [was] between nomos and phusis; law and nature." McKeon emphasizes later in this paragraph that *phusis* is the word which Aristotle uses for man's political "nature." The same term is also the origin of the modern English term *physics*.

9. In McKeon's notes for this lecture ("Concepts and Methods 202 [VIII] 3,2."), he elaborates slightly on the issues treated in this paragraph. In part, those notes on reflexive principles read as follows:

> The state and society are natural because man cannot live by himself alone; he depends on other men—this is the sense of Aristotle's man is by nature a political animal. (In the same way as an individual has an internal source of action over and above "nature"—voluntary as well as natural action.) He organizes different states with distinct constitutions. Freedom is the condition of the polity or democratic state; it is also the end of such a state. The state provides the circumstances of individual action—and freedom is the condition required for virtuous action, which likewise is the product of action—virtuous action is action according to the rule of right reason.

10. As frequently occurs throughout this—and, of course, every other—lecture, McKeon is systematically working out the implications of his basic knowledge matrix (see fig. 1).

11. In the *Theaetetus*, Socrates identifies the position that knowledge is perception—a position he will go on to refute—as being equivalent to that of Protagoras, who argued, "Man is the measure of all things."

12. That is, the knowledge matrix of figure 1.

13. In his lecture notes ("Concepts and Methods 202 [VIII] 3,2."), McKeon includes under actional principles the famous maxim "Might makes right."

14. In his lecture notes ("Concepts and Methods 202 [VIII] 3,3."), McKeon describes these three simples as "atoms, simple ideas, undefined terms."

15. In his lecture notes (see "Concepts and Methods 202 [VIII] 3,3."), McKeon describes in the following way the two kinds of meroscopic principles as they relate to freedom:

> Actional freedom is power simply leading to what pleases. Simple freedom is power flowing from one's nature, and pleasure has a natural basis—[one] may be mistaken in what one conceives to be pleasurable (false pleasures or lowly pleasures). Two kinds of convention, likewise—simple power relations and balances, and an interplay of natures underlying the manifestations of power.

This distinction between freedom as merely power and as based on underlying nature provided the editors with the two meroscopic distinctions of table 5.

DISCUSSION. Spinoza (Part 1)

1. The text of Spinoza's *Ethics* quoted in this discussion is from Benedict de Spinoza, *Works of Spinoza*, vol. 2, trans. R. H. M. Elwes (New York: Dover, 1951).

2. Figure 14 is in student notebooks.

3. As in the case of Hobbes, McKeon prepared extensive notes in preparation for his discussions, starting with early versions of this course (see endnote 3 in the discussion of Hobbes, part 1, for a brief description of these notes in general, and the foreword for a history of the course). Those notes are here and in the succeeding discussions laid out and reproduced as typed, with any changes to that original typing being noted in square brackets, except for a few regularizations of spelling, which are not noted. *Italics* are used to indicate McKeon's penciled additions, which, most usually, were revisions made for later versions of the course.

4. After writing "Insert" in pencil, McKeon crossed out the following section on his note card with a large *X* from the preface through all of prop. LXVI, up to the concluding words, "the latter is *free*." Presumably, the note card which follows next, entitled "Spinoza Freedom Ethics IV.," which was found in his files right after this note card, is intended to be what he wished to insert at this point, because it covers book IV from the preface through proposition LXVI.

5. In the margin of his note, McKeon has penciled a bracket around the whole of proposition LXXIII and added an additional vertical line for emphasis.

DISCUSSION. Spinoza (Part 2)

1. Table 6 is in students' notebooks.

2. The text of Spinoza's *Ethics* quoted in this discussion is from Benedict de Spinoza, *Works of Spinoza*, vol. 2, trans. R. H. M. Elwes (New York: Dover, 1951).

3. Some editions of the *Ethics* translate the Latin *scholium* into English, using "note."

DISCUSSION. Spinoza (Part 3)

1. The text of *Tractatus Theologico-Politicus* quoted in this discussion is from Benedict de Spinoza, *Works of Spinoza*, vol. 1, trans. R. H. M. Elwes (New York: Dover, 1951).

2. McKeon originally numbered this sheet as "2" but later penciled it in as "5." It was found in his files immediately following the preceding note.

3. This note card is included here because on the previous one, McKeon has added a fourth kind of principle, the comprehensive, to his originally typed three principles that could be combined with a logistic method. Note that the preceding card above (which was filed immediately before this card on Hume and Leibniz) gave Hume (an atomist) and Leibniz as examples of the way that one could combine simple or comprehensive principles, respectively, with a logistic method, in addition to the examples covered in class of combining the same method with the actional (Hobbes) and reflexive (Spinoza) principles. See all four possible combinations in appendix D. Also note in appendix J that McKeon at one time had a different method for Hume.

4. From Kant, *Critique of Pure Reason*: "Transcendental Aesthetic," section 2, part 8: "General Observations on Transcendental Aesthetic."

DISCUSSION. Spinoza (Part 4)

1. The text of *Tractatus Theologico-Politicus* quoted in this discussion is from Benedict de Spinoza, *Works of Spinoza*, vol. 1, trans. R. H. M. Elwes (New York: Dover, 1951).
2. Figure 15 is in one of the student's class notes.
3. On the rationale for including this note card, see the discussion of Hobbes, part 2, endnote 6.

LECTURE 5. Freedom: Selection

1. The tape recording begins slightly after McKeon starts his lecture. The editors have created an introductory sentence to approximate those opening remarks.
2. Table 7 is in students' notes.
3. Figures 16, 17, and 18 are an expansion by the editors of a condensed sketch in one student's notes. They are intended to help clarify the relation among the modes of thought with regard to interpretation, method, and principle. Compare these, respectively, to figures 12, 5, and 13, above where McKeon is relating his foundational knowledge matrix (fig. 1) to the specific terms involved in each of the four different aspects of interpretation, method, and principle.
4. Table 8 has been created by the editors from McKeon's lecture to schematize what he is saying. It is not in students' notes.
5. Figures 19, 20, 21, and 22 are in students' notes.
6. The date of Aristotle's death.
7. The semantic profile in figure 23 has been created by the editors as a visual representation of Hobbes, while that in figure 24 has similarly been created for both Machiavelli and Mill. Neither figure is in students' notes. Notice, these profiles can act as a shorthand representation of a thinker and thereby provide an initial basis for demonstrating the relations among various individuals.
8. The editors have created table 9 from McKeon's discussion of the changes in orientation of the basic selection during different historical periods to help schematize his points. The table is not in students' notes.
9. Descartes published his *Discourse on Method* in 1637.
10. The German terms can be roughly translated as follows: *Geistesgeschichte* (literally, "spirit" [vs. material] plus "history") as "intellectual history," *Geisteswissenschaft* (literally, "spirit" plus "knowledge" or "science") as "human (or social) science," and *Naturwissenschaft* (literally "nature" plus "knowledge" or "science") as "natural science."
11. The semantic profile in figure 25 has been created by the editors as a visual representation of Spinoza and is not in students' notes.

12. The *Oxford English Dictionary* (often referred to as the *OED*), a multivolume work, first began publication in 1884 and has grown to become the largest English-language dictionary in print.

LECTURE 6. Freedom: Selection (Part 2)

1. The tape recording of this lecture begins at this point, presumably shortly after McKeon starts speaking.

2. The editors think this is a key sentence for McKeon's treatment of selection. It emphasizes that his approach is based on a conception of terms and their referents which holds that they are not univocally defined or fixed; rather, both are aspects of language and experience which are to be understood in relation to other terms and referents similarly viewed. Thus, the various tables and figures he uses to show what he is doing are fundamentally about the relationships among the terms taken ambiguously. The tables and figures, then, are not to be seen as fixed pigeonholes of meaning: they are neither statements/propositions/definitions nor arguments nor organizing beginning points of what he is saying. They are, rather, demonstrations/exhibitions of relationships, including all the ambiguity that demonstration inherently entails. Consequently, the rest of lecture 6 is not merely a repetition of lectures 2, 3, and 4 but a re-view from the perspective of selection, emphasizing the role that terms and their ambiguous relations play in McKeon's conception of interpretations, methods, and principles.

3. Alfred North Whitehead published his *Process and Reality* in 1929, helping found process philosophy.

4. Table 10 has been created by the editors to pull together the various aspects of freedom treated in lectures 2 through 5 (see tables 3, 4, and 5), and to relate them from the perspective of selection, that is, in a single structure of terms. It is not in students' notes. Of the ambiguous questions at the top of table 10, the first two (for interpretation and method) are from the text of this lecture, but editors have created the third (for principle) from table 12 below. Also, note that the lines between the columns connect terms that grow out of each respective mode of thought. However, as McKeon repeatedly says, it is important to remember that any term in any column can go with any term in another column, even though the latter is associated with a mode of thought different from that of the former.

Table 11 is included here to summarize in one place the basic set of terms McKeon is using in his semantic analysis. The table, with the editors' addition of the initial column containing the relevant modes of thought, is from a paper entitled "Philosophic Semantics and Philosophic Inquiry," which he delivered at the Illinois Philosophy Conference held in Carbondale, Illinois, on February 26, 1966. This paper had been previously reproduced and distributed among his students and colleagues. It was first published posthumously in Richard McKeon, *Freedom and History and Other Essays: An Introduction to the Thought of Richard McKeon*, ed. Zahava K. McKeon (Chicago: University of Chicago Press, 1990), pp. 242–56. The schematism appears on page 253.

5. The editors have constructed table 12 from the text to focus on the central pairs of topics McKeon is using to create his analysis of freedom. This table is not in student notes in this form, though all the distinctions are written down. Notice that the table provides a clear example of the operational method, as McKeon uses it, something about which he was explicit toward the end of lecture 2.

6. A section of one of McKeon's notes prepared for this lecture summarizes these points as follows:

Concepts and Methods 212 6.5.

. . .

4. Principle. Basic aspects of the meaning of freedom on the grounds of discourse or action. Why or for what reason or on what basis is freedom possible and desirable? What are the properties of freedom which make it an end or a means?

Question of principle—What is freedom as a cause or what is its value?

Problem of the relation of known to knowledge (holoscopic) the internal organization of freedom as property of whatever is free.

Problem of the relation of knower and knowable (meroscopic) the external problem of how freedom establishes values.

If knowledge-known, coincidence of what is and what is known—the values involved in action are found among the objects of knowledge; value is a property of objects which arouses desire and leads to action.

If knower-knowable—values are arbitrary projections or decisions of the knower: called good because they are desired.

. . .

---

7. H. A. Prichard published his essay "Does Moral Philosophy Rest on a Mistake?" in 1912.

DISCUSSION. Kant (Part 1)

1. Figure 26 is in students' notebooks.

2. The version of the *Metaphysics* the editors have mainly used in this discussion is Immanuel Kant, *Fundamental Principles of the Metaphysics of Morals*, trans. T. K. Abbott (New York: Liberal Arts, 1949).

3. See McKeon's discussions of Galileo after lecture 5 and of Newton after lecture 7 in Richard McKeon, *On Knowing—The Natural Sciences,* ed. David B. Owen and Zahava K. McKeon (Chicago: University of Chicago Press, 1994).

4. Although not in students' notes, figure 27 is typical of illustrations McKeon used to illustrate the schematic character of the operational method, which Kant is using, and has been created by the editors to help clarify the fourfold distinction used here.

5. In the Beck translation, which students also frequently purchased for the course, this is on the third page of the preface, page 52. See Immanuel Kant,

Foundations of the Metaphysics of Morals, trans. Lewis White Beck (Chicago: University of Chicago Press, 1949). This edition represents a selection from a more extensive collection of Beck translations and retains that larger work's pagination. In parts 2 through 4 of the Kant discussions, the equivalent pagination in the shorter Beck translation will be included in the text within square brackets, as [B:52] is here. See appendix F.

6. This McKeon's customary shorthand in his notes for reflexive principle, operational method, ontological interpretation.

7. For this full note by McKeon, see the end of the following discussion, the second one on Kant.

DISCUSSION. Kant (Part 2)

1. This and the following discussion of Kant are from the only tape recordings of discussions in this course that are known to exist. In these two discussions, ellipses (. . .) are used to indicate one of the following: extended pauses after McKeon asks a question and receives no immediate response, a sentence which trails off and remains incomplete, or an interruption of one speaker's remarks by a second speaker. In a number of instances, students' comments are partially unintelligible on the tape, and in those cases the editors have tried to interpolate the essence of what was said. In extreme cases, where comments are completely unintelligible, the editors have indicated such by square brackets, ellipses, and a question mark—[. . . ?]. Otherwise, this is a literal transcription, with only minor changes made to assist ease of reading. Finally, students' laughter is represented by [L!].

2. Here McKeon evidently looks at the copy of Kant the student has brought to class, probably a version of Immanuel Kant, *Fundamental Principles of the Metaphysic of Morals*, trans. T. K. Abbott (New York: Liberal Arts, 1949). Pagination in this and the following discussion evidently refers to this edition. The equivalent pages from the Beck translation will immediately follow the Abbott references in class and are contained in square brackets, *e.g.*, [B:55–58].: Immanuel Kant, *Foundations of the Metaphysics of Morals*, trans. Lewis White Beck (Chicago: University of Chicago Press, 1949). This edition represents a selection from a more extensive collection of Beck translations and retains that larger work's pagination. For a more complete list of page equivalents, see appendix F.

3. All students' names have been changed, but each pseudonym has been used consistently throughout all the discussions so that if the reader wishes, one can follow different patterns of thinking. Where it is not clear from the tape recording which student is speaking, the speaker is identified generically as "Student."

4. In the Beck translation, the following quotation appears at the beginning of paragraph three [B:56].

5. In Beck, paragraph four of the first section (p. 56).

6. Springfield is the capital of Illinois, in which the University of Chicago is located, and is the seat of elected state government.

7. For clarity, the editors have constructed figure 28, which is not in students' notes, along the lines of figure 29, which is in their notes.
8. McKeon is referring to Plato's *Phaedrus*, where a speech by Socrates describes the soul's ascent to heaven and perception, however dim, of statues representing the eternal Ideas, such as Truth, the Good, and Beauty.
9. Figures 29, 30, 31, 32, and 33 are all in students' notes.
10. Although not in student notebooks, figure 34 represents McKeon's description of how, at its most abstract, the operational method often works.
11. For an overview of the distinctly different purposes of the various methods, see figure 6 and the end of the first lecture.
12. Observe the penciled "*Op*" and "*Ref*" toward the end of this note card where McKeon draws attention to specific instances, respectively, of the operational method and the reflexive principle.

DISCUSSION. Kant (Part 3)

1. See part 2 of the Kant discussion, endnote 1.
2. The version of the *Metaphysics* the editors have mainly used in this discussion is Immanuel Kant, *Fundamental Principles of the Metaphysics of Morals*, trans. T. K. Abbott (New York: Liberal Arts, 1949). Page references within square brackets are to Immanuel Kant, *Foundations of the Metaphysics of Morals*, trans. Lewis White Beck (Chicago: University of Chicago Press, 1949). This edition represents a selection from a more extensive collection of Beck translations and retains that larger work's pagination. See appendix F.
3. For "principled springs," the Beck translation reads, "sensuous incentives."
4. Figure 35 has been filled out from partial diagrams in student notes.
5. At this point, a break occurs in the tape recording, and the recording resumes for only the last two paragraphs at the end of this discussion. What follows here, therefore, as in the case of the other discussions for which a recording does not exist, is a compilation of what was discussed in class (during the break in the recording) that is based on students' notebooks as emended by McKeon's own notes on Kant's *Fundamental Principles*.
6. The editors have created table 13 both from elements in students' notes and from McKeon's own notes.
7. The editors have created figure 36 to clarify the distinctions McKeon is making. Compare the analysis of duties here with figure 33 from part 2 of the Kant discussion.
8. At approximately this point in the discussion, the tape recording resumes, and the final two paragraphs are a transcription of the taped ending of the discussion.
9. McKeon typed two asterisks in his notes, as they appear here.

DISCUSSION. Kant (Part 4)

1. This part of the discussion of Kant marks the return to a summary of what transpired in class, because no tape recording of it is known to exist. It is,

therefore, as heretofore customary, a compilation of three students' notebooks describing what was discussed in class but without the benefit of the precision of McKeon's customary question-and-answer dialectic.

2. Page references within square brackets are, first, to Immanuel Kant, *Fundamental Principles of the Metaphysics of Morals*, trans. T. K. Abbott (New York: Liberal Arts, 1949); and second, to Immanuel Kant, *Foundations of the Metaphysics of Morals*, trans. Lewis White Beck (Chicago: University of Chicago Press, 1949). The former edition is the one the editors have mainly used in this discussion. The latter edition represents a selection from a more extensive collection of Beck translations and retains that larger work's pagination. See appendix F.

3. See at the end of the discussion of Kant, part 3, McKeon's note headed "Kant . . . 2,2" and the section under it entitled "II. Question—how are these imperatives possible?," including items 1 through 3 immediately following. In general, McKeon followed very closely his own note cards for Kant numbered 2,2 through 2,6, which appear at the end of this and the preceding discussions, and which the reader will find most helpful in clarifying the structure of Kant's argument that McKeon is elucidating in class.

4. Figures 37, 38, and 39 are in students' notes.

5. McKeon's last penciled word in this sentence is not fully legible.

LECTURE 7. Power: Selection and Interpretation

1. Figure 40 is in students' notes, although the editors have added arrows for the terms' mutual implications.

2. The material for the first column of figure 41 is in students' notes. The editors have formalized it here and have added the middle and last columns to suggest the schematic manner in which McKeon is treating the relation of freedom and power. See endnote 5 below.

3. The Universal Declaration of Human Rights was adopted by the United Nationals General Assembly in 1948 and grew directly out of the experience of World War II. As a member of the United States delegation, McKeon was actively involved with the preparatory work for the declaration, which was undertaken by the just-formed UNESCO. See McKeon's discussion of this work in his "Philosophy and History in the Development of Human Rights" in *Selected Writings of Richard McKeon*, vol. 1, *Philosophy, Science, and Culture*, ed. Zahava K. McKeon and William G. Swenson (Chicago: University of Chicago, 1998), pp. 447–67.

4. In the United States, the Civil Rights Act of 1964 was a major and broad piece of legislation which outlawed discrimination against racial and other minorities and against women, banning inequalities in voter registration requirements, at work, and in public accommodations, such as education, transportation, and hotels.

5. The editors assume here that McKeon means that the relationship of figure 41 to the knowledge matrix, figure 1, is as follows: *a* refers to the *knower* (or mode of thought discrimination), *b* refers to *knowledge* (assimilation), *c* refers to the *known* (resolution), and *d* refers to the *knowable* (construction).

6. Bishop John Bramhall (1594–1663), a defender of the Church of England, entered into a lengthy public debate with Hobbes in the 1650s following the publication of the latter's *Leviathan* in 1651.

7. The editors assume that McKeon is referring to the *knowable* (construction) position in figure 41.

8. Figure 42 is in students' notes.

9. Presumably, McKeon is referring to section 405 in book III of the *Republic*.

10. The reference here is likely to 423d–424a in book IV and 549b in book VIII of the *Republic*.

11. Socrates says that perfect state will exist only in thought, not action, at the end of book IX in the *Republic* 592a–b.

12. The main elements of table 14 appears in students' notes. The editors have organized them and have added the first column on modes of thought and the column on selection, because McKeon works with these terms in the following lecture, lecture 8.

LECTURE 8. Power: Interpretation (Part 2) and Method

1. See the discussion on Spinoza, part 2, the fourth paragraph from the end, *i.e.*, before McKeon's notes begin, on page 78.

2. See Richard McKeon, *On Knowing—The Natural Sciences*, ed. David B. Owen and Zahava K. McKeon (Chicago: University of Chicago Press, 1994), pp. 233–34.

3. See McKeon's discussion of Galileo in his *On Knowing—The Natural Sciences*, pp. 130–84.

4. See McKeon's discussion of Maxwell in his *On Knowing—The Natural Sciences*, pp. 304–29. For McKeon's notes in preparation for discussing Einstein, which he did not do in the version of the course that appears in *On Knowing—The Natural Sciences*, see appendix F in that volume.

5. McKeon is using his proportion in its existentialist interpretation form to show how it works, moving from the second term—*law*—to the third—*nature*.

6. A portion of one of McKeon's notes prepared for class contains the following remarks.

Concepts and Methods 212 Power 8.3.

. . .

4. Existentialist interpretation—discrimination.

Power as initiation or change. (not as in entitative power as motion, but power as change of motion). Action or actual power in exercise or operation. Relative to frame of reference and perspective.

Only one variety of power—power as action or innovation—no power except actually exercised power. Every thing is and is known relative to the observer or agent—indeed established by his power and initiative.

Nature is power—a thing is what it does, and knowledge and law are judged as instrumentalities or power.

Perspective or frame of reference.

Example of Darwin's doctrine of aggregate of independent determining agents—occurrence of variation. Statistical laws can be formulated. This is what nature is and constitutes knowledge of nature or the known.

Strictly speaking only living things have this spontaneous initiative or actual power. Continuing motion or rest merely objects for the exercise of power. Laws of motion as laws of [shock?].

. . .

---

7. The editors have constructed table 15 for clarity in relation to table 3.
8. As McKeon mentions in lecture 7, this occurs at the end of book IX of the *Republic* at 592a–b.
9. Most famously, this distinction occurs in Augustine of Hippo's work, *The City of God*. For him, that city was represented by the Roman Catholic Church and was, therefore, separated from the city of man. The influence of Plato's *Republic* can be seen throughout Augustine's work.
10. Karl Marx's work might be an example of what McKeon has in mind here.
11. The editors have constructed table 16 from what McKeon says in class at the end of this lecture and the review at the beginning of lecture 9 in order to clarify with an example how one mode of thought in method can be connected with any of the other modes of thought reflected in differing interpretations of power.

DISCUSSION. Mill (Part 1)

1. McKeon's note cards for this discussion indicate that he first typed the page numbers for the Everyman Library edition [John Stuart Mill, *Utilitariansim, Liberty, and Representative Government* (London: J. M. Dent, 1910; reprint, New York: E. P. Dutton, 1947)] and subsequently added pagination in pencil for the Library of Liberal Arts edition [John Stuart Mill, *On Liberty*, ed. Currin V. Shields (New York: Liberal Arts, 1956)]. Also note the clear reference to Kant in Mill's opening sentence in the text. See appendix G.
2. At this point, the student notebooks refer to either page 95 or page 9, presumably because they are using different editions of Mill's work than McKeon is. The editors have not been able to identify the edition one student is using. The other is using John Stuart Mill, *On Liberty* (New York: Appleton-Century-Crofts, 1947). Again, see appendix G.
3. In order to help clarify the formal structure of Mill's use of the operational method here, the editors have created figure 43 from both students' and McKeon's notes. They have also added the contrary terms *Freedom* and *Power*, as well as *Different* and *Same*, to suggest the exhaustive character of Mill's distinctions to which McKeon refers. He further explores this formal character of method in part 3 of the discussion on Mill.

4. In several earlier versions of this course, McKeon used Hegel's *Reason in History, trans. Robert S. Hartman* (New York: Liberal Arts, 1953) as one of the readings in the discussion part of the course.

5. See endnote 1.

6. McKeon typed an asterisk in his notes, as it appears here.

7. This and the following two notes were found filed in the section of McKeon's reading and lecture notes devoted to J. S. Mill.

8. The reader can see in this and the following notes that McKeon makes a number of distinctions to help clarify the ones separating the different kinds of principles, methods, and interpretations.

9. This note was found filed in the section of McKeon's reading and lecture notes devoted to I&M 212. It was typed for an the earlier version of 212 (Concepts and Methods 202, later renamed Ideas and Methods 202) but, as was frequently the case, was used where appropriate in subsequent versions of the course.

10. This note uses the shorthand profiles for philosophers first discussed in lecture 5. See, for examples, figures 19 through 25. The editors have added the proper terms for principle, method, and interpretation, which the arrows symbolize. Note that one can see from figure 23 that McKeon's analysis of Hobbes's interpretation changed from the existentialist of this earlier note card to the entitative used in figure 23 for the current course from 1965.

DISCUSSION. Mill (Part 2)

1. For a slightly expanded treatment of the "value" of McKeon's approach, see appendix H.

2. McKeon's note cards for this discussion indicate that he first typed the page numbers for the Everyman Library edition [John Stuart Mill, *Utilitarianism, Liberty, and Representative Government* (London: J. M. Dent, 1910; reprint, New York: E. P. Dutton, 1947)] and subsequently added pagination in pencil for the Library of Liberal Arts edition [John Stuart Mill, *On Liberty*, ed. Currin V. Shields (New York: Liberal Arts, 1956)]. To follow the outline of this discussion, see appendix G.

3. See figure 36. Also see McKeon's note at the end of the next discussion for a fuller comparison of Mill and Kant.

4. One student's notes have page 104.

5. One student's notes have page 34.

6. See E:96–97; L:44–45. One student's notes have p. 128.

7. This note was found filed in the section of McKeon's reading and lecture notes devoted to J. S. Mill.

DISCUSSION. Mill (Part 3)

1. McKeon begins this class by announcing that the course's final examination will be on Tuesday, March 16, not Friday, March 19, and will be given at the announced time of 4:30 to 6:30 p.m. in Swift Hall, Room 201, as previously scheduled.

2. One student has page 17.
3. One student has page 126; another has page 34.
4. One student has pages 20 and 38.
5. One has page 140; another has page 45.
6. One has page 148; another has page 52.
7. Figure 44, Mill's matrix of distinctions, appears both in the students' notes and in McKeon's note reproduced at the end of this discussion.
8. In figure 45, the arrows are in McKeon's note reproduced at the end of this discussion, and their labels come from one student's notes, which also adds the two-headed arrow for the third hypothesis.
9. Figure 46 is from one of the students' notes and reflects, though slightly rearranged, the same figure in McKeon's note reproduced at the end of this discussion.

DISCUSSION. Mill (Part 4)

1. McKeon's note cards for this discussion indicate that he first typed the page numbers for the Everyman Library edition [John Stuart Mill, *Utilitarianism, Liberty, and Representative Government* (London: J. M. Dent, 1910; reprint, New York: E. P. Dutton, 1947)] and subsequently added pagination in pencil for the Library of Liberal Arts edition [John Stuart Mill, *On Liberty*, ed. Currin V. Shields (New York: Liberal Arts, 1956)]. See appendix G.
2. For this first step, one student has page 153; another has page 56.
3. One student has page 162; another has page 63.
4. In their notes, students have the basic diagram for figure 47; but to that figure one student has added "(as reasons)" under "End" as well as the two-headed arrow and connecting line between "spontaneity" and "variety," as shown.
5. Students have the basic diagram for figure 48; however, they have reversed "Duties" and "Non-interference," putting them on the lower level of the diagram. The editors have chosen to put the two terms on the upper level of the diagram not only because one student's note states that the "two parts" of Mill's argument in chapter IV are "now up top of the chart"—that student also puts a two-headed arrow between "Duties" and "Non-interference," as is reflected in the figure—but also because it appears to make sense in terms of McKeon's emphasis upon exhaustiveness in the form of the argument.
6. One student has page 84.
7. Since all three philosophers have the same principle, McKeon is possibly making a point, in passing, about how a principle operates—in this case, the reflexive.
8. For the final exam, see appendix I.
9. The following brief, handwritten schematism on a separate piece of paper was found within this folded, typed note on Mill. McKeon presumably wrote it in preparation for one of the earlier versions of this course, as is indicated by the "202" course number. Note the focus on both formal and material aspects.

LECTURE 9. Power: Method (Part 2)

1. In the republican period of Rome, which immediately preceded the empire, a consul was the highest elected official. Two consuls were elected each year to serve one-year terms in which they alternately led the state.

2. *The Federalist Papers* are a set of eighty-five essays written by Alexander Hamilton, James Madison, and John Jay which appeared serially in 1787 and 1788. They argued in support of the ratification of the recently drafted Constitution of the United States.

3. McKeon makes a similar point in his lectures on the natural sciences. See Richard McKeon, *On Knowing—The Natural Sciences*, ed. David B. Owen and Zahava K. McKeon (Chicago: University of Chicago Press, 1994), pp. 70–71 and figure 11.

4. McKeon is referring to president Dwight Eisenhower's secretary of defense from 1953 to 1957, Charles Erwin Wilson, who had formerly been president of General Motors, from which he earned his nickname, "Engine Charlie" Wilson. In his Senate confirmation hearings, he was questioned about his large stock holdings in GM and whether he would be able, as secretary of defense, to make a policy decision that would be against GM's interests. He replied that he would, in fact, be able to do so, but that he could not conceive of such a situation, "because for years I thought what was good for our country was good for General Motors, and vice versa." In the newspapers this quotation was reversed, and after the hearings he was widely characterized as saying that "what's good for General Motors is good for the country."

5. As he frequently does, McKeon is here distinguishing between all four modes of thought, specifically with respect to method, in a single sentence. He does something similar in the first sentence of the second paragraph after this one.

6. Significantly, the framers of the United States Constitution were all classically educated, and therefore were careful to include a procedure for amending their document, article V, as a central feature. So far, twenty-seven amendments have been ratified since 1789, the first ten of which are collectively known as the Bill of Rights.

7. The rest of this paragraph comes from McKeon's teaching notes entitled "Concepts and Methods 202 (VIII) 7.3." The editors have added these comments to the lecture in order to help clarify the structure of the sets of distinctions being laid out in the text at the end of this lecture. Note the relation to the equivalent distinctions laid out for freedom in table 12.

8. This brief, passionate defense of the importance of exploring the full diversity of conceptions of power, formal and material, in relation to rights and freedom was frequently repeated by McKeon during the social unrest and protest movements of the 1960s growing out of the Vietnam War, the civil rights movement, and other, broadly antiestablishment issues raised both in the United States and in Europe. In the late 1960s, McKeon even hosted numerous informal gatherings of students, undergraduate and graduate, and faculty regarding the importance of such broad understanding in the practical context

of the student protests on campus, which included the seizure of the University of Chicago's main administrative building in January–February of 1969. For his concern with this problem, see, for example, his "Spiritual Autobiography" in *Thirteen Americans: Their Spiritual Autobiographies*, ed. Louis Finkelstein (New York: Harper, 1953), pp. 77–114; his essay "The Philosophic Bases and Material Circumstances of the Rights of Man," which appeared in *Ethics* 58, no. 3, part 1 (Apr 1948): 180–87; and volume 3 of *The Selected Works of Richard McKeon* (Chicago: University of Chicago Press, forthcoming).

LECTURE 10. Power: Principle; and History: Interpretation

1. McKeon is referring to the format of the course's final exam, which he described in the last paragraph of the discussion of Mill, part 4, saying that students would be expected to analyze something from the first forty-nine pages of Hegel's *Reason in History*. For the exam itself, see appendix I.

2. McKeon is presumably referring, as he often did, to Hans Vaihinger, a German philosopher whose *The Philosophy of "As If"* appeared in 1924. In it, Vaihinger argued that we cannot really know the external world, and that therefore, we construct models of it, treating these "as if" they were reality.

3. McKeon may be referring to lecture 4, the end of lecture 6, or possibly to both, where he discusses the role of principle in the differing definitions of *freedom*.

4. The editors have created table 17 in order to summarize McKeon's treatment of power in lectures 7–10. This table can be compared with table 10 above, which does the same for freedom.

5. Figure 49 is in students' notes. However, their arrowheads have been switched here to point to the basic term in order to conform to all the preceding figures. Compare with figure 41.

6. Hegel's *The Philosophy of History*, based on lecture notes first published posthumously in 1837, argues that history is progressive, and that the account of it tells how the power of a transcendental reason works itself out through human action.

7. The title of Croce's collection of essays, first published in 1938, is *La storia come pensiero e come azione*, which translates literally as "History as Thought and as Action."

8. Georg Wilhelm Friedrich Hegel, *The Philosophy of World History*, ed. John Sibree (New York: Dover, 1956). See the introduction.

9. Since McKeon is using Hegel on the course's final exam (see appendix I), he is being careful not to prejudice the students' essays. In fact, he views Hegel's interpretation as being entitative and his method as dialectical (see Hegel's profile in appendix J).

10. In the *Laws*, Plato has the Athenian Stranger (often interpreted as being Socrates) tell the myth of Cronos, the leader of the gods, who appointed demigods to be the first rulers of cities and give them order and justice in the golden age of humanity, much as a shepherd governs his flock.

DISCUSSION. Machiavelli (Part 1)

1. The basis of figure 50 appears in one student's notes: he has drawn a rectangle and three inverted *V*s, with the left arm of each V extending into the rectangle. The editors have kept that geometric form but have added the word *Discourses* to the rectangular box and the terms that are being dichotomously distinguished; this was done to reinforce the intent of the diagram, which is to show that Machiavelli's full position requires understanding how *The Prince* and *The Discourses* treat different aspects of the whole argument.

2. The editors have created figure 51 to schematize the structure of the argument in *The Prince* as McKeon is describing it here and just below. Although this diagram is not in students' notes, the substantive points are all described.

3. Figure 52 appears in students' notes. One student has added onto his diagram the last two lines, that is, the subdivision of the mixed principates.

4. Page references in the text, preceded by ML, are to the Modern Library edition of *The Prince*, which has appeared in several versions. The editors have used Niccolò Machiavelli, *The Prince and the Discourses*, trans. Luigi Ricci and E. R. P. Vincent [*The Prince*] and Christian E. Detmold [*Discourses*] (New York: Random House, 1950), an edition that McKeon clearly used for page references on several of his note cards.

5. Figure 53 appears in one student's notes, to which the editors have added the term *self* for clarity.

6. In chapter XVIII of the Modern Library edition, these five adjectives are listed as "merciful, faithful, humane, sincere, religious" [ML:65]. Since the five used in class, which are given here, come from McKeon's own notes (see his note below, "Machiavelli Prince 2."), McKeon is probably using his own translation. He both read Italian and published in it.

7. This and the following three notes were found in McKeon's reading and class files. The editors have not been able to identify the edition to which the pagination of this and the following notes refers.

8. The editors have not been able to decipher the term used here.

9. Again, the editors have had difficulty deciphering these written words, so they may not accurately reflect McKeon's intention here.

10. This note (#3) and the following (#4) contain the pagination from the Modern Library edition used by McKeon in this class discussion (see endnote 4).

11. This is another example of McKeon changing his interpretation of an author over time. He had originally viewed Machiavelli as having an actional principle, but by the time of the current course interprets his principle as reflexive. Several such instances can be seen in the Semantic Profiles in appendix J.

12. This is probably mistyped. It actually appears on page 61.

DISCUSSION. Machiavelli (Part 2)

1. Page references to the *Discourses* are to the Modern Library edition, which binds it with *The Prince:* Niccolò Machiavelli, *The Prince and the*

Discourses, trans. Luigi Ricci and E. R. P. Vincent [*The Prince*] and Christian E. Detmold [*Discourses*] (New York: Random House, 1950).

2. For figure 54, students have the basic form of this diagram in their notes. The editors have used one student's version, which includes explanatory phrases in three of the cells, and have added the term *imitation* to the other student's "doing" in the fourth cell.

3. Figure 55 is in student notes.

4. The following selection of eight McKeon notes, all of which were found filed under the heading of "Machiavelli" in McKeon's files of notes prepared from reading and for classes and lectures, is divided into three sets. The first three notes are typewritten analyses in some detail of the first ten chapters of the first book of the *Discourses*. The next three notes are handwritten analyses of the *Discourses*, with the first of the three, although also on the beginning of that text, being found within McKeon's folded, typewritten note entitled "Machiavelli The Prince" (for this last note, see the first of McKeon's notes reproduced at the end of the previous discussion, the first on Machiavelli). The last two notes are typewritten comparisons of central features of *The Prince* and the *Discourses* and were found immediately after the three typewritten notes on the *Discourses* described at the beginning of this endnote.

5. Where McKeon has circled a word in pencil for emphasis, the editors have printed it not only in italics but also in underlined, bracketed ***[bold]***.

6. In this and the following two handwritten notes, the editors have tried to decipher McKeon's handwriting, which is often difficult to make out.

7. The editors have not been able to decipher this handwritten term.

8. The editors have added sequential numerals to this and the following handwritten note to indicate the order in which they were found.

9. These last two notes are particularly explicit about how McKeon's treatment of an argument can be based on a use of the four main topics of things, thoughts, action, and language (from his schema of philosophic semantics—see table 11 in lecture 6) and on how these can be, in turn, connected to any one of the four methods.

10. These three elements of rhetoric can be seen in figure 51, where they are related to the analysis of the structure of *The Prince* as presented in the previous discussion.

LECTURE 11. History: Method and Principle; and Conclusion

1. The editors have created table 18 from this lecture and the end of the previous one in parallel with tables 10 and 17 on freedom and power, respectively. For principle, see endnotes 7 and 13 below.

2. For the different historians McKeon mentions in what follows, see their entries in appendix B.

3. McNeill was a younger colleague of McKeon's at the University of Chicago from the 1940s onward.

4. This latter is a reference to Karl Marx's view of history, where economic issues and conflict over the means of ownership and of production provide

the dynamics of development, as opposed to Hegel's conception of Reason working itself out in a history of Ideas.

5. For Plato's use of myth, see the latter part of lecture 10.

6. Paul Janet and Gabriel Séailles, *Histoire des problemes de la philosophie*. Presumably, McKeon had read this edition when he was in Paris studying with Étienne Gilson in the 1920s, and did not know that a translation had been made by Ada Monahan and edited by Henry Jones: *A History of the Problems of Philosophy* (London: Macmillan, 1902).

7. McKeon does not have time to cover the heading of Principle under history and now turns to his concluding remarks. To complete the schematism for history, therefore, the editors have included selected notes at the end of this lecture which cover principle from the last two times he prepared that topic for this course. Those notes were used to complete the Principle column in table 18. See endnote 13.

8. Table 19 appears in one student's notes, though in three separate steps; for simplicity, the editors have joined them together. In addition, since it figures importantly in McKeon's comments, they have added a column on selection for clarity.

9. From the genitive case of the Latin *crux*, "cross," *crucis* can, figuratively, mean a testing or an examining, as in the English expression of a "test case."

10. *Utilitarianism* appeared in 1863.

11. McKeon read this and the following quotations from Mill and Kant directly from his note entitled "Concepts and Methods 212 Conclusion 11.2."

12. McKeon is referring to Hobbes's *Elements of Philosophy*, a proposed work of which three parts were written: *De Cive* (1642), *De Corpore* (1655), and *De Homine* (1658).

13. Because McKeon does not have time in the lecture to get to principles for history (although he touches on them briefly in the final discussion), the editors have included here the following lecture notes from two of the later versions of the course for which he prepared notes. They were found filed with the other notes prepared for use in the final lecture presented here. They are presented in an abridgment of those last complete notes prepared on history for use in class in 1960 (version VI) and 1963 (version VIII). These two notes, then, were reused the last two times he taught the course, as Ideas and Methods 212 in 1964 and in 1965.

DISCUSSION. Review

1. This class is devoted to answering various questions that the class has raised; as a result, no notes prepared by McKeon directly for this class were found in his files. However, he did type several different groups of notes in preparation for the concluding class in the various versions he taught of this course. Regarding his notes on principles in history, for example, see the notes at the end of lecture 11, including endnote 13. More broadly, for the notes he prepared to give an overview of what he is doing in the course in general, see his notes at the end of this discussion summary; he prepared these for three different versions of the Social Sciences.

2. Notice that McKeon treats the authors read in the reverse order in which they were presented in the course. Regarding the possible reasoning for doing so, see his notes reproduced at the end of this chapter.

3. See lecture 11, toward the end.

4. This is the literal meaning of the terms *analysis* and *synthesis*, respectively.

5. To help the reader follow in outline what McKeon is saying in the discussion, the editors have created table 20 by combining Kant's profile from table 19 with the profiles of Hume and the others McKeon refers to below as they appear in appendix J—with the exception of Peter Ramus (1515–1572), for whom no profile card was found.

6. Between 1781 and 1790, Kant published three major works: the *Critique of Pure Reason*, the *Critique of Practical Reason*, and the *Critique of Judgment*.

7. For a somewhat more extended summary of how the history of science changes, see lecture 1, "An Introduction to Philosophic Problems," as well as the last discussion, "Review," in McKeon, *On Knowing—The Natural Sciences*, ed. David B. Owen and Zahava K. McKeon (Chicago: University of Chicago Press, 1994), pp. 1–11 and 342–56, respectively.

8. The following nine notes are grouped in sets of three, all created to act as a conclusion to various versions of the Social Sciences course's lectures and discussions. The first three notes, all labeled as "Conclusion," were presumably prepared for the first version of I&M 212 in 1964 and reused in 1965 (the year of the course contained in this book). The first note of that first set of three begins with an explicit reminder McKeon made to himself to refer to the version VII taught in 1962 ("Conclusion; see 202 [VII]"), and the second set of three notes presented here is the one created for version VII. Finally, the last three notes are presented here because they also are referred to by an explicit reminder on the third of the three cards from version VII ("Concepts and Methods 202 [VII] 11.3") where McKeon has typed, "insert 202 (II) 9.1–3 on Method—advantages and errors," the version the editors estimate was probably taught in 1956. The close connection of the first two sets of notes is reinforced by their being found filed together sequentially toward the end of McKeon's files for this course. The last set, however, was found filed well ahead of the first two sets, about a third of the way through the entire course's files.

All three sets of notes are included here complete because of the different emphases each provides in developing McKeon's views on the value of what he has been engaged in during the course, which extends beyond the treatment of the authors read in class. As he makes explicit in these notes, he views the careful, precise intellectual analyses the class has been engaged in as essential not only retrospectively with respect to insightful semantic and historical interpretation of what individuals have written but also prospectively and creatively with respect to the discovery of common courses of action and policy among individuals of diverse, even conflicting, intellectual positions, whether they be economic, social, political, educational, religious, and so on. Thus, these three sets of note cards begin to develop his view of both the importance and the value of such disciplined thinking.

That view can also be seen in greater detail in his earlier publication, *Freedom and History: The Semantics of Philosophical Controversies and Ideo-*

logical Conflict (New York: Noonday Press, 1952), especially chapter 6. The work was republished posthumously in Richard McKeon, *Freedom and History and Other Essays: An Introduction to the Thought of Richard McKeon*, ed. Zahava K. McKeon (Chicago: University of Chicago Press, 1990). For a brief summary of what McKeon thought the purpose was of his book, an overview evidently prepared for a lecture given independently of this course, see appendix H.

9. The editors have made slight changes to the following notes for ease in reading. As is customary, McKeon's penciled changes are represented here by *italics*.

10. The alert reader will observe that three years earlier (in 1962), McKeon characterized Hobbes's interpretation as *existential* rather than *entitative*, which is his view in this 1965 version of the course. This is a further reminder that the profiles of appendix J should be taken as tentative, not definitive, statements of interpretation.

11. This typed list of five authors and their semantic profiles was found on a small sheet of paper tucked inside the folded note which it here concludes.

12. In some earlier versions of the course, McKeon used selections from Hegel's *Lectures on the Philosophy of History*, first published in German in 1831. Note that McKeon uses a passage from *Reason in History*, a general introduction to this large work, for the course's final examination (see appendix I).

13. The editors cannot decipher what McKeon penciled in after "operational history."

14. For one tentative approach to putting together all the variables McKeon has treated topically in the course, see appendix K.

APPENDIX A. Class Schedule

1. This schedule of class meetings is based on actual classes held and topics covered. It has been reconstructed from comments on the tape recordings and in students' notebooks and has been laid out to reflect the typical McKeon syllabus. An actual syllabus from this class has not been found.

APPENDIX C. One Alternate Introduction to the Course

1. In the initial lecture of the immediately preceding versions of this course in the social sciences, McKeon briefly introduces possible relations between it and the course in the natural sciences taught the term before. In the earlier courses, these relations are grouped under headings based on the same four questions used in the current (1965) course: principle, method, interpretation, and selection. However, in these earlier instances the main similarities and differences within each of those four questions as they are treated in the initial lecture are based on substantive issues and thereby provide a contrasting, though parallel, equivalent to the formal, topical distinctions organizing the 1965 social sciences course (see endnote 19 of lecture 1 above). This appendix presents two sheets of McKeon's notes prepared for a preceding version of the

course, identified as "Concepts and Methods VII (1962)," in order to give the reader a sense of what an approach different from that of 1965 might look like. All the notes here are laid out and reproduced as typed, with any changes being noted in square brackets, except for a few regularizations of spelling, which are not noted. Penciled additions are noted in *italics*.

For the schematism composed of topics that underlies all the later courses and formalizes what appears in these lecture notes, see appendix D.

APPENDIX D. Schema of Philosophic Semantics

1. This complete semantic schema is reprinted from the posthumously published paper entitled "Philosophic Semantics and Philosophic Inquiry," which McKeon delivered at the Illinois Philosophy Conference held in Carbondale, Illinois, on February 26, 1966. This paper had been previously reproduced and distributed among his students and colleagues. (See Richard McKeon, *Freedom and History and Other Essays*, ed. Zahava K. McKeon [Chicago: University of Chicago Press, 1990], pp. 242–56. The schema appears on page 253.) To the original four-column schema the editors have added a first column on modes of thought. In the resulting schematism, the lines connect each mode of thought with its related specification. For instance, the mode of thought resolution is expressed in a reflexive principle, problematic method, essentialist interpretation, and a selection of kinds; thus, the lines represent the *pure* expression of the mode of thought. However, as McKeon frequently emphasizes throughout this course, these pure connections are *not necessary* ones; that is, a thinker can connect one mode of thought expressed in principles with *any* of the four modes of thought expressed in methods or interpretations or selections. In fact, McKeon frequently stated in his lectures that he had found no major Western thinker after Aristotle's death in 322 BCE who used any of the complete sets of the *pure* connections, *e.g.*, actional, operational, existentialist, types. For some examples of these intellectual profiles, see appendix J.

APPENDIX E. Reading Selections from Hobbes

1. What follows is an exact copy of the mimeographed passages from Hobbes handed out to students in the class. This is McKeon's own copy, which was found filed with other materials used in the course and which contains a number of his penciled notations. The most visually prominent notations are penciled and circled numbers (shown by italicized, underlined, bracketed bold—for instance, ***[1]***) at the beginning of paragraphs on his mimeograph copy, except for a ***[4]*** which appears in the middle of the third paragraph of chapter XIV; these numbers coordinate with his typewritten notes found at the end of part 1 and part 2 of the Hobbes discussions. The editors have also indicated within each paragraph where McKeon penciled in further numbers pointing at the structure of Hobbes's argument (numbers shown in parentheses with *italics*), where he underlined keywords in the text with pencil (shown here by *italic underline*), where he either circled or boxed in with pencil particular

words or phrases (shown here by italicized, underlined, bracketed ***[bold]***), and where he added a large bracket for emphasis (at the bottom of the sixth paragraph of chapter XXI). The reader should be aware that a substantial portion of the mimeograph copy's text is underlined and numerous words are wholly capitalized, and that the orthography of that original has been reproduced here without alteration where McKeon has not added pencil marks.

APPENDIX F. Kant, *Fundamental Principles*: Three Editions with Major Sections' Pagination

1. The editors have created this outline based on the pagination in McKeon's discussion notes, with the latter adjusted for his verbal references in parts 2 and 3 of the Kant discussions. In the event of inconsistencies, we have tried to interpolate the proper pages in question. McKeon's notes contain typewritten pages that refer to an unknown edition. His notes also contain penciled references which are within a page or two of the Abbott edition which we have consulted. Presumably, he was working with one or another printing of that edition. The version we consulted is Immanuel Kant, *Fundamental Principles of the Metaphysics of Morals*, trans. T. K. Abbott (New York: Liberal Arts, 1949).

For the Beck edition, see Immanuel Kant, *Foundations of the Metaphysics of Morals, and What Is Enlightenment*, trans. Lewis White Beck (Chicago: University of Chicago Press, 1949).

APPENDIX G. Mill, *On Liberty*: Four Editions with Major Sections' Pagination

1. The editors have created this outline and pagination based on McKeon's discussion notes plus the student notes of Betz, whose edition is unknown to the editors, and of Gould, whose edition is known. In the event of inconsistencies, the editors have tried to interpolate the proper pages in question. For full citations to the relevant editions, see the discussion of Mill, part 1, endnotes 1 and 2.

APPENDIX H. McKeon Notes on *Freedom and History*

1. This appendix contains notes McKeon evidently prepared for a single lecture and discussion of his book, *Freedom and History: The Semantics of Philosophical Controversies and Ideological Conflicts* (New York: Noonday Press, 1952), but they were found filed toward the end of the set of notes prepared for the lectures in I&M 202/212. They are presented here to suggest something of the practical, as well as theoretic, value of the kind of analysis of freedom and history undertaken in this course.

2. He was deeply involved in the early years of the United Nations Educational, Scientific and Cultural Organization. "Richard McKeon was adviser to the United States delegation at the first three sessions of the General Conference of UNESCO. After its establishment in 1947 he served as the first acting

counselor on UNESCO affairs attached to the United States Embassy in Paris. In the first year of UNESCO's existence, McKeon, with Julian Huxley, provided material for the drafting of the Universal Declaration of Human Rights in 1948." See Zahava K. McKeon, introduction to *Selected Writings of Richard McKeon*, vol. 1, *Philosophy, Science, and Culture*, ed. Zahava K. McKeon and William G. Swenson (Chicago: University of Chicago Press, 1998), p. 4.

3. Published more than a decade before the current course was taught, *Freedom and History* and its related notes here reflect a threefold analysis of the terms *freedom* and *history* rather than the fourfold approach used in this course. (The reader will note that the "operational" approach was to be added to the other, initial three.) This variation suggests something of the operational character of the method McKeon is using, which can lead to a diversity of approaches. A careful study of all the notes he prepared for the various versions of the 202/212 class would reveal something of the chronology and nature of that shift in his thinking. Also, a former student who studied with him in the 1940s, George Kimball Plochmann, wrote an analysis of his work which makes use of the earlier threefold treatment and has published it in *Richard McKeon: A Study* (Chicago: University of Chicago Press, 1990).

4. This final paragraph was typed on the back of the preceding note.

APPENDIX J. Semantic Profiles of Selected Western Thinkers

1. The lists of intellectual characteristics in this appendix are derived from a set of 3" × 5" note cards which McKeon typed for each individual and which were found filed in alphabetical order in a wooden box after his death. The main lists, including the various sorts, are all constructed from the revised profile cards and so, presumably, represent his final judgment on the individuals in question. For these revisions, see the table accompanying the second footnote (indicated by a single dagger) to table Appendix J.

One should take these "profiles" not as a set of fixed characteristics that absolutely define each thinker for all time but, rather, merely as suggestions for investigation of similarities and differences among them, as provocations to further inquiry. Their tentative nature is indicated, first, by the fact that McKeon did not publish them during his life, suggesting that he did not want others to get fixed on just a single view of a writer as the only and the "true" interpretation of his or her work. Second, he himself changed his thoughts on a number of points, as evidenced by penciled corrections of the original typed profiles. For instance, Adams's original profile was typed as "Reflexive," "Operational," and "Entitative"; but penciled changes of the Principle to "Simple" and of the Interpretation to "Ontological" indicate that he revised his initial views. Or, with respect to Interpretation, his view of Burke changed from "Existentialist" to "Entitative," of Dewey from "Essentialist" to "Entitative," of Heidegger from "Dialectical" to "Entitative," of Hobbes from "Existentialist" to "Entitative." He also changed Jefferson's Method from "Problematic" to "Operational." On other occasions, a penciled question mark after a change indicated his ambivalence about the potential switch, for instance, whether he should change the Interpretation of Berkeley from "Existentialist" to "Entitative," or of Collingwood from "Existentialist" to "Ontological," or whether he should modify Epicurus's Method from "Logistic" to "Dialectical." Most provocatively, perhaps, is a note questioning whether he should change Freud's Method from "Logistic" to "Problematic" and his Interpretation from "Ontological" to "Entitative."

In addition, McKeon added a Selection to several cards. For instance, Darwin's is "Functional" [= Action], Feuerbach's is "Material" [= Thing], and Merleau-Ponty's is "Functional" [= Action].

APPENDIX K. Alternative Definitions of *Freedom, Power*, and *History*

1. The editors have created appendix K, based on tables 10, 17, and 18 in the text, only to suggest one of a number of possibilities for working with the structure of topics that McKeon used in this course in order to open up the diversity of meanings possible when examining the themes of freedom, power, and history. The purpose is to give the reader one way to begin to integrate the various meanings possible for each term by combining them into sentences that give greater definitiveness than just an ambiguous listing of topical distinctions as occurs in the various tables. The appendix is constructed so that a term in any of the four major columns, from Principle to Selection, can be combined with any other in order to give an initial approach to defining and applying one of the main themes. Thus, for example, one could make the connections to create the following description of freedom: "Self-rule sets the conditions to deliberate, which results in the voluntary actions of humans in institutions." That would be sticking with the mode of thought resolution all the way across—Aristotle's approach. However, one could just as easily make the following sentence describing freedom: "Self-rule sets the conditions to choose, which results in the wisdom of rational beings." This would be mixing the modes of thought—resolution, discrimination, and assimilation, respectively—as one moved across the table—such as has been seen in Kant's approach. The alert reader will observe that McKeon's treatment actually allows for a large variety of alternative treatments of each of the three themes, in fact, 256 alternatives for each one (a set of 4 variables can be combined in any fashion with the other 3 sets of 4 variables each, or $4^4 = 256$). Consequently, as he carefully observes in his lecture notes beginning with "Concepts and Methods 202 (VII) Conclusion 11.1," which are reproduced toward the end of the last discussion, McKeon's approach is *not* relativistic, where any action or any intellectual argument is of the same value as any other; rather, he is arguing for an intellectual and cultural pluralism where values can be appropriately asserted or denied; where arguments can be defended or refuted and errors of beginning point, logic, statement, and fact are entirely possible; and where actions can be justified as creative and beneficial or as not useful and even destructive.

As for the table set out in this appendix, the reader needs to recognize several critical limitations inherent in it. In the first place, it is the editors' creation, not McKeon's, and what it represents should not be attributed to him merely because of its appearance here. Second, it is important to remember that his tables of variables, the sets of four topics occurring under each of the headings when treating his main themes, are *by their very character* a consciously ambiguous invention designed to "open up" investigation of the themes involved; by contrast, appendix K sets as its purpose the transforming of those heuristic matrices of variables into specifications, however numerous and loose, pointing at particular interpretations of the themes investigated—the exact opposite of his deliberate preservation of ambiguity. Third, even if such specification of a variety of interpretations of the themes involved were something that he might have done, the terms the editors have chosen with which to do it as well as the character of the connecting phrases between the columns might well not be how he would have approached this aspect of his work and are, in any case, on occasions grammatically awkward. In short, *caveat lector* ("Let the reader beware!").

INDEX

The letter *f* or *t* following a page number denotes a figure or table, respectively.